MODERN
SHIPS

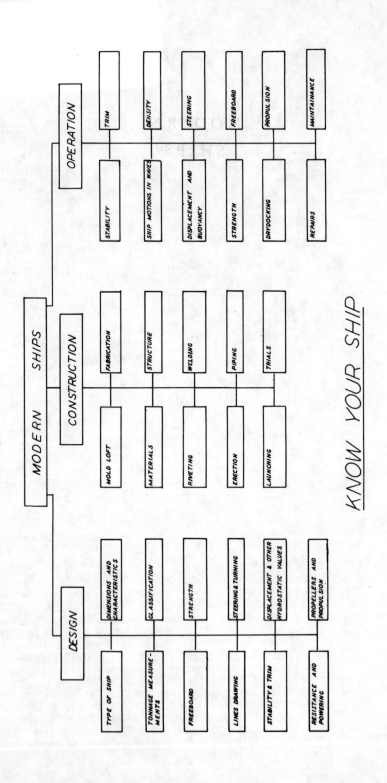

KNOW YOUR SHIP

MODERN SHIPS

Elements of Their Design,
Construction and Operation

SECOND EDITION

by
John H. La Dage, Lt. Comdr. USMS
Associate Professor of Naval Architecture, U.S.M.M.A.

Illustrations by
Frank X. Schuler, Lt. Comdr. USMS

CORNELL MARITIME PRESS
Centreville   Maryland

ISBN 0-87033-065-9
Library of Congress Catalog Card Number: 65-21747

Manufactured in the United States of America
First edition, 1953. Second edition, 1965; Fifth printing, 1982

DEDICATED TO

Those two most important "ladies in my life"
MY WIFE BRENDA AND THE SHIP

TABLE OF CONTENTS

Chap. 1: Principal Dimensions and Characteristics 1

Preliminary Definitions 1
Longitudinal, transverse, and vertical Dimensions . 2
Other Dimensions and Characteristics 4
Displacement Tonnages 5
Deadweight Tonnage 5
Gross and Net Register Tonnages 6
Power Tonnage 6
Equipment Tonnage 7
Questions 7
Bibliography 8

Chap. 2: Modern Types of Ships 9

Trends in Design 9
Classification System for Maritime Commission
Designs 13
Dry Cargo Types 15
Tanker Types 25
Passenger Vessels 26
Special Merchant Types 28
Questions 33
Bibliography 33

Chap. 3: Tonnage Measurement 34

Tonnage History 34
Gross Tonnage 36
Net Tonnage 42
Tonnage Calculations 45
Suez and Panama Canal Tonnages 49
Questions 49
Bibliography 51

Chap. 4: Classification 52

History of Classification Societies 52
Modern Organization of ABS 54
The Effect of Classification on Ship Design 58
Questions 64
Bibliography 65

Chap. 5: Freeboard and Load Lines 67

History of Freeboard Regulations 67
The Technical Background of Load Line Regula-
tions 68
Load Line Regulations 73
Load Lines for Steamers Carrying Timber 81
Load Lines for Tankers 84
Load Lines for Great Lakes Vessels 86
Load Lines for Passenger Vessels 87
Questions 90
Bibliography 91

Chap. 6: Strength of Materials and Ships 93

Strength of Materials 93
Stresses on a Loaded Beam 98
Measures of Sectional Strength 102
Strength of Ships 107
Strength Curves 110
The Principle of Continuity in Strength 118
Scantlings of Ship's Plating 119
Structural Tests on Ships 123
Strength Provisions of the Load Line Regulations . 124
Table for Estimating Stresses 126
Questions 127
Bibliography 130

Chap. 7: Lines, Offsets, and the Mold Loft 131

The Theory of the Lines Drawing 134
Drawing the Lines 135
Table of Offsets 138
The Mold Loft 142
Questions 145
Bibliography 146

Chap. 8: Riveting and Welding 147

Rivets and Riveting 147
What is Welding? 156
Welding Methods Employing the Fusion Process .. 157
Welding Methods Employing Pressure 163
Welding Versus Riveting 167
Welding Technique 171
Inspection of Welding 175
A Comparison of the Welded and Riveted Ship ... 176
Questions 178
Bibliography 179

Chap. 9: Tanks, Bilges, and Piping Systems 181
    Bilge and Clean Ballast Systems 183
    The Fuel Oil and Oily Ballast System 192
    The Fire System 196
    Sanitary System 197
    Fresh Water Systems 197
    Questions 198
    Bibliography 199

Chap. 10: Turning and Steering 200
    The Turning Circle 200
    Heeling During a Turn 204
    Factors which Influence Steering 206
    Rudders and Their Characteristics 207
    Questions 212
    Bibliography 214

Chap. 11: Launching 215
    Declivity Angles 215
    Construction of the Ways 217
    Construction of the Launching Cradle 222
    Launching Calculations 223
    Description of the Launch 226
    Side Launchings 228
    Questions 230
    Bibliography 231

Chap. 12: Drydocking 233
    The Graving Dock 233
    The Floating Drydock 235
    Docking a Vessel 241
    Advantages and Disadvantages of Floating and
      Graving Docks 250
    Deck Officers Duties 251
    Engineers Duties 252
    Work Done While in Drydock 252
    Questions 254
    Bibliography 255

Chap. 13: Ship's Calculations 256
    Rules for Integration 256
    Calculation of Displacement 261
    Calculation of Wetted Surface 264
    Change of Draft with Density 264
    Coefficients of Form 269

Centers of Areas and Volumes 275
Tons Per Inch Immersion 277
Height of Metacenter Above Keel 279
Change in Displacement for trim 282
Moment to Change Trim One Inch 284
Questions 286

Chap. 14: The Ship in Waves 293
The Nature of Ocean Waves 293
Rolling 298
The Virtual Upright Position 302
Clinometer Error 304
Anti-rolling Devices 305
Questions 309
Bibliography 310

Chap. 15: Resistance and Powering 312
Hydrodynamic Principles Relating to Resistance ... 312
Frictional Resistance 320
Wave Resistance 322
Eddy and Air Resistance 325
Resistance and Powering Considerations in Hull
   Design 325
The Effect of Speed on Draft and Trim 331
The Effect of Shallow Water on Resistance 332
Resistance Under Sea Conditions 332
Calculation of Ship Horsepower 332
Questions 334
Bibliography 336

Chap. 16: Propellers and Propulsion 337
Propeller Definitions 337
Propulsive Efficiency 346
Factors Effecting Propeller Performance 349
Example Pitch Problem 353
Questions 355
Bibliography 357

Chap. 17: Ship Trials 358
Dock and Builder's Trials 359
Standardization Trial 359
Endurance and Fuel Economy Trials 363
Maneuvering Trials 363
Questions 369
Bibliography 370

Index 371

PREFACE

THIS text has been written to satisfy the special requirements of personnel in the Merchant Marine and students of ship operation. These requirements are, in many ways, unique. The present or prospective ship's officer is not required to be a ship designer or shipwright and the many fine texts on design and construction, therefore, are not completely suitable; nor are the texts on nomenclature and other elementary phases of the study of ships suitable for a comprehensive professional approach to the problem.

In satisfying the requirements of a course for professionally educated merchant marine officers, it is hoped that the requirements of many other people interested in the design, construction, and operation of merchant vessels will be met. These include office staffs who must be keenly aware of the capabilities and limitations of ships, students of Naval Architecture who must be conscious of the close relationship of design to operation, and students in college courses in Marine Transportation who are interested in ship design but do not have the time to devote to an intensive study of the subject.

The author, with his background of experience as a ship's officer and an instructor of prospective ship's officers, has attempted to present from the general field of Naval Architecture and Ship Construction those theories and practices which can be applied most practically to the problems of those people engaged in the operation of merchant ships. The format of the text has been arranged so as to place emphasis on those phases of ship design and construction which, in the opinion of the author, have not been accorded the importance they deserve in the education of a ship's officer. The study of Nomenclature has been largely omitted, not with any intent to minimize its importance but recognizing the existence of well-written texts on the subject. Information on the practical application of the theories of stability and trim have been given in a companion text "Stability and Trim for the Ship's Officer" by La Dage and Van Gemert.

The author has been assisted in his task by many individuals and agencies. Credit is given at the appropriate place in the text where assistance was rendered. Special mention, however should be made of Frank X. Schuler, Lt. USMS, who spent many a weary hour in drawing the original illustrations; Peder Gald, Captain, USMS, whose encouragement and advice helped materially in making a dream a reality; and the author's colleagues, Lt. N. Steiner and Lt. Comdr. C. Sauerbier whose criticism and suggestions were very helpful. Also, of the agencies who willingly provided requested photographs and information, the following deserve special mention: The American Bureau of Shipping; Todd's Shipyards, Inc.; Lincoln Electric Company; United States Maritime Administration; and the Bethlehem Steel Company.

It is hoped that the footnotes and the bibliographies which appear in each chapter will assist the interested student in pursuing further any element of the subject which appeals especially to him.

JOHN H. LA DAGE

Kings Point, N. Y.

MODERN SHIPS

Chapter 1

PRINCIPAL DIMENSIONS AND CHARACTERISTICS

The principal dimensions of his vessel should be as familiar to the ship's officer as his age. These dimensions are required by many officials upon entering a port, for example. It is obvious that a ready knowledge of them is of great assistance at these times. Also, the dimensions are used in many of the ship's calculations an officer is called upon to make.

Preliminary Definitions

As an aid in locating points for the purpose of designing and building a vessel, certain reference planes are designated.

Base Line Plane (BL) is established somewhere near the base of the ship, usually running through the upper edge of the flat plate keel and parallel to the *waterplanes*. Almost all vertical dimensions are referred to this imaginary plane.

Centerline Plane (₵) is a longitudinal plane at right angles to the base line plane, and parallel to *buttock* planes port and starboard. A vessel is symmetrical on either side of the centerline.

Transverse vertical planes are established at equal intervals along the length of the vessel. These are known as *frame stations*. The forwardmost frame station is called the *forward perpendicular* (FP) and is usually located at the intersection of the designer's load water line (DLWL) and the forward part of the stem. The aftermost frame station is called the *after perpendicular* (AP) and is usually located at the after end of the stern post. (When a vessel is so constructed as not to have a stern post, the A.P. runs through the middle of the rudder stock.) That frame station halfway between the forward and after perpendiculars is called the *midship section.* (⧢).

Thus any point may be located in three dimensions by reference to the buttock planes, the waterplanes, and the frame stations.

The *Lines Drawing* or *Lines Plan* showing the lines (form) of a vessel uses these three types of planes to define a vessel in three dimensions on a two-dimensional plan.[1]

In drawing up the Lines Plan of a vessel it is convenient to create what is called a *molded surface*. The molded surface is almost exactly the shape which a thin piece of sheet rubber would take if stretched tightly over the shell and deck framing with no plating in place. The molded surface has

---

[1] See Chapter 7.

1

no thickness and is fair and smooth. The molded surface thus enables a designer to ignore in his vessel's lines, the small irregularities caused by plating, rivets, and the like. All *molded dimensions* are referred to the molded surface of a vessel.

Longitudinal Dimensions

Length-over-all (LOA) is the linear distance from the most forward point of the stem to the aftermost point of the stern, measured parallel to the base line.

Length between Perpendiculars (LBP) is the linear distance between the forward and after perpendiculars measured parallel to the base line.

Length on the Load Waterline (LWL) is the linear distance from the most forward point of the LWL to the aftermost point of the LWL. The Load Waterline may represent a slightly different draft than the DLWL, since the latter is the designer's estimate of the load draft. The actual load draft is calculated according to the "Load Line Regulations" of the United States [1] and is assigned by the American Bureau of Shipping. Length on the load waterline is apt to be very close to or equal to LBP on a vessel with a counter stern since the load waterline usually intersects the stern at the stern post on this type of stern. With a cruiser stern, however, the waterline intersects the stern aft of the stern post, and LWL will be greater than LBP.

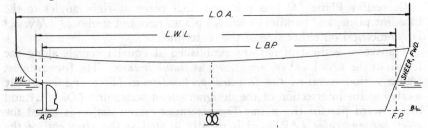

Figure 1.   Linear Dimensions

Each different length definition has its own purpose (as is true of the various breadth and other dimensions). LOA is obviously useful for maneuvering information; LBP is used by ship designer's as an average "under the water" or *effective length.* Where LBP as defined above (as the American Bureau of Shipping defines "length" for purposes of assigning required scantlings) does not produce a good effective length, the designer may designate another length as effective length. This length is then used in ship's calculations. In assigning Registered Tonnage, the regulations specify a *Registered Length* which may be regarded as the "official" or governmental length. In actually measuring the vessel for tonnage, the term *Tonnage Length* is also used.

---

[1] See Chapter 5.

Transverse Dimensions

Extreme breadth is the linear distance from the most outboard point on one side to the most outboard point on the other side of a vessel's hull. Extreme breadth includes any projections on the ship's side and is used with Length-over-all to determine the maximum space occupied by the vessel.

Molded breadth is the linear distance from the molded surface on one side to the molded surface on the other side measured at the widest portion of a vessel's hull parallel to the waterlines. This dimension is used in ship calculations.

Breadth by ABS is similar to the definition of molded breadth given above. The tonnage regulations also specify a *Registered Breadth*.

Tumble home is the inward slope of the ship's side. It is also a transverse linear dimension since, at any point, it is the transverse distance separating the side at its widest portion and the side at that point. *The* tumble home of a vessel is measured at the deck.

Flare is the outward slope of a ship's side. It is the opposite of tumble home.

Vertical Dimensions

Draft is the vertical distance from the lowest point of the hull to the waterline. This dimension is indicated on the sides of the vessel forward and aft by the draft marks. *Molded Draft* is measured from the base line.

Depth is the vertical distance from the lowest point of the hull to the side of the deck to which it is referred. (Depth to main deck, depth to Promenade deck, etc.) Depth will vary from amidships to the ends depending on the amount of sheer and camber. *Molded depth* is the vertical distance from the base line to the molded line of the upper deck (or the deck to which it is referred) at the side. For purposes of listing the principal dimensions of a vessel, depth is measured amidships.

Freeboard at any point along the ship's side is the vertical distance from the waterline to the upper deck at that point. Officially, freeboard is measured amidships. Calculation of statutory or legal freeboard is a difficult technical matter. (See Chapter 5). Freeboard can be considered, at any point, to be the difference between draft and depth at that point.

Sheer, at any point, is the vertical distance between the ship's side amidships and the ship's side at that point. It is the longitudinal curvature of a vessel's deck. Sheer is usually much greater forward than aft. It's purpose is to increase bouyancy at the ends. The Load Line Regulations specify a reduction in required freeboard for sheer and thus where additional draft is desirable, the upper deck will have sheer.

Camber, at any point, is the vertical distance between the side of the deck and the deck at that point. It is the transverse slope of the deck. A deck may have *straight camber* or *knuckled camber*. The purpose of camber is to direct water on deck out to the side where it can be drained by the scuppers. Camber does not provide additional transverse strength. Appearance is a secondary consideration.

Dead rise or **rise of bottom,** at any point, is the vertical distance between the bottom at the centerline and the bottom at that point. The total dead rise of a vessel is the vertical distance that the bottom rises in one half the beam. (See Figure 2 for an illustration of how this distance is found). Dead rise causes a shift upwards of the center of buoyancy, and is therefore principally concerned with the stability aspect of hull design.

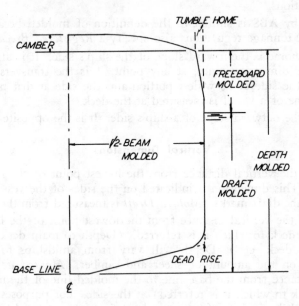

Figure 2.　Linear Dimensions

Other Principal Dimensions and Characteristics

The definitions which follow are commonly included in a list of ship's dimensions:

Girth is the linear distance from the intersection of the upper deck with the side, around the hull of the vessel to the corresponding point on the opposite side.

The hull of a vessel can be considered to be divided into three separate bodies longitudinally:

Middle Body is the midship portion of a vessel throughout the length of which a constant cross-sectional shape is maintained. On almost all merchant ships, a *Parallel Middle Body,* where the sides are vertical, is employed.

Entrance of a vessel is that portion of a vessel which lies forward of the middle body and under the load waterline.

Run of a vessel is that underwater portion of the after body that is fined off to the stern. On most merchant types the run is apt to be finer than the entrance in form.

TONNAGES

A ship is more than a three-dimensional body. It is that, of course, and as such can be defined to some extent by dimensions. But a ship is a *floating* body which must be designed to transport cargo, crew, and passengers as rapidly, safely, and economically as possible. A broader definition of a ship is necessary than mere lengths and breadths. This broader definition includes the various type of ship tonnages. A study of ship's tonnages not only helps to express the size and/or weight of a vessel but answers many questions of importance to the ship's officer.

Why a Ship Floats

When any object is placed in a liquid, the liquid is displaced as the object submerges. When the volume of displaced liquid is equal in weight to the weight of the object, the latter ceases to submerge and is said to be floating.[1] The upward force of the displaced water, or buoyancy, is then exactly equal to the downward force of weight. The term displacement can be considered to be synonymous with the term weight.

Displacement Tonnages

It is possible to obtain the weight of a vessel by calculating the volume of displaced water in cubic feet and multiplying that volume by the known weight per cubic foot of the water in which the vessel is floating (or by dividing the volume of displacement by the number of cubic feet which one ton of that water occupies).[2] The weight of a vessel is known as *displacement tonnage.* ($\triangle$)

The weight of a vessel and everything in her when she is floating at her deepest permissible draft (summer draft) is known as *load displacement.*

When the vessel is completely empty, her weight is known as *light displacement.* The weight of a vessel is always expressed in long tons. (2240 pounds).

Deadweight Tonnage

The weight of cargo, fuel, water and stores necessary to submerge a vessel from her light draft to her load draft is called deadweight tonnage.

---

[1] This is a statement of the well known Archimedes Principle. The entire subject of displacement will be considered in detail in Chapter 13.

[2] Salt water weighs approximately 64 pounds per cubic foot and one ton of salt water occupies 35 cubic feet of space. Fresh water weighs approximately 62.5 pounds per cubic foot and one ton of fresh water occupies approximately 35.9 cubic feet of space.

It is the difference between light and load displacement. This tonnage is not to be confused with the weight of the ship. It is the "dead" weight of the cargo, and so on, in distinction to the "live" weight of the ship.

Gross and Net Register Tonnage

One is accustomed to think of tonnage in terms of weight so that an understanding of displacement and deadweight is not difficult. But when one is asked to think of a ton as representing 100 cubic feet of *space,* the eye reads the words, and the brain rejects their meaning. Nevertheless, one "registered" ton, by law, represents 100 cubic feet of a ship's internal space.

Whenever a vessel is berthed at a pier, enters a drydock; goes through a canal, and so forth, fees must be assessed on that vessel. Registered tonnage is used to obtain an equitable basis for assessing fees.[1]

Gross Register Tonnage is calculated by measuring in cubic feet the total internal volume of a vessel (less certain exempted spaces) and dividing by 100. These exempted spaces are of considerable importance to the shipowner in this measurement type of tonnage as he naturally wishes to keep his Gross Tonnage down as low as possible in order to reduce the fees. In general, those spaces on a vessel which afford comfort to the crew and safety for the ship are exempted from Gross Tonnage. The ship owner is not penalized, therefore, for erecting large galleys, water ballast spaces, wheelhouses, and so on. The design of a vessel is determined in no small measure by the tonnage laws.

Net Register Tonnage is determined by deducting from Gross Tonnage most spaces which are not used for the carriage of cargo or passengers. This, one might think, leaves the volume of cargo carrying spaces. Well, it is not quite that easy since, for one thing, the machinery space deduction is considerably larger than its actual space. Here again, tonnage laws effect design, since in general, the larger the machinery space in relation to the vessel, the larger the deduction allowed for the space and the lower the Net tonnage.

The Certificate of Admeasurement, issued by the U. S. Customs, shows those spaces which are exempted, from, or included in Gross tonnage and those which are deducted from Gross to obtain Net tonnage.

Power Tonnage

Power tonnage is arrived at by adding to the Gross tonnage of the vessel her I.H.P. (Indicated Horsepower). Since this type of tonnage takes into consideration not only a relative indication of the vessel's size

---

[1] For a complete discussion of Register Tonnages, see Chap. 3.

but her power (and thus her type) it is sometimes used as a basis for determining the salary of ship's officers.[1]

Equipment Tonnage

Equipment tonnage is a type of measurement tonnage since one equipment ton is equal to various units of space. It differs from Gross tonnage in that there are no exempted spaces, and is therefore, a truer criterion of size and internal volume. However, the ship's officer should be primarily interested in the *use* for equipment tonnage. The American Bureau of Shipping uses this tonnage as a basis for determining the scantlings (size and strength) of such ground tackle as anchors and cables.

QUESTIONS

1. What are the symbols for: Base Line; centerline; midship section; length-over-all; length between perpendiculars; forward and after perpendiculars; length on the load waterline; displacement in tons.
2. What agency is responsible for the definition of the location of perpendiculars as given in the text?
3. What is the purpose of "molded" dimensions?
4. In what Plan would one find the molded lines of a vessel?
5. In what way is DLWL different from LWL?
6. State the purpose for each major longitudinal and transverse dimension.
7. What agency assigns freeboard to U. S. vessels? ABS, See p. 68.
8. Explain the relationship of camber and sheer to depth.

---

[1] As an illustration of how power tonnage is used in arriving at ship's officers wages, the following information is taken from the Agreement between the International Organization of Masters, Mates & Pilots and Atlantic and Gulf Coast Dry Cargo and Passenger Companies, effective 6/16/64.

Vessels are defined into the following classifications depending upon the power tonnage. Power tonnage here is defined as the number of gross tons added to the horsepower of the vessel as shown in "Merchant Vessels of the United States," published by the Bureau of Navigation of the United States Coast Guard. How wages vary with class and power tonnage is shown for Master only (Single Screw) and Chief Mate (Twin Screw).

Class	Power Tonnage	Monthly Wages
	Single Screw	
A-1	25,001 and over	
A	17,001 to 25,000	$1,353.14
B	12,001 to 17,000	1,292.38
C	7,501 to 12,000	1,230.02
D	5,001 to 7,500	1,230.02
E	Less than 5,001	1,230.02
	Twin Screw	
A-3	35,001 and over & P2's	948.31
A-2	28,001 to 35,000	857.19
A-1	20,001 to 28,000	829.24
A	15,001 to 20,000	798.85
B	9,001 to 15,000	769.25
C	5,501 to 9,000	738.88
D	3,501 to 5,500	723.72
E	Less than 3,501	708.50

9. How does sheer affect the assigned freeboard?

10. Show by a sketch how the following linear dimensions are found: Tumble home; camber; dead rise; molded breadth, draft, depth, and freeboard.

11. a) How many pounds are there to the long ton?

     b) What is the weight in pounds of a cubic foot of salt water? a cubic foot of fresh water?

     c) How many cubic feet of space make up one registered ton?

     d) What is the volume in cubic feet of a ton of salt water? a ton of fresh water?

12. Does Net Tonnage represent the cargo carrying capacity of a vessel? Explain.

13. Derive a formula for volume of displacement in cubic feet (V), which contains tons displacement ($\triangle$). $V = 35 \triangle$ $a \ 35.9 \triangle$

14. A vessel displaces 140,000 cubic feet of salt water in a light condition. After loading 7500 tons of cargo, and 2000 tons of fuel, water, and stores, she is down to her marks. Find:

     (a) Light displacement in tons.   ANS.   4000

     (b) Deadweight, in tons   ANS.   9500

     (c) Load displacement in tons   ANS. 13,500

15. What is the capacity in tons of salt water of a double bottom tank with a volume of 7350 cubic feet? ANS. 210.

16. What is the purpose of power tonnage? How is it computed?

17. Why would registered tonnage, either gross or net, be an unreliable basis for arriving at the necessary size and strength of ground tackle?

18. From a financial point of view, would you rather serve on a single screw or a twin screw vessel with a power tonnage of 16,000? 18,000?

BIBLIOGRAPHY

NOTE: The student should look up the listing of *Principal Dimensions and Characteristics* for several ships. This listing can be found in many places. For example, most ships plans; papers written on the design of new or altered vessels and published in marine literature; Trial Trip reports, etc.

Rossell & Chapman, *Principles of Naval Architecture*, Vol. I, Chap. 1, Society of Naval Architects and Marine Engineers, New York, 1942.

Baker, *Introduction to Steel Shipbuilding*, McGraw-Hill Book Company, Inc., 2nd Ed., New York, 1953.

D. Arnott, *Design and Construction of Steel Merchant Ships*, Society of Naval Architects and Marine Engineers, New York, 1955.

Chapter 2

MODERN TYPES OF SHIPS

While there has been no radical revolution in the design of merchant vessels in the last few decades, there have been significant and distinctive changes. Most of these changes have occurred in the last ten or fifteen years; many are due to the acceleration of development experienced during the preparation for, and participation in, the last great war. One of the most tremendous effects of the war was the standardization of ship types. Never before have so many ships of exactly the same design carried the commerce of the world. The former Maritime Commission's designs make up a large percentage of the U. S. Merchant Marine, as well as the merchant fleets of the whole world. Standardization of types has lead to standardization of construction, sub-assembly, and more efficient fabrication. Meanwhile, welding has caused vast changes in the methods of constructing vessels and the members which compose their structure. Experiments have been made successfully with different structural materials. Changes in hull form while not extensive, have refined and improved hull design. This work has been aided by the development of the science of Hydrodynamics. The experiments carried on in the U. S. Experimental Model Basin near Washington and the Stevens Institute's towing tank are illustrative.

In this chapter, a discussion of design trends and ships which they have produced is offered.

Trends in Design

Distinctive changes in a vessel's appearance and design have occurred in bows, sterns, superstructure, rigging, speed, power, and structure.

Bows and Sterns: Yesterday's bow—the *plumb bow*—was straight, undistinctive, and unscientific. Its massive stem bar was exactly vertical and when collisions occurred, made a long deep slash above and below the waterline of the unfortunate vessel. The entrance was not as fine, hence resistance was greater with more pitching tendencies. Today's sloping bows—the *raked* or *raking bow*, the *spoon bow*, the *clipper bow*, and the *Meierform* type (See Figure 3)—have added beauty, economy and safety to their functions. The stem bar is gone, having been replaced by a fabricated or plate bow which crumbles well above the waterline of the vessel struck. Finer entrances combined with a wide flaring upper bow section have improved the sea behavior of vessels. Resistances have been reduced by the use of finer forms combined with better hull design, thereby increasing the average speed of merchant cargo vessels from about 10

9

knots to 16 knots. One interesting development in bow design is the
bulbous forefoot or so-called *bulbous bow*. This large bulge at the lower
part of the stem has been found to decrease resistance at certain speeds
(for merchant vessels, speeds between 16 or 17 knots and 22 or 23 knots).
Thus, some high-speed tankers, passenger liners, and naval vessels are
so constructed.[1]

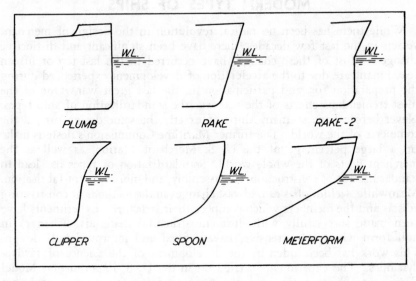

Figure 3. Types of Bows

Older type sterns were as unattractive and unscientific as the bows. The
prototype was the *counter stern*. This type of stern, characterized by its
ugly knuckle, has been largely replaced on merchant ships by the *merchant
cruiser stern* (sometimes called the *cruiser-spoon stern*), or the full *cruiser
stern*. (Figure 4). These sterns are gracefully rounded without the
knuckles typical of the counter stern. These newer sterns also have been
designed to reduce resistance thus increasing speed. This is mainly due
to the increase in waterline length obtained by reducing the overhang of
the stern above the water. (Length is an important factor in wave-making
resistance: See Chapter 15.)

The merchant vessels of the World War I period were mainly of the
"three island" type; that is, three separate and distinct groups of houses
or erections were found on the main deck. These were the forecastle head;
the bridge and midships house (with a small No. 3 hatch between them);
and the poop house, usually a steering engine room. World War II period
vessels have brought these sprawling houses together in a composite house

---

[1] See Chapter 15 for a discussion of the effect of the bulbous bow on wave-making
resistance.

situated amidships or slightly abaft amidships. The forecastle head is retained on some ships since the increase in reserve buoyancy and increased height of platform permits a decrease in assigned freeboard.

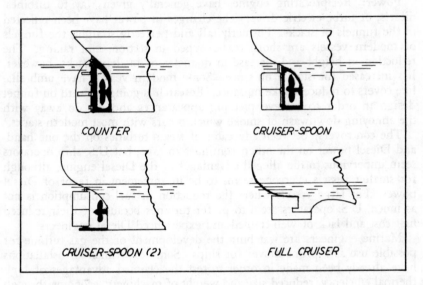

Figure 4. Types of Sterns

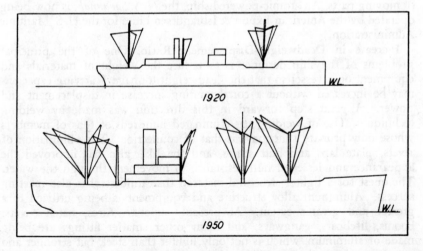

Figure 5. Changes in Ship Profiles

The former rigging of most vessels consisted of a foremast around which the winches and booms were clustered, and a similar arrangement aft, with a set of kingposts amidships for No. 3 hatch. The rigging of today generally has substituted a great number of kingposts for masts, double rigging several or all hatches. The gear generally is heavier and stronger.

Power: Reciprocating engines have generally given way to turbines, diesels, or turbo-electric drive. The changes in power have been reflected in the funnels or stacks. Formerly tall and perfectly straight, the funnels of modern vessels are short, tear-dropped in section, and raking. The reduction in height and increase in diameter of modern stacks, however, has increased the smoke nuisance. Some modern vessels have umbrella-like covers to reduce smoke nuisance. Research is going forward on funnel design in order to achieve pleasing appearances and yet do away with the annoying downwash of smoke which occurs with most modern stacks.[1]

The controversy between advocates of steam turbines on the one hand, and Diesel power on the other, continues to rage; but U.S. ship operators seem impervious to the alleged advantages of the Diesel engine, although for smaller vessels everyone seems to be in agreement in favor of Diesel power. For large vessels where the reduction in fuel consumption is not as much, U.S. operators seem to prefer turbines because of their reduced first cost and lack of well-trained and experienced Diesel engineers.

Marine engineers are watching the development of the gas turbine for possible use as a prime mover for ships. Some experimental installations have already been made in order to test the claimed advantages of high thermal efficiency, reduced size and weight of machinery, economy through use of a low-cost fuel such as bunker "C" oil or even coal, and absence of moving parts. An atomic-powered ship, the *N. S. Savannah*, is now being operated by the American Export & Isbrandtsen Lines for the U. S. Maritime Administration.

Increase in Deadweight-Displacement Ratio: One of the principal problems of the ship designer is to reduce the weight of materials and equipment on a vessel so that the deadweight tonnage (carrying capacity) may be increased without a corresponding increase in displacement and power. A great step forward in this direction was made by welding techniques. Use of welding has eliminated hundreds of tons of members whose only primary function was that of connection. The elimination of rivets, plate laps and butt straps, and the like, also has improved the appearance and lessened hull resistance to movement through the water. The quest for a lighter structural material than mild steel is also meeting success. Aluminum alloy structure and equipment is being utilized to a greater and greater extent. At present, superstructures, hatch covers, booms, lifeboats, gangways, and many other smaller fittings are being made of aluminum, which is not only lighter than steel, but stronger and more corrosion resistant. With reductions of cost in aluminum production and advances in the technique of welding aluminum, one may look for a continuation of this trend. Corrugated plating has also contributed to

---

[1] See "Design of Stacks to Minimize Smoke Nuisance" by R. W. Nolan, *Transactions of the Society of Naval Architects and Marine Engineers*, Vol. 54, 1946.

the increasing ratio of deadweight to displacement since a considerable weight reduction is effected with the elimination of stiffeners and framing. This trend also is one which should be watched. At present, bulkheads and superstructures are being made of corrugated or fluted plating.

Classification System for Maritime Commission Designs

Maritime Commission (Administration) vessels are classified by a series of letters and numbers which are often confusing to the uninitiated. All of these numbers and letters have a definite meaning. Since there are literally thousands of such vessels afloat, it is apparent that the mariner should understand the classification system.

The system is based on three groups of letters and numbers. The first group indicates the type of vessel, such as cargo, passenger, tanker, etc., and its approximate length. The second group indicates the type of machinery, number of screws, and whether or not the vessel carries over twelve passengers. The third group indicates the particular design of the type of vessel and modifications of the same.

SEE TABLE I & TABLE II

It is necessary to refer to Tables I and II for the meaning of the letters and numbers. Using the C2-S-AJ1 should serve as an example of how the system works. In the first group a letter is used in conjunction with a number. Referring to Table I, it is seen that the C2-S-AJ1 is a cargo vessel with a length on the load waterline between 400 and 450 feet. Also, referring to Table II, that the vessel has a single screw, steam machinery, and carries twelve or fewer passengers. There may be many vessels with the above characteristics and it is necessary, therefore, to have a design letter that will fix the particular vessel under consideration. A third group is used and the design letter is fixed regardless of any change that may be made. The design letter of our example is therefore "AJ." The number 1 after the "AJ" indicates the original arrangement of this particular design. This number can be varied to reflect changes of a major nature such as addition of passengers, conversion to troopship, etc. An example is as follows: Let us assume that accommodations for 50 passengers were added to this particular vessel. As this would be a major change, the third group would become "AJ2." Since accommodations for more than 12 passengers had been added, the second group would become "S1," and as these accommodations were for less than 100 passengers, the first group would not change. Since there are already many "C2" vessels and may be many more, it is important to realize that the "nickname" for this particular vessel should be "AJ" and not "C2."

Occasionally another letter is added to the first group to indicate other things. For example, the basic Liberty ships are designated EC2 and the Victory ships VC2. The A in C1A stands for shelter deck type and the B in C1B stands for full scantling type.

Maritime Commission designed vessels may sometimes be identified by their names. For example, C1A and C1B types are sometimes named for capes; the C1-M-AV is named for knots; some C2's are named for

TABLE I

Type of Vessel		Length on the L. W. L. in feet						
		1	2	3	4	5	6	7
C	Cargo—Unlimited Service (under 100 pass.)	Under 400	400-450	450-500	500-550			
P	Passenger— Unlimited Service (over 100 pass.)	Under 500	500-600	600-700	700-800	800-900	900-1000	Over 1000
T	Tanker	Under 450	450-500	500-550				
N	Coastwise Cargo	Under 200	200-250	250-300	300-350	350-400	400-450	450-500
B	Barge	Under 100	100-150	150-200	200-250	250-300		
R	Refrigerated	Under 400	400-450	450-500	500-550			
V	Towing Vessels	Under 50	50-100	100-150	150-200			
S	Special	Under 200	200-300	300-400	400-500	500-600	600-700	

TABLE II

Type of Machinery	No. of Propellers	Under 12 Pass.	Over 12 Pass.
Steam	Single	S	S1
Motor	Single	M	M1
Turbo Electric	Single	SE	SE1
Diesel Electric	Single	ME	ME1
Steam	Twin	ST	S2
Motor	Twin	MT	M2
Turbo Electric	Twin	SET	SE2
Diesel Electric	Twin	MET	ME2

[1] In 1950, a new system of classification for the Maritime Administration was inaugurated. In this system, the third group of letters and numbers are altered so that the hull design is indicated by numbers, the conversions by lower case letters. The "Mariner" type ship was the first vessel to be so classified (C4-S-1a). It was given the number 1, the original design being identified by the letter "a". Subsequent alterations to the ship are given the letters "b, c, d," etc. Vessels designed subsequent to the "Mariner" are identified by numbers 2, 3, 4, etc.

famous clipper ships; C3 vessels are sometimes named for birds, fish, and animals in combination with the prefix "Sea," such as the "Sea Otter."

The original C4's (C4-S-A & C4-S-B types) are generally named for birds, fish, and animals too, but the prefix Marine is used. The new "Mariner" class C4's (C4-S-1a) have the nickname of States with the suffix "Mariner," such as "Lone Star Mariner." T2 tankers are named for American battles or for national landmarks. Liberty ships were named for famous deceased Americans; Victory's for the various United Nations, or for small U.S. cities and towns, or for colleges. Liberty colliers are named for major coal seams in the U.S. In all of these cases, however, after the ships were sold to private companies, their names were changed.

MODERN TYPES OF SHIPS

The development of the modern standard vessel was instigated by the Merchant Marine Act of 1936 which gave to the Maritime Commission (now the Maritime Administration of the Commerce Department) the responsibility for rehabilitating our deteriorating Merchant Marine. The original Commission program contemplated the construction of some 500 cargo and passenger vessels as well as several hundred tankers over a period of 10 years. The Commission was fairly launched on this program when war broke out in 1939. The program was revised; revised again; and then again; so that in the period from 1939 through 1945, American shipyards completed over 5,000 merchant vessels of 2,000 gross tons or more. This comprised a total of over 54,000,000 deadweight tons. (Table III). The overwhelming majority of this stupendous fleet was of Commission design.

With the war over, the reserve fleet acts as a drag to construction of new vessels. To prevent block obsolescence, a sustained program of new construction should be maintained. The passenger ship picture is particularly dark. A postwar boom in oil demand, however, has lead to the construction of great numbers of large, fast tankers.

Liberty Ship: The Liberty ship program, which started early in 1941 when the keel of the PATRICK HENRY was laid, produced over 2,600 vessels of the standard design EC2-S-C1. In addition, there have been scores of Liberty hulls built or converted to special types. These include: Oil tankers, colliers, tank carriers, hospital ships, troop transports, training vessels, and several types of special service naval auxiliaries.

It was in the construction of the Liberty ship that prefabrication and sub-assembly reached its amazing peak. Huge sub-assemblies such as whole deckhouses complete with wiring and piping, were constructed off the ways and then lifted bodily and put in place. Naturally it was welding that permitted such extensive use of sub-assembled sections. The standard ship of the first World War, the "Hog Islander" never approached the Liberty in ease and speed of erection. The average time for the completion of a Liberty was 61.9 days.

TABLE III

UNITED STATES MARITIME ADMINISTRATION CLASSED SHIPS (1950-1965)

Designation	Remarks	Designation	Remarks
C4-S-1a	20 knot cargo ship—the MARINER	EC2-S-22a	Navy conversion of Liberty hull
C4-S-1b	Navy AKA	S2-ST-23a	MSTS cargo ship (dock)
C4-S-1d	Navy APA	T1-MET-24a	MSTS small Arctic tanker
C4-S-1f	Pacific Far East Lines Mariner	S2-S-RM28a	Coast & Geodetic survey vessel
C4-S-1h	APL Lines. PRESIDENT JACKSON class	C3-S-33a	Moore-McCormack. MORMACPRIDE class
P2-S1-1g	Oceanic liner MONTEREY	C3-S-37a	Lykes Bros. JAMES LYKES class
C4-S-1m	U. S. Lines, American Pioneer conv.	C3-S-37b	Lykes Bros. Improved 37a
C4-S-1p	APL conversion	C3-S-37c	Lykes Bros. Improved 37a
C4-S-1qa	APL conversion	C3-S-37d	Gulf & South America
C4-S-1sa	American Mail Lines	C3-S-38a	American Export Lines
C4-S-1t	Pacific Far East Lines	T4-SE-39a	Jumboized Red Hill Corps. tanker
C4-S-1u	States Steamship Co.	P2-N1-MA40a	Nuclear-powered SAVANNAH
P2-S1-1v	American Export. S. S. ATLANTIC.	C3-S-43a	Mississippi Ship. Co. DEL RIO class
T5-S-RM2a	"Pipeline" class tanker	C3-S-45a	Container ship
R3-S-4a	Navy reefer (turbine)	C3-S-46a	American Export. EXPORT BANNER class
R3-ME-4b	Navy reefer (Diesel-electric)	C3-S-46b	American Export. EXPORT COURIER class
C3-S-7a	SCHUYLER OTIS BLAND conversion	C4-S1-49a	Grace Lines. SANTA MAGDALENA class
C3-M-7b	Same as 7a but Diesel	B2-MA51a	Nuclear servicing vessel
EC2-S-8a	Liberty turbine. GEN CHEN	C4-S-57a	U. S. Lines. CHALLENGER class
EC2-M-8b	Liberty Diesel. THOMAS NELSON	C4-S-58a	Farrell Lines. AFRICAN COMET class
EC2-G-8f	Liberty gas turbine. JOHN SARGENT	S1-MT-59a	Coast & Geodetic survey vessel
EC2-G-8h	Liberty gas turbine. WM PATTERSON	C4-S-60a	Moore-McCormack. MORMACARGO class
P2-S2-9a	Moore-McCormack. BRASIL class	S1-MT-MA63a	Coast & Geodetic survey vessel
P2-S2-11a	Grace Lines. SANTA ROSA class	C4-S-64a	U. S. Lines. AMERICAN RACER class
T5-S-12a	MSTS tanker	C4-S-65a	Grace Lines. SANTA LUCIA class
T5-S-12b	Same as 12a but 7 ft. more amidships	C4-S-66a	Lykes Bros. LOUISE LYKES class
C1-ME2-13a	Small Navy cargo ves., ice strength.	C4-ST-67a	MSTS vehicle cargo vessel
C3-ST-14a	Roll-on, roll-off ship for MSTS	S1-MT-MA72a	Coast & Geodetic survey ship

U.S. Maritime Commission

Figure 6. Hog Islander

U.S. Maritime Commission

Figure 7. Liberty Ship

U.S. Maritime Commission

Figure 8. Liberty collier: EC2-S-AW1

Although there has been some criticism of the Liberty, mainly due to the many cracks which the ships sustained and the loss of a few due to cracking, the fact remains that the Liberty program was successful in achieving its goal of providing a sufficient number of vessels to carry through our war effort. About 150 Liberties were lost due to enemy action. The fleet now remaining has been sold to U.S. and foreign operators, laid up in reserve, or scrapped. By 1965, the Liberties were all over 20 years old, but hundreds of them were still in service under U. S. and foreign flags with scores of conversions to special types.

Victory Ship: The Victory ship, another war-emergency type, was designed as a high speed cargo vessel. In the period from 1943 through 1945 when the program was completed, a total of 531 ships was constructed. Four types, which differ principally as to propelling machinery and size of machinery space, were constructed. The hull form and size on all four types is identical. In 272 ships, of the VC2-S-AP2 type, geared-turbine machinery was installed with a shaft horsepower of 6,000 producing a

U.S. Maritime Commission

Figure 9. Victory Ship

speed of 15½ to 16 knots. The AP3 type, of which 141 were constructed, has geared-turbine machinery with shaft horsepower of 8,500, producing a speed of 17 to 17½ knots. The AP5 type were constructed as troop transports. The VC2-M-AP4, of which only one was constructed, is powered by Diesel machinery.

The Victory ship, a full-scantling type, has, with its higher speed, been even more successful than the Liberty in avoiding the scrap yard. But, like the Liberty, her days are numbered and by 1970 most of these ships will disappear from the oceans of the world.

"C" types: The various types of Commission designed cargo vessels are known as the "C" types. All of these vessels belong to the long range program in distinction to emergency designs such as the Liberty and the Victory.

C1 types: Two of the earlier Commission designs were the C1-A and the C1-B types, both relatively small flush deck vessels being specially

Figure 10. The USNS *Kingsport*, a Victory ship conversion to a Satellite Communications ship. It is characterized by a giant radome aft and a multiple array antenna aft.

Figure 11. The USNS *Mirfak*, a C1-ME2-13a, used in MSTS Arctic operations.

Figure 12. C1-M-AV1

adapted for service not requiring excessive speeds. The C1-A is a shelter deck vessel, while the C1-B is full-scantling.[1] The midship housing on both types of C1's is very distinctive, extending out to the vessel's sides, forming a box-like superstructure, with the cargo ports on the C1-A located at Nos. 2, 3, and 4 hatches, helping to identify this vessel. Most of the C1-A's are Diesel powered, while most of the C1-B's are turbine driven.

Military Sea Transportation Service

Figure 13.   The USNS *Josiah Gibbs*, oceanographic vessel. Its deep sea winch can handle up to 40,000 feet of wire rope and twenty tons of equipment.

A later C1 design is the C1-M-AV1. This class of vessel is the result of a directive from the Joint Chiefs of Staff for small cargo vessels (LOA of 338 feet) for use in the Pacific theatre of operations. They were requested because much of the smaller tonnage had been lost to enemy action and had been replaced by larger ships which could not utilize their full capacity in such a service. Following a recent trend in ship design, the machinery space was located well aft with only one small compartment aft of the machinery space. These vessels are proving very popular in postwar operation, with a number being converted to army transports, and others sold to foreign and domestic operators. Some two hundred of this type are in operation.

There are other C1 designs including: Ocean-going barges, self-propelled concrete ships (C1-S-D1 type), a lumber vessel (C1-MT-BU1), and small transports (C1-S-AY1). There has been only one small ocean-going cargo vessel built in the post-war building program, the ice-strengthened C1-ME2-13a for MSTS.

C2 types: The first Maritime Commission design was a medium-size cargo vessel called simply the C2. This design, a shelter deck type, presented a fine blend of speed, cargo capacity, and economy of operation; and immediately achieved popularity among the shipping fraternity and the U.S. Navy. In ensuing years, with many medium-size cargo vessels being designed by the Commission, it was necessary to classify these vessels.

---

[1] The definition of what constitutes a shelter deck vessel and what a full-scantling vessel is not an easy one, since it is involved with three very technical design factors—tonnage measurements, freeboard regulations, and strength. These factors are explained fully in subsequent chapters. However, shelter deck vessels are designed to operate at relatively small drafts. Volumetric capacity is, therefore, more important than deadweight, and the shelter deck ship carries light, bulky types of cargo.

The two most numerous of the C2 designs are the C2-S-AJ1 and the C2-S-B1. These vessels have the distinctive appearance of the original C2. Both have raised shelter decks with deck line being raised slightly at the forecastle head and at the poop. A number of the B type built at North Carolina are designated as full-scantling types, since the tonnage well is omitted, thus permitting an addition to the draft. However, these ships do not qualify for minimum freeboard due to their light scantlings, and are better designated as scantling-draft ships than full-scantling ships.

U.S. Maritime Commission

Figure 14.   C2-S-B1

Most of the C2 types are driven by turbines, but a few are Diesel powered.

There are many C2 types now in operation: the C2-S-E1, the C2-S-A1, the C2F, and the C2SU, to name but a few. These vessels may be entirely different in appearance from the AJ and B types. It is apparent that a vessel can no longer be identified completely by stating that it is a C2. (Both Liberty and Victory types are also C2's). There have been no vessels of the C2 length built in the post-war program of ship construction.

C3 types: The C3, a cargo vessel between 450 and 500 feet in length— not being of an uncommon length—has many types. Also, in common with all Commission designs, the owners frequently modify their vessels so that the vessel as originally designed is quite unlike the finished product. These alterations in design may be in the type of rigging, the superstructure (forecastle and bridge housing), and stack, as well as conversion of tanks and holds for various uses. Almost all C3's, however, are shelter deck vessels designed for greater cargo capacity and speed than the C2's; and can be identified by a forecastle with the remainder of the upper deck being flush. C3's tend to have a great number of kingposts, a square, box-like housing, and the usual raked bow, cruiser spoon stern, and tear drop stack. Propelling machinery is usually turbine with a few Diesel drives. The most numerous of the C3 types are the C3-S-BH and the C3-S-A.

Moore-McCormack Lines

Figure 15. The *Mormacpride*, a C3-S-33a, designed for Great Lakes and Seaway as well as ocean voyages, uses extensively aluminum (bridge house, etc.), hydraulic power for cargo handling and deck gear, plastics (lifeboats, ventilators), and has no cargo hold pillars.

U. S. Lines

Figure 16. The *American Racer*, a C4-S-64a, highly automated, crew of only 38, sustained sea speed of 21 knots, triple hatches, 70-ton heavy-lift boom serves both Nos. 3 & 4, polyurethane insulation, stainless steel or plastic-lined tanks, etc.

Moore-McCormack Lines

Figure 17. The *Mormacargo*, a C4-S-60a, highly automated, service speed over 24 knots, 75-ton heavy-lift Stulcken rig, etc.

The C3 passenger and cargo type is roughly similar to the C3 in dimensions, but has the massive midship housing common to the passenger vessel. Only a few of the C3 P & C vessels have been constructed.

By reference to Table III, page 16, one may observe the various classes of vessels of C3 length which have been constructed in the post-war building program. They include a Navy reefer class, the C3-S-7a ("Schuyler Otis Bland", a prototype ship), a roll-on, roll-off ship for MSTS, the "Mormacpride" class, and cargo vessels for Lykes, Gulf & South America, American Export, Mississippi, as well as a container ship.

Figure 18.   C4-S-1a   U.S. Maritime Commission

Figure 19.   The *Santa Lucia*, a C4-S-65a, in service in 1966.   Grace Lines

C4 types: During World War II, two variations of the C4 type were built—the C4-S-B and C4-S-A types. Many of these large cargo vessels are still in operation. Most have undergone extensive conversion work. It is the C4 length and size which has proven most popular in the post-war building program. The new C4's are not only big—they are fast (upwards of 20 knots) and they have been automated extensively with such things as quick-opening steel hatch covers, machinery controls on the bridge, constant tension winches, automatic datalogging both on the bridge and in the engine room, bow-thrusters, etc. Table III reveals the popularity of the

C4-S-1 type, the "Mariner" which has been converted by various U. S. companies to their own particular requirements. Then, there are the "Challenger" class C4's for U. S. Lines, the "Mormacargo" class for Moore-McCormack, the "African Comet" class for Farrell, the "Santa Lucia" class for Grace, the "Louise Lykes," and several others.

In 1951, construction was started on a new class of C4's: the C4-S-1a, or "Mariner" class. These vessels are to be very fast (20 knots) and equipped with helicopters in time of war.

C5 type: There are only a few C5's operating: the C5-S-AX1, an ore carrier.

Military Sea Transportation Service

Figure 20.   The USNS *Marine Fiddler*, a heavy-lift cargo ship, conversion of war-built C4.

Farrell Lines

Figure 21.   The *African Comet*, a C4-S-58a, one of six fast vessels in Farrell Lines "Third Fleet."

N3-S-A: The N3-S-A1 is a dry cargo vessel, but since it is a small coastal cargo type it is given the designation "N". It was designed to fill a real need for a general service coastal vessel. Ninety-five of this type were built during the war. The type reminds one of the old "three island" vessels, since it has a very high forecastle, midship, and poop erections. However, for the service in which the vessel is engaged this design is considered economical.

The Future: A great deal of the more lucrative cargo is being carried on aircraft now than previously. This partially accounts for the fast, automated ships now being built. Also, a great deal of experimentation in hydrofoil vessels is going on, with the Maritime Administration "Denison" and the Grumman "Dolphin" class hydrofoil vessels coming to mind most prominently. Some day, hydrofoils may recapture some of the high priority cargo. Meanwhile, they are mainly useful for passengers on short (up to a hundred miles) voyages. Hovercraft or "ground effect" type vessels are also attracting some attention.

Tanker Types

Tankers, which comprise a large part of our operating Merchant Marine, are assuming great importance in this age of motor cars, aircraft, and modern oil-heating plants. The tanker has not been standardized as completely as the cargo vessels since shipping companies generally prefer their own designs. It was necessary, however, to construct a relatively large number of standard tankers during the war. Also, a large number of Liberty hulls were converted (62 Liberty tankers of the ZET1-S-C3 type).

T2 type: By far the most numerous of all standard tanker designs are the T2-SE-A types. Over five hundred of these single screw turbo-electric tankers have been constructed. These vessels have a single deck, raked stem, cruiser spoon stern, with the conventional arrangement of forecastle, bridge, and poop. The T2-SE-A1 design develops a maximum of 7240 shaft horsepower, while the maximum for the A2 and A3 designs is 10,000 SHP. Many of the T2's have been "jumboized," that is, lengthened by the inclusion of an extra section amidships. But the T2's are slowly disappearing under the pressure of age and the new economical mammoth size vessels.

T1 and T3 types: The Commission designed various other types of tankers in the T1 and T3 class which were used by private companies and the Navy. Thirty twin screw vessels of the T3-S2-A type; 21 of the T3-S-A1 type; and 24 T1-M-BT vessels were built. In addition, some one hundred tankers of various design were built during this period by private interests and the Commission.

Postwar Construction of Tankers: At the war's end it had been thought that a surplus of tankers would exist due to the vast wartime construction program. But a tremendous demand for petroleum developed in 1946 and 1947 and the war-built tankers were not sufficient to satisfy the need for ships. (Even the lowly Liberty tankers were brought out of the reserve fleet for a while). A new program of tanker construction was started by the major oil companies and independent owners. Most of these new tankers were of the so-called "supertanker" class. Most supertankers, built to operate on the long haul to the Persian gulf, are of mammoth proportions with a length overall of about 625 feet, a draft of 33 feet, and a carrying capacity of 28,000 tons.[1] The largest tankers in the world, how-

---

[1] For a fine description of these vessels, see "The Design of a Class of 28,000 ton Tankers", by H. de Luce and W. I. H. Budd, a paper read before the New England Section of the Society of Naval Architects and Marine Engineers, October, 1949.

ever, as of 1965, have carrying capacities of 160,000 tons, and tankers of about 100,000 deadweight tonnage are rather commonplace.

Passenger Vessels

In the post-war years, the passenger fleet of the U. S. Merchant Marine drew mainly upon the war-built vessels which were easily converted. The building program (see Table III) has produced very few vessels, certainly not enough to bring the Merchant Marine back to its prewar status. The following vessels are representative of the small fleet of passenger vessels under the U. S. flag. (In 1965, the fleet consisted of only 13 large commercial ships.)

Grace Lines

Figure 22. The *Santa Mercedes*, a C4-S1-49a, passenger and cargo vessel fitted with gantry cranes for carrying containers both on deck and below.

The United States: The *S.S. United States*, the fastest passenger vessel in the world, made its maiden voyage in July, 1952, completing the eastbound run from Ambrose, L.V. to Bishop Rock in 3 days, 10 hours and 40 minutes for an average speed of 35.59 knots. Since that time it has been continuously in service compiling an enviable record of safety and efficiency on the North Atlantic run.

Constitution, Independence: These sister ships went into operation for the American Export Lines in 1951 on the Mediterranean service. They are more typical of U. S. passenger ships with their moderate speed (23 knots) and size. The *Atlantic*, a Mariner conversion, is in the same service.

Brasil, Argentina: The Moore-McCormack Lines built these two ships in 1958 and 1959 for service on the East Coast of South America-New York run.

Santa Rosa, Santa Paula: The *Santas*, which went into operation in 1958 for Grace Lines, were designed primarily for cruises to Caribbean ports. As is the case with most of the newer passenger vessels, they are equipped with fin stabilizers.

President Cleveland, President Wilson: These ships, built in 1947 and

Figure 23.   The *Santa Paula*, P2-S2-11a.   Grace Lines

Figure 24.   S.S. Panama   U.S. Maritime Commission

Figure 25.   The *Brasil*, P2-S2-9a.   Moore-McCormack Lines

1948, are the only important U. S. entries in the transpacific service. Operated by the American President Lines, they are relatively slow speed and size, but very popular with tourists traveling to the Far East. The *President Roosevelt*, a conversion of a war-built P2, is also in this service.

C2, C3 and C4 type vessels are all being utilized as passenger and cargo vessels, some of them with very luxurious accommodations for 12 passengers. Some, however, have been converted to carry 50 or more passengers.

Future Construction: The picture is very gloomy here. American Export & Isbrandtsen may replace the *Independence* and *Constitution;* American President is planning on two or three new liners. Although the nuclear vessel, the *Savannah*, has no difficulty in booking passengers, there are no plans at present for building any large nuclear-powered passenger vessels. If the Government abandons subsidies for passenger vessels, U. S. flag passenger ships will disappear.

Special Merchant Types

Specialized vessels, equipped to handle some particular type of cargo (as opposed to the general dry cargo carrier), are assuming an increasingly important role in our Merchant Marine. Among these, in addition to the oil tanker are the following types:

U.S. Maritime Commission

Figure 26.   Great Lakes ore carrier: L6-S-A1

The Refrigerated Vessel: The "reefer", as a refrigerated ship is called, is a vessel with a future. The United Fruit Company's *Fra Berlanga* is a good example. The *Fra Berlanga* is the world's largest reefer, with a length over-all of 455 feet, refrigerated cargo capacity of 318,000 cubic feet, and shaft horsepower of 12,000, producing a speed of 18½ knots. The *Fra Berlanga* was delivered in February, 1945, as the first of a class of six vessels. She was primarily designed to serve a new route between U. S. West Coast ports, Central America, the United Kingdom, and Continental Europe. During the war, however, she served in the Pacific.

The Car Carrier: A fleet of car carriers, owned by Seatrain Lines, operates between East Coast and southern ports.   Typical of the car carriers

Figure 27.   T2-SE-A2   U.S. Maritime Commission

Military Sea Transportation Service

Figure 28.   The USNS *Chattahoochee*, one of seven small MSTS Arctic tankers.

Manhattan Tanker Co., Inc.

Figure 29.   The *Manhattan*, largest U. S. merchant ship, can carry over 106,000 tons at a speed of 17.75 knots.

is the *Seatrain Texas*. This vessel can carry 100 freight cars. The advantage of a car carrier lies in the reduction of port time, stevedoring costs, and the rapid shipment of perishable goods. However, the car carrier can only be used economically on short runs, where quick turnaround in port assumes great importance. Since special terminal facilities are needed, the vessels can only load and discharge at a few ports where the special piers are located.

The *Seatrain Texas* has her machinery space aft with an uninterrupted compartment from forward collision bulkhead to forward machinery space bulkhead. There are four decks, including a superstructure deck, which extends the length of the vessel. Only one loading hatch, 57 feet long, is available. The cars are loaded and discharged through the one hatch

Military Sea Transportation Service

Figure 30. The USNS *Comet*, a C3-ST-14a, vehicle (roll-on, roll-off) cargo ship, can load through five ramps, two on each side and one at the stern.

by means of cranes at each terminal. There are four cradles at each deck and tank top and one on the superstructure deck for handling the cars. These cradles are situated in the loading hatch or cradle space and when the ship is fully loaded, a car is on each cradle except the one on the superstructure deck which is used as a gangway between the break of this deck. All decks and the tank top are laid with steel rails, welded in place. At the center of the main rails, hauling rails are fitted for moving the cars into position. This is accomplished by cables; the power for these cables being supplied by two steam winches, one forward of and one abaft the hatch on the superstructure deck. The winches are connected by vertical driving shafts to the 'tween decks and lower hold. These shafts operate continuously with the engine; but at each deck a wire rope drum is located which may be cut in and out of use by separate foot-operated clutches.

The *Seatrain Georgia* and the *Seatrain Louisiana* were constructed in 1951.

The Ore Carrier: Ore carriers include some of the largest cargo vessels afloat. An example of a modern ocean-going ore carrier is the *Venore*, which was placed in service in July, 1945. She is the first of a class of eight vessels. The *Venore* has a deadweight capacity of 24,376 tons, and is 583 feet in over-all length. She will operate primarily in the U.S.-Chile, and U.S.-Venezuela trades. Other classes of ore carriers are being planned to exploit the widening ore trade with Venezuela and Liberia.

On the Great Lakes, the most common type of vessel is the bulk ore carrier. One of the most modern of these is the *Wilfred Sykes* which was launched on June 28, 1949. The *Wilfred Sykes* is 678 feet in length, and can carry 20,000 tons of Mesabi ore at a top speed of 16½ knots. During the war, the Commission built the L6-S-A and L6-S-B type ore carriers. In the postwar period, conversions of C4's (and one Victory ship) to ore carriers are adding to the Lakes fleet.

The Trailership: A proposed ship to carry truck-trailers between San Francisco and Los Angeles is the so-called trailership, designated the Q8-S2-DW1 by the Maritime Administration. This vessel, to be operated by the Pacific Coast Steamship Company, is 563 feet in length and will have a speed of about 25 knots. About 175 trailers can be carried, as well as some 380 passengers. This vessel may be the prototype of a fleet of such vessels if the venture is successful.

Special Liquid Cargo Vessels: The term tanker is commonly taken to mean a vessel designed to carry crude oil or its products. However, the economies available in water-borne movement of this liquid are also finding application in the bulk carriage of other liquids including chemicals, liquified petroleum gas and molasses.[1]

About twenty-five different types of liquid chemicals are now being shipped in chemical tankers. Chemical tankers have all the characteristics of the regular oil tanker, but structurally must have a number of cofferdams, both longitudinally and transversely, to isolate the tanks so that different types of chemicals may be carried on the same voyage. Chemicals have specific gravities ranging up to 1.7 and therefore only the centerline tanks are usually used. These are separated from the wing tanks by longitudinal cofferdams. Inner bottoms must also be used so that there is no possible contamination from contact with the outer shell. Externally, it is possible to identify a chemical tanker by the additional piping on deck, as well as large pump motors on deck.

Vessels designed to carry liquified petroleum gas (LPG) such as propane and butane are rapidly increasing in numbers as the use of LPG

---

[1] An interesting example of a liquid cargo vessel is the *Canteleu,* a sixteen-knot, 490-foot wine "tanker" which operates in the wine trade between North Africa and France. Two pump rooms direct the flow of wine into the 22 tanks distributed on either side of the ship aft below the holds and below the holds forward. The ship also carries dry cargo in the holds.

as domestic and industrial fuel has increased considerably in recent years. LPG "tankers" are generally conversions of dry cargo vessels and are very easy to identify since the cylindrical tanks are arranged vertically and project above the weather deck. In one C1-A conversion, the *Natalie O. Warren,* 68 tanks ranging in size from eight to thirteen feet in diameter and from twenty-five to forty-eight feet in length were fitted. The void space around the tanks is ventilated thoroughly by fans.

Tankers used to carry molasses usually serve only part of the year in this trade and the rest of the time resume their function as an oil tanker. Crude molasses has a relatively high specific gravity and must be heated to maintain fluidity; and therefore, these vessels require heavier scantlings and greater heating coil surface than a normal tanker. An inner bottom is usually fitted as well.

Military Sea Transportation Service

Figure 31. *Dolphin* class hydrofoil (1965), can carry 90 passengers at 50 knots with a range of 200 miles with her gas turbine engine.

QUESTIONS

1. Explain the advantages of modern bow and stern types.
2. What is the function of the bulbous bow?
3. What is the relationship of waterline length to resistance? How has the shift from the counter to the cruiser stern affected waterline length?
4. List the changes in ship's profiles in the last 30 years.
5. Why is a forecastle head included in the design of some modern vessels?
6. A vessel weighs 4000 tons light. Its carrying capacity is 8500 tons. What is its deadweight-displacement ratio? Ans: 17/25.
7. In what ways has the deadweight-displacement ratio of modern vessels been increased?
8. What is the purpose of corrugated or fluted bulkheads?
9. What is preventing a more general use of aluminum as a structural material?
10. Compose a classification for the following mythical ship: A medium size passenger vessel with twin screws, turbo-electric drive and the third modification of a BT hull design. Ans: P2-SE2-BT4.
11. What type of vessel is sometimes named after famous American battles?
12. What is the meaning of "A" in C1A? "B" in C1B?
13. Why was E used in the classification of the Liberty ship?
14. What length is used in the Maritime Commission classification system?
15. How would you identify the following mass produced ships? Hog Islander, Liberty, Victory, C1A, C1B, C1-M-AV, C2-S-AJ, C2-S-B, C3-S-BH, C4-S-B, N3-S-A, T2-SE-A?
16. How would you identify a Car Carrier? Explain, in detail, how a Car Carrier is loaded?
17. Give the name or type of the largest of the following classes of U. S. ships: Passenger, tanker, ore carrier, refrigerated ship, freighter.
18. What type of tankers are required to have inner bottoms? Why?

BIBLIOGRAPHY

Information relating to the dimensions and characteristics of types of ships can be found in:

Record, American Bureau of Shipping
Lloyds Register of Shipping
Trial Trip Reports, U. S. Maritime Administration
Construction Specifications for the ship concerned.

Papers presented on the ship concerned before such technical societies as the Society of Naval Architects and Marine Engineers and included in their Transactions, or published in the various marine periodicals such as Marine Engineering and Shipping Review.

J. La Dage & Associates, A Pictorial Study of Merchant Ships, Cornell Maritime Press, Inc., Cambridge, Md., 1955.

Chapter 3

TONNAGE MEASUREMENT

All merchant vessels of the world are assigned a Gross Register Tonnage and a Net Register Tonnage by their respective governments. The principles involved; that is, the measurement of spaces within a vessel, are the same for all nations. The laws, although differing in some details, produce tonnages which are approximately the same. The basic intent of tonnage measurement is to establish an equitable basis for the assignment of fees. The search for a tonnage system which would be entirely equitable and workable has extended over centuries; has resulted in many varied and interesting results and an equal number of disturbing anomalies; has aroused criticism from many quarters and is still continuing to do so. A mass of detailed regulations has been accumulated over the years through legislative and administrative actions. These regulations are contained, for the United States, in a book entitled "Measurement of Vessels." The Commissioner of Customs is charged with the supervision of the regulations contained in this book. The work of measurement is undertaken by officers of the U. S. Customs.

Tonnage History

It appears that attempts to establish a tonnage system were made as early as the thirteenth century. The capacity of a vessel in barrels of wine was judged to be her tonnage. Thus the original meaning of the word "ton" was not a weight unit, but a measurement unit, since the word is probably a corruption of the old English word "tun" meaning barrel or cask, or the Latin word "tunna" meaning barrel.[1]

Later on, acts of the English Parliament established the tonnage as simply "length times breadth times depth divided by 94." Since depth was defined as breadth divided by two, designers tended to build deep, narrow ships. Vessels were subsequently lost because of this poor design.[2] Tonnage regulations promulgated since then, although not leading to such disastrous results, have had pronounced deleterious effects on design.

The basis for modern tonnage regulations was started in England in 1854. A Mr. George Moorsom, charged with evolving a new system for tonnage assignment, laid down the basic principle that assessment of fees

---

[1] Rossell & Chapman, *Principles of Naval Architecture*, Vol. I, page 72.
[2] Ibid, page 72.

for services rendered to a vessel should be based on a measurement of the vessel's potential earning capacity. The "Moorsom System" underlies the thinking embodied in all modern tonnage systems.

U. S. Registered Tonnage

Gross tonnage may be defined as the total internal volume of a vessel in units of one hundred cubic feet, less the volume of certain spaces which are exempted to encourage the use of spaces devoted to the safety of the ship or the comfort of her crew and certain spaces which are exempted because they are not "closed-in" spaces according to regulations.

Net Tonnage may be defined as the Gross Tonnage less the volume of certain specified spaces which are not available for the carriage of cargo or the accommodation of passengers.

These definitions of Gross and Net Registered Tonnages are very general. In order to understand how these tonnages are arrived at and how the design of a vessel is affected by the regulations, one must struggle through the complexities of these regulations as given in "Measurement of Vessels." The regulations are so complex, yet so important, that large Naval Architect firms must employ the talents of "tonnage experts" who are able to embody in the design of a vessel those features which will reduce the tonnages of the vessel to an absolute minimum.

In the following discussion of the calculation of Gross and Net Registered Tonnages and the regulations governing such calculations, direct reference shall be made wherever necessary to "Measurement of Vessels," Part 1 (Regulations for the tonnage measurement of vessels) by article number.

The first step in the process of tonnage measurement and the acquisition of the Marine Document or Certificate of Admeasurement and the registering of a vessel is to apply in writing to the Collector of Customs before the engine is installed and compartments partitioned off, (16.10), that is, at an early stage in the construction of the vessel. Admeasurers can then commence the actual measuring of the ship's internal volume. It is not considered necessary in this text to enter into a discussion of the exact methods and instruments used in measuring a vessel for tonnage. However, certain dimensions which are used in the computations and which appear on the Marine Document are quoted from the regulations.

The *Register Length* is the length measured on the tonnage deck from the fore end of lap of outer plating to the after side of the sternpost. (16.18) The tonnage deck is the upper deck to the hull in vessels having not more than two decks and the second deck from the keel in vessels having more than two decks. (16.26)

The *Register Breadth* is the measure taken from the outboard face of the outer skin on one side to the same point opposite, taken at or below the upper deck and at the widest portion of the hull. (16.19)

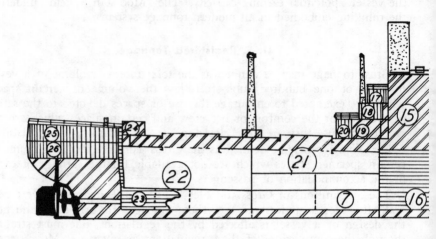

1. BOS'NS STORES	6. SHELTER DECK - NO 2. HOLD	11. GALLEY
2. BOS'NS STORES	7. DEEP TANKS	12. DINING SALOON
3. FORE PEAK TANK	8. NO. 3. HOLD	13. CAPTAINS OFFICE
4. CHAIN LOCKER	9. MAST HOUSE	14. WHEEL HOUSE
5. NO. 1 HOLD	10. CREWS MESS	15. LIGHT & AIR

▨ EXEMPTED   ▥ INCLUDED + DEDUCTED   ☐ INCLUDED

Figure 32.   Tonnage Profile

The *Register Depth* is taken at the middle of the tonnage length from the under side of the tonnage deck to the top of the inner bottom; if a ceiling is fitted the depth is measured to top of same and the thickness of the support for the ceiling is added. (16.20)

Gross Tonnage

The measurement of spaces for gross register tonnage is taken and entered on the Marine Document in the following manner: (16.5)

1. "The cubical capacity below the tonnage deck, excluding exemptible water ballast spaces.

2. "The cubical capacity of each between-deck space above the tonnage deck.

3. "The cubical capacity of the permanent closed-in spaces on the upper deck available for cargo or stores, or for the accommodation of passengers and/or crew.

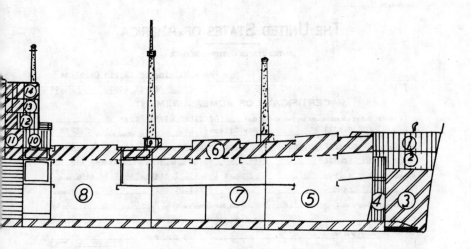

16. MACHINERY   20. FAN ROOM   24. DECK LOCKER
17. FAN ROOM   21. NO. 4 HOLD   25. STORE ROOM
18. ELECTRICIANS ROOM   22. NO. 5 HOLD   26. STEERING ENGINE ROOM.
19. TOILETS   23. SHAFT TUNNEL

▤ POWER SPACE (INCLUDED & DEDUCTED)   ▦ FITTINGS

4. "All permanent closed-in spaces situated elsewhere available for cargo or stores, or for the accommodation of the crew, or for the charts, except cabins or staterooms for passengers constructed entirely above the first deck which is not a deck to the hull.

5. "The excess of hatchways."

In item 1, above, it should be noted that *all* space below the tonnage deck is included except certain water ballast spaces. Water ballast spaces are exempted only when they are not available for the carriage of cargo, stores, supplies, or fuel. Adaptation for water ballast consists of having the space or spaces properly constructed and tested as ballast tanks; that the pumps, pipes, etc., for filling and emptying such tanks must be connected to the ballast system and completely independent of the cargo, fuel-oil, feed, or domestic water-pumping apparatus. (16.43, h). Thus, for example, if the fore peak tank is to be exempted it cannot be used to carry fresh water nor can pipes be fitted to enable it to carry fresh water. *All* double bottom spaces, are, in effect, exempted since they do not form

Certificate No. ....

THE UNITED STATES OF AMERICA

UNITED STATES CUSTOMS SERVICE

Port of __Wilmington, North Carolina__

__April 4th.__ , 19__44__

CERTIFICATE OF ADMEASUREMENT

I CERTIFY that an admeasurement has been made of the [1] __American Steam Screw__

called the __(C2-S-AJ1)__ of __New Orleans, La.__ , official number __245373__

which was built by __North Carolina Shipbuilding Company__ in the year 19__44__, at __Wilmington__,

State of __North Carolina__ , of __Steel__ ; and has been known as builder's hull No. __112__ ;

that she has __Two__ deck s, 1 mast, 1 signal mast, 10 king posts mast

__Raked__ stem, and __Elliptical__ stern;

that her register length is __441.2__ TE feet, her register breadth is __63__ __2__ TE feet

her register depth is __30.7__ TE feet, her height under upper deck is [3] TE feet,

and that her tonnage is as follows:

	TONS	100THS
Capacity under tonnage deck [5]	7347	18
Capacity between decks, above tonnage deck		
Capacity of enclosures on the upper deck, viz:		
Forecastle [4] , bridge , poop , break		
deckhouses __692.05__ , Trunk __42.72__ , Raised decks , chart house __62.40.__		
radio house , excess hatchways __20.77__ , light and air [5] __93.15__	911	09
GROSS TONNAGE.	8258	27
Deductions under Section 4153, Revised Statutes, as amended (Section 77, title 46, United States Code):		
Crew space __580. 63__ , master's cabin __38. 80__ , steering gear __53.45__	672	88
anchor gear __24. 43__ , boatswains' stores __65.06__ , chart house __8.60__	98.	09
donkey engine and boiler , radio house __12.12__	12	12
storage of sails , propelling power (actual space [6] __988.69__) 32%Gross	2642	65
TOTAL DEDUCTIONS	3425	74
NET TONNAGE.	4832	

The following-described spaces, and no others, have been omitted, viz:

Forepeak __2 .05__ , afterpeak __22.73__ , other spaces (except double bottoms) for water ballast ; open fore-

castle , open bridge , open poop , open shelter deck , cabins [7]

companions __3.04__ , galley __30.32__ , skylights [8] __2.33__ , wheelhouse __21.27__ , water-closets __27.67__ ,

anchor gear , condenser , donkey engine and boiler , steering gear , light

and air spaces, including skylights, over propelling machinery __64. 82__ , other machinery spaces __37.24__ lookout houses

Admeasurer. (SEAL) ....

Collector of Customs.

I agree to the above description and admeasurement.
__North Carolina Shipbuilding Company__

Owner, Master, or Agent.

Figure 33. Certificate of Admeasurement

part of the measurable portion of the ship, register depth being taken to the top of the inner bottom.

The wording of item 3, above, is very important since only those spaces which are *permanently closed-in* are included in gross tonnage. The interpretation of what constitutes a permanently closed-in space has given rise to regulations permitting such peculiarities as the tonnage well and tonnage openings. This element of the tonnage regulations is discussed further on. The following spaces, on or above the upper deck are exempted in line with the regulation in item 3. It must be emphasized that these spaces are exempted only if they are on or above the upper deck. The definition of upper deck to the hull is important and is quoted directly from the regulations: (16.21)

"The uppermost complete deck, which extends from stem to stern and from side to side at all points of its length and below which there are no openings through the hull as required in shelter deck spaces and also having its hatchways or other openings provided with means for closing them against the action of the sea and weather upon the space below inclosed by the sides of the vessel, making the said space a fit place for the stowage of general cargo, is to be considered the upper deck to the hull."

Spaces on or above the upper deck which are exempted: (16.43)

1. *Companions:* All companions and booby hatches protecting companionways leading to spaces below, whether such spaces are exempted or not.

2. *Galleys:* All galleys and bakeries.

3. *Machinery spaces:* This includes all auxiliary machinery spaces such as steering engine rooms, resistor houses, etc. If part of the space is below the upper deck, that part is not exempted.

4. *Skylights:* That portion of skylights above the upper deck.

5. *Water closets:* All toilets which are public. A crew water closet is considered public if it serves more than one member of the crew.

6. *Wheelhouse:* If the space is a combined wheelhouse and chart room, only such space as is necessary for the proper steering of the vessel shall be exempted.

7. *Light and air:* This term is applied to the skylight space above the propelling machinery space. Although the space is exemptible, it may be included at the owner's option in order to achieve a larger deduction from gross tonnage. Details on this option are given in a succeeding section.

8. *Passenger spaces above the first deck which is not a deck to the hull:* (16.44). This is the very significant and important Special Passenger accommodation exemption, and dates back to an obscure law of 1865 which apparently was meant to apply only to river and lake steamers. The rule, however, has been applied to all U. S. vessels. Since this rule results

in a considerable reduction of tonnage for U. S. vessels, some foreign countries do not accept the exemption and U. S. passenger vessels must carry, therefore, a "Special Appendix to the Certificate of Registry of American Passenger Vessels" which notes the tonnage which has been excluded and the special gross and net tonnages. (16.61). This exemption results in a tendency to place as many passenger spaces as possible above the first deck which is not a deck to the hull.

9. *Open superstructures on or above the upper deck:* (16.45) "Nothing shall be added to the gross tonnage for any sheltered space on or above the upper deck which is under cover and open to the weather; that is, not enclosed."

Cadet-Midshipman R. D. Lezcano, Class of 1951, US Merchant Marine Academy

Figure 34.   Tonnage hatch on a cargo ship.

The regulations surrounding this rule make it possible to create a "sheltered space, not enclosed" by providing tonnage openings in the end and intermediate bulkheads of the space. The size and closing arrangements of the openings are carefully specified in the regulations. The openings can be covered by "temporary" means, but no gaskets, bolts, etc., can be installed on the coamings of openings. Plates with hook bolts are permitted on the end bulkheads but not on the intermediate bulkheads. Thus, by this regulation, a deck space with an end bulkhead can be made exemptible by a purely fictional "open" space. Cargo can, and is carried in these spaces with perfect safety.

10. *Open shelter deck space:* By this rule entire deck space under a complete deck can be made technically "open" and a shelter deck space, and thus exempted. The rules for achieving this happy situation are long and detailed but in general the tonnage well must be at least 4 feet in length; equal in width to the width of the after cargo hatchway on the same deck; must be not less than 1/20th of the register length from the

Cadet-Midshipman R. D. Lezcano, Class of 1951, US Merchant Marine Academy
Figure 35. Tonnage opening in Bulkhead between tonnage well and No. 5 hold.

stern post or 1/5th of the length from the stem. The regulations on coamings, covers, etc. for the well provide that no permanent means of closing the well can be installed on the coamings. The well must be *kept clear* at all times. All bulkheads forward of the well (if it is aft) must have two tonnage openings, each 3 feet wide by four feet high.

A majority of modern vessels take advantage of this shelter deck exemption to reduce their register tonnages. It should be noted, however, that the installation of a tonnage well results in putting the freeboard deck one deck below the upper deck and thus increasing the freeboard. A shelter deck ship of this type, therefore, is designed to carry relatively, light, bulky cargo and can relinquish the deeper draft without any real penalty.

Excess of hatchways: (16.41)

There is one more space which remains to be discussed in connection with exemptions. Hatchways which are out in the open or in open spaces on the upper deck to the hull are normally exempted. However, in order to prevent the building-up of hatch coamings to unreasonable heights in a search for exempted cargo space, the regulations provide that so-called "excess of hatchway" space shall be included in gross tonnage. The regulations in this regard are quoted: (16.41)

> "The cubical contents of the hatchways shall be obtained by multiplying the length and breadth together and the product by the mean depth taken from the top of the beam to the underside of the hatch cover. From the aggregate tonnage of the hatchways there shall be deducted one-half of 1 percent of the gross tonnage of the vessel exclusive of the tonnage of the hatchways, and the remainder only shall be added to the said gross tonnage as excess hatchways."

The rule has the effect of eliminating hatchway space in excess of one half of 1 percent of gross tonnage, since any space past that volume will result in an increase in the gross tonnage of the vessel.

The discussion of exemptions from Gross Tonnage given above illustrates the complexity of the modern method of arriving at an equitable basis for assessing fees. A system which results in such ridiculous structural abnormalities as tonnage wells, tonnage openings, and excessive passenger spaces on certain upper decks, etc. is certainly in need of overhaul. Such important regulations as these which have affected the design of every ship afloat, however, cannot be changed easily. What might be fair to one shipowner would be disastrous to another. If changes are to be made, it is certain that they will be made slowly and carefully.

Net Tonnage

After the gross tonnage has been obtained, the volume of certain spaces which are not available for the carriage of cargo, and which has been previously included in gross tonnage, is obtained. This volume, with the exception of the machinery space and the boatswains storerooms, is divided by 100 to obtain the deductible tonnage. The deductions permitted for the propelling machinery space and boatswains storerooms are found by rather involved and somewhat outmoded methods. These methods are outlined below.

Certification of deducted spaces: (16.49)

"No space shall be deducted unless . . . . the certification showing the exclusive use for such purpose is permanently cut in a beam, over the doorway, within the space, with these words: 'Certified to accommodate - - - - seamen,' 'Certified for the accommodation of master,' 'Certified messroom', 'Certified W. C.,' 'Certified for boatswain's stores,' 'Certified chart house,' 'Certified for steering gear,' etc. as the case may be."

Spaces deductible from gross tonnage to obtain net tonnage:

1. *Crew spaces:* Spaces used exclusively by officers and crew including such spaces as showers, sleeping rooms, smoking and recreation rooms, messrooms, hospitals, etc. (16.49)

2. *Private water closets:* A private water closet is defined as one serving not more than one member of the crew. (Public water closets below the upper deck are also deductible).

3. *Master's cabin:* This includes any space exclusively for the use of the master.

4. *Anchor gear:* This includes the chain locker and any space below used for the capstan, windlass, etc. (16.50)

5. *Chart room and Radio room:*

6. *Boatswain's storerooms:* These spaces are given special treatment by the regulations since there is a tendency on the part of some owners to use them for carrying cargo despite their certified category. In order to limit the size of what may become in effect, a deductible cargo-carrying space, the deduction can never be greater than 100 tons regardless of the volume of the spaces. Normally the deduction is 1 percent of gross tonnage or the actual tonnage of the space, whichever is smaller.

7. *Propelling machinery space:* The deduction for this space is by far the largest of all deductions from gross tonnage. The deduction is never the actual tonnage of the space, but is always much greater than actual tonnage.

The propelling machinery space is considered to consist not only of the engine room, but also such spaces as the shaft tunnel or tunnels, the escape shaft, the settling tanks, and the engineers stores and workshops. (16.52)

The deduction for propelling machinery space is found by comparing the actual space occupied by the propelling machinery with gross tonnage. (16.58)

If this percentage is	*The deduction is*
13% or less	175% of the machinery space[1]
Above 13%, below 20%	32% of the gross tonnage
20% or more	32% of the gross tonnage; or at owner's option, 175% of machinery space

The "32% of gross tonnage" deduction is usually much larger than the "175% of space" deduction, and it is, therefore, greatly to the owner's advantage to bring the machinery space volume up to the point where it represents more than 13% of gross tonnage. This is true even though technical requirements do not indicate the necessity of all such space.

[1] In 1957, this provision was altered. The deduction is now 32/13 of the machinery space, making the incentive to design a large machinery space far less urgent.

The regulations on this section of the tonnage laws are becoming increasingly irritating to the shipping fraternity.[1]

To add to the involved character of the machinery space deduction, the shipowner may elect to *include* the light and air space in the machinery space in order to bring the latter space up to 13% of gross tonnage. If he so elects, however, the light and air space is then included in gross tonnage. (16.59) This results in a small increase in gross tonnage, but enables the owner to achieve a substantial reduction in net tonnage. Only that portion of the light and air space which is required to bring the machinery space up to exactly 13.1 percent of the final gross tonnage is included. Since the gross tonnage is increased by this amount of light

---

[1] The following excerpt from the 1948 *Transactions of the Society of Naval Architects and Marine Engineers* is illustrative. The quotation is from the paper "Modern Tankers" by H. F. Robinson, J. F. Roeske, and A. S. Thaeler.

"Modern tankers are characterized generally by the fact that they can be loaded with gasoline to the international summer freeboard draft in the domestic trades, notwithstanding the high ratios of deadweight to displacement which are now obtainable. These characteristics require large volumetric cargo capacity and it has become increasingly difficult to satisfy this requirement and at the same time, obtain minimum United States net tonnage admeasurement; in fact, it would seem that, under the present measurement regulations, the attainment of minimum United States net tonnage cannot always be justified in the case of tankers.

"There now exists the paradoxical situation wherein the machinery casing is being increased in height, thereby increasing the gross tonnage, for no other reason than to obtain a volume of propelling machinery space equal to 13 percent of the gross tonnage volume in order that the net tonnage may have the benefit of a 32 per cent deduction from the gross tonnage. This points to the need for reconsideration of the legal requirements for measurement of vessels. These requirements, so far as net tonnage is concerned, were adopted in the United States in 1895 and include that feature of the British rules which, at an even earlier date, penalized the net tonnage of vessels having a volume of machinery space less than 13 per cent of the gross tonnage volume. This requirement was intended presumably to insure adequate working access around machinery, but it is now becoming increasingly apparent that the space required for satisfactory operation is not a simple function of the size of ship as defined by the gross tonnage.

"The large tankers which are now being built with modern geared-turbine propelling machinery have adequate working space at the operating levels, and the space which is added at the top of the machinery casing to satisfy the requirements for minimum United States net tonnage can be justified only if the tolls which are based on United States net tonnage are an appreciable proportion of the cost of tanker operation. Propelling machinery space which is obtained in this manner is not useful space from the point of view of machinery operation and does not add to the safety or comfort of the ship's personnel."

However, in the discussion of the above quotation, Rear Admiral H. C. Shepheard, USCG, has this to say:

"I agree that an ideal set of rules for tonnage admeasurement would contain nothing which would encourage the construction of useless enclosed space. Likewise such rules should not require ship designers to sacrifice seaworthiness and safety to obtain reduced tonnages. Our present rules contain both of these faults.

"The only way in which the rule regarding machinery space deductions could be made equitable between different types of ships would be to remove the *bonus* given to vessels in the 13 to 20 per cent category, thus applying the "actual measurement" principle to all ships. This automatically would remove the conditions which bring about the unnecessary expansion of machinery casings, but it would increase the net tonnage of a large percentage of all merchant ships.

"Until the day comes when shipowners will not object to an increase in the net tonnage of their ships, there probably will continue to be considerable opposition to any change in these rules."

and air space added, it is not sufficient simply to take the difference between the actual machinery space and 13.1 percent of the gross tonnage.
The regulations give a simple rule for finding the amount of light and
air space which must be added: (16.49, d)

"Find 13.1 percent of the gross tonnage inclusive of excess of hatchways. Find the difference between this percentage and the tonnage of
the propelling machinery space below the upper deck to the hull. Increase
this difference by 15 percent of itself, which gives approximately the
amount of light and air space or spaces to be added to the gross tonnage
defined above, and also to the propelling machinery space below said
upper deck."

Examples of tonnage calculations:

1. Calculation of Gross Register Tonnage:

Given: Capacity under tonnage deck ...... 7347.18 tons

　　　Capacity, enclosures on upper decks:

　　　　Deckhouses ....　692.05
　　　　Trunk ....　　42.72
　　　　Raised decks ....　62.40

　　　　　　　　　　　　　　　　　797.17

　　　Hatchway space ....　61.96

　　　Light and air:
　　　　(over 100 tons)
　　　Propelling machinery
　　　　space ....　988.69

Calculations

Gross tonnage, exclusive of light and air and hatchways ..	8144.35
Excess of hatchways (based on the above)	21.24

Gross tonnage, inclusive of excess of hatchways and ex-
　clusive of light and air ....

13.1 percent of 8165.59 .... 1069.69

Machinery space below the upper deck to the
　hull 988.69

Difference 81.00
15 percent of difference 12.15

Difference plus 15% of itself 93.15

Gross tonnage inclusive of light and air and excess of hatch　8258.74
Additional exemption for hatchways (.005 x 93.15) .... 　.47

GROSS REGISTERED TONNAGE .... 8258.27 tons

In this calculation, the first step is to find the gross tonnage exclusive of hatchway space. One half of one per cent of this gross tonnage is then figured and any hatchway space in excess of this tonnage is included in gross tonnage. In this case 1/200th of 8144.35 is 40.72 tons; and since hatchway space is 61.96 tons, there is an excess of 21.24 tons which must be included in gross tonnage and is therefore added to 8144.35. Light and air space is normally exempted unless part of it is to be used to bring the machinery space up to 13.1 per cent of gross tonnage. Therefore, it is necessary to find first, whether or not it will be necessary to use part of Light and Air, and second, how much of it will be necessary to include in gross tonnage. The rule for finding this was given above. In this case, 93.15 tons of Light and Air are included in the machinery space, and hence, in the Gross Tonnage. One final step must be taken. Since the gross tonnage has been increased by the addition of some light and air space, it is apparent that the value of one half of one per cent of gross tonnage has increased. Therefore, there is a slight additional exemption for hatchway space. This additional exemption is found by taking 1/200 of the addition to gross tonnage due to inclusion of some Light and Air. Here this amounts to .47 ton and is *subtracted* from 8258.74. It is subtracted because the original figure for excess of hatchways was too large by this amount.

2. Calculation of the propelling machinery deduction (old Rules):

Case A: Machinery space less than 13% of G. T.

Given: Gross tonnage: 7101.04 tons
   Actual propelling power space: 860.20 tons
   Light and air space: 52.80 tons

Find: Maximum machinery space deduction:

Ans: 13.1 percent of 7101.04 tons is 930.24 tons. Machinery space of 860.20 tons is less than this figure. There is not enough light and air space to bring the machinery space up to 930.24 tons. Therefore, the deduction is:
   175% of 860.20, or: 1505.35 tons

Case B: Machinery space less than 13% of G. T., but with inclusion of Light and Air, greater than 13%.

Given: Tonnages as in Calculation 1 (Calculation of Gross Tonnage.)

Find: Machinery space deduction.

Ans: Since the machinery space is now over 13% of G. T. (13.1%) the deduction is:
   32% of 8258.27 tons, or 2642.65 tons

Note: If Light and Air had not been included in G. T., the deduction would have been 175% of actual space, or: 1730.21 tons. This is a difference of 912.44 tons! Net tonnage is not decreased by exactly this amount, however, since the inclusion of Light and Air results in an increase of 93.15 tons in the Gross tonnage (less the increased hatchway exemption) and thus is a corresponding increase in Net tonnage. Thus the increase in Gross tonnage is 92.68 tons (93.15 — .47) and the decrease in Net tonnage is 819.76 tons (912.44 — 92.68).

Case C: Machinery space 20% or more of G. T.

Given: Gross tonnage: 6220.8 tons
   Actual machinery space: 1248.6 tons (which is 20.07 per cent of the G. T.)

Find: Maximum machinery space deduction

Ans: 175% of actual space: 2185.05 tons
   32% of Gross Tonnage: 1990.66 tons
   Therefore, since the shipowner may elect either of these choices, the deduction chosen will obviously be 2185.05 tons.

   3. Calculation of boatswain's stores deduction.

Given: Gross tonnage: 8258.27 tons
   Boatswain's stores: (actual space): 65.06 tons

Find: Deduction for boatswain's stores:

Ans: Since the deduction is the smallest of three possibilities; that is, actual tonnage, 1 per cent of gross tonnage (82.58 tons) or 100 tons, the deduction is 65.06 tons.

Note: If the boatswain's stores had a tonnage over 82.58 tons (with the same G. T.) the deduction would be 1 per cent of gross tonnage, in this case, 82.58 tons. If the gross tonnage were over 10,000 tons the deduction could not be 1 per cent of G. T., but would be equal to the actual tonnage or 100 tons, whichever figure were smaller.

The Certificate of Admeasurement:

The Certificate of Admeasurement: After all calculations for Gross Tonnage have been made, and the deductions from Gross Tonnage to obtain Net Tonnage, have been arrived at, they are entered upon the "Certificate of Admeasurement." The vessel upon being registered, receives an official number, and is said to have been documented. An example of this Certificate is shown. The vessel is first described and identified; next the spaces included in Gross Tonnage are listed; then the deductions totaled and subtracted from Gross to obtain Net Tonnage; and finally the exempted spaces are listed. Footnote 7 at the bottom of the certificate is worthy of repetition:

   "To be exempted, cabins and staterooms for passengers must be on a deck which is not a deck to the hull; all other spaces except forepeak, afterpeak, and other water-ballast spaces must be *on* or *above*

the upper deck to the hull. A cellular double bottom is not included in tonnage."

Miscellaneous information and regulations on U. S. Register Tonnage:

1. It should be noted that certain spaces are included in Gross Tonnage, but not deducted from Gross to obtain Net Tonnage, even though they are non-cargo carrying spaces. These spaces include tanks which are not exempted; that is, tanks which are not used exclusively for water ballast.

2. Net tonnage is not necessarily a measure of the earning capacity of the vessel, since an entire shelter deck space which carries cargo may be exempted from Gross Tonnage (and hence from Net Tonnage). Also, the propelling machinery space deduction which is much larger than the actual tonnage of the space leaves a net tonnage which is likely to represent a volume of space which is less than the actual volume of cargo carrying space. For example, the net tonnage of the C2-S-AJ vessel in the Certificate of Admeasurement illustrated here is 4832 or at 100 cubic feet to the ton, 483,200 cubic feet. The actual grain capacity of this vessel, however, is 582,845 cubic feet. On the VC2-S-AP design (the Victory Ship), on the other hand, these figures of net tonnage volume and actual capacity are almost the same. In this design, this equality can be traced to the presence of large deep tanks in Nos. 4 and 5 which are not deductible and therefore make up for the large machinery space deduction. Also, there is no shelter deck in this design. One must be careful, therefore, before defining net tonnage as a measure of earning capacity. In general, it is likely not to be such a measure.

3. Almost all charges on a vessel are based on Net rather than Gross Tonnage. One exception to this is drydocking where fees *are* based on Gross Tonnage. Since this is so, the designer will make every effort to decrease the net tonnage even if it means an increase in gross tonnage, (as is the case when part of Light and Air is added to the machinery space).

4. A vessel can be constructed as a full scantling type, but with provisions for shelter deck arrangements if the owner should so desire. An example of this type of construction is the C3-S-DX1 (the U. S. Maritime Commission prototype ship). The following quotation is from the USMC Specifications for this vessel:

"The vessel shall be constructed as a full scantling type with minimum freeboard to the Main Deck. In order to facilitate ready conversion to shelter deck type, there shall be incorporated the necessary structure for later installation of tonnage hatch and well and tonnage openings. Further to this purpose, nine inch hatch coamings shall be fitted in way of all Second Deck hatch openings, and the arrangement of Second Deck shall not impede required access to tonnage openings."

5. The Net Tonnage and Official Number are required to be marked in a conspicuous place on the main beam (hatch coaming) at the forward end of the largest hatch on the weather deck. (16.60a). The official number is preceded by the abbreviation "NO" and the net tonnage by the word "NET" in Arabic numerals at least three inches in height.

6. Almost all maritime nations of the world have adopted similar measurement tonnages and U. S. tonnage being accepted by these nations, like courtesy is extended to vessels of these nations. Therefore it is directed (16.63) "that merchant vessels of those countries, the registers of which indicate their gross and net tonnage under their present laws, shall be taken in the ports of the United States to be of the tonnage so expressed in their documents. Vessels of foreign countries other than the aforesaid are to be measured according to the laws of the United States."

7. The term "register" tonnage derives from the fact that, following the institution of the Moorsom system in Great Britain, the new tonnages were required to be registered at the Custom House, and hence came to be known as Register tonnage.

SUEZ AND PANAMA CANAL TONNAGES

Vessels transiting the Suez and Panama Canals are charged on a basis of a tonnage measurement system set up by the respective canals. The Moorsom principle is adhered to, just as it is in U. S. tonnage, but the regulations vary in detail.

Owners of U. S. vessels may apply to the Collector of Customs for Suez and Panama Canal Certificates since Customs officers are authorized to measure vessels according to the Canal rules.

Since the Canal rules are somewhat more strict in the definition of exempted and deducted spaces, these tonnages are larger than U. S. Gross and Net Tonnages. As an example, the tonnages of the C2-S-AJ design referred to above are given:

	United States	Suez Canal	Panama Canal
Gross	8,258.27	8,376.74	8,373.03
Net	4,832.00	6,141.06	5,647.94

At present, the Panama Canal tolls are 90 cents per net Panama ton when the vessel is loaded and 72 cents when neither cargo nor passengers are carried. Warships, American and foreign are charged 50 cents per ton of displacement.

QUESTIONS

1. What agency is responsible for the supervision of tonnage regulations? What agency is responsible for the actual measurement of vessels for tonnage?
2. What is the title of the booklet containing the laws and regulations pertaining to tonnage measurement? Where can this booklet be obtained?

3. Whose name is most intimately associated with the evolution of modern tonnage measurement systems?
4. Show by means of a sketch why old British tonnage regulations defining depth as one-half the beam resulted in the construction of deep, narrow ships.
5. Define as simply as possible: Gross and Net Register tonnage.
6. When are vessels usually measured for tonnage?
7. Define: Register length, breadth, and depth.
8. What are the five categories of spaces included in Gross tonnage?
9. What two important characteristics must a space possess in order to be exempted from Gross tonnage?
10. What is the only type of space below the upper deck to the hull which can be exempted? Why are double bottom spaces, although not included in Gross tonnage, not considered as exempted spaces?
11. Define: Upper deck to the hull.
12. Make a list of all spaces on a ship classifying the spaces as: (1) *Included* in Gross tonnage (and not deductible from Gross tonnage) (2) *Exempted* from Gross tonnage (3) *Included* in Gross tonnage and *deductible* from Gross to obtain Net.
13. Explain fully the role of "Light and Air" space in the computation of Gross and Net tonnage, and the effect of this role on ship design.
14. What is the "Special Passenger Accommodation Exemption" and how does this rule affect the design of U. S. passenger vessels?
15. Classify the following spaces according to the categories given in Ques. 12: Steering engine room (below upper deck); Fore peak tank used for storage of washing water; chain locker; Water closet for passengers (on upper deck).
16. Differentiate between an open superstructure on or above the upper deck and an open shelter deck space.
17. Can stores or cargo be carried legally in a tonnage well?
18. What is the difference between a tonnage well and a tonnage opening?
19. How is the freeboard of a vessel effected by the exemption of a shelter deck space?
20. What is the purpose of providing for the inclusion of "excess" hatchway space?
21. In what way do tonnage regulations make for less seaworthy ships?
22. Are all non-cargo carrying spaces deductible on a cargo ship? What is the principal type of non-cargo carrying space which is not deductible?
23. All tank spaces devoted exclusively to the carriage of water ballast are exempted, but if they carry other types of liquid are not only included in Gross tonnage but are not deductible. What is the logic of this rule?
24. How is the deduction for the boatswain's storerooms calculated? Explain the logic of the rule.
25. What is the largest deduction from Gross tonnage?
26. Explain why it is virtually imperative for ships to have machinery spaces with tonnages greater than 13% of the Gross tonnage?
27. Why are owners given an option of 175% of actual machinery space or 32% of Gross tonnage as the deduction for machinery spaces with tonnages over 20% of the Gross tonnage?

28. Explain why Net tonnage is not necessarily a measure of the earning capacity of a vessel.
29. Why is it sometimes desirable to construct a vessel so that it can be converted to a shelter deck design by opening up a tonnage well, the structure of which has been provided in the original design.
30. Compare U. S., Suez Canal, and Panama Canal Register tonnages.
31. A vessel has an internal volume (less exempted spaces) of 1,000,000 cubic feet. The volume of space inclosed by the hatchways is 12,000 cubic feet. What is the excess of hatchways? What is the final Gross tonnage? Ans: 70 tons; 10,070 tons.
32. A C2 has the following internal capacities in cubic feet:

Capacity under tonnage deck	427,043
Capacity 'tween decks	177,838
Capacity inclosed spaces above deck	50,216
Capacity of all hatchways	7,898
Propelling power (actual space)	89,607
Other deductions	56,074

What is the Gross tonnage? Ans: 6597.2 tons.
What is the Net tonnage? Ans: 3925.4 tons.
33. A vessel is measured for tonnage as follows:

Capacity under tonnage deck	6,450 tons
Capacity, encl. on upper deck	672 tons
Hatchway space	58 tons
Light and air	140 tons
Propelling machinery space	846 tons

Find: Gross Register tonnage: Ans: 7247.3 tons.
34. What is the deduction of a bosn's storeroom that has 9200 cubic feet of space if the Gross tonnage of the vessel is 8800 tons? if the Gross tonnage is 9400 tons? Ans: 88 tons; 92 tons.
35. The Gross tonnage of a vessel is 8,200 tons. The propelling machinery space, including Light and Air, is measured at 820 tons. Find the machinery space deduction using the new (1957) regulations.

BIBLIOGRAPHY

Measurement of Vessels, United States Government Printing Office.

Rossell & Chapman, *Principles of Naval Architecture,* Vol. I, Society of Naval Architects and Marine Engineers, New York, 1942.

Comstock, J. P., *Introduction to Naval Architecture,* Chap. IV, Simmons-Boardman Publishing Company, New York.

Baker, *Introduction to Steel Shipbuilding,* McGraw-Hill Book Company, Inc., 2nd Ed., New York, 1953.

Walton & Baird, *Steel Ships, Their Construction and Maintenance,* Chap. VI, Charles Griffin and Company, Limited, London, 1944.

Robinson, Roeske & Thaeler, "Modern Tankers", *Transactions of the Society of Naval Architects and Marine Engineers,* Vol. 56, 1948.

Walton, *Know Your Own Ship,* Chap. VIII, Charles Griffen and Company, Limited, London, 1942.

D. Hudson, *Design Conflicts Resulting from Regulations Based on the Tonnage Measurement,* SNAME Pacific Northwest Section, April, 1956.

Chapter 4

CLASSIFICATION

In this age of mass-production and complicated economies, the need for specialization has manifested itself in all branches of nations' economies. The shipbuilding and ship operating industry is no exception. Marine insurance is a highly specialized field, and marine insurance in turn, looks to the classification society for the extremely technical information necessary regarding the strength and seaworthiness of vessels which are to be insured. The modern function of a classification society therefore, is to survey all elements of ship design and operation:—materials used in construction, the size and distribution of all members comprising the structure, the adequacy of all equipment, etc.—and report, when requested to do so, on the "class" of vessels. The organization and multifarious activities required to accurately classify vessels will be outlined in this chapter.

History of Classification Societies[1]

The origin of classification societies can generally be traced to the influence and need of Underwriters for information regarding prospective risks. The brief account here of the historical development of the American Bureau of Shipping and Lloyd's Register of Shipping—two of the most important classification societies today—illustrates the control exercised by Underwriters in the formation of these societies.

Lloyd's Register of Shipping: The origin of Lloyd's, as is well known, dates back to the middle of the eighteenth century in the meetings of Underwriters in Lloyd's Coffee House in London. The discussions there relating to the seaworthiness of ships, led directly to the formation of a Register of ships controlled by, and for the private use, of those Underwriters who belonged to the Society. The extension of functions of the Society, amalgamations with rival societies, the admittance of shipowners and merchants to the Society, and a steady increase in the influence of Lloyds, characterized the two hundred years which followed. The British Corporation Register of Shipping which was founded in 1890 was an important rival of Lloyd's until recently (March, 1949) when the two

---

[1] The source for this account of the history of classification and for much of the following information on classification is: "Classification of Ships", by David Arnott, a paper read before the New York Metropolitan Section of the Society of Naval Architects and Marine Engineers on September 29, 1944 and "American Bureau of Shipping: 1862-1943" by J. L. Luckenbach, *Transactions of the Society of Naval Architects and Marine Engineers, 1943.*

societies combined to form the Lloyd's Register of Shipping United with the British Corporation Register. This society and the American Bureau of Shipping cover now some 80 percent of the merchant tonnage of the world.[1] It should be pointed out that Lloyd's Underwriters and Lloyd's Register are separate entities and that the insurance of ships or the controlling of rates of insurance are not functions of Lloyd's Register (or any other classification society).

History of the American Bureau of Shipping: In 1860, an organization known as the American Shipmaster's Association was formed. Its purpose was to encourage the development of efficient ship's officers of good character. This organization was sponsored by the Atlantic Mutual Insurance Company, and illustrates not only the interest of marine insurance companies in classification, but also the interest in the development of competent ships officers. "There is no such thing as a fool-proof ship and in the last analysis most accidents at sea can be traced to some failure on the part of the personnel." [2]

The American Shipmaster's Association from 1862 to 1900 issued Commissions of Competency and Service to ships officers and since the U. S. Steamboat Inspection Service which ordinarily licensed masters and mates was suspended from 1860 to 1870, the Association was the only organization during this time which offered a standard of efficiency for ships officers.

In 1867, the Association issued a "Record of American and Foreign Shipping" with information on the ratings and surveys of vessels. The Record has been issued annually ever since. In the preface to the 1869 Record it was stated that the Association proposed "to establish a record of the character and rating of vessels; and, in entering upon the performance of this work, it will bring to its aid and assistance the best and the most efficient men whom it can procure. The importance of this work can hardly be over-estimated. The underwriter and shipowner are equally interested. If the examination of a vessel be thorough and complete, and the judgment passed upon her be without bias, the shipowner will know what ought to be the measure of premium to be paid, and the underwriter will be limited to the proper measure to be charged. So far as possible, a perfect record will be kept of every vessel, whether repaired rebuilt, or newly constructed." [3] This statement of the function of a classification society and its Record of Shipping is just as excellent a statement today as it was in 1869.

---

[1] N. Y. Times, March 28, 1949.
[2] David Arnott, op. cit., page 6.
[3] J. L. Luckenbach, op. cit.

The next step in the development of the American Shipmasters Association was the preparation and publication of Rules governing the survey of vessels. The first official *"Rules for the Survey and Classing of Iron Vessels"* was published in 1877.

In 1898, the corporate name of the Association was changed to its present name, the American Bureau of Shipping. Since that time, the ABS has made persistent progress in becoming one of the really outstanding technical organizations of the world.

Modern Organization of the American Bureau of Shipping: The ABS is, and has been, since its inception a corporation under the laws of the State of New York. It must be emphasized, however, that the Bureau is a non-profit organization; it has no capital stock and pays no dividends. All fees charged for its services are used for maintenance, extension, and improvement of these services. There are some 150 prominent maritime persons who are members of the American Bureau. Its governing body consists of a Board of Managers elected from the membership. There are Committees on Standing and Finance; Classification; Great Lakes; and Pacific Coast. Two very important committees on Naval Architecture and Engineering, made up of preeminent naval architects and marine engineers, offer sound technical background. Special committees such as the Sub-Committee on Welding which was established in 1943 to investigate the soundness of welded ship construction, are also formed. The routine work of the ABS is carried on by a technical staff and by surveyors established in all principal ports of the United States, and in a great number of ports scattered about the world.

Relationship of the American Bureau to the Government: As long ago as 1891, the American Shipmasters Association was authorized to survey and rate the first vessels built for transatlantic service under the Ocean Mail Act of that year. The American Bureau is officially recognized by the United States Government in the Merchant Marine Act of 1920. This Act directs all departments of the Government to recognize the ABS as their agency for classification and other proper functions of a classification Bureau as long as the Bureau continues to be a non-profit organization. The Act also specifies that two representatives of the Government shall serve on the Board of Managers of the Bureau. These representatives today usually come from the Coast Guard and the Maritime Administration.

After the passage of the Load Line Act of 1929 the American Bureau of Shipping was designated as the assigning authority for load lines under this Act.

In addition to these connections with the Government, the ABS also has representation on most international Conferences relating to merchant shipping. For example the Bureau was represented at both the International Conferences for the Safety of Life at Sea (1929 and 1948) and the International Load Line Conference of 1929.

There is some duplication of effort in the activities of the American Bureau and many government agencies concerned with the regulation of merchant shipping. This is especially true of the surveys carried on by the U. S. Coast Guard's division of merchant marine inspection and the ABS surveys. Government regulations, in this respect, influence the ABS Rules since it would be futile for the Bureau to have less stringent rules than the government bodies.

In spite of all these connections with the government, it must be remembered that the American Bureau is a private corporation and except for its loadline work cannot force legal compliance with its Rules. Nor is such force necessary. The strength of a classification society lies in its technical reputation and the need of shipowners, Underwriters, and shippers for assurance on the seaworthiness of vessels in which they are interested.

Modern Publications and Functions of the American Bureau: The primary purpose of the ABS is, of course, the establishment of standards of ship construction and maintenance of "class." In performing this function and others, it is necessary to issue various publications which give details of how these functions are organized and carried out. A list of these publications and the related functions follows:

1. *"Rules for Building and Classing Steel Vessels."* This is an annual publication, which in many ways is the "Bible" of American ship production. The *"Rules"* give first, details of requirements of the various structural elements which make up the ship's hull and superstructure. For example, such elements as Double Bottoms, Panting Arrangements, Shell Plating, Cementing and Painting, and Welding are discussed. In the back of the book, Tables of Scantlings offer the designer, as well as the ABS surveyor, an exact listing of the scantlings required for a vessel of certain principal dimensions. There are Rules for the Construction and Classification of Machinery, Rules for the Inspection and Testing of Materials, and Rules for the various surveys which are required to maintain a vessel in "class," There are three types of surveys which are conducted: (a) The annual survey which is conducted at least three times during each four year period. At this survey such important parts of a vessel as require constant attention such as steering gear, watertight arrangements, and all parts particularly liable to rapid deterioration, are inspected. (b) Special Periodical Surveys are made at intervals of four years from date of build. These special surveys are very strict and become even more so with succeeding surveys. The ship must be placed in drydock for Special Surveys. The scantlings of all members may be inspected by drilling holes in the members. (c) Surveys must be held after damage (or suspected damage) to a classed vessel. The Master of the vessel is responsible for reporting damage to the nearest ABS office.

Materials which enter into the construction of hull and machinery are tested by ABS inspectors right at the steel mill, factory, etc.

2. The *"Record."* (Fig. 36) This is an annual publication wherein important dimensions and characteristics of all vessels classed by ABS are given. Also, the classification of each vessel; the dates when the various surveys were made; particulars of vessels of the United States not classed with the Bureau and of the larger foreign vessels which regularly visit U. S. ports; vessels which have had their name changed.

The highest hull classification given by ABS, as listed in the *Record* is: ✠ A1 Ⓔ. The Maltese Cross means that the vessel was surveyed during its construction. If the Bureau surveyed a vessel after its construction, this symbol would be omitted. A1 stands for the highest hull classification. Ⓔ means that the Equipment of the vessel meets the requirements of the Rules. The highest machinery classification is ✠ AMS. Once again, the Maltese Cross means that the machinery was built under the survey and supervision of the Bureau; AMS is for the highest machinery classification. Other symbols of class which may appear in the Record are: ✠ RMC for refrigerating installation; EAC for auxiliary electrical installation. Also following the classification symbols may be some qualification of class such as "Oil Carrier" meaning that the vessel is given the classification only when it is used as an Oil Carrier; "River Towing Service"; "with freeboard" meaning that the vessel is in class only with a certain specified freeboard.

The *Record* is of great value to all persons operating, or shipping on, or underwriting, vessels, since it informs them at a glance of the opinion of a highly respected technical organization of any particular vessel.

3. The *"Bulletin."* This is a monthly publication of a pamphlet containing statistical information on vessels under construction and other intelligence regarding the work of the Bureau.

4. In addition to the functions enumerated above, the Bureau has been designated to assign load lines for all United States vessels. The surveys, in this regard, are made according to the laws and regulations in *Load Line Regulations,* a U. S. government booklet issued under the supervision of the United States Coast Guard. In addition to U. S. load line surveys, the Bureau has been granted authority by various foreign countries to issue load lines to vessels of those countries registry. These countries include: Belgium, Denmark, Finland, France, Norway, Sweden, Greece, Panama, Honduras, Brazil, Canada, Liberia, Pakistan, and the Philippine Republic. Details of the computation of freeboard and the assigning of loadlines under U. S. regulations are given in Chapter 5.

5. The Bureau issues, after the survey of a vessel and its equipment and machinery, a number of certificates of character. These include:

    a) Certificate of Classification For Hull (Fig. 37)

    b) Certificate of Classification For Machinery (Fig. 38)

    c) Equipment Certificates (for bower and stream anchors, cables and chains for the anchors, and towlines) (Fig. 39, 40)

ALH

1 No. OFF. No. SIG. LTR.	2 NAME OF VESSEL / FORMER NAME / OWNER / FLAG PORT OF REGISTRY	3 TYPE / WATER BALLAST / SIZE TANK TONS	4 CONSTRUCTION / BULKHEADS / No. OF HATCHES / No. OF HOLDS / LARGEST HATCH / LONGEST HOLD	5 FUEL AND CAPACITY APPLIANCES / FIRE PROTECTION APPARATUS / EQUIPMENT	6 DIMENSIONS MOLDED REGISTERED / LGTH. BDTH. DPTH. / DECK ERECTIONS BALE CUB. / DRAFT BALE CUB. / FREEBOARD DEADRISE	7 TONNAGE GROSS NET DEAD DISPL.	8 BUILDERS / SHIP PLACE ENGINE BOILER / HULL No. DATE BUILT	9 TYPE AND PARTICULARS OF MACHINERY	10 HULL CLASSIFICATION; DATE OF LAST SURVEY; AND DATE OF LAST PERIODICAL SURVEY MACHINERY: CLASSIFICATION; DATE OF LAST SURVEY MCH. AND DATE OF LAST SURVEY TAIL-SHAFT DRAWN; ETC. OTHER CLASSIFICATION
568	ALHAJUELA............. / United States of America / (The Panama Canal) / Washington, D.C. / United States	Sgl Sc MV Tug	Steel; 1 Dk / Trans Frmg / 3 WT	Oil / 33 tons	110'6"OA 25'6"	265 / — / 457	Panama Railroad Co. 1936 / Balboa, C.Z. / Ingersoll-Rand Co.	Oil Eng;Elec Mot / BHP 750	✠A1⑬ 6-46
569 247340 ANNP	ALHAMBRA VICTORY... / U.S. Maritime Commission / Washington, D.C. / United States Los Angeles, Cal.	Sgl Sc / AP2 / DT 133' / DB 306'6" / FP / 34 / 1648 / 1524 / 106	Steel; 3 Dks / Orlop Dk / Metal Arc Welded / (Gunwale Bar riveted) / Trans Frmg / 7 WT to Fbd Dk / 2 WT to 3rd Dk / 5 Ha 36'x22'4" / 5 Ho 81' / FreonSys 11M Ref	Oil / 2882 tons / Rad Tel / Rad DF / DS;GC / Radar / C-39(S)	436'6" 62' 38' / 439.1' 62.1' 34.5' / Dft 28'6½" F87' / Fbd 9'7" 453M / Dr 0'	7607 / 4561 / 10709 / 15200	California S.B. Corp. V47 / Los Angeles, Cal. 2-1945 / General Electric Co. 2-1945 / Babcock & Wilcox Co 2-1945	2 Cyl Stm Turb / SHP 6600;DR Gears / 2 WTB;HS 12120;WP 525 Lbs / FD;SH / SBP;CL	AS 2-46;Dkd 6-46 / ✠AMS 9-46 / An MS 2-46 BS 2-46 / RMC 2-46 TS Drn 6-46
	south Dredge Co. Duluth, Minn. / Duluth, Minn. / United States								
576 5WAA	ALIKI............... / ex Louis Joliet / Linardos Bros. Maritime Co., Ltd. / Piraeus, Greece / Greek Piraeus, Greece	Sgl Sc / AP2 / DT 20' / DB 345'9" / DTl 60'9" / FP / 152 / 762 / 1258 / 652 / 138	Steel; 3 Dks / Orlop Dk / Metal Arc Welded / (Frames riveted) / (Gunwale Strap riveted) / Trans Frmg / 7 WT to Fbd Dk / 1 WT to 2nd Dk / 5 Ha 35'x20' / 5 Ho 72'6"	Oil / 1834 tons / Rad Tel / Rad DF / DS / C-28(S)	417'81" 56'10½" 37'4" / 422.8' 57' 34.8 / Dft 27'8½" 468M / Fbd 9'8½" Dr 6'	7194 / 4383 / 10700 / 14100	Richmond Shipyard 449 / Number One of the / Permanente Metals / Corp. 1-1943 / Richmond, Cal. / Joshua Hendy Iron 1-1943 / Works / Combustion Engineer- 1-1943 / ing Co., Inc.	3 Cyl TE 24½" 37" 70"x48" / IHP 2500 / 2 WTB;HS 10232;WP 240 Lbs / FD;SH / SBP;CL 2	✠A1⑬ 8-49 / SS No. 1 Alexandria 9-47 / AS 8-49; Dkd 9-48 / ✠AMS 8-49 / MS 9-47; BS 9-48 / An MS 8-49 / n TS 3-46; TS Drn 2-48 / EAC
577 212,822	ALIQUIPPA............. / Jones & Laughlin Steel Corp. / Pittsburgh, Pa. / United States Pittsburgh, Pa.	StW Towboat	Steel; 1 Dk	Coal	152' 29.1' 4.8'	191 / 191 / — / —	J. Rees & Sons Co., Inc. 1914 / Pittsburgh, Pa.	2-2 Cyl Comp 14" 28"x84" / IHP 600 / 4 Bkrs;WP 204 Lbs	
578 107,636 WA2241	ALITAK............. / Otis L. Shively / Seattle, Wash. / United States Seattle, Wash.	Sgl Sc MV Pass	Wood; 1 Dk	Oil / Rad Phone	91' 23.5' 10'	115 / 73 / — / —	United Engineer- / ing Wks. 1901 / Alameda, Cal. / Atlas-Imperial Diesel 1924 / Engine Co.	Oil Eng 6 Cyl 11½"x15" / SA;4 Cyc / BHP 300	

The ✠ and ✛ prefixed to the Classification symbols denote vessels built under the supervision of the Bureau, the latter being applicable only to Great Lakes Vessels. The publication of the particulars of unclassed vessels is for general information only. While extreme care is used in the preparation of all information, the Bureau accepts no responsibility for any errors or omissions.

American Bureau of Shipping

54

ALI

Figure 36. Sample page: ABS "Record"

d) International Load Line Certificate
e) A number of individual certificates certifying that an ABS inspector has surveyed the construction of various machinery at the place of construction and has approved the machinery for installation aboard ship. (Fig. 41)

The Effect of Classification on Ship Design

Shipowners find it advantageous as a general rule to have their vessels built to class, not only as a more convenient method of obtaining insurance but also to ensure the construction of their vessels according to the Rules of a classification society which has developed its requirements through years of experience and through the continuing investigation of competent technical staffs. However, some vessels are not classed. This does not indicate that the ship's structure and design is less sound than under classification requirements but merely the preference of the owner, either for self-insurance of his vessels, or for the work of his own design staff. The point here, however, is that a great majority of vessels *are* classed for various reasons. The rules and requirements as well as the policy of classification societies, therefore, have considerable effect of the design of vessels.

One of the principal effects on design due to classification is a tendency toward *uniformity* of design. This is a result of the method by which ships have to be built in order to meet requirements. For example, in the ABS *Rules,* the designer is not given too much latitude in the determination of scantlings. Once his principal dimensions (length, breadth, depth, and freeboard) have been established, the Tables of Scantlings will indicate exactly what the dimensions, weights, spacings, etc. of the structural elements of his ship must be. A small amount of discretion is permitted the designer in determining, for example, whether an increase in frame spacing can be substituted for the usual spacing by increasing the scantlings of shell plating. Also, the designer can submit plans which do not follow the *Rules* and these plans will receive special consideration from the Bureau. In general, though, the *Rules* are generally followed with the result that a uniformity of structure exists in most vessels. This may be considered a healthy situation, since a great divergency in designs might lead to uncertain results. On the other hand, classification requirements which have been developed over many years of experience can be counted on to produce reliable results. Any deficiency in the *Rules* which is revealed by experience is quickly remedied by a change in the *Rules.*

It is sometimes maintained that progress is limited by the conservatism of classification societies. New developments in materials, construction methods, and design are scrutinized and tested carefully by classification societies before they are approved for use on classed vessels. There is a tendency, therefore towards slower development of new ideas than might occur otherwise. It must be remembered however that a classification

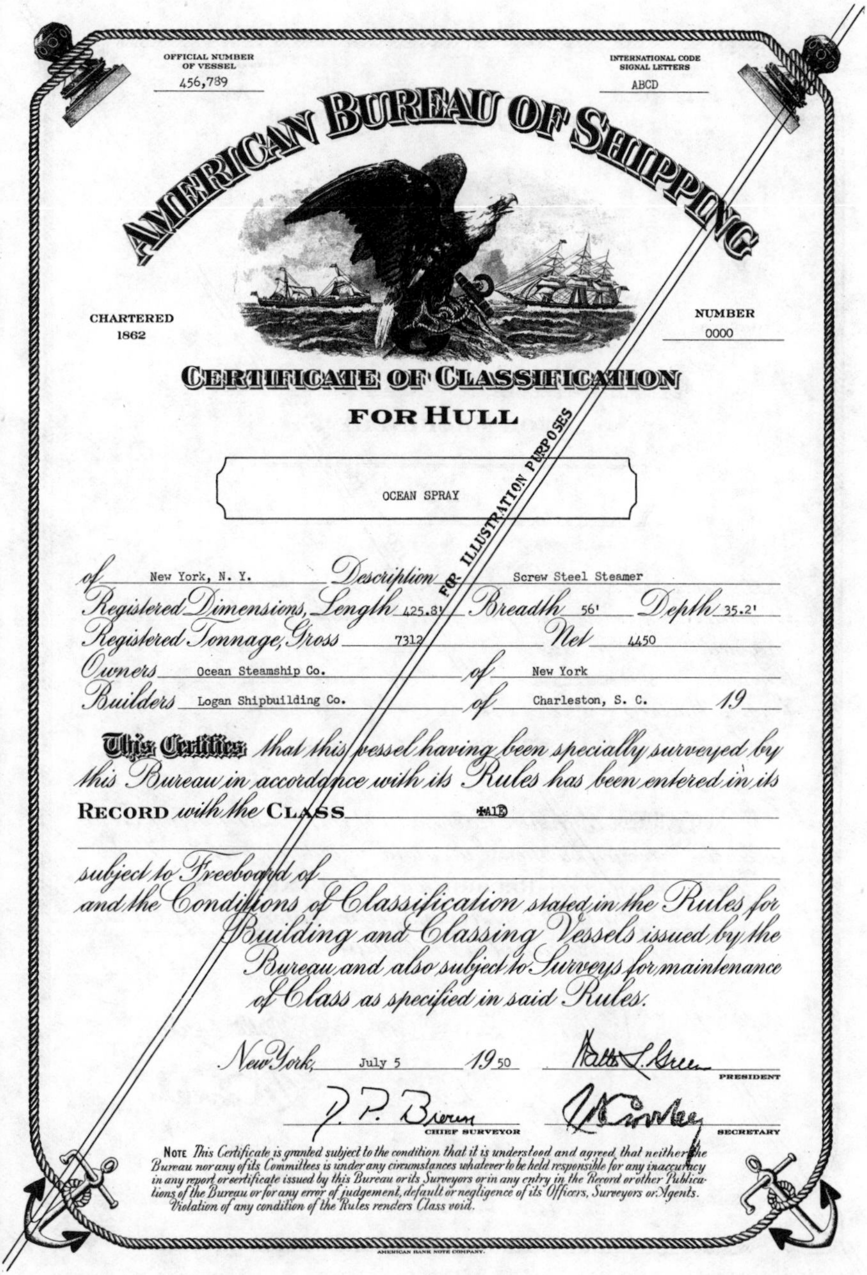

Figure 37. Certificate of Classification for Hull

OFFICIAL NUMBER
OF VESSEL

456,689

INTERNATIONAL CODE
SIGNAL LETTERS

ABCD

AMERICAN BUREAU OF SHIPPING

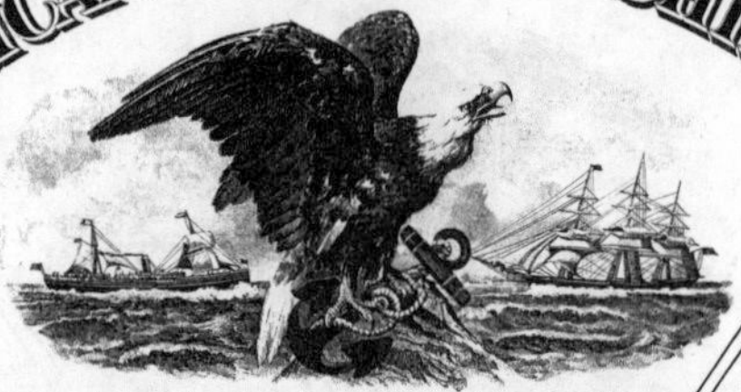

CHARTERED
1862

NUMBER

0001

CERTIFICATE OF CLASSIFICATION

FOR MACHINERY

OCEAN SPRAY

of New York, N. Y. *Description* Screw Steel Steamer
Registered Dimensions, Length 425.8' *Breadth* 56' *Depth* 35.2'
Registered Tonnage, Gross 7742 *Net* 4450
Owners Ocean Steamship Co. *of* New York
Engine Builders Evans Engineering Corp. *of* Leslie, Mass. *19*
Boiler Builders Standard Boiler Corp. *of* Newton, Pa. *19*

This Certifies *that the Machinery of this Vessel having been specially surveyed by this Bureau in accordance with its Rules has been entered in its* **RECORD** *with the* **CLASS** ✠AMS *subject to Surveys for maintenance of Class as specified in said Rules.*

New York, June 5 *19*50

Walter L. Green
PRESIDENT

J. P. Brown
CHIEF SURVEYOR

SECRETARY

American Bureau of Shipping

Figure 38.   Certificate of Classification for Machinery

Form AB 130

AMERICAN BUREAU OF SHIPPING

CERTIFICATE NO.	PORT OF
212	PHILADELPHIA, PA.

EQUIPMENT CERTIFICATE

DATE MARCH 18, 1950

This is to Certify *that the following Equipment has been tested and inspected in accordance with the Rules of this Bureau, at the request of* THE JONES ANCHOR AND CHAIN COMPANY, PHILADELPHIA, PA., ONE (1) STOCKLESS ANCHOR OF AN ACTUAL WEIGHT OF 8390 POUNDS (SPECIFIED WEIGHT OF 8400 POUNDS) TO A PROOF STRAIN OF 125690 POUNDS.

Markings:

212

A.B. 8390#

AMERICAN BUREAU OF SHIPPING

J. P. Brown — CHIEF SURVEYOR

By S. F. Smith — SURVEYOR

This Certificate is granted subject to the condition that it is understood and agreed that neither the Bureau nor any of its Committees is under any circumstances whatever to be held responsible for any inaccuracy in any report or certificate issued by this Bureau or its Surveyors or in any entry in the Record or other publication of the Bureau or for any error of judgment, default or negligence of its Officers, Surveyors or Agents.

Verified on board the SS Ocean Spray May 15, 1950

H. R. Jones
Surveyor
American Bureau of Shipping

Figure 39. Equipment Certificate

Form AB 130

AMERICAN BUREAU OF SHIPPING

CERTIFICATE NO.	PORT OF
210	PHILADELPHIA, PA.

EQUIPMENT CERTIFICATE

DATE MARCH 18, 1950

This is to Certify ***that the following Equipment has been tested and inspected in accordance with the Rules of this Bureau, at the request of*** THE JONES ANCHOR AND CHAIN COMPANY, PHILADELPHIA, PA., TWENTY 15 FATHOM SHOTS OF 2-1/16" CAST STEEL STUD LINK ANCHOR CHAIN, SIXTEEN 2-1/16" CAST STEEL CONNECTING LINKS AND FOUR 2-1/16" CAST STEEL ANCHOR CONNECTING LINKS TO A PROOF TEST OF 243930 POUNDS AND A BREAKING TEST OF 341510 POUNDS WEIGHT 73032 POUNDS

Markings:

JD 210 3-50

341510 AB 243930

AMERICAN BUREAU OF SHIPPING,

J. P. Brown
CHIEF SURVEYOR

By S. F. Smith
SURVEYOR

This Certificate is granted subject to the condition that it is understood and agreed that neither the Bureau nor any of its Committees is under any circumstances whatever to be held responsible for any inaccuracy in any report or certificate issued by this Bureau or its Surveyors or in any entry in the Record or other publication of the Bureau or for any error of judgment, default or negligence of its Officers, Surveyors or Agents.

Verified on board the SS Ocean Spray May 15, 1950

H. R. Jones
Surveyor

American Bureau of Shipping

Figure 40. Equipment Certificate

AMERICAN BUREAU *of* SHIPPING
CHARTERED 1862

CERTIFICATE FOR REFRIGERATING PLANT
✠ R.M.C.

CERTIF. NO. 1111   NEW YORK, July 5, 1950

THE REFRIGERATING MACHINERY AND INSULATION OF THE

_____ SS "OCEAN SPRAY" _____ OFF. NO. 456,789 _____

WERE SPECIALLY SURVEYED DURING CONSTRUCTION BY SURVEYORS TO THIS BUREAU

IN ACCORDANCE WITH THE RULES AND REPORTED TO BE ON June 2, 1950 _____

IN GOOD AND EFFICIENT CONDITION AND THE SPARE GEAR IN ACCORDANCE WITH THE

REQUIREMENTS. A NOTATION ✠ R.M.C. HAS BEEN MADE IN THE RECORD OF THE

AMERICAN BUREAU OF SHIPPING SIGNIFYING THAT THE REFRIGERATED SPACES ARE

FIT FOR THE CONVEYANCE OF_____ chilled and frozen products _____

SUBJECT TO PERIODICAL SURVEY AND TO THE REQUIREMENTS OF THIS BUREAU.

DESCRIPTION OF MACHINERY, _____ 2 - 10 ton freon 12 refrigerating units with brine circulation to diffusers

" " INSULATION, _____ 12" zerocel, 2 layers felt paper, T & G spruce sheathing

NO. OF CARGO SPACES INSULATED_____ 2

STATED CAPACITY _____ 3150 _____ BALE CUBIC FEET

J. P. Brown
CHIEF SURVEYOR

Walter L. Green
PRESIDENT

J. K. Cowley
SECRETARY

NOTE.—The continuance of classification of refrigerating plant is subject to survey of the plant at the end of each voyage of more than 3 months duration, or in the case of vessels making shorter voyages at intervals not exceeding 3 months. The Bureau uses its best endeavors to ensure that its rule requirements are properly executed, but it is to be understood that the Bureau is not to be held responsible for any error of record or judgment or negligence on the part of its surveyors or agents.

American Bureau of Shipping

Figure 41.   ABS Certificate for Equipment

63

society cannot afford to gamble with the confidence reposed in it by the shipping community. Its technical committees and staffs examine any new suggestions on ship construction carefully and their competence cannot be questioned. Their natural conservatism must be regarded as a small price to pay for the assurance of proper construction which they offer in return.

Classification Societies of the World

Although the American Bureau and Lloyd's, between them do most of the classification work in the world, most countries have societies which are essentially national in character. These societies do a great proportion of the classification in their own areas, although both ABS and Lloyd's are active in the classification of vessels of many nations. In some case, shipowners find it advantageous to have dual-classification; that is classification by two societies. Sometimes, classification societies will enter into agreements with each other, whereby the surveyors of one society can assume the functions of the other society when the need arises. This reduces the need for placing surveyors in foreign ports. Thus, in many foreign ports Lloyd's handles classification problems for ABS.

The following is a list of Classification Societies: [1]
  Lloyd's Register of Shipping—London
  Bureau Veritas International Register of Shipping—Paris
  Registro Italiano Navale—Genoa
  American Bureau of Shipping—New York
  Det Norske Veritas—Oslo
  Germanischer Lloyd's—Berlin
  Teikoku Kaiji Kyokai (Imperial Japanese Marine Corp.)—Tokyo
  Register of Shipping of U.S.S.R.—Moscow
Summary: Classification societies perform the specialized function of classing vessels as to their soundness of design for the service for which they are intended. This information is of value to marine insurance companies, shipowners, and others interested in the seaworthiness of ships. The rules and policies of these societies affect, in no small measure, the design of modern ships. The classification society represents, in effect, a cross-section of the entire marine industry and its rules, therefore, a composite opinion of what constitutes sound ship design.

In other Chapters the American Bureau rules on various structural elements will be given wherever pertinent.

QUESTIONS

1. Define as simply as possible the meaning of the term "classification."
2. What economic group was influential in initiating the formation of classification societies?
3. What are the two most important classification societies in the World?

---

[1] David Arnott, op. cit.

4. What was the original name of the American Bureau of Shipping? What was the purpose for which this organization was founded?
5. What are the dates associated with these important milestones in the development of the American Bureau of Shipping?
   a) The original organization of the Bureau.
   b) The issuance of the first *Record of Shipping?*
   c) The issuance of the first official *Rules?*
   d) The use of the name "American Bureau of Shipping".
   e) Official recognition by the United States Government.
   f) Designation as assigning authority for load lines for U. S. vessels.
6. Explain, in detail, the modern organization of the American Bureau of Shipping.
7. The statement has been made that:[1] "A modern Classification Society like the American Bureau of Shipping represents a practical expression of the desire on the part of the shipping industry to regulate itself in matters in which the shipowner has a predominant interest." Explain.
8. Explain the relationship of the American Bureau of Shipping to the United States Government.
9. Why are many regulations issued by both Government agencies and the American Bureau exactly the same?
10. What are the three important publications of the Bureau?
11. What, briefly, is the format of the three publications?
12. List the work performed in each of the three different types of surveys performed by the ABS.
13. List all information which can be found in the *Record* concerning an ABS classed vessel.
14. What are the classification symbols for the following?
    a) Hull
    b) Machinery
    c) Equipment
    d) Electrical equipment
    e) Refrigeration equipment.
15. What is the meaning of each individual symbol in Ques. 14?
16. Explain the effect of Classification on ship design?

BIBLIOGRAPHY

R. Renni, *The Classification of Ships*, Pacific Northwest Section, SNAME, March, 1954.

D. Arnott, *Classification of Ships,* American Bureau of Shipping, New York, 1944.

J. L. Luckenbach, "American Bureau of Shipping: 1862-1943", *Transactions of the Society of Naval Architects and Marine Engineers,* Vol. 51, New York, 1943.

Rules for Building and Classing Steel Vessels, issued annually by American Bureau of Shipping.

The Bulletin, issued monthly by the American Bureau of Shipping.

---

[1] David Arnott, op. cit.

Rules and Regulations for the Construction and Classification of Steel Vessels, issued annually by Lloyd's Register of Shipping, London.

Lloyd's Register of Shipping, issued annually by Lloyd's Register of Shipping, London.

Walton & Baird, *Steel Ships,* Chap. IV, Charles Griffin and Company, Limited, London, 1944.

J. P. Comstock, *Introduction to Naval Architecture,* Chap. V, Simmons-Boardman Publishing Company, New York, 1944.

Chapter 5

FREEBOARD AND LOAD LINES

Freeboard, which may be defined simply as the distance from the waterline to the weather deck, (but which becomes a more difficult definition when the legal or statutory element is considered) is a dimension of vast importance to all concerned with shipping. Underwriters are interested in freeboard since it affects the degree of their risk; classification societies are interested since freeboard is such an essential element of seaworthiness; government is interested due to its responsibility towards the safety of passengers and crew; and shipowners are interested in the obvious relationship of restriction of draft to diminishment of carrying and earning capacity as well as the effect on their competitive position when freeboard regulations are not uniform for ships of all nations.

The development of freeboard legislation and the compulsory marking of load lines is a comparatively recent development in the history of shipping. Restriction of drafts, prior to the twentieth century, was mainly limited to underwriter's and classification societies' rules. The latter rules were haphazard, unscientific, and not uniform among the nations. The development of modern international agreement and national legislation on this subject was a slow and difficult proposition. This is readily understood when one considers the conflicting national and international interests involved, as well as the complicated technical considerations affecting freeboard. A brief history of this development is helpful in understanding the need for, and make-up of, modern load line regulations.

History of Freeboard Regulations

The year 1870 in Great Britain marks the inception of great interest in load lines. Prior to that time drafts had been restricted by underwriters' and classification societies' rules. These rules were usually based on freeboard requirements of a number of inches per foot of depth of hold. The number of inches varied from 2 to 4 depending upon the depth of the vessel with the larger figures applied to the deeper ships. Merchant Shipping Acts of 1871, 1875, and 1890 provided for the marking of drafts and load line marks. The Act of 1875 was promoted by a Mr. Plimsoll, a Member of Parliament and provided for the compulsory marking of foreign vessels. Load lines since that time have come to be known as Plimsoll marks. This Act left the position of the mark to the owners. The Act of 1890, however, required the load line to be marked in accordance with freeboard tables prepared by the Board of Trade. In succeeding years, the Plimsoll mark developed into its modern appearance with seasonal, zonal, and fresh water marks in addition to the line through the disk. Meanwhile, various committees were continuing to study the problem of freeboard in preparation for an international agreement. This agreement was to be realized finally in 1930.

In the United States progress was somewhat slower than in Great Britain and other prominent maritime nations. Early rules of the American Bureau specified freeboards according to the "inches per foot of depth of hold" method. Thus, U. S. vessels were loaded to drafts which the owner desired except for this restriction and in some cases, restrictions imposed by the regulations of countries to which the vessels were bound. The first government restriction on drafts of U. S. vessels appears to be a U. S. Shipping Board requirement in 1917 that all their vessels be assigned load lines by the American Bureau in accordance with British Board of Trade regulations. Load line legislation was introduced in Congress in 1920 but was not passed.

The International Load Line Conference, 1930: In the years prior to the convening of this conference in London on May 20, 1930, a great amount of work had been done by Load Line Committees both in the U. S. and Great Britain.[1] The work of U. S. Load Line Committees from 1919 to 1921 and 1928-1930 had lead to the enactment by Congress of the Load Line Act of 1929 which specified the American Bureau of Shipping as the assigning authority. This Act marks the first load line legislation of the U. S. Government. The work of the U. S. Load Line Committee also formed the basis of the International Load Line Convention. The regulations of this Convention were almost identical with the U. S. Act, and since this Act was effective on September 2, 1930, the United States was the first nation to adhere to the new international agreements. Congress ratified the Convention on February 27, 1931. In 1935, the Coastwise Load Line Act was passed by Congress, which extended load line regulation to vessels in coastwise service and the Great Lakes.

The Technical Background of Load Line Regulations

Before entering on a discussion of the Load Line Regulations, it would be well to understand the complexity of the technical background which had to be considered before the regulations could be promulgated. Many factors enter into the assignment of a freeboard which will be technically proper and fair to the interested parties. This section will not attempt to give a complete technical explanation of these factors since they concern elements of design which are explained in other Chapters. A mere recitation of the factors should prove sufficient at this time to indicate the difficulty of the problem of freeboard assignment:

---

[1] For an excellent account of this work see: David Arnott, "Load Line Regulations with Special Attention to the International Load Line Conference, 1930" *Transactions of the Society of Naval Architects and Marine Engineers,* 1930.

1. *Structural strength:* It is obvious that the deeper the draft of a vessel, the greater the weight the structure is called upon to take. Thus the structural strength of a vessel is related intimately to its freeboard.

2. *Subdivision and reserve buoyancy:* Reserve buoyancy, which is that portion of the enclosed and watertight portion of a vessel above the waterline, varies directly with the freeboard and is important in case of flooding since a greater amount of reserve buoyancy increases the extent of flooding which can be suffered without causing the foundering of a vessel. Subdivision, that is, the subdividing of the hull by transverse, watertight bulkheads, limits the loss of reserve buoyancy in case of damage. More concern for passengers in this respect is evidenced by the Load Line Regulations and as will be seen, special subdivision load lines are required for passenger vessels.

3. *Height of platform:* The height of the weather deck above the waterline, or height of platform as it is sometimes called, determines, of course, the extent to which heavy seas will sweep across the weather deck. Thus the security of passengers, crew, and equipment is a function of the height of platform.

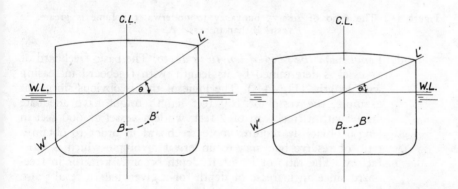

Figure 42. Greater freeboard produces a larger angle of deck edge immersion. B continues to move out until deck edge is immersed thus increasing stability.

4. *Transverse stability:* Freeboard is one of the important dimensions of a vessel which determine its overall stability. Although the initial resistance of a vessel to the force of the seas is not determined by the freeboard directly, the stability at larger angles of inclination is influenced greatly by the angle at which the deck edge is submerged and hence the freeboard. (Fig. 42.)

5. *Geometric form of the hull:* In this category may be included:

   a. *Camber.* The greater the "round of beam," the easier it becomes to rid the vessel's decks of water.

b. *Sheer.* Since a vessel's freeboard is measured amidships, the more the rise of the deck from that point (sheer) the more freeboard the vessel possesses at the ends, and the greater the addition to the vessel's seaworthiness.

c. *Fullness:* Fullness, which is measured by the block coefficient (volume of displacement/length x breadth x draft) must be considered since the ratio of reserve buoyancy to underwater volume is less in a fuller vessel than it is in a finer vessel. (Fig. 43.)

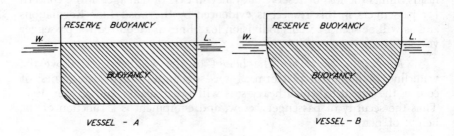

Figure 43. The ratio of reserve buoyancy to underwater volume is greater in vessel B than in vessel A.

d. *Length and the ratio of length to depth:* The basic freeboard of a vessel is determined by its length, with freeboard increasing with length. (Fig. 44.) The logic of this is obvious since, for example, the vessel of 100 feet length might have adequate safety with a freeboard of 2 feet, while a vessel of 600 feet in length obviously requires more freeboard in order to obtain a ratio of reserve buoyancy to underwater volume which is satisfactory. The ratio of length to depth becomes a factor in freeboard since an increase of depth for a given length results also in a decrease of the ratio of reserve buoyancy to underwater volume. (Fig. 45.)

6. *Superstructures:* If we define superstructure as enclosed and watertight space on or above the freeboard deck and stretching from side to side, it can be seen that this space contributes to almost all the factors which control the assignment of freeboard. That is, it increases reserve buoyancy; it raises the height of plaform, etc. This is especially true when a complete superstructure exists extending from bow to stern. This is the case when the freeboard deck is established one deck below the uppermost deck. Since freeboard is measured from the freeboard deck, superstructure results in a decrease of freeboard so measured.

7. *Type of vessel:* In the assignment of freeboard, the type of vessel concerned is an important factor. Differentiation must be made as to pas-

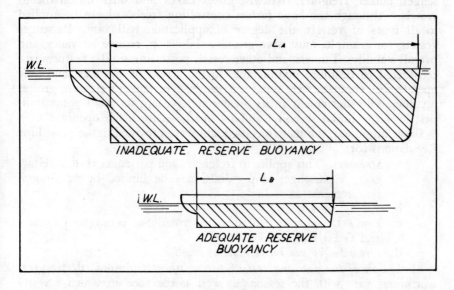

Figure 44

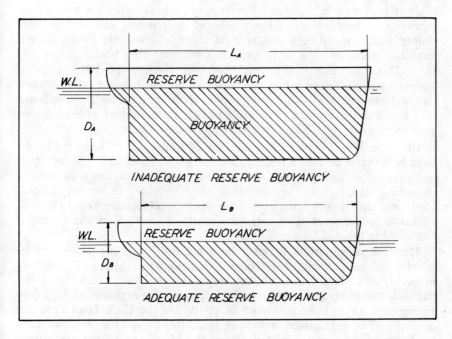

Figure 45

senger, tanker, freighter, coastwise Great Lakes, and small miscellaneous vessels. Although the basic factors controlling freeboard can be applied to all types of vessels, the degree of application will vary. Passenger vessels, for example, must have greater subdivision, reserve buoyancy, and overall stability. Tankers, and other vessels possessing similar features, are considered to be more invulnerable to the action of the seas, and may operate with comparatively small freeboards. The tanker's claim to greater invulnerability lies chiefly in its greater subdivision; its small permeabilities; its large initial stability; and its small, secure hatch openings.

Basic, minimum, summer freeboard tables are provided in the Load Line Regulations for:

- a. *Steamers.* This applies to freighters and passenger vessels. However, a passenger ship's draft may be limited by subdivision requirements as well.
- b. *Sailing vessels.*
- c. *Tankers.* Separate tables are provided for oceangoing tankers and Great Lakes tankers.
- d. *Great Lakes and miscellaneous small vessels.*

8. *Season of the year and zone:* Since weather conditions effecting seaworthiness vary with the seasons' as well as the zone in which a vessel is steaming, it is necessary to vary the freeboard accordingly in some cases. However, seasonal and zonal lines may not apply in cases where the draft is restricted by another consideration such as structural strength or subdivision. In these cases the freeboard assigned is sufficient to offer proper structural strength and/or subdivision and is more than sufficient from the points of view of other factors effecting freeboard.

9. *Density of water:* Since the freeboard which a vessel has at sea in salt water is decreased when the vessel enters fresh water, it is evident that a fresh water allowance is proper when considering the freeboard of a vessel in fresh water. Therefore vessels are permitted such an allowance from whatever load line mark would determine their draft otherwise.

10. *Carriage of timber:* The carriage of timber on deck, in the holds, or in both places entitles a vessel to a reduction of freeboard. The increased buoyancy of a lumber cargo, and the value of a deck cargo of lumber in adding, in effect, to the freeboard, are recognized by the regulations. However, the timber carrying vessel must meet certain regulations in regard to proper securing of cargo and safety of crew before the decreased freeboard is granted.

The foregoing, although not a complete list of all the factors which govern the assignment of freeboard, does contain the major elements involved, and should indicate the enormous problem which faced the technical committees considering the question of international load line agreements before the Conference of 1930, and the U. S. Load Line Act of 1929. The regulations stemming from the Load Line Act will now be discussed. As was indicated above, the U. S. regulations are almost identical with the Convention requirements, and a U. S. vessel which meets U. S. requirements also meets the international standards as set forth in the International Convention of 1930. The U. S. regulations are set forth in a booklet entitled *"Load Line Regulations,"* issued by the United States Coast Guard. The regulations which are considered pertinent to the purposes of this text will be discussed and the section number of each pertinent regulation will be given:

Load Line Regulations

Administration: Load lines are established by the regulations for merchant vessels, both ocean-going and coastwise, which have a gross tonnage of 150 or more tons. (43.01-1)

The Commandant of the Coast Guard is vested with the responsibility for administration of the regulations. (43.01-5)

The American Bureau of Shipping is appointed by the Load Line Acts as the assigning authority. It issues a Load Line Certificate (Fig. 46) after calculating the freeboard according to the regulations. (43.01-40) The Bureau makes an annual inspection of all vessels regulated by the Load Line Acts to check protection of openings, guardrails, freeing ports, means of access to crew's quarters, and to see that there have not been alterations which would effect the position of the load lines. (43.01-55) Also, the ABS makes a survey every five years "to determine that the load lines are then correctly placed as required by the regulations." The load line certificate may then be renewed, usually for another five years. (43.01-75).

The regulations require the master to note in the vessel's *official log* "before departing from her loading port or place, the position of the load line mark, port and starboard, as applicable to the voyage and the actual drafts of the vessel forward and aft at the time of departing from port as nearly as the same can be ascertained." (43.01-95)

Vessels of foreign countries which have ratified the provisions of the International Load Line Convention of 1930 have their load lines recognized by our government if U. S. vessels are similarly treated in the foreign country in question. The Coast Guard has the responsibility of upholding the freeboard regulations for these foreign vessels and may detain and order a survey of a foreign vessel if there is reason to believe that these regulations are not being adhered to. (43.01-97)

Determination of Minimum Freeboard of Merchant Vessels (except tankers): The definition of freeboard according to the regulations, that is, the statutory freeboard or assigned freeboard is: The distance measured vertically downward at the side of the vessel amidships from the upper edge of the freeboard deck line to the upper edge of the load line. (43.05-1) (See Fig. 47). The definition of freeboard deck is very important since the assigned freeboard is measured from this deck. The rules define this deck as the "deck from which the freeboard is measured, and is the uppermost complete deck having permanent means of closing

Form L. L. 9E-L-8-50

International
Load Line Certificate

Issued under the authority of the
United States of America, Commandant, U. S. Coast Guard
under the provisions of the International Load Line Convention, 1930

Name of Ship.......... SS OCEAN SPRAY ....

Certificate No.... I-1234 ....   Official Number.... 456,789 ....

Gross Tonnage.... 7312 ....   Port of Registry.... New York, N.Y. ....

Freeboard from Deck Line   Load Line

Tropical.......... Nine .... feet. one, -- -- -- ....inches. T. seven, -- -- -- ....inches above S

Summer.......... Nine .... feet. eight, -- -- -- ....inches   Upper edge of line through
center of disc

Winter.......... Ten .... feet. three, -- -- -- ....inches. W. seven, -- -- -- ....inches below S

Winter { North Atlantic { .... -- feet. -- -- -- -- ....inches. WNA -- -- -- ....inches below S

†Fresh Water Allowance for all freeboards..........seven, one quarter..........inches
All measurements are to the upper edge of the respective horizontal lines.

The upper edge of the deck line from which these freeboards are measured is.......... No ....inches above

the top of the.......... Steel Upper ....deck at side.

OFFICIAL ILLUSTRATION PURPOSES

THIS IS TO CERTIFY that this ship has been surveyed and the freeboards and load lines shown above have been assigned in accordance with the Convention.

*This certificate remains in force until.......... June 3, 1955 ....

Issued at New York on the.......... 3 ....day of.......... June 19 50

D. P. Brown
CHIEF SURVEYOR.

Bett L Green
PRESIDENT.

J. K. Cowley
SECRETARY.

NOTE:—In accordance with the Load Line Regulations the disc and lines must be permanently marked by center punch marks or cutting.
†Where seagoing steamers navigate a river or inland water, deeper loading is permitted corresponding to the weight of the fuel, etc., required for consumption between the point of departure and the open sea.
*Upon the expiration of the certificate renewal must be obtained as provided by the Load Line Regulations and the certificate so endorsed. Endorsement should also be made in the spaces provided on the occasion of each annual inspection required by the Load Line Regulations.

American Bureau of Shipping

Figure 46

all openings in weather portions of the deck in accordance with [requirements]." It is the upper deck in flush-deck vessels and vessels with detached superstructures. (43.05-1) A flush deck vessel is defined as one which has no superstructure on the freeboard deck; (43.05-1) and superstructure is defined as a decked structure on the freeboard deck extending from side to side. (43.05-1).

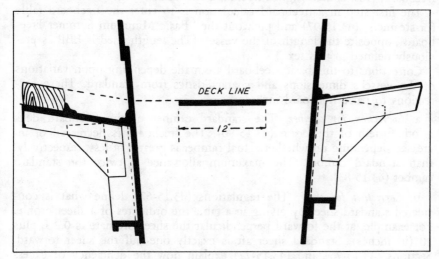

DECK LINE

12"

Load Line Regulations

Figure 47. Location of deck line

An understanding of the term "minimum freeboard" is vital to an understanding of how the load line regulations operate. The following requirements must be met if a merchant vessel is to receive an assigned freeboard which is the minimum possible under the regulations:

a. The vessel must comply with the highest standard of the rules of a classification society recognized by the Coast Guard. (43.15-17). The assigning authority is guided in this respect by strength moduli given in the regulations. If a vessel does not meet the requirements for minimum freeboard due to relatively light scantlings, its freeboard will be increased appropriately. Its permissible draft in all seasons and zones will be determined by the maximum weight which can safely be loaded. Only one load line is assigned, therefore. The fresh water allowance, however, is permitted since this does not effect the weight aboard. Figure 50 illustrates the type of load lines assigned a "scantling draft" vessel, as it is called. This element of freeboard regulations will be covered in the chapter on Strength.

b. Certain requirements on subdivision and stability must be met by passenger vessels. These requirements will be discussed below, in connection with subdivision load lines.

c. The vessel must be structurally efficient and provide effective protection to the crew. Section 43-10 lists these requirements for such things as protection of hatchways and other openings in deck and sides, guardrails, and freeing ports, and are known as *conditions of assignment*.

Let us assume, then, that a vessel meets the requirements for minimum freeboard. How is the assigned freeboard arrived at?[1]

The first step in a freeboard calculation is to enter the freeboard table for steamers, (43.15-97) and pick out the "Basic Minimum Summer Freeboard" opposite the length of the vessel. (The length used is LBP as previously defined in this text.)

Corrections to this basic freeboard are made depending upon variations of the vessel's dimensions and characteristics from standard. These corrections to basic freeboard include:

a. *Correction for camber.* The standard camber of the freeboard deck is one-fiftieth of the beam (43.15-80). The freeboard is decreased or increased depending on whether actual camber is greater or less, respectively, than standard camber. The maximum allowance is twice the standard camber (43.15-83).

b. *Correction for sheer:* The regulations (43.15-67) define what is considered standard sheer by giving in a table the ordinates of a sheer profile. For example, at the forward perpendicular the sheer ordinate is 0.2 L plus 20 (in inches). Standard sheer aft is exactly one-half the sheer forward. Sections (43.15-75) and (43.15-77) explain how the deficiency or excess of sheer is computed and the correction to basic freeboard arrived at. Excess sheer under certain conditions permits a reduction in freeboard not to exceed 1½ inches for each 100 feet of length (43.15-85). Deficiency in sheer results in an increase of freeboard equal to the correction for deficiency of sheer (43.15-83). Where sheer aft is greater than standard, and the sheer forward less than standard, only the deficiency forward is considered. Where the sheer forward is greater than standard and the sheer aft less than standard, credit is given depending upon the extent of the deficiency aft. These provisions illustrate the importance attached to forward sheer in contrast to after sheer.

c. *Correction for fullness:* Standard fullness is defined by a block coefficient of 0.68 taken at a draft equal to 85% of the depth (43.15-97). Freeboard is increased if the coefficient exceeds 0.68. However, no decrease of freeboard is granted if the coefficient is less than 0.68 (43.15-15, b).

d. *Correction for depth:* Standard depth is defined as one-fifteenth of the length. If the depth exceeds L/15 the freeboard is increased; and

---

[1] The explanation of freeboard calculation to follow does not present enough information to make an involved calculation for an actual ship. This is considered beyond the scope of this text. The interested student should refer to a copy of the *Load Line Regulations* for the exact method of obtaining corrections to the basic freeboard for differences from standard dimensions.

under certain conditions the freeboard is decreased if the depth is less than L/15 (43.15-97).

e. *Correction for superstructures:* If a vessel has no superstructures, i.e., a flush-deck vessel, the freeboard is increased by 1½ inches for every 100 feet of length. The decrease in freeboard when superstructures do exist depends upon the "effective length" of the superstructure. Effective length depends, in turn, upon:

1. *Efficient construction of the end bulkheads:* The regulations (43.15-35) set forth in detail the required scantlings of the bulkhead plating and framing for bridge front bulkheads and after bulkheads of bridges and forecastles; and poop bulkheads.
2. *The type of closing appliances in the bulkheads:* Class 1 closing appliances are, in general, steel fittings permanently attached (43.15-37). Class 2 closing appliances are, in general, wooden doors or shifting boards.

Depending, then upon the type of closing appliances and the length of the superstructure, varying percentages of the poop (43.15-47), of the bridge (43.15-37), of the forecastle (43.15-55), and of a complete superstructure with a tonnage well (43.15-60) are considered to be effective. The effective length of the superstructures is also effected by deck structures that do not extend to the sides of the vessel (trunks or deckhouses) but to a lesser degree than do side to side erections (43.15-57).

The actual deductions from basic freeboard for superstructures are, then: (43.15-63) Where the effective length is 1.OL, the deduction varies with the length of the ship. (For vessels 400 feet in length or over, the deduction is 42 inches.) Where the total effective length is less than 1.OL, the deduction is a percentage of the deduction permitted for a superstructure which has an effective length of 1.OL. The percentage varies depending upon whether the vessel has a forecastle and/or a detached bridge. (The percentage is reduced by 5 where no forecastle exists. Thus for a vessel over 400 feet in length, the absence of a forecastle means, in effect, an increase in required freeboard of more than two inches plus the normal allowance received for an effective forecastle. For this and other reasons the incentive to include a forecastle in the design of a merchant vessel is strong.).

The provisions in regard to superstructures are of great importance to the designer in determining the type of vessel to select. For example, a shelter deck ship, i.e., one with a tonnage well and openings, has what amounts to a complete superstructure. The Load Line regulations require (43.15-43) that cargo hatchways in the freeboard deck within superstructures which are fitted with Class 2 closing appliances are to have coamings at least 9 inches in height and means for securing these hatches (cleats on the coamings). Outboard scuppers may also be required on the freeboard deck (43.10-87).

Thus the tonnage requirements which must be met in order to have a shelter deck space exempted (tonnage well and openings) lead to load line regulations requiring 9 inch coamings and scuppers on the freeboard deck within the shelter deck space. Also, the freeboard of the shelter deck vessel is reduced considerably.

To recapitulate: Freeboard is calculated by entering the freeboard tables and selecting the basic freeboard which varies with the length of the vessel. Corrections to the basic freeboard are made in accordance with variations of camber, sheer, fullness, depth, and superstructures from certain standard values for these dimensions and characteristics. These corrections may be additive to or subtractive from, the basic freeboard. The net value of the corrections is applied to the basic freeboard. It is also well to stress the fact that the final freeboard thus obtained is the *minimum* freeboard and as indicated above, a vessel must meet certain requirements of strength and subdivision in order to qualify for this minimum freeboard.

We are now ready to use this final or assigned freeboard to obtain the position of the load line marks on the side of the vessel.

Example of Freeboard Calculations: [1]

GIVEN:

Suppose a steamer (dry-cargo vessel) to have a length of 465 feet; a depth to freeboard deck of 34 feet; an inclosed superstructure on the freeboard deck with tonnage well. The basic freeboard from the table is 91.7 inches. Corrections to the basic freeboard are as follows:

Depth: (Greater than standard)	9.0 in.
Superstructure correction:	41.0 in.
Sheer: (Deficient)	4.0 in.
Camber: (Less than standard)	0.5 in.
Block coefficient: (0.67)	0.0 in.

FIND:

a) *Minimum* summer freeboard
b) Summer draft, maximum
c) Winter and tropical freeboards
d) Fresh water allowance if the displacement at the summer draft is 17,600 tons and tons per inch immersion at this draft is 60.0 tons.

---

[1] This example is not meant to simulate an actual freeboard calculation for any particular vessel or design. Therefore the corrections for variations in standard conditions are only representative of actual corrections.

SOLUTION:

Table freeboard at 465 ft. length:	91.7	in.
Depth correction:	plus 9.0	in.
	100.7	in.
Superstructure correction:	minus 41.0	in.
	59.7	in.
Camber correction:	plus .5	in.
	60.2	in.
Sheer correction:	plus 4.0	in.
	64.2	in.
To nearest $\frac{1}{4}''$	64¼	in.
Minimum summer freeboard:	5' 04¼	in.
Depth:	34' 00	in.
Summer draft:	28' 07¾	in.
T and W: [1] 28.647/4	07³⁄₁₆	in.
Tropical Freeboard: [1]	4' 09¹⁄₁₆	in.
Winter Freeboard: [1]	5' 11⁷⁄₁₆	in.
Fresh Water Allowance [1] $\dfrac{17{,}600}{40 \times 60}$	07⁵⁄₁₆	in.

The Load Line Marks: Figure 48 shows the load lines assigned a vessel which qualifies for minimum freeboard.

The deck line is 12 inches in length and 1 inch in breadth. It is marked amidships (middle of the length of the summer load water line) on each side of the vessel. It's upper edge is located at the intersection of the upper surface of the *freeboard deck* and the outer surface of the shell plating (43.05-5) (Fig. 47).

All load lines are 1 inch in breadth; their length is indicated on the figure.

The assigned freeboard is measured from the top of the deck line to the top of the line through the disk.

The seasonal and zonal lines are forward of the disk (43.05-15).

The summer line is simply an extension of the line through the disk. The winter line (W) is located below the summer line by a distance

---

[1] See below for explanation of how seasonal and zonal marks and fresh water mark are obtained.

equal to one-fourth inch per foot of summer draft (measured from the top of the keel to the center of the disk) (43.15-90). The tropical line (T) is located the same distance above the summer line (43.15-87). The winter North Atlantic line (WNA) is located two inches below the winter line and applies only to vessels not exceeding 330 feet in length (43.15-93).

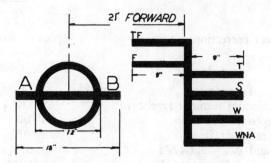

FREIGHTER MINIMUM FREEBOARD

Figure 48

The dates which determine what is considered to be winter and what summer are given in section 43.40 and on a chart which appears in the back of the *"Load Line Regulations."* (Fig. 49). The areas which comprise the various zones are also indicated. It is to be noted that the zones vary with the seasons. For example, in the Atlantic north of Latitude 36°N., there is a winter zone from 1 November to 31 March. The rest of the year this area is a summer zone. A vessel may never be loaded so as to submerge the load line then applicable to her voyage. If the vessel's intended voyage will necessitate entering a zone where freeboard must be increased, this must be taken into account in the loading (43.01-90). Where an ocean-going vessel (except a passenger ship) is loading in inland water, the reduction in draft expected due to consumption of fuel, etc. on the way to the sea permits an increase in draft over the applicable mark to the amount of this reduction.

In addition to the seasonal and zonal lines, two fresh water lines appear. The summer fresh line is simply marked F and represents the decrease in draft that the vessel will experience when passing from fresh water into salt water. The tropical fresh line (TF) indicates the decrease in draft in a similar fashion. The expected decrease is calculated by the formula: Displacement/40T, where the displacement is in tons of salt water displacement at the summer draft and T is the tons per inch immersion in salt water at the summer draft (43.15-95). It should be noted that there are no fresh water marks for the winter or winter North Atlantic. This does not mean that a vessel may load to the F mark when in fresh water and these lines are applicable. If this were done the vessel would be at the summer line instead of the winter line, for example. The method employed is to apply the fresh water allowance calculated according to the above formula, to the winter freeboard (43.05-15). The fresh water allowance is reduced appropriately for brackish water.[1]

The mark of the assigning authority (AB) *may* be indicated by letters measuring about 4½ by 3 inches marked alongside the disk and above the center line (43.05-20).

The load lines must be painted in white or yellow on a dark background and in black on a light background. They must be indicated in a permanent fashion by cutting or center punching (43.05-25). A welding bead is used for this purpose sometimes.

The seasonal and zonal lines as described above do not always appear on the load lines of vessels. When a vessel does not qualify for minimum freeboard due to a deficiency of structural strength, only one line is provided which applies to all seasons and zones. However, a fresh water line is provided. Since the structural strength of a vessel depends upon its displacement and not upon the zone in which the vessel is located, the use of only one load line is logical. (Fig. 50). The seasonal and zonal lines may also be omitted in the case of a passenger vessel when her draft is limited by subdivision or stability considerations.

Load Lines for Steamers Carrying Timber Deck Cargoes: The decreases of freeboard permitted vessels of this type are shown in Figure 51, the load line marks for vessels carrying timber deck cargoes. The decrease in the summer freeboard is accomplished in the rules by increasing the allowance for total effective length of superstructures (43.25-70). The vessel is required to have a forecastle at least 7 percent of the length, and a poop (43.25-15). Also, the vessel must be fitted with permanent bulwarks at least 3 feet 3 inches high or efficient, strongly constructed rails of the same height (43.25-30). The timber must be stowed in the wells to at least the standard height of the bridge superstructure; and in winter to a height not greater than one-third the extreme breadth of the vessel (43.25-40). Other requirements which a vessel must meet in order to qualify for this reduction in freeboard are: (a) proper protection to the crew in the form of safe access to quarters and efficient life lines on top of the deck cargo (43.25-45), and (b) efficient securing of the deck cargo.

The special lines are marked aft of the disk. The winter line (LW) is located below the summer line a distance equal to one-third of an

---

[1] See Chapter 13 for methods of computing allowance for different water densities.

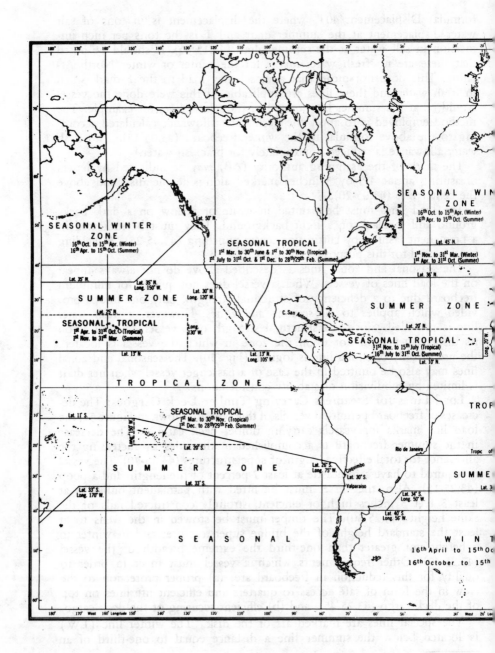

SEASONAL WINTER
ZONE
16th Oct. to 15th Apr. (Winter)
16th Apr. to 15th Oct. (Summer)

Lat. 35° N.

Lat. 35° N.
Long. 150° W.

SUMMER ZONE

Lat. 30° N.
Long. 120° W.

SEASONAL TROPICAL
1st Apr. to 31st Oct. (Tropical)
1st Nov. to 31st Mar. (Summer)

Lat. 25° N.

Long.
130° W.

Lat. 13° N.

Lat. 13° N.
Long. 105° W.

SEASONAL TROPICAL
1st Mar. to 30th June & 1st to 30th Nov. (Tropical)
1st July to 31st Oct. & 1st Dec. to 28th/29th Feb. (Summer)

SEASONAL WIN
ZONE
16th Oct. to 15th Apr. (Winter)
16th Apr. to 15th Oct. (Summer)

Lat. 45° N.

1st Nov. to 31st Mar. (Winter)
1st Apr. to 31st Oct. (Summer)

Lat. 36° N.

SUMMER ZONE

Lat. 20° N.

SEASONAL TROPICAL
1st Nov. to 15th July (Tropical)
16th July to 31st Oct. (Summer)

Lat. 10° N.

Long. 20° W.

C. San Antonio
C. Catoche
C. Corrientes

TROPICAL ZONE

Lat. 11° S.

SEASONAL TROPICAL
1st Mar. to 30th Nov. (Tropical)
1st Dec. to 28th/29th Feb. (Summer)

Long. 150° W.

Lat. 20° S.

TROP

SUMMER ZONE

Lat. 26° S.
Long. 75° W.

Rio de Janeiro

Tropic of

Coquimbo

Valparaiso

Lat. 30° S.
Long. 50° W.

SUMME

Lat. 33° S.
Long. 170° W.

Lat. 33° S.

Lat. 34° S.
Long. 50° W.

Lat. 3

Lat. 40° S.
Long. 56° W.

SEASONAL

WINT
16th April to 15th Oc
16th October to 15th

82

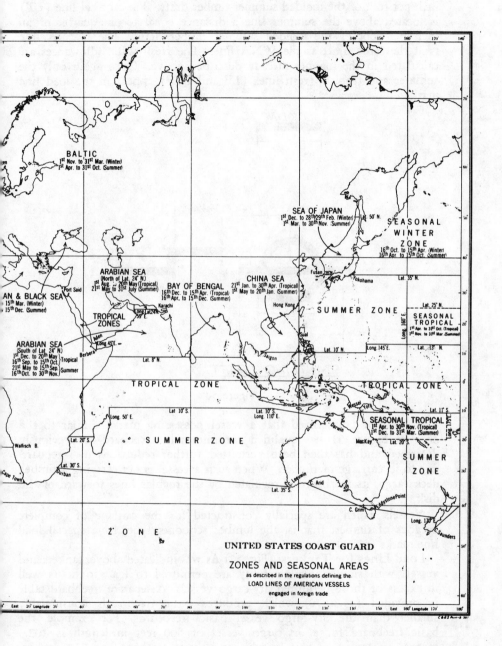

BALTIC
1st Nov. to 31st Mar. (Winter)
1st Apr. to 31st Oct. (Summer)

SEA OF JAPAN
1st Dec. to 28th/29th Feb. (Winter)
1st Mar. to 30th Nov. (Summer)

Lat. 50° N.

SEASONAL
WINTER
ZONE
16th Oct. to 15th Apr. (Winter)
16th Apr. to 15th Oct. (Summer)

ARABIAN SEA
(North of Lat. 24° N.)
1st Aug. to 20th May (Tropical)
21st May to 31st July (Summer)

BAY OF BENGAL
16th Dec. to 15th Apr. (Tropical)
16th Apr. to 15th Dec. (Summer)

CHINA SEA
21st Jan. to 30th Apr. (Tropical)
1st May to 20th Jan. (Summer)

Fusan

Yokohama

Lat. 35° N.

AN & BLACK SEA
15th Mar. (Winter)
15th Dec. (Summer)

Port Said

Karachi

Lat.24°

Hong Kong

SUMMER ZONE

Lat. 25° N.

SEASONAL
TROPICAL
1st Apr. to 31st Oct. (Tropical)
1st Nov. to 31st Mar. (Summer)

TROPICAL
ZONES

Long.45°E.

Men

59°E

Suai

Long 160° E.

ARABIAN SEA
(South of Lat. 24° N.)
1st Dec. to 20th May
16th Sep. to 15th Oct.
21st May to 15th Sep.
16th Oct. to 30th Nov.

Tropical

Summer

Berbera

Saigon

Lat. 10° N.

Long 145° E.

Lat. 13° N.

Lat. 8° N.

TROPICAL ZONE

TROPICAL ZONE

Walfisch B.

Lat. 20° S.

Lat. 10° S.
Long 50° E.

Lat. 10° S.
Long. 110° E.

C. Wessel

York

Darwin

C. Arnhem

Lat. 11° S.

SEASONAL TROPICAL
1st Apr. to 30th Nov. (Tropical)
1st Dec. to 31st Mar. (Summer)

SUMMER ZONE

MacKay

Lat. 20° S.

SUMMER
ZONE

Cape Town

Durban

Lat. 30° S.

C. Leeuwin

C. Arid

Lat. 35° S.

C. Grim

Eddystone Point

ZONE

C. Saunders

Long. 170°

UNITED STATES COAST GUARD

ZONES AND SEASONAL AREAS
as described in the regulations defining the
LOAD LINES OF AMERICAN VESSELS
engaged in foreign trade

East   20°   Longitude   30°   40°   50°   60°   70°   80°   90°   100°   110°   120°   130°   140°   150°   East   160°   Longitude   170°   180°

Load Line Regulations

Figure 49

83

inch per foot of the molded summer timber draft. The tropical line (LT) is located above the summer line a distance equal to one-quarter of an inch per foot of the molded summer timber draft. The LWNA line is at the same draft as the WNA line. The fresh water allowances are calculated in the manner already described above. Once again only the summer and tropical fresh lines (LF and LTF) appear in the load line marks.

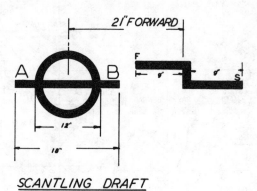

SCANTLING DRAFT

Figure 50

It must be emphasized that a vessel possessing marks similar to the ones in Figure 51 has qualified for minimum freeboard as previously described and has then been permitted further reductions in freeboard due to its carriage of timber. When such a vessel is not carrying a timber deck cargo, its freeboard is regulated by the regular lines forward of the disk.

Vessels which are specially constructed for the carriage of complete cargoes of timber; that is, the lumber schooner type, have special load line marks (43.35).

Load Lines for Tankers: (Fig. 52) As was indicated above, tankers and vessels with similar invulnerability are permitted to load to drafts well in excess of those permitted dry-cargo vessels. A separate freeboard table is provided (43.30-70) which produces basic freeboards considerably smaller than the dry-cargo vessel basic freeboards. For example, the basic freeboard for a dry-cargo vessel of 500 feet in length is 102.3 inches. A tanker of this length has a basic freeboard of 87.5 inches. Corrections to this basic freeboard are computed in the same way as for

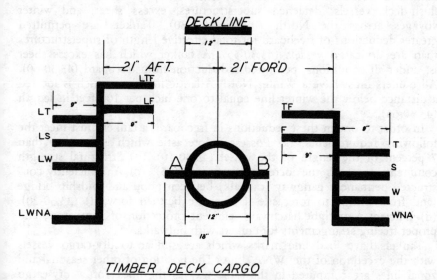

TIMBER DECK CARGO

Figure 51

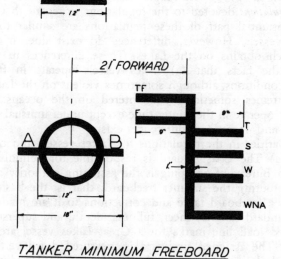

TANKER MINIMUM FREEBOARD

Figure 52

minimum freeboard for dry cargo vessels, except those corrections for flush-deck vessels, detached superstructures, excess sheer, and winter voyages across the North Atlantic (43.30). Tankers are permitted greater deductions of freeboard for total effective length of superstructures than are dry-cargo vessels (43.30-55). A tanker which has excess sheer is, under all conditions, permitted a deduction from freeboard (43.30-60). All tankers must have a Winter North Atlantic load line which is located a distance below the winter line equal to one inch per 100 feet in length (43.30-65).

In order to obtain these reductions in freeboard, a tanker must meet the following requirements: (a) Possess a forecastle which is not less than 7 percent of the length of the vessel (43.30-10). (b) Structural strength commensurate with the increased draft (43.30-5). (c) An efficiently constructed permanent gangway (catwalk) between poop and midship bridge (and from bridge to forecastle if crew are berthed forward) (43.30-20). (d) Efficient watertight hatchways, efficient protection of ventilators, and proper freeing arrangements for tankers with bulwarks.

Tankers have load line marks which are similar to dry-cargo vessels with the exception of the WNA line. The position of other seasonal and zonal lines are computed in the same way as the lines for a dry-cargo vessel.

Tankers above 600 feet in length must be dealt with specially by the Coast Guard.

Load Lines for Great Lakes vessels: Load lines for merchant vessels of the Great Lakes are established by the Coastwise Load Line Act, 1935, (and amended in 1936). Although there is a separate Part in the *Load Line Regulations* devoted to the regulations in regard to Great Lakes vessels, a substantial part of these regulations are similar to those for ocean-going vessels. However, differences do exist due to the special situation which obtains on the Lakes. These differences in the regulations reflect the facts that (a) Lakes vessels operate in fresh water. (b) Weather conditions, although sometimes violent on the Lakes, do not reach the extremes sometimes encountered on the oceans. (c) Lakes vessels do not operate in the winter time except under unusual conditions. (d) Structural and operational differences exist.

Major similarities in the regulations for Lakes vessels and ocean-going vessels are: (a) The Coast Guard is responsible for administration (b) The American Bureau of Shipping is the assigning authority and (c) the *method* of computing the summer freeboard; that is, the basic freeboard is taken from a freeboard table and corrections to it are made for variations from standard camber, sheer, fullness, depth, and superstructures.

The required load line marks for a Great Lakes vessel are illustrated in Figure 53. The assigned freeboard is measured down vertically from the top of the deck line to the top of the line through the load line diamond. There are four seasonal lines required: (45.05).

Winter (W): November 1 to April 15

Intermediate: April 16 to April 30 and October 1 to October 31
Summer: September 15 to September 30
Midsummer: May 1 to September 15.

These lines are given vessels which qualify for minimum freeboard. Scantling draft vessels and passenger vessels with subdivision load lines are assigned a single mark in somewhat similar fashion as ocean-going vessels. This mark is the line through the diamond and is applicable to all seasons.

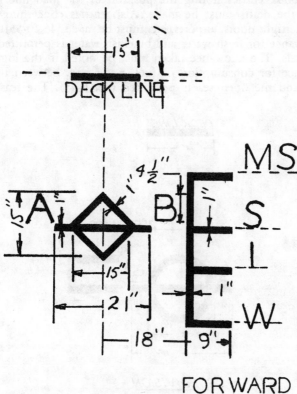

Figure 53

Tankers on the Great Lakes have the same type of lines as the dry-cargo types on the Lakes. However, freeboards are reduced in the same way as they are for ocean-going tankers by using a separate freeboard table.

Subdivision Load Lines for Passenger Vessels: As has been mentioned previously, passenger vessels which do not meet certain requirements in regard to subdivision and stability, are assigned subdivision load lines, which represent an increase in freeboard over minimum freeboard lines. These regulations were established in 1937 after ratification by the United States Senate in 1936 of the provisions of the International Conference for Safety of Life at Sea held in London in 1929, in regard to subdivision. They relate to all passenger vessels[1] over 150 gross tons making ocean, coastwise, or Great Lakes voyages (46.01-15).

The regulations state that for a passenger vessel:

1. Weekly drills are necessary for operation of watertight doors, side ports, etc. All watertight doors and hinged doors in main transverse bulkheads in use at sea must be operated daily (46.10-50).

2. Log book entries noting the position of the load line mark applicable and the drafts must be made. Also entries concerning the operation of watertight doors, airports, etc. must be made (46.10-55).

3. Allowance for fresh water and brackish water is permitted on oceangoing vessels. The allowance taken must be noted in the log. However, no allowance for consumption of fuel, water, etc. between the point of departure and the open sea is permitted (46.10-45). The reasoning here

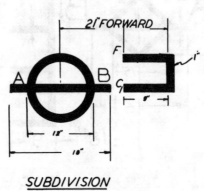

SUBDIVISION

Figure 54

is that, in case of damage, as far as subdivision and stability are concerned a vessel can founder or capsize in inland waters just as well as she can at sea.

4. Certain structural requirements must be met.

Figure 54 is an illustration of subdivision load lines (46.15-10). The method of computing the assigned freeboard in this case is very compli-

---

[1] A passenger vessel, by definition, carries more than 12 passengers (ocean) or 16 passengers (coastwise or Great Lakes).

cated and is considered beyond the scope of this text. A fresh water allowance is permitted; therefore, the F line is included. The C1 stands for the principal passenger condition. This line is applicable for all seasons and zones. When a vessel has spaces used for cargo and passengers alternatively, the vessel may be given a C2 line (and in rare cases, a C3 line) representing a condition requiring additional freeboard.

It is possible that the assigned freeboard for subdivision may produce a line which falls among the regular minimum freeboard lines. In this event, the lines above the subdivision line do not apply and are not marked. The load lines below the subdivision line, however, represent limiting freeboards and must be marked. Thus it is possible to have a situation resulting in marks of the type appearing in Figure 55.

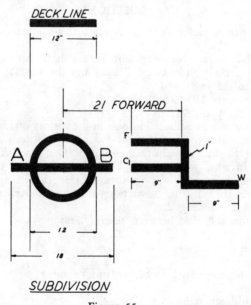

Figure 55

Miscellaneous

1. The American Bureau of Shipping charges a fee for Assignment of Load Lines and for renewal of certificates and annual inspections. The fees vary with the gross tonnage and the status of the vessel as to classification. For example, a classed vessel of 7000 gross tons would be charged $110 for load line assignment; an unclassed vessel, $260. Renewals are half of these amounts. The fee for annual inspections for unclassed vessels is $25. There is no fee for classed vessels.

2. Enforcement of the load line regulations: Customs officials are empowered by law to detain a vessel violating any provision of the

regulations. The owner or master of a vessel violating the regulations may be fined $500 for each offense. Failure to make the log entries as required may result in a fine of $100 for each offense.

3. In the Appendix of the *Load Line Regulations* a list of ports is given along with the percentage of the Fresh water allowance permissible. In New York, for example, this percentage varies with the location of the pier and the state of the tide, high or low. This list is for the guidance of load line inspectors. Where there is a question as to the legality of the vessel's loading and a possibility of a fine is present, the density of the water must be obtained by hydrometer.

4. A copy of the *Load Line Regulations* may be obtained by writing to the U. S. Coast Guard, Treasury Dept., Washington, D. C.

QUESTIONS

1. List all parties interested in freeboard assignment and the reasons therefor.
2. Explain how drafts of merchant vessels have been controlled in the following periods: (In Great Britain and the U. S.).
   a) Prior to the year 1870
   b) In the years 1870 to 1931
   c) After the year 1931.
3. What is the role of Samuel Plimsoll in the history of load line legislation?
4. What date marks the initiation of federal legislation in the United States pertaining to the compulsory marking of load lines for U. S. merchant vessels? In what year was this U. S. Load Line Act effective?
5. Explain how the scantlings (structural strength) of a vessel are related to its freeboard? In this connection, differentiate between a full scantling vessel and a scantling draft vessel.
6. Explain how the ratio between reserve buoyancy and underwater volume is affected by:
   a) Camber
   b) Sheer
   c) Form of the vessel (whether full or fine)
   d) Length
   e) Length-depth ratio
   f) Superstructure.
7. How does subdivision affect the volume of reserve buoyancy necessary to provide reasonable safety in case of flooding?
8. What is "height of platform" and how does it affect the freeboard?
9. Why is angle of deck edge immersion (and hence freeboard) related to stability?
10. Name five geometric elements of hull form which effect the assignment of freeboard.
11. Explain why passenger ships are given large assigned freeboards while tankers are permitted to sail with relatively small freeboards.
12. In what two cases will the season of the year and the zone in which the vessel is sailing have no effect on the freeboard assigned the vessel?
13. What is meant by the term "fresh water allowance"?

14. What is the maximum gross tonnage which a vessel may have without becoming subject to the assignment of load lines?
15. Who administers load line regulations? What agency is the assigning authority?
16. A foreign vessel enters a U. S. port loaded over its international load line mark applicable. Describe all action which would be taken.
17. Define completely: Freeboard deck.
18. Which of the following ships are flush deck ships, according to the definition given in the load line regulations? Victory ship, Liberty ship, C1-M-AV1, C2-S-AJ1, C1-A, C3-S-A1.
19. Name the three broad requirements which must be met before a vessel is eligible for the assignment of minimum freeboard.
20. What are "conditions of assignment"?
21. What is the "standard" for the following dimensions and characteristics?
    a) Camber
    b) Sheer
    c) Fullness
    d) Depth.
22. What is the rule for finding the position of tropical and winter load line marks? When is a freight vessel required to have a winter North Atlantic mark? How is the fresh water allowance obtained?
23. Explain by reference to the superstructure correction, how the draft of a vessel is affected by incorporating a tonnage well and openings in its structure.
24. Explain how the draft of a vessel loading, say in Albany, in the winter time, would be determined.
25. A vessel may load to the TF line in tropical fresh water and to the F line in summer fresh water. How deeply may the vessel load in winter fresh water?
26. Outline the requirements which a vessel carrying a timber deck cargo must meet in order to obtain a reduction in freeboard. In what situation is such a vessel not granted a reduction in freeboard?
27. What important requirements must a tanker meet in order to qualify for its very small freeboards? How is the WNA line for a tanker placed?
28. What are the differences in conditions on the Lakes which result in lesser freeboards than those assigned ocean-going vessels? Describe the load lines marked on Lakes vessels.
29. When were the regulations in regard to subdivision load lines for passenger vessels effective for U. S. vessels?
30. Why, for passenger vessels, is no allowance permitted for consumption of fuel between the point of departure and the open sea?
31. Describe the usual appearance of subdivision load lines.
32. Why is it possible to have a situation resulting in the assignment of the regular subdivision load lines plus the winter line usually found for minimum freeboard marks?
33. How is enforcement provided for in the Load Line Regulations?

BIBLIOGRAPHY

Load Line Regulations, issued by the Treasury Department, United States Coast Guard, U. S. Government Printing Office, Washington, D. C.

Rossell & Chapman, *Principles of Naval Architecture*, Vol. I, Chap II, Society of Naval Architects and Marine Engineers, New York, 1942.

Walton & Baird, *Steel Ships, Their Construction and Maintenance*, Chap. VI, Charles Griffin and Company, Ltd., London, 1944.

Walton, *Know Your Own Ship*, Chap. IX, Charles Griffin and Company, Ltd., London, 1942.

Comstock, *Introduction to Naval Architecture*, Chap. IX, Simmons-Boardman Publishing Corporation, New York.

D. Arnott, *Design and Construction of Steel Merchant Ships*, SNAME, New York, 1955.

Chapter 6

STRENGTH OF MATERIALS AND SHIPS

Ship's officers are intimately concerned with the problem of their vessel's strength. The stresses placed upon the structure of a vessel even when the vessel is in still water are tremendous; but when the vessel is at sea, exposed to the ferocity of storm conditions the stresses which a vessel must successfully resist sometimes stagger the imagination. Consider a modern vessel weighing, say, thirty thousand tons in a load condition, being buffeted by waves thirty or forty feet in height and seven or eight hundred feet in length; the vessel heaving, rolling, yawing, and plunging its bow against thousands of tons of water; where the seas attack the vessel now at this point, now at another; where hundreds of tons of water are hurled on the deck, at the sides, at the superstructure; where the vessel literally is suspended on the crest of a gigantic sea and then slides crazily into its trough. This is the problem which confronts the ship designer in considering the amount and disposition of material in a ship's structure. What is the answer to this problem? Can a naval architect accurately predict the stresses resulting from the maelstrom into which a ship must proceed? Can the materials of which a ship's structure is composed successfully resist these stresses without becoming so massive as to preclude an economic carrying capacity? Obviously, the designer can and does provide satisfactory answers to these questions. The ship's officer, however, must realize the extent of any vessel's ability to resist stress. He must not expose his vessel to any condition where the design stress is exceeded.

It is readily seen that the scantlings of a vessel depend upon two major considerations: These are:

(1) The strength of the material or materials which are used in the structural members of the vessel.

(2) The stresses, structural and local, which the vessel must resist.

Thus, if relatively strong material is used, the scantlings may be reduced proportionately; or, if the expected stresses are relatively small, the scantlings also may be reduced proportionately. These two major considerations will now be discussed.

STRENGTH OF MATERIALS

The subject of "Strength of Materials" can and does, under certain conditions, entail many months of study and the careful perusal of many full-length texts for a comprehensive knowledge of the subject. In this

93

text, however, we must fit the extent of our investigation into the theories of "Strength of Materials" to our need for them. This text is primarily directed towards ship's officers. The ship's officer is not required to design a vessel. He is only required to use that design in the best possible manner. With this purpose in mind, the following analysis of the subject is written.

Preliminary Definitions: All structures and all members making up a structure are exposed to stresses of varying character and extent:

Tension or tensile stress is a result of two forces acting in opposite directions on the same line. When tensile stress is applied to a material, it tends to pull the material apart, lengthening it in the process. A simple illustration of this stress and its result is the stretch of a rubber band when force is applied. Tensile stress is measured in *force per unit area,* ie., pounds per square inch or tons per square inch, for example. Assume a deck beam has a total force of 90 tons attempting to pull it apart, and the cross-sectional area of the beam is 15 square inches. The tensile stress on the beam will be 6 tons psi.

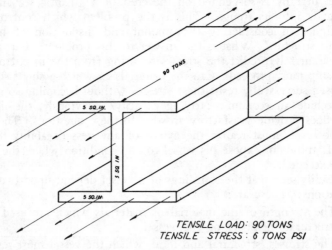

TENSILE LOAD: 90 TONS
TENSILE STRESS: 6 TONS PSI

Figure 56

Compression or compressive stress is a result of two forces acting in opposite directions on the same line. Here however, the forces tend to compress or push the material together. If the force of 90 tons on the beam had been so acting, the compressive stress would also be 6 tons psi.

Shear stress is a result of two forces acting in opposite directions and along parallel lines. The tendency of shearing stress is to tear the material between the two forces. If, for example, the total shearing force or pull across the shank of a rivet in a lap joint is 4 tons and the shank has a diameter of 1 inch, the shear stress can be determined by dividing the total force by the cross-sectional area of the rivet or 4 tons divided by (3.14×0.5^2) giving a shear stress of 5.1 tons psi.

The term *load* refers to the total force acting on a member or a structure and is expressed usually in tons or pounds. Load may be statically induced as in the case of water pressure (hydrostatic pressure) or dynamically induced as in the case of propeller vibration.

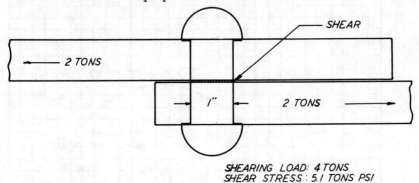

SHEAR

2 TONS

1″   2 TONS

SHEARING LOAD: 4 TONS
SHEAR STRESS : 5.1 TONS PSI

Figure 57

Strain is the lengthening or distortion of a member due to stress.[1] It is usually measured in inches.

Properties of Metals: A generalized knowledge of the mechanical properties of metals is useful to a ship's officer who commands a metal vessel, specifies repairs to metal members, and uses metals in various ways aboard ship.

Some of the most important properties of metals can be seen by reference to a *Stress-Strain diagram*. (Figure 58). This diagram results from a test of a specially prepared test-piece in a machine which literally pulls the piece apart. It can be observed from the diagram that as stress is applied initially, it remains proportional to strain. However the end of this range of proportionality or *elastic limit* is difficult to locate since the curve does not deviate sharply from the straight line. If the stress is removed within this limit, the material will return to its original length; if the material is stressed beyond its elastic limit, however, it will be permanently distorted and will sustain what is known as a *permanent set*. It is obvious that a designer must provide enough material so that the expected stress will not strain the material beyond this limit. The designer must stay within the "working range". Another property of metals can be derived from the relationship between stress and strain within the proportional limit. A metal's *"Modulus of Elasticity"* is a measure of the

---

[1] The use of the term "strain" here is quite different from its common use aboard ship where such expressions as "take a strain on the line" mean to tauten or *stress* the line.

stiffness or *rigidity* of the metal and is defined as the ratio of the stress (lb. psi.) to the unit strain (in. per sq. in.). The steeper the initial slope of the curve, the greater the stiffness. In some cases, the property of

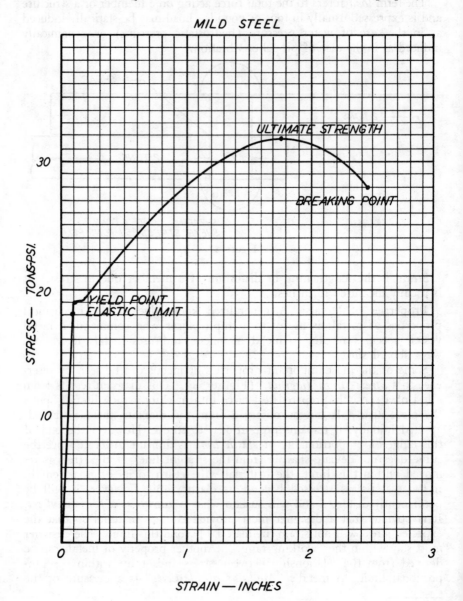

Figure 58. Stress-Strain Diagram

stiffness is more important than the property of tensile strength. For example, a shaft strong enough for a given job might not be rigid enough, that is, it might bend excessively. In this case, a metal with a higher modulus could be used without increasing the size of the shaft or the number of bearings.

If the test piece is loaded beyond the elastic limit it will strain more or less proportionately for a slight increment of stress. Then, a sudden yielding will take place with strain disproportionate to stress. This point is known as the *yield point*. This point, like elastic limit is difficult to locate exactly in the testing process. However, as the stress is continued, a point will finally be reached when the contraction of the test piece which started somewhat after the yield point had been reached, will result in a fracture of the piece. The stress necessary to achieve this failure of the test specimen is known as *ultimate strength* and can be measured very accurately on the testing machine. Thus the purpose of a tension test is to find ultimate strength, not elastic limit or yield point. However, the elastic limit can be deduced with fair accuracy since it has been found from experience that this limit is approximately one-half the ultimate strength. Using this criterion is not a careless practice since an adequate factor of safety is used in any case. It is common in ship design to allow a factor of safety of four based on ultimate strength. This is, in effect, a factor of safety of two based on elastic limit. To put in another way, members are commonly made twice as strong as they have to be to stay within the working range. This not only offers a generous allowance for the approximation of elastic limit, but also allows for corrosion and a factor of safety of two based on elastic limit. Put in another way, members are commonly made twice as strong as they have to be to stay within the working range. This not only offers a generous allowance for the approximation of elastic limit, but also allows for corrosion and wastage of the material in service.

The ultimate strength of mild steel in tension is approximately 30 tons psi and in shear, 22 tons psi. With this in mind, what would be the necessary cross-sectional area of a girder which is expected to withstand a maximum load of 75 tons in tension? Using a factor of safety of four (based on ultimate strength) it is apparent that a square inch of mild steel should not be called upon to take more than 7.5 tons psi. of tension. Therefore, the girder should have 10 square inches of cross-sectional area.

Also revealed by the stress-strain diagram is a very important property of metal called *ductility*. Lack of ductility is usually called brittleness. It is revealed in the tensile test by measuring the percent elongation and the reduction of cross-sectional area of the test piece. Good ductility in a metal means that the metal can be cold-worked with relative ease without rupture.

Tests required by the American Bureau of Shipping for structural steel used in shipbuilding reveal the importance attached to the properties of tensile strength and ductility. Details of these tests specify that:

(a) The tensile strength of plates not intended for cold flanging must be between the limits of 58,000 and 70,000 lbs. psi, and that for shapes between the limits of 60,000 and 72,000 lbs. psi. Plates intended for cold flanging must have a tensile strength of 55,000 to 65,000 lbs. psi.

(b) The minimum percent elongation in 8″ of the test piece must be 1,500,000 divided by the tensile strength. (Roughly between 21 and 26 percent).

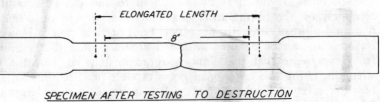

TENSION SPECIMEN

ELONGATED LENGTH

SPECIMEN AFTER TESTING TO DESTRUCTION

Figure 59

(c) A cold-bend test specimen must bend cold through 180 degrees around a pin the diameter of which varies with the thickness of the specimen (two or three times the thickness) without cracking on the outside of the bent portion.

Other properties of varying importance for ship construction include: (1) *Hardness,* which is that property of a metal which enables it to resist plastic deformation. Resistance to erosion by steam, oil and water, for example, generally increases with hardness. Hardness testing usually consists of impressing a steel ball on the flat surface of a test specimen and measuring either the diameter or the depth of the impression. (2) *Toughness,* which is a measure of the ability of a metal to withstand a sudden shock (in distinction to the slow building-up of stress). Toughness may be measured by an impact test usually consisting of the release of a hammer at the end of a pendulum and recording the energy absorbed by the test specimen. (3) *Fatigue strength,* a property relating to the ability of a metal to withstand continuing changes in the direction of application of the stress. For example, a metal may now be stressed in tension, then in compression, then in tension, etc.

Stresses on a Loaded Beam

It is necessary now to investigate the type and intensity of stresses which fall upon a loaded beam. The theories of strength which result from a study of this kind are used not only to arrive at the proper scantlings of individual ship's frames, beams, girders, etc. but also are used to arrive at the strength of the entire ship's hull. In the latter case, the entire hull of the ship is considered to be a single girder and the strength of the *"hull girder"* is calculated by using the "beam theory".

All stress on a loaded beam results from differences in the force or weight moving in one direction and the resistance or support operating in the opposite direction. If no difference exists, no stress exists. The study of stresses on a loaded beam must then start with·an investigation of differences in weight and support, and find the type of stress resulting and the intensity of these stresses. There are, of course, an infinite number of possible variations in weight and support. Here, we can only investigate some of the more simple variations. Let us consider first a simple rectangular beam loaded in such a way that the supporting forces are less in the middle of the beam than the forces of weight. (The forces of support are then greater than the forces of weight at the ends). (Figure 60). The beam obviously will bend. The upper and lower surfaces of the beam

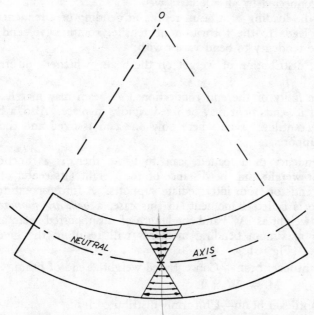

Figure 60. Formation of Stresses on a Loaded Beam

are now curved but are still parallel while the ends of the beam are no longer parallel. (Tangents run through the ends of the beam would meet at a point above the beam. This point will represent the center of curvature of the upper and lower surfaces of the beam). It is obvious that the upper surface of the beam has been shortened and the lower surface has been lengthened. It is equally obvious that there must be a surface halfway between the upper and lower surfaces which is still the same length. This surface is generally designated as the plane of the *neutral axis*. In this case, all material above the neutral axis must have been in compression and material below the axis, in tension. Also the stresses of tension and compression increase in intensity with the distance from the neutral axis, reaching their maximums at the topmost and lowermost fibres of the beam. Another type of stress also develops when a beam bends (or tends to bend). Since the forces of tension and compression vary from top to bottom of the beam shearing forces must be operating along the length of the beam. These forces have the same value from the upper to the lower surfaces since the difference in the tension (or compression) forces is uniform from top to bottom.

From the above it should be apparent that the reason for constructing structural shapes in the form of I beams is to place as much of the material in the beam as possible at the upper and lower surfaces or flanges where it will do the most good in resisting bending. However, the flanges must be connected by an adequate web.

While the loading of a beam results in bending or a tendency to bend and thus leads to the formation of tensile, compressive, and shearing forces, the tendency to bend varies with:

a) The distribution of weight on the beam, whether uniform or concentrated.

b) The fixity of the end connections. A beam may merely rest on a support at its ends or it may be fixed rigidly in place. Also, a beam may be of the cantilever type where only one end is fixed and there are no further supports.

The tendency of a loaded beam to bend, then, is a function of the amount of weight and the distance of the weight (its center of gravity) from the ends or from intermediate supports. A force operating through a distance is called a moment; in this case, a *bending moment*. If we designate weight as "W" and the length of unsupported beam as "L" the following maximum bending moments will result in the given simple situations: (Fig. 61.)

A.　Cantilever beam—Concentrated weight at end of beam.

$$M = W \times L$$

B.　Cantilever beam—Uniformly distributed load.

$$M = \frac{W \times L}{2}$$

C.　Free-ended beam—Concentrated load in middle of beam.

$$M = \frac{W \times L}{4}$$

D. Free-ended beam—Uniformly distributed load.

$$M = \frac{W \times L}{8}$$

E. Fixed-ended beam—Concentrated load in middle of beam.

At ends: $M = \dfrac{W \times L}{8}$ At middle: $M = \dfrac{W \times L}{8}$

F. Fixed-ended beam—Uniformly distributed load.

At ends: $M = \dfrac{W \times L}{12}$ At middle: $M = \dfrac{W \times L}{24}$

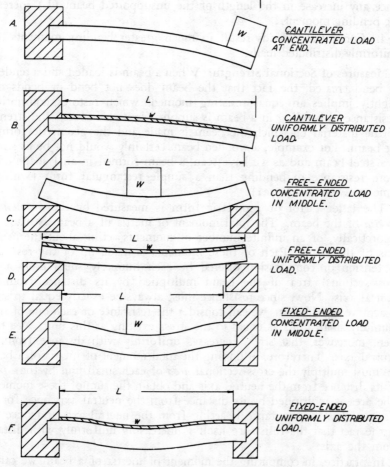

Figure 61. Various Simple Methods in Which a Beam May Be Loaded

Of course, the load on a beam can be and usually is more complicated than the simple situations outlined above. However, the bending moment formulas for many of these complicated loads are given in Handbooks on Strength of Materials. These simple formulas point up some interesting principles. It should be observed that:

1. The bending moment for a concentrated load on a free-ended beam is twice that of the moment on the fixed-ended beam. Framing on a ship can be fairly well fixed by the use of brackets and continuity over supports.

2. For a uniformly distributed load on a fixed-ended beam, the bending moment at the ends is twice that at the middle. The need for brackets at the ends of beams and girders is explained by this fact.

3. The need for intermediate supports for a loaded beam is shown since any increase in the length of the unsupported beam (L) increases the bending moment.

4. Concentrated loads result in much greater bending moments than uniformly distributed loads.

Measures of Sectional Strength: When a beam is loaded and a tendency to bend created, the fact that the beam does not bend or bends only slightly implies an equal resisting moment which restores equilibrium. Resistance to bending in a beam is supplied by two factors—the strength of the material of which the beam is made and the geometric form of the beam. For example, a wooden beam certainly would not be as strong as a steel beam and as we have seen, a beam formed in an I shape offers more resistance to bending than a simple rectangular form (with the same cross-sectional area).

The latter factor of geometric form is measured by the *moment of inertia* of the beam. The total moment of inertia of a beam is made up, theoretically, of an infinite number of moments acting about the neutral axis of the beam. Each of these moments is made up of the resistance to tension or compression offered by each infinitely small unit of the cross-sectional area of the beam multiplied by its distance from the neutral axis. Now, since resistance must always be exactly equal to stress to achieve equilibrium, we can consider the resistance of each one of these infinitely small units as equal to the stress existing at this unit. We have seen, moreover, that stress increases uniformly with distance from the neutral axis. Therefore, in finding the total moment of inertia of a beam, we must multiply the cross-sectional *area* of each small unit by the *square* of its distance from the neutral axis and obtain the sum of these moments. The area is multiplied by its distance from the neutral axis once for the distance that the resistance is acting from the neutral axis and once due to the fact that the resistance itself is increasing uniformly with distance from the axis.

In practice, in computing the moment of inertia of a beam we cannot use infinitely small units of area. However, it is sufficiently accurate to divide the beam up into convenient units such as flanges and webs and multiply these units by the square of their distance from the neutral axis. Since the moment of inertia is a geometric property of a beam, the moments of inertia of all standard structural shapes have been computed and can be found in any Handbook on the subject. However, for unusual shapes (built-up shapes) it is necessary to calculate this value. The following are the steps in such a calculation:

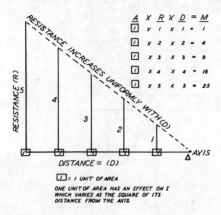

Figure 62.   How Moment of Inertia is Developed

1.   Compute the center of gravity of the girder. The plane of the neutral axis passes through this center. The center of gravity is found by multiplying the areas of convenient sections by their distance from a base line. These moments are summed and divided by the total cross-sectional area to find the distance of the center of gravity from the base line.

2.   The areas of all sections are then multiplied by the square of their distance from the neutral axis. In determining the distance of each section from the axis the geometric center of the section is used. Therefore a distinction must be made as to whether the section is horizontally disposed or vertically disposed. If for example we took two sections of equal cross-sectional area, and each having its center the same distance from the neutral axis, but one section being disposed horizontally and one vertically, it can be seen that the vertical section offers more resistance to bending due to its depth. Therefore, it is necessary to compute the moment of inertia of each individual vertical section around its own axis and add these to the total moments. For rectangular sections, the formula for moment of inertia around an axis through its center is:

$$I = \text{Width of section x (depth of section)}^3$$
$$12$$

Example of a Moment of Inertia Calculation:

Calculate the Moment of Inertia of the girder in Fig. 63.

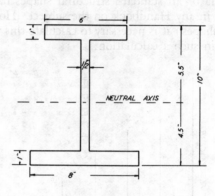

Figure 63

STEP 1:   *Find C.G. of girder:*

Section	Scantlings	Sectional Area	Section Above BL	Moments
Lower Flange	8″ x 1″	8	0.5	4.0
Web	8″ x 0.5	4	5.0	20.0
Upper Flange	6″ x 1″	6	9.5	57.0
		18		81.0

$$\frac{81}{18} = 4.5 \text{ (C.G. of Girder above Baseline)}$$

STEP 2:   *Find Moment of Inertia about Neutral Axis:*

Section	Sectional Area	Center of Sections From Axis	Area x (Dist)²	Depth of Vert. Sections	Depth²	Area x (Depth)² / 12
Lower Flange	8	4.0	128.0			
Web	4	0.5	1.0	8	64	21.3
Upper Flange	6	5.0	150.0			
			279.0			21.3
			21.3			
		Moment of Inertia:	300.3			

From the above calculation it should be observed that:

1. The plane of the neutral axis lies below the mid-depth of the girder due to the greater length of the lower flange.

2. The moment of inertia of the web about the neutral axis of the girder is small because the center of the web is very close to the axis.

3. The moment of inertia of the web about its own neutral axis is an appreciable figure due to the depth of the web.

4. The last column of the form for finding I of the girder is the formula for finding the moment of inertia of the web about its own neutral axis, since area is equal to width times depth.

Section Modulus: With a given cross-sectional area to work with, it would be possible to create two sections. One could have a much greater I than the other because of a greater distance of its flanges from the neutral axis. This greater I would be achieved by reducing the area of the flanges. If the area is reduced by too much, however, the flanges of the girder might be inadequate to withstand the tensile and compressive stresses resulting from bending. Thus, the distance of the upper flange (or the lower flange) from the neutral axis (a distance which we will designate "y") is an indication of the efficiency with which the flange can resist these stresses. If the moment of inertia, then, is divided by y, the resultant expression of I/y can be used as a standard or modulus" of the ability of the section to withstand not only bending, but tensile and compressive stresses as well. Section modulus (S) is strictly a geometrical consideration and hence can be calculated in advance for all standard shapes, and listed in Handbooks on Strength of Materials. For unusual built-up shapes (or for the hull girder of a ship), S must be calculated by finding the moment of inertia and dividing I by y.

For the example problem above, then:

$$S = \frac{I}{y} = \frac{300.3}{5.5} = 54.6 \text{ (to the upper flange)}$$

$$\text{and } S = \frac{I}{y} = \frac{300.3}{4.5} = 66.7 \text{ (to the lower flange)}$$

The Strength Equation: As indicated above, the geometrical distribution of material in a section is a measure of the strength of the section. It is obvious however, that the material used in a section also determines the strength of the girder. The greater the strength of the material, the greater will be the resistance to bending. Now, we know that resistance to bending implies stress; that is, if a loaded beam does not break, it is obvious that the stress has been opposed by an equal amount of resistance. The maximum stress occurs at the uppermost and lowermost fibers of the loaded beam. We designate this stress as "p". Thus if we combine I/y (which is a measure of the stiffness of a beam from a geometric point of view) and p (which is a measure of the resistance offered by the material of which the beam is made) then I/y x p represents the total resistance to bending. Since the moment tending to bend a girder is equal to the moment tending to resist bending:

$$M = I/y \times p \qquad (1)$$

The function of "y" in the strength equation can be understood when it is remembered that the stress p (thus the resistance) increases uniformly with distance from the neutral axis. As "y" increases in the formula for a given bending moment and as I/y decreases uniformly, p will increase uniformly thereby satisfying this requirement.

This formula is basic to problems involving beam stresses, thus basic to the problem of structural strength of ships. The formula can be expressed and used in various ways. For example, if we are dealing with a beam of given section modulus and want to know what is the maximum bending moment which the beam can take (with a proper factor of safety) we may use (1).

Of, if we propose to place a known bending moment on a mild steel structural shape: We know that the maximum stress which we can permit on the flanges of the shape (with a proper factor of safety) is around 7.5 tons psi. We may then divide the known bending moment by 7.5 and the proper Section Modulus is indicated:

$$M/p = I/y \qquad (2)$$

It is a simple matter then to select a standard shape with a Section Modulus at least equal to that required.

Or, with a given bending moment and a given section modulus, we may find the resultant maximum stress:

$$p = My/I \qquad (3)$$

Sample Problems in the Use of the Strength Equation:

1. Suppose the beam for which I was calculated above is a fixed-ended beam with a length between supports of 30 feet, and a uniformly distributed load of 10 tons. Find the tensile stress at the upper flange and the compressive stress at the lower flange (at the ends).

Step 1: Find Bending Moment (M): $M = \dfrac{10 \times 30}{12}$

= 25 foot-tons

25 foot-tons is equal to 300 inch-tons.

Step 2: p (upper flange) $= \dfrac{My}{I} = \dfrac{300 \times 5.5}{300.3}$

= 5.495 tons psi. ANS

p (lower flange) $= \dfrac{My}{I} = \dfrac{300 \times 4.5}{300.3}$

= 4.496 tons psi. ANS

2. What is the maximum bending moment in inch-tons which the beam in Problem 1 can withstand (with a proper factor of safety)? What is the maximum uniformly distributed load?

$$M = I/y \times p = \frac{300.3}{5.5} \times 7.5 = 409.5 \text{ inch-tons. ANS.}$$

409.5 inch-tons is equal to 34.125 foot-tons.

$$W = \frac{34.125 \times 12}{30} = 13.65 \text{ tons ANS.}$$

Note: In all problems, the units of distance and weight selected must be used consistently throughout. In the above problems, since I was calculated in terms of inches, the inch is the unit of distance used. The ton is the unit of weight used.

3. If the maximum bending moment for a beam with a uniformly distributed load is WL/8 (with freely supported ends) and a six inch channel with an I of 28.0 inch units is to be used for such a job, what is the maximum load which can be placed on the beam if the unsupported span is 20 feet?

Maximum stress is 7.5 tons (15,000 lbs.) for mild steel. y is 3.0 inches; L is 240 inches

$$p = My/I = \frac{WL/8 \times y}{I} \text{ or } W = \frac{8 \times 15,000 \times 28}{240 \times 3}$$

$$= 4,666.6 \text{ lbs.}$$

4. If the ends of the beam are fixed in Problem 3, what will be the maximum load?

$$W = 12pI/Ly \text{ or } 1.5 \text{ times as much: } 7,000 \text{ lbs. } ANS$$

STRENGTH OF SHIPS

With the foregoing outline of theory in the general field of Strength of Materials understood, we may now proceed to a study of Strength of Ships where this theory may be applied to an explicit problem of design.

The study of strength in a ship may be divided into two rather broad considerations:

1. *Local stresses.* It is apparent that each individual member of the structure of a vessel be adequate to withstand with a proper margin of safety the load due to such local stresses as hydrostatic pressures; concentrated weights like machinery, masts, propeller vibration and dynamic effects of liquids; special stresses encountered in drydocking and launching a vessel and so on.

2. *Structural stresses on the complete hull girder.* The problem here is to investigate the stresses which result from inequalities between weight acting down and buoyancy acting up along the length of the ship. These inequalities create shearing and bending forces, both longitudinal and transverse on the entire hull of the vessel. Just as a loaded beam must possess a resisting moment potentially large enough to resist any reasonable bending moment, so must a ship possess a reasonable resisting moment in order to withstand the loads placed upon it.

In this section it is proposed to study only the longitudinal stresses acting on the hull of vessels, since the provision of material adequate to resist longitudinal stresses will, in general, automatically provide for the transverse stresses.

The "Beam Theory" of Ship's Strength: We have seen that it is possible to ascertain the necessary dimensions of a beam if the type and extent of the load to be placed upon it, the material of which it is made, and the fixity of the end connections are known. This same procedure is applied by ship designers to the problem of obtaining the necessary longitudinal scantlings of a ship's hull. Now, of course, the hull of a vessel moving through seas is not directly analogous to the static load placed upon a beam in the structure of a building. However, the use of the "beam-theory" of ship's strength does not presume to produce an exact answer to the problem of obtaining the bending moment produced on a vessel in a given condition of loading and a given wave condition. The results from this method are only approximate. The important thing to remember is that if the calculations of strength for all vessels *are made in a similar manner,* the results may be accurately analyzed. Thus, if the scantlings of a vessel are arrived at by the beam theory and a failure occurs, the scantlings may be appropriately increased for future vessels. Through many years of experience, classification groups and others have found that the beam theory *does* produce a satisfactory tentative basis on which the strength of the vessel can be based.

In applying the beam-theory of strength to ships, then, it is necessary to make the following calculations:

1. The maximum *reasonable* load which the hull of a vessel considered as a girder or beam will be called upon to assume. This load will consist of (a) a reasonably severe condition of loading and (b) a reasonably severe sea condition.

2. The bending moment and shear resulting from this maximum reasonable load. These stresses are computed by the use of strength curves.

3. The section modulus necessary to withstand with a proper margin of safety, the calculated bending moment, and the resulting tensile and compressive stresses in the upper and lower flanges of the hull girder.

Let us consider first what the ship designer considers a reasonably severe condition of loading.

If a vessel were loaded in such a way that all of the possible deadweight were loaded in the midship section of the vessel, it is apparent that a very severe bending condition would be induced. The vessel would tend to *sag*. On the other hand, if all the deadweight were loaded in the end compartments, the vessel would tend to *hog*. Extremely high tensile and compressive stresses would result in the flanges of the hull girder. However, these suppositions are for unreasonably severe loading conditions. The designer does not build enough strength into a ship's hull to assume such stresses. What then, are reasonably severe conditions?

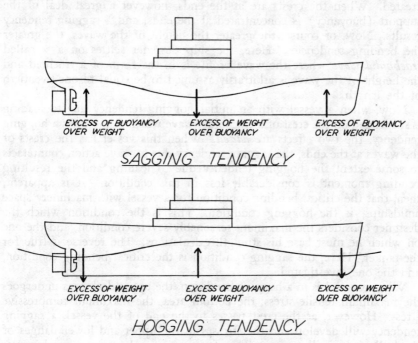

EXCESS OF BUOYANCY OVER WEIGHT   EXCESS OF WEIGHT OVER BUOYANCY   EXCESS OF BUOYANCY OVER WEIGHT

SAGGING TENDENCY

EXCESS OF WEIGHT OVER BUOYANCY   EXCESS OF BUOYANCY OVER WEIGHT   EXCESS OF WEIGHT OVER BUOYANCY

HOGGING TENDENCY

Figure 64. Hogging and Sagging

For a dry cargo vessel with machinery amidships, a loading condition which assumes the cargo compartments full, the midship tanks empty, and the end tanks full, and the ship down to her marks is usually adopted. This results in an initial hogging tendency for this type of vessel. For a tanker with machinery space aft, a loading condition which assumes the cargo compartments full, the end tanks empty, and the ship down to her marks is adopted. This results in an initial sagging tendency for this type of vessel. These can be considered as the maximum reasonable loading conditions, although it is possible for a vessel to achieve greater bending moments in some ballasted conditions. It is interesting to observe that the advent of oil fuel and double bottom tanks has made it possible to reduce the extreme bending moments which used to obtain on coal-burning ships in the load burned-out condition. Oil may be spread out over the length of the ship instead of being concentrated amidships as in the case of coal.

Next, we shall consider what constitutes a reasonably severe sea condition.

Suppose a vessel to be heading into waves equal in length to the length of the vessel. When the crest of the wave is amidships the ship is suspended, as it were, on the crest and a maximum hogging tendency is created. When the crests are at the ends, however a great deal of the support (buoyancy) is concentrated at the ends, and a sagging tendency results. Now, of course, the greater the height of the waves, the greater the bending tendencies. Here, the ship designer settles on a so-called *trochoidal wave* where the wave profile is in the form of a trochoid and the height of the wave is arbitrarily assumed to be equal to one-twentieth of the length.

Now, when a vessel with an initial hogging tendency due to loading is suspended on the crest of a trochoidal wave which also creates a hogging tendency, the two effects are *added*. When this vessel has the crests of the waves at the ends, the sagging tendency due to wave action counteracts to some extent the hogging tendency due to loading and the resulting bending moment is considerably less in this condition. It is apparent, then, that the critical bending condition for a vessel with machinery space amidships, is the hogging condition. This is the condition which the designer considers the maximum reasonably severe condition, and the one on which he must base his strength calculations. The reverse is true for the tanker. Here, the sagging condition is the critical bending condition, and the one investigated.

When a vessel is in a hogging condition, the upper deck area undergoes the maximum tensile stress; the bottom area, the maximum compressive stress. However, as the crest passes to the end of the vessel, a sagging tendency will develop and the stresses in the upper and lower flanges of the hull girder will reverse. Therefore as a vessel passes through waves there is a constant shifting in the direction of stresses along the flanges of the hull.

Longitudinal shearing stresses are also developed since tension and compression vary uniformly from the top of the hull girder to its bottom. The small difference in tension (and compression) from layer to layer results in shearing forces between the layers. All this is in conformance with the beam theory of strength.

We have seen then, what constitutes reasonably severe bending moments. The next problem is that of calculating the bending moments and the shearing stress which result from these bending conditions.

Strength Curves: We have seen that when the force of buoyancy acting upwards is greater than the force of weight acting downwards in the midship section (which means that the force of buoyancy at the ends is less than the force of weight at the ends), the vessel tends to hog. This illustrates in a general way the principle that bending moments exist due to a difference or differences in the forces of buoyancy and weight along the length of the vessel. Therefore, in finding the bending moment for any given condition of both weight and buoyancy distribution, we must

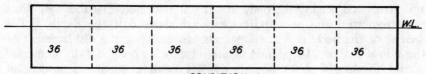

CONDITION A

SIX BLOCKS EACH. I'X I'X I' AND EACH WEIGHING 36 POUNDS AND CONNECTED BY SIDE STRIPS 6' X I'

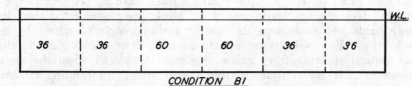

CONDITION BI

SIX BLOCKS EACH. I'X I'X I' THE FOUR END BLOCKS WEIGHING 36 POUNDS, THE TWO MIDDLE BLOCKS WEIGHING 60 POUNDS AND CONNECTED BY AND TO SIDE STRIPS.

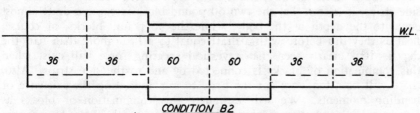

CONDITION B2

SIX BLOCKS EACH I'X I'X I' THE FOUR END BLOCKS WEIGHING 36 POUNDS, THE TWO MIDDLE BLOCKS WEIGHING 60 POUNDS EACH BLOCK IS FREE TO SEEK ITS OWN LEVEL, BEING LOOSELY CONTAINED BY THE TWO SIDE STRIPS.

Figure 65

find first the exact extent of the force of weight acting downwards, and the exact extent of the force of buoyancy acting upwards at all points along the length of the vessel, and then find the difference between these forces. Plotting these differences, in turn, will reveal the extent of shearing stress and bending moments existing for the given condition.

These principles can be illustrated by the following simple example. (See Figure 65).

Suppose that a floating body be constructed a series of six blocks, each 1' x 1' x 1', and each connected by and to, thin side strips in such a way that blocks of varying weights can be made part of the floating body in any combination desired.

Now let us consider a combination of blocks which we will designate Condition A. In this condition the floating body will consist of six blocks all weighing 36 pounds apiece. Connecting the blocks by and to the side strips and placing the body in salt water we note that the body floats with zero trim and at a draft somewhat above half the depth. (The weight of the body is 6 x 36 pounds, disregarding the displacement of the side strips, or 216 pounds, while the floating body if fully immersed would displace 6 x 64 pounds or 384 pounds, leaving a reserve of displacement of 168 pounds.) It may ·be observed that the weight of *each* block is opposed by an equal buoyant force. Since there is no difference between weight and buoyancy at any point of the length of the body, no load exists on the body, and no shearing force or bending moment exists. This may be clearly seen if the blocks are disconnected from the side strips and made separate floating bodies loosely contained by the side strips. Each will assume exactly the same draft, showing clearly that no vertical shearing force existed between the blocks when they were connected. If no vertical shearing force existed, no bending moment existed.

Now, if two 60 pound blocks are substituted for the two middle blocks of the floating body and the four end blocks of 36 pounds each and the two middle blocks of 60 pounds each are inserted loosely between the side strips, it is seen that the two 60 pound blocks assume a draft almost equal to the depth of the body, while the 36 pound blocks, of course, float as they did before with a draft equal to a little more than half the depth. It is clearly seen that a vertical shearing force will exist when this combination of blocks is connected by and to the side strips. Also, there will be a tendency for the body to sag, indicating the existence of bending moments. We will designate this combination of blocks as Condition B1, and attempt by the drawing of strength curves to ascertain the exact extent of the shearing forces and the bending moments on the floating body in this condition.

First to be plotted is the *Weight Curve*. We will calculate the weight per inch of length. For the 36 pound blocks there will be a weight of 36/12 or 3 pounds per inch of length. For the 60 pound blocks a weight of 5 pounds per inch of length results.

Next, the *Buoyancy Curve* is plotted. Since the body is rectangular, floats at zero trim, and has a total buoyant force equal to the total weight or 264 pounds, the buoyancy curve will be a straight line indicating a buoyancy force of 264/72 or 3.67 pounds per inch of length.

It is immediately apparent that differences between weight and buoyancy exist. These differences are plotted as the *Load Curve*. Plotting from left to right, it is seen that an excess of buoyancy over weight to the extent of 0.67 pounds per inch exists for the first two feet of length. Then an excess of weight over buoyancy to the extent of 1.33 pounds per inch exists for the next two feet, and finally, an excess of buoyancy over weight

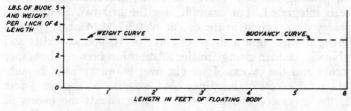

STRENGTH CURVES FOR CONDITION A

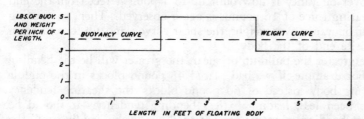

WEIGHT AND BUOYANCY CURVES FOR CONDITION BI

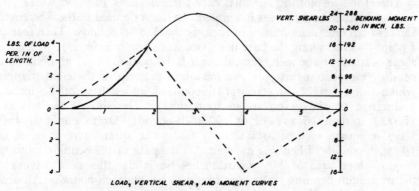

LOAD, VERTICAL SHEAR, AND MOMENT CURVES

STRENGTH CURVES FOR CONDITION BI
Figure 66

of 0.67 pounds per inch is observed for the last two feet. Excess of buoyancy over weight is usually plotted above the base line, the reverse being true for excess of weight over buoyancy.

We may now obtain the vertical shearing force from the load curve by merely "adding up" the excess of buoyancy over weight or vice versa. The greater the length of body over which buoyancy continues to exceed weight, the greater the shearing tendency. The logic of this can be seen by merely noting that in order for a person to tear (shear) even a piece of paper, it is necessary for him to exert an excess of force over resistance in opposite directions with each hand.

Therefore in plotting the next curve, the *Shear Curve,* the area under the load curve is integrated. For example, for the first two feet, a total excess of buoyancy over weight to the extent of 0.67 x 24 or 16 pounds is built up. Thus, at this point a shearing force of 16 pounds exists and is so plotted. Now, a sudden change in the relationship between buoyancy and weight occurs and the excess of weight over buoyancy must be subtracted from the total excess of buoyancy over weight. At a point 3 feet from the end, the excess of buoyancy over weight equals the excess of weight over buoyancy and the shear curve crosses the base line. Excess of weight over buoyancy is now built up to a point 4 feet from the end where a shearing force of 16 pounds is again observed. Then, subtracting the excess of buoyancy over weight, the shear curve slants up to zero again at the opposite end of the body.

Now, the greater the build-up of shear, the greater will be the bending tendency. For example, if we had placed 48 pound blocks in the middle of the floating body instead of 60 pound blocks, the shearing tendency would have been less, leading to less bending tendency. It should be apparent that bending moments are obtained simply by "adding up" the shearing tendencies.

Therefore, in plotting our final curve, the *Bending Moment Curve,* the area under the shear curve is integrated. In the scale used in these Strength Curves each one inch ordinate of shear is equal to 16 pounds. Therefore at a point two feet along the base line (two inches on the curves), where the shear ordinate *is* one inch, vertical shear is 16 pounds. Now to obtain the bending moment at this point we must find the area of the right triangle which has a height of 1 inch (16 pounds) and a base of 24 inches. (Abscissae on the graph are in foot units). The area of the triangle (bh/2) is then 16 x 24/2 or 192 inch-pounds. Or to put it another way: A square inch of area actually under the shear curve is equal to 192 inch-pounds of bending moment. At the peak of the bending moment curve, a total area of $1\frac{1}{2}$ square inches lies under the shear curve and the maximum bending moment is found to be 288 inch-pounds. All area between the base line and the shear curve now represents a reduction in the bending moments and the curve once again comes back to zero at the opposite end.

Important characteristics of Strength Curves: The following important characteristics of strength curves should be noted:

1. Total area under the weight curve should equal total area under the buoyancy curve, since total weight is equal to total buoyancy.

2. The geometric center of the weight curve should be vertically in line with the geometric center of the buoyancy curve, since the center of

gravity of a vessel is always in a vertical line with the center of buoyancy when the vessel is in equilibrium.

3. Whenever the buoyancy curve crosses the weight curve, a peak value of shear occurs and the shear curve changes its direction.

4. Peaks of shear occur approximately at the quarter-lengths.

5. When the excess of buoyancy over weight is equal to the excess of weight over buoyancy, the shear curve crosses the base line.

6. When the shear curve crosses the base line, the bending moment curve reaches a maximum value. (Or a peak value, in more complicated loadings.)

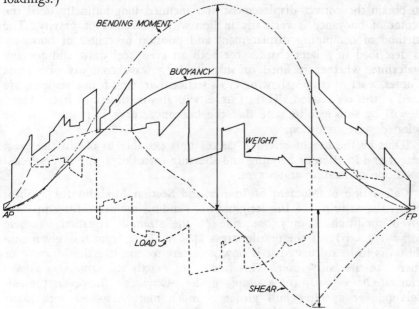

Figure 67. Typical Strength Curves for Ship in Waves

Strength Curves for a Ship in Waves: The drawing of strength curves for a simple rectangular form floating in still water is obviously less complicated than the drawing of curves for a ship with an involved distribution of weights along its length and an involved buoyancy distribution due to the form of the ship and the wave formation. The theory, however, is similar; that is, weight and buoyancy curves are plotted and from these, the intensity and location of shearing and bending forces can be derived.

The weight curve is drawn by plotting the number of tons per foot of length. This is done first for the light ship and then for all the deadweight items (cargo, fuel, etc.). The two are combined to produce the total weight curve. The calculation of each individual weight in a foot of length is an extremely tedious job and it is customary to resort to approximate methods involving the use of geometric figures. The description of these methods is beyond the scope and purpose of this text. Suffice it to state that the weight curve is drawn for the design loaded condition considered to be a reasonably severe condition.

The buoyancy curve must now be drawn for the wave condition producing the maximum bending tendencies. This, as previously described is a trochoidal wave equal in length to the length of the ship, with a height equal to one-twentieth of the length, and with the crest amidships (when machinery is amidships) and crests at the ends (when machinery is aft). The wave contour is laid out on a profile of the vessel and moved vertically to obtain the correct displacement and inclined longitudinally until the center of buoyancy is vertically in line with the center of gravity. The method of computing displacement and position of center of buoyancy is described in a later chapter for both an even keel draft and for any waterline, whether inclined or shaped along wave contours. Bonjeans Curves, a set of curves showing cross-sectional areas at frame stations, are used in this connection. These Curves will also be described later. Here, it will be sufficient to state that the buoyancy curve is plotted for the selected wave condition.

Thus by the use of strength curves it is possible to obtain the exact extent and location of bending and shearing forces of a ship in a selected condition of loading and waves.

Calculation of Moment of Inertia and Section Modulus for a Ship: Now, the securing of the longitudinal bending moments for ship in a given condition is only one side of the strength equation. (where $M = I/y \times p$). If the tensile stress (p) resulting from this given condition is to be calculated it is now necessary to calculate the Moment of Inertia of the hull girder. This is done in exactly the same way as was illustrated previously for a simple girder. Obviously, however, the calculation for a ship's hull girder is much more involved with many members making up the hull girder. This is simply a question of more arithmetic. Another more difficult question arises, however. What members are to be included in the calculation of moment of inertia? There is some difference of opinion in this respect among Naval Architects. In general, however, only continuous longitudinal members are included. Figure 68 shows the longitudinal members commonly included in the calculation of moment of inertia. Such members as the hatch coamings, discontinuous deck girders, deck plating between hatches, and other discontinuous longitudinal members are excluded. The question of rivet holes has stirred some controversy, since these discontinuities are effective in compression but not in tension (as are some discontinuous longitudinal members). Generally, no deductions are made for rivet holes. It must be remembered that this whole process of obtaining longitudinal stress is approximate in nature and therefore small discrepancies resulting from the exclusion of members which may offer some longitudinal strength are important. What *is* important is uniformity of method so that there may be uniformity of analysis of results.

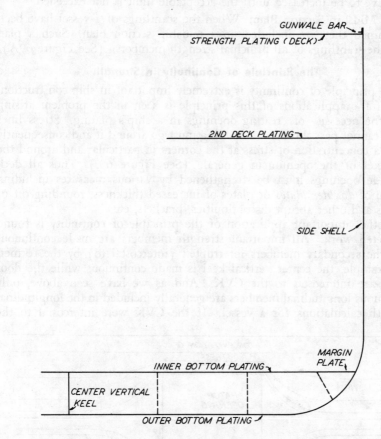

Figure 68.   Longitudinal Strength Members—Dry Cargo Vessel

Summary of Longitudinal Strength Calculations: To find the unit tensile (or compressive) stress resulting from the placing of a vessel in a given condition of loading and waves, it is necessary first to calculate the bending moment. This can be done by the use of Strength Curves. (Sometimes in preliminary work an approximation of the bending moment is arrived at by some simple formula such as: $M = bL^2Bd/35^2$ where b is the block coefficient, L the length in feet, B the breadth in feet, and d the draft in feet.) Next, the section modulus is calculated by finding the Moment of Inertia and the distance from the neutral axis to the uppermost and lowermost points of the hull girder. The strength formula: $M = I/y \times p$ is then used to find unit stress (p) at the upper flange and the lower flange of the hull girder. If this unit stress exceeds the acceptable limit for the material used (around 7 or 8 tons psi for mild steel[1]) the scantlings used in the calculations are not sufficient and they will have to be increased until the acceptable limit is not exceeded.

The Midship Section Plan: When the scantlings of a vessel have been determined they are included on a midship section plan. Such a plan gives the scantlings of all principal strength members. (See Figure 69A).

The Principle of Continuity in Strength

The principle of continuity is extremely important in ship construction. One of the applications of this principle is seen in the problem arising from the necessity of creating openings in a ship's plating. Stress lines which cannot pass through an opening must go around it and consequently create a concentration of stress at the corners in particular and around the perimeter of the opening in general. (See Figure 69.) Thus all deck and side openings must be strengthened by various measures including the use of *doubler plates* or plates of increased thickness, rounding off of corners and other abrupt discontinuities, brackets, etc.

Another important application of the principle of continuity is found in riveted work. All important strength members are made continuous with the secondary members interrupted (intercostal to) by the former. For example, the center vertical keel is made continuous while the floor plates are intercostal to the CVK. And as we have seen above, only continuous longitudinal members are generally included in the longitudinal strength calculations for a vessel. If the CVK were intercostal to the

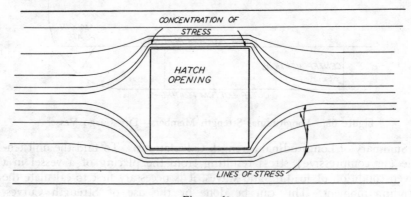

Figure 69

---

[1] The acceptable figure for "p" actually, in practice, varies depending upon the length of the vessel. A greater *calculated* value is permitted for vessels of greater length, and a smaller *calculated* value is required for vessels of smaller length. This is due to the use of a standard height of 1/20th of the length of a trochoidal form wave assumed to have a length equal to that of the ship. For long vessels, it is extremely unlikely that a wave of, say, 800 feet will be encountered, and even if it were, it is even more unlikely that it would have a height of 40 feet. The calculated value of "p" is, therefore, unrealistic and can be adjusted upwards in line with experience.

floors for example it could not be considered a longitudinal strength member.

Superstructure Scantlings and Expansion Joints: Since superstructure is located at a great distance from the neutral aixs it is subjected to very great stresses even though it is not considered to be part of the hull girder in some cases. Since it is not desirable to have heavy structure in the upper part of a vessel (due to stability considerations) a problem exists in how to obtain proper strength in superstructure without unduly increasing weight. One method of treating this problem is to install expansion joints in very long ships. These joints extend across the superstructure and down to the main deck at intervals of about 100 feet. Another method is to utilize high tensile steel in the superstructure decks instead of mild steel thus reducing the weight of steel required. Still another method (and the most widely used) is to maintain the section modulus required for the main or strength deck for all superstructure decks. This results in a redistribution of material in such a way as to give superstructure decks sufficient strength without overly increasing the weight in the upper parts of the vessel. In other words, superstructure decks are considered to be strength decks where they extend the length of the vessel, thus reducing the scantlings required in the main deck.

Scantlings of Ship's Plating: Vertically, plating must be thicker at the upper and lower levels of a ship. Therefore the deck plating, bottom plating, sheer and bilge strakes are heavier than the side plating in between the sheer and bilge strakes. This is due to the higher tension and compression stresses at points vertically away from the neutral axis. Longitudinally, plating must be heavier amidships than at the ends due to the greater bending moments amidships.

The American Bureau requires that midship scantlings be maintained through the midship one-half length.[1] End scantlings which cannot extend for more than 0.1 L from each end of the vessel are given in the Rules in addition to the midship scantlings. The latter are gradually reduced from the midship one-half length to the end scantlings.

Some of the principal longitudinal strength members of a Liberty ship, along with their amidship and end scantlings are cited as an example:

Member	Scantlings amidships	Scantlings at ends
Upper deck stringer	.71″	.40″
Other deck plating	.71″	.40″
Sheer strake	.70″	.45″
Bottom plating	.64″	.64″
Side plating	.63″	.45″
Inner bottom	.44″	.40″
Margin plate	(.54″ in holds and ER; .60″ in B.S.)	
Keel plate	.88″	.88″
Rider plate	.52″	.44″

[1] For vessels with machinery aft. For vessels with machinery amidships, through the midship 0.4L.

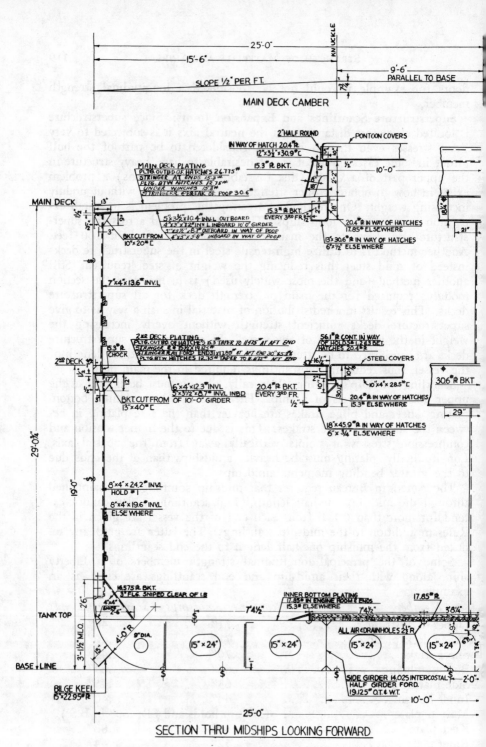

SECTION THRU MIDSHIPS LOOKING FORWARD

Figure 69A.   Midship Section Plan: C1-M-AV1

120

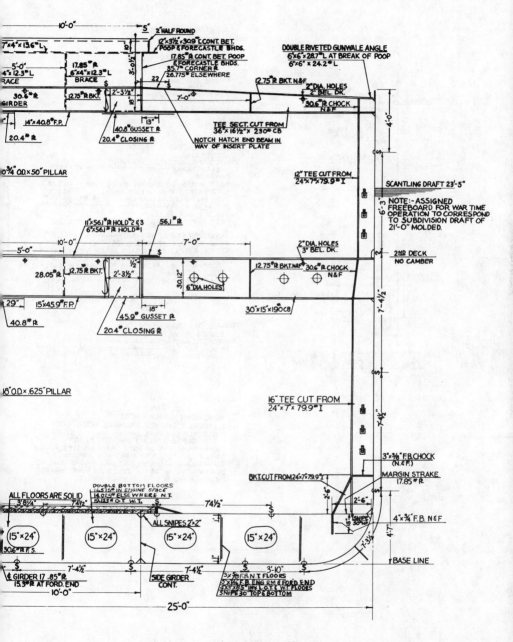

Figure 69A. *(Continued on next page)*

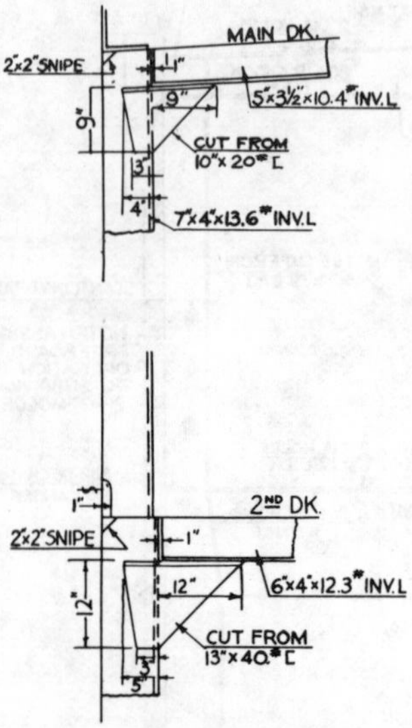
MAIN DK.
2"x2" SNIPE
1"
9"
9"
5"x3½"x10.4# INV. L
CUT FROM
10"x20# L
3"
4"
7"x4"x13.6# INV. L
1"
2ND DK.
2"x2" SNIPE
1"
12"
12"
6"x4"x12.3# INV. L
CUT FROM
13"x40.# L
3"
5"

ALTERNATE DET. OF FR. & BEAM CONN. AT MAIN & 2ND DECKS

FRAME SPACING
F.P. TO FR. #1 — — — — 1'-9"
FR#1 TO FR#4 — — 24" — — 26'-0"
FR#14 TO FR#135 — 27" — — 272'-3"
FR#135 TO A.P. — — 24" — — 20'-0"

SHELL PLATING
MIDSHIP 1/2 L
BOTTOM & SIDE SHELL PLATING — — — — 21.675#
SHEER STRAKE — — — — — — — — — — 48"x25.5#
FORWARD
BOTTOM PLTG. MIDSHIP 1/2 L TO 3/5 L FWD. 24.225#
BOTTOM PLTG. FWD. OF MIDSHIP 3/5 L 24.225#
FORE END PLTG. BELOW L.W.L. 24" FR. SP. — 26.775#
SIDE PLTG. AT FORE END — — — — — — 21.675#
FOC'SL'E SIDE PLTG. — — — — — — 16.575#
PLTG. IN WAY OF HAWSE PIPE — — — — 30.6#
AFT.
POOP SIDE PLTG. AT AFT ENDS — — — — — 12.75#
POOP SIDE PLTG. AT FORD. ENDS — — — — 20.4#
OTHER PLTG. AT AFTER END 24" FR. SP. — 16.575#
SHEER STRAKE EACH SIDE OF BREAK OF POOP — 33.15#
AFTERMOST PLS ATTACHING TO STERN FR. 21.675#
BOSS PLTG. — — — — — — — — — 22.95#
FLATKEEL THRUOUT — — — — — — 26.775#

PRINCIPAL DIMENSION
LENGTH BETWEEN PERP. — — 320'-0"
BREADTH MOLDED — — — — 50'-0"
DEPTH MOLDED — — — — — 29'-0¾"
SCANTLING DRAFT — — — — 23'-5"

EQUIPMENT
EQUIPMENT NUMERAL C33
2-STOCKLESS BOWER ANCHORS 6090# EACH
1-STOCKLESS SPARE BOWER ANCHOR 5150#
1-STOCKLESS STREAM ANCHOR 2240#
270-FATHOMS 1 13/16" DIA. (CAST OR FORGED STEEL) CABLE
90-FATHOMS 5/8" DIA. 6/12 STEEL WIRE-STREAMLINE
120-FATHOMS 11/16" DIA. 6/12 STEEL WIRE ROPE TOWLINE
2-58 FATHOMS 1 1/8 DIA. 6/12 STEEL WIRE ROPE HAWSER
2-75 FATHOMS 6" CIRC. MANILA WARPS

Figure 69A. *(Concluded)*

Of course, plating must be increased in thickness at some local points in order to take care of local stresses. For example, it should be noted that the bottom plating scantlings are maintained throughout the length of the ship. This may be ascribed to drydocking requirements, allowance for corrosion, etc.

Shearing Stresses: We have seen that horizontal shearing stress exists at all points along the length of a vessel; that a maximum of vertical shearing stress exists at the quarter lengths. In these areas connecting members must be strengthened. Particularly is this true of the areas where vertical shear is at a maximum; that is, at the quarter-lengths. For example, the ABS requires additional riveting in these areas.

It should be observed that horizontal shear leads to the formation of vertical shear and vice-versa. This can be understood when it is remembered that, for equilibrium, an opposing force equal to the shearing stress must be generated. For example, in Figure 70, let us suppose that a shearing force has been created in a horizontal direction. This couple immediately gives rise to an opposing couple or in this case, vertical shear.

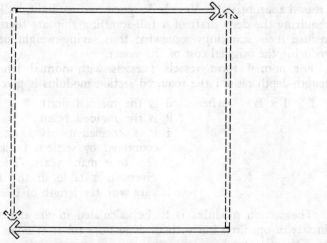

Figure 70. Formation of Shear Stress

Structural Tests on Ships: Partly as a result of the partial failure of the welded ship, several full-scale structural tests of ships have been made during and since World War II.[1,2,3] These tests are conducted by subjecting a vessel to various hogging and sagging moments by means of ballasting the vessel and then measuring the stress and strain at numerous points in the plating by means of strain gages. These tests have confirmed the essential validity of the beam theory of strength. They have confirmed

[1, 2, 3] See footnotes next page.

the presence of concentrations of stress at structural discontinuities and led to improved design of such discontinuities. In regard to superstructure, however, it has been shown that short deckhouses contribute practically nothing to the hull girder strength with the stress decreasing instead of increasing with distance from the neutral axis;[1] longer deckhouses do assume part of the hull girder stresses but even here, only a moderate fraction of the theoretical values.[2]

Strength Provisions of the Load Line Regulations

As has been noted in the Chapter on Freeboard, the Load Line regulations specify that a vessel in order to qualify for minimum freeboard must meet certain strength requirements. These requirements are now discussed:

First, if a vessel has complied with the highest standards of the ABS, it is regarded as having sufficient strength for the assignment of minimum freeboard. For other vessels, the Rules specify certain required section moduli. If the modulus is less than that required, the freeboard is increased appropriately. Vessels designed to carry light, bulky cargo and not requiring the deep draft of a full-scantling ship are thereby permitted to reduce their scantlings somewhat thus saving weight of hull steel and reducing the original cost of the vessel.

For normal form vessels (vessels with normal length-breadth and length-depth ratios) the required section modulus is given by:

$f \times d \times B$ where: d is the molded draft
B is the molded beam
f is a coefficient based on experience encountered by sections built to ABS standards over many years. The coefficients are given in a table in the Regulations and vary with the length of the vessel.

The section modulus is to be calculated in the normal way, that is, in way of openings but without deductions for rivet holes. All continuous longitudinal members other than such parts of underdeck girders as are required entirely for supporting purposes are included. Above the strength deck only the gunwale bar and the extension of the sheer strake are included. Areas are measured in square inches and distances in feet.

---

[1] John Vasta, "Structural Tests on the Liberty Ship S.S. Philip Schuyler", *Transactions of the Society of Naval Architects and Marine Engineers*, 1947.

[2] John Vasta, "Structural Tests on the Passenger Ship SS President Wilson—Interaction Between Superstructure and Main Hull Girder", *Transactions of the Society of Naval Architects and Marine Engineers*, 1949.

[3] "Structural Investigation in Still Water of the Tanker Newcombia, *Transactions of the North East Coast Institution of Engineers and Shipbuilders*, April, 1947 and *"Report of Hogging and Sagging Tests on All-Welded Tanker M.V. Neverita"*, The Admiralty Ship Welding Committee, H.M. Stationery Office, 1946.

The Rules also specify the Frame modulus using a somewhat similar system. The frame modulus required depends upon the molded draft and the vertical dimensions of the floor, frame, depth, and superstructure height.

Example Problem in Finding the Required I/y under Load Line Regulations:

Given: A vessel with dimensions as follows: (Dimensions defined as in Rules:)

Length:	436 feet	Note: These dimensions produce length-breadth and length-depth ratios within the range prescribed by the Rules.
Breadth:	62 feet	
Draft:	26 feet	

Find: Required section modulus for minimum freeboard:
1) In the "Load Line Regulations" (Section 43.37,e) for a length of 436 feet, f is 12.71.
2) 12.71 x 26 x 62 = 20,489 in²-ft. *ANS:*

Loading Instructions to Minimize Stress: It is time now to consider some practical applications of the theories of strength to the problem of operating a vessel. In recent years designers have begun to show increasing interest in providing information by which the ship operator and ship officer can be guided in loading their vessels. This has been especially true in the case of tankers.[1] This concern can be traced to the following reasons:

1. The crackings experienced by numerous welded ships, especially the all-welded tanker.

2. The increasing length of the modern tanker bringing with it an accentuation of the loading problem.

3. The tendency in modern tanker design to provide enough volumetric capacity to load "full and down" with a low density cargo like gasoline. When heavier density cargoes are carried and the available cubic is not all utilized, a problem naturally arises on the best location of the cargo.

Table IV, for estimating stresses in the weather deck of a T2 tanker is illustrative of designer's efforts in this field.

The use of the table is self-explanatory. However, the following comments might be helpful:

1. The design stress, both hogging and sagging is given at the top of columns 5 and 7. These are the stresses which will result on the weather

---

[1] For an especially fine paper on this subject, see "Investigation of Cargo Distribution in Tank Vessels" by J. H. McDonald and D. F. MacNaught, *Transactions of the Society of Naval Architects and Marine Engineers,* 1949. The authors present recommendations for loading and ballasting various type tankers.

TABLE IV

T2 Tanker Example

Table for estimating stresses in weather deck in
STANDARD HOGGING AND SAGGING POSITIONS

	Full load (1)	Any condition (2)	Change— hundreds of tons (3)	HOGGING		SAGGING	
				Change per 100 tons (4)	Change in stress psi (5)	Change per 100 t. (6)	Change in stress psi (7)
Full Load			217.70		10,500		14,600
A.P. Tank	0			+470		−350	
F.W. Aft	29			+432		−318	
Dist. Tank ...	36			+410		−296	
F.F.W. Aft ..	73			+370		−263	
Crew, STS. aft.	40			+330		−232	
R.F.W. Fwd. .	166			+238		−148	
F.O. aft	692			+175		− 97	
Cargo #9 ...	1714			+ 50		+ 10	
Cargo #8 ...	1803			− 65		+112	
Cargo #7 ...	1813			−182		+218	
Cargo #6 ...	1814			−302		+322	
Cargo #5 ...	1814			−218		+218	
Cargo #4 ...	1812			−110		+ 98	
Cargo #3 ...	1784			0		− 25	
Cargo #2 ...	1620			+102		−142	
Cargo #1 ...	529			+178		−230	
Crew & F.W. .	81			−160		+155	
F.O. Fwd. ...	728			+236		−317	
Stores fwd. ...	20			+330		−402	
F.P. tank	0			+355		−430	
TOTALS							

With the above table, stresses for any condition may be closely predicted for both HOGGING and SAGGING by following the steps described below:

A. List the load distribution in column (2).

B. Enter difference from full load in column (3) retaining algebraic sign.

C. Multiply entries in column (3) by figures in column (4) & (6) and enter results in columns (5) & (7) respectively, observing rules for algebraic sign.

D. Add algebraic sum of entries in columns (5) & (7) to the stresses heading these columns, thereby obtaining the resultant stresses.

IN NO CASE SHOULD THESE RESULTANT STRESSES EXCEED 18,000 lbs. PSI.

deck if the vessel is loaded as in Column 1. The stresses are in pounds per square inch of tension or compression. It should be noted that the maximum stress condition is reached in the sagging position. This, of course, is typical of tankers. In almost all cases, therefore, the problem will be one of reducing the tendency to sag rather than one of reducing the tendency to hog, although a problem of high hogging stresses may arise in the ballasted conditions.

2. Although the calculation of the exact figures in Columns 4 and 6 is involved since strength curves must be drawn for the various possibilities, the logic of the table is clear. For example, if 100 tons are loaded in the Fore Peak tank, the figure +1 is entered in Column 3. When +355 is multilied by +1, the hogging stress will be increased by 355 psic and when −430 is multiplied by +1, the sagging stress will be reduced by 430 psi. The effect of weight loaded or discharged at the end of the vessel has a large effect in altering the sagging and/or hogging stresses. Similarly, weight loaded or discharged amidships has a considerable effect on sagging and hogging. Weight loaded or discharged at the quarter-lengths has a minimum effect.

Another form of information which is of value to the ship operator is the maximum unit deck load in pounds per square feet. This information may be provided by the designer on the Capacity Plan in this form or given as the maximum number of tons to be loaded in a given area (or both).

QUESTIONS

1. What are the two major factors determining the scantlings of a vessel?
2. Define: Tension, compression, shear, load, and strain.
3. If a girder is subjected to a compressive load of 60 tons and its cross-sectional area is 10 sq. in., what is the compressive stress? ANS: 6 tons psi.
4. A girder, at a certain point, is subjected to a shearing load of 80 tons. Its cross-sectional area is 20 sq. in. What is the shear stress? ANS: 4 tons psi.
5. Define the following properties of materials: Elastic limit, yield point, ultimate strength, modulus of elasticity, ductility, hardness, toughness, fatigue strength. Which two of these are generally most important for shipbuilding steel?
6. A beam is to be installed in a structure and is expected to assume, with the proper factor of safety, a total load of 60 tons. If the beam is made of mild steel, what is the proper cross-sectional area for the beam? ANS: 8 sq. in.
7. It is calculated that a rivet will assume a maximum shear load of 2 tons. What should the diameter of the rivet shank be if the rivet is made of mild steel and the proper factor of safety is used? ANS: 0.68 in.
8. What is the approximate ultimate strength of mild steel in tension? in shear?
9. How is ductility revealed in a stress-strain diagram?
10. How does the ABS assure itself that the mild steel intended for ships building to its class has proper tensile strength and ductility?
11. A ruler lies flat on the top of a desk. Is the ruler subjected to any stress? Explain. Now lay the ruler down so that it creates a bridge between two books. What stresses now exist and where? Explain.
12. Explain fully why structural shapes are built with flanges and webs instead of a simple rectangular shape.

13. A fixed-ended beam is 40 feet long. A concentrated load of 20 tons is placed on the middle of the beam. What is the resulting bending moment? ANS: 100 foot-tons.

14. If a uniformly distributed load of 20 tons is placed on the beam in Ques. 13, what is the resulting bending moment at the ends? in the middle? ANS: 66.7 and 33.3 foot-tons.

15. What would be the result on beam scantlings if ship's deck beams were not supported at intermediate points by pillars and girders? Explain fully.

16. Explain the need for brackets at the ends of ship's beams and girders.

17. Explain in terms of bending moments why it is better to distribute cargo evenly over the compartment rather than concentrating it in one spot.

18. Prove empirically that *the strength of a rectangular beam varies as the square of its depth* by computing the stress p on beams 1″ x 3″ and 1″ x 5″, if the beams are assumed to be fixed ended beams with a length of 10 feet and concentrated weight of 2 tons in the middle of the beams. ANS: p on 1″ x 5″ is 14,402 lbs.
           p on 1″ x 3″ is 40,000 lbs.
           or: 1″ x 5″ will support $(5/3)^2$ times as much load as the 1″ x 3″.

19. Find the height above base of the center of gravity of the section illustrated in Figure 71. ANS: 8.4 inches.

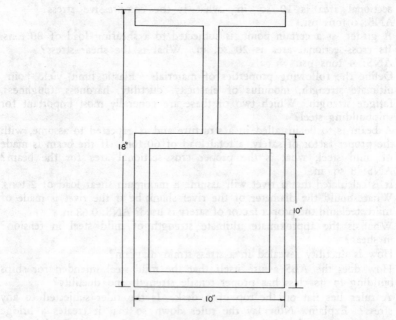

18″

10″

10″

NOTE: ALL MEMBERS 1″ THICK

Figure 71

20. Find the moment of inertia of the section in Question 19.
ANS: 1945.25 in.^{4}

21. If the maximum bending moment on the section in Question 19 is 1,600 inch-tons, what will the stresses be at the upper and lower flanges of the section?
ANS: 7.9 tons per sq. in.   6.9 tons per sq. in.

22. Discuss the "beam theory" of ship's strength with relation to the assumptions used and the validity of the theory.

23. What is considered to be the maximum condition of loading for a freighter for purposes of drawing the weight curve? What is considered to be a reasonably severe sea condition?

24. Why is the critical bending condition for a tanker considered to be sagging?

25. In the floating body described in the text, draw strength curves for the following condition:
1st compartment: 30 lb. block.
2nd compartment: 36 lb. block.
3rd compartment: 48 lb. block.
4th compartment: 48 lb. block.
5th compartment: 36 lb. block.
6th compartment: 30 lb. block.

26. In regard to strength curves, explain why:
a) Total area under the weight curve is equal to total area under the buoyancy curve.
b) The centroid of the weight curve is vertically in line with the centroid of the buoyancy curve.
c) Difference between weight and buoyancy lead to the development of shearing stress, both vertically and horizontally.
d) Bending results from an accumulation of vertical shear.

27. List the longitudinal members commonly included in longitudinal strength calculations. What longitudinal members are not included? Why?

28. Explain, step by step, how a ship designer finds the necessary scantlings of longitudinal plating and framing.

29. How are the problems intendent on the high direct stresses in superstructure decks solved by ship designers?

30. Structurally, how does the shell plating on ships vary vertically and longitudinally? Explain why in terms of location of maximum stresses.

31. Explain why the development of shear in one direction leads to the development of equal and opposing shearing stresses.

32. Outline the method required by the Load Line Regulations for finding section moduli.

33. Using the "Table for Estimating Stresses in the Weather Deck" find the hogging and sagging stresses resulting from the following loading condition of a T2 tanker:
1. All tanks and storerooms except the F.P., A.P. and cargo tanks filled.
2. 1200 tons in Cargo #7; 1400 tons in Cargo #5; 1200 tons in Cargo #3.
3. Other cargo tanks empty.
ANS: 17,711 (hogging)
     6,217 (sagging)

BIBLIOGRAPHY

Load Line Regulations, issued by U. S. Coast Guard, Government Printing Office, Washington, D. C. (Section 43.32.)

Rules for Building and Classing Steel Vessels, issued annually by the American Bureau of Shipping.

Rossell & Chapman, *Principles of Naval Architecture*, Vol. I, Chapter VI, Society of Naval Architects and Marine Engineers, New York, 1942.

Comstock, J. P., *Introduction to Naval Architecture*, Simmons-Boardman Publishing Company, New York.

Walton & Baird, *Steel Ships, Their Construction and Maintenance*, Charles Griffin and Company, Ltd., London, 1944.

Walton, *Know Your Own Ship*, Charles Griffin and Company, Ltd., London, 1942.

Timoshenko and MacCullough, *Elements of Strength of Materials*, D. Van Nostrand Company, Inc., New York, 2nd Edition, 1940.

J. H. McDonald and D. F. MacNaught, "Investigation of Cargo Distribution in Tank Vessels", *Transactions of the Society of Naval Architects and Marine Engineers*, Vol. 57, 1949.

Vasta, J., "Structural Tests on the Liberty Ship S.S. Philip Schuyler", *Transactions of the Society of Naval Architects and Marine Engineers*, Vol. 55, 1947.

Vasta, J., Structural Tests on the Passenger Ship SS. President Wilson—Interaction Between Superstructure and Main Hull Girder", *Transactions of the Society of Naval Architects and Marine Engineers*, Vol. 57, 1949.

"Structural Investigation in Still Water of the Tanker Newcombia", *Transactions of the North East Coast Institution of Engineers and Shipbuilders*, April, 1947.

"Report of Hogging and Sagging Tests on All-Welded Tanker M.V. Neverita", The Admiralty Ship Welding Committee, H. M. Stationery Office, 1946.

Baker, *Introduction to Steel Shipbuilding*, McGraw-Hill Book Company, Inc., 2nd Ed., New York, 1953.

Jasper & Church, *Structural Seaworthiness Studies*, Transactions of the Society of Naval Architects and Marine Engineers, Vol. 71, 1963.

Evans & Khoushy, *Optimized Design of Midship Section Structure*, SNAME Transactions, Vol. 71, 1963.

D'Arcangelo, *A Guide to Sound Ship Structures*, Cornell Maritime Press, Inc., Cambridge, Md., 1964.

D. Arnott, *Design and Construction of Steel Merchant Ships*, SNAME, New York, 1955.

Chapter 7

LINES, OFFSETS, AND THE MOLD LOFT

One of the most interesting and important tasks of Naval Architecture is the drawing of the vessel's lines. As we have seen in the section on Dimensions and Characteristics, the form of a vessel may be delineated to some extent by its principal dimensions, such as length, breadth, and depth. Further on, in our study of ships, we shall see that a vessel's form may be delineated even more by its form coefficients such as block, prismatic, and waterplane coefficients. But all of these form characteristics are only guides in completely delineating a ship's form by means of the *Lines Drawing* or *Lines Plan*.

The Problem: The problem confronting the Naval Architect here is that of delineating completely on a blueprint, (in two dimensional form) the involved curvilinear form of a ship (a three dimensional body). This problem was not always solved by a strictly two dimensional process. When man first started constructing vessels, they were formed on the ways (or on a beach) by using only a practiced and judicious eye. Later, with advances in technique and need for a more certain procedure, models were constructed first and shaped to the desired form. From these models the lines could be taken and put in blueprint form. Today, however, the completely scientific techniques of modern shipbuilding dictate the drawing and fairing of lines first. Only then, if at all, is a model constructed from these lines.

Preliminary Work: Before work on the actual drawing of the lines can be started, the principal dimensions, form characteristics and ratios must be, at least, tentatively established. These are based on:

1. Obviously, the *type of ship desired* by the owner. The latter will specify the approximate deadweight, speed desired, etc. This will in turn establish approximately the principal dimensions and form characteristics. For example, the faster the ship to be built, the finer the lines.

2. *Experience with previous successful designs.* It must be stressed that no designer works in a vacuum of knowledge. Through many years of experience with the construction of and operation of ships the approximate dimensions and forms best suited for a particular type of ship have been evolved. The designer of a new ship will base his design, to a great extent, on previously built ships. The new ship will vary only in detail from the older ships. However, these details may be of great importance.

131

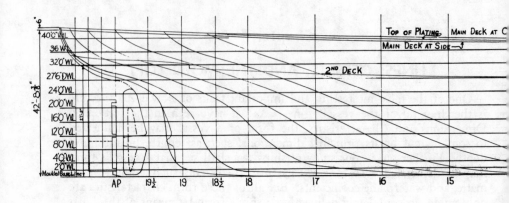

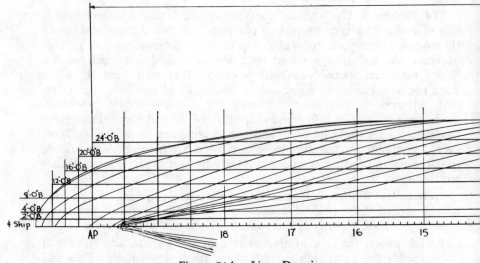

Figure 71A.   Lines Drawing

3. *Research in model basins.* Ship's lines have been altered considerably by research on hull form conducted in model basins around
the world. Findings are published in the literature and are available to all ship designers. Also, for a particular design, the owner
may find it advantageous to test the preliminary lines by model
basin trials. Final lines may be altered in conformance with the
results of these trials.

The following dimensions and form characteristics must be established
tentatively before work is started on the drawing of the lines:

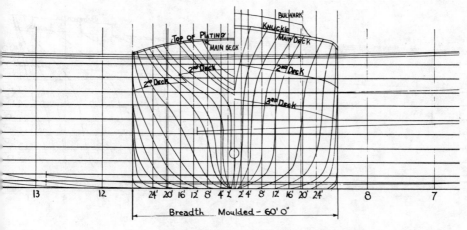

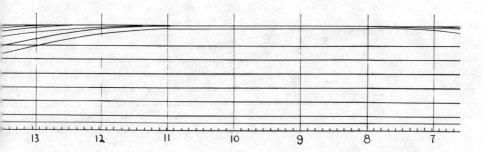

Figure 71A. (*Continued on Next Page*)

1. *Principal Dimensions:* Length, breadth, depth, freeboard, draft, and the lesser dimensions of camber, sheer, dead rise and tumble home. These, in turn, are dictated by such design factors as strength, freeboard rules, stability and resistance. Desired ratios of beam to draft, beam to length, length to depth, etc., are established.

2. *Form Coefficients:* Block, prismatic, waterplane, and midship section coefficients are decided on tentatively. The speed-length ratio and displacement-length ratio must be at least approximately fixed. These ratios will be discussed in a later chapter and need not concern us here.

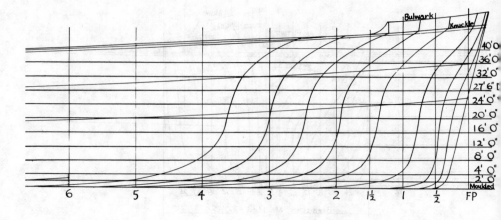

LENGTH OVERALL ... 417' 9¼"
LENGTH BET. PERP'S. ... 395' 0"
BREADTH MOLDED ... 60' 0"
DEPTH MOLDED TO MAIN DCK AT SIDE ... 37' 6"
DRAFT MOLDED TO D.W.L. ... 27' 6"

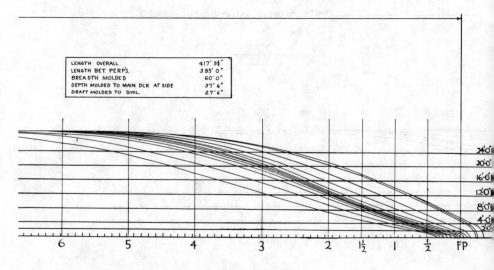

Figure 71A. (*Concluded*)

3. *Sectional-Area Curve:* This curve provides information as to the cross-sectional area desirable at every transverse section along the length of the vessel. A great deal of research has gone into the development of these curves and is available to designers.

The Theory of the Lines Drawing: Consider a ship model divided into a series of transverse planes perpendicular to the base plane and uniformly spaced along the length. If now, we actually cut a thin transverse plane at each of these sections and place the thin planes together so that the base line and centerline of each plane are superimposed, we can immediately see how the form of the model changes from bow to amidships and from amidships to the stern. The same thing can be done by dividing the model into a series of horizontal planes parallel to the base plane, or by a series of vertical planes parallel to the centerline plane. Let us call the transverse planes *frame stations,* the horizontal planes, *waterplanes,* and the vertical planes, *buttocks.* If we now drew three separate plans showing the appearance of these frame stations, waterplanes, and buttocks, we would have a Lines Drawing, and another model to replace the one we have cut up, could very easily be made from these Lines. The Plan showing the appearance of the frame stations is called the *Body Plan;* that showing the form of waterplanes, the *Half-breadth Plan,* and that showing the form of the buttocks, the *Sheer or Profile Plan.* It should be observed that, since the vessel is symmetrical on either side of the centerline, the Body Plan can show the port side forward of amidships on the right-hand side of the plan, and the port side aft of amidships on the left-hand side. For the same reason, only one half of the waterplanes must be shown and the profile plan can be of one side only.

Now, if in drawing up an original Lines Plan we drew in frame stations on the Body Plan, waterplanes on the Half-breadth Plan and buttocks on the Profile Plan, drawing each set of curved lines separately with no reference to each other, a ship or model constructed from these lines would not have a smooth, fair form. For example, we may have drawn the waterplanes on the Half-Breadth Plan with greater or less breadth than the waterplanes have on the Body Plan, or we may have drawn the frame stations on the Body Plan with less height at a buttock than that buttock has on the Profile Plan at the same frame station. It is obvious that *any point* on *any* plan must have the same breadth (or half-breadth) and height, the same height and distance forward or aft of a particular frame station, and/or the same half-breadth and distance forward or aft of a particular frame station as the same point on the other two plans. Accomplishing this rather difficult and tedious task is known as *fairing the lines.*

The dimensions mentioned above, that is; half-breadths, heights, and distances forward or aft of some particular frame station, are known as *offsets* since they represent the distance that some point in the molded form of a vessel is set off from some reference plane such as the base plan, the centerline plane, or frame station.

Drawing the Lines: Techniques involved in drawing the lines may vary in detail but are always similar in general.

Step 1: Establishing coordinates for the "graph" of each Plan of the Lines Drawing:

A. *Profile Plan.* A base line is drawn first with a length (to the desired scale) somewhat greater than the desired length. Waterplanes are then drawn parallel to the base line and identified by their distance in feet above the base. For example: 2' WL, 4' WL, 6' WL, etc. Frame stations are then drawn at right angles to the waterplanes with uniform spacing. They are identified by numbers starting with Station No. 0 or the forward perpendicular, then Sta. 1, Sta. 2, and so on, aft to the after perpendicular which may be Sta. 10, 20, 30, etc. depending upon the length of the ship involved and the accuracy desired. It is customary to use half stations forward and aft at the locations of greatest fineness.

We may now lay off the molded depth to the upper deck at side amidships. The line of the upper deck may then be continued forward and aft with the desired sheer. This may vary from standard sheer as given in the freeboard regulations according to the desires of the designer.

Next, the tentative assigned freeboard can be calculated by the use of the Load Line Regulations and measured down from the side amidships, thus establishing the load waterline.

Then, the bow and stern profiles can be drawn with the perpendiculars located properly. (The forward perpendicular must pass through the intersection of load waterline and stem profile and the after perpendicular must be located at the after edge of the stern post or the middle of the rudder stock depending on the type of stern desired.)

B. *Half-Breadth Plan.* The first line to be drawn is the centerline. This line is usually drawn below the Profile Plan. Its length will be the same as the length of the base line on the Profile Plan. Buttock lines are drawn parallel to the centerline and identified by their distance from the centerline. For example: 2′ Butt, 4′ Butt, 6′ Butt., etc. Frame stations are then drawn by simply extending the stations on the Profile Plan down to the Half-Breadth Plan. The line of the upper deck can now be drawn using desired half-breadth amidships, length as indicated by the Profile Plan, and a logical form forward and aft.

C. *Body Plan.* This Plan is usually superimposed on the Profile Plan using the midships station as the centerline of the Body Plan. Thus, the waterlines are already drawn, and it is only necessary to draw in the buttocks parallel to the centerline and label them correctly. The midships station (usually Sta. 10) can now be drawn using the half-breadth indicated by the half-breadth plan, desired dead rise and bilge radius. The line of the upper deck can be drawn in now by establishing the points where the frame stations cut the upper deck line. The coordinates of these points are the half-breadths on frame stations as revealed by the half-breadth plan, and the heights of these frame stations as revealed on the profile plan. However, when these points are connected by a curved line, the latter may not be smooth and fair. This line may be faired by drawing a smooth curve through as many points as possible. Then the offsets of height and half-breadth may be measured from this smooth curve, transferred back to the two plans, new smooth curves drawn here, transferred back to the body plan, and so on. The process is continued until the offsets used produce smooth curves for the upper deck line on all three plans.

Step 2: Drawing the Frame Stations on the Body Plan:

The most important single step in establishing the form of the ship is now undertaken. The frame stations are drawn on the Body Plan using predetermined sectional areas at frame stations. These predetermined areas are found on the sectional area curve. It is in this step, particularly, that experience and familiarity with ship's lines is necessary. The lower and upper terminus of each frame station can be taken from the Half-Breadth Plan and the Profile Plan by measuring the corresponding half-breadths and heights. The sectional area at each station is also known from the sectional area curve. The designer, however, within these limits must determine the shape of the sections both below the load waterline and above it. Once again, it should be noted that the form of the port side forward is drawn on the right hand side of the centerline; the form of the port side aft is drawn on the left hand side of the centerline. On most merchant ships a good many frame stations have the same shape due to the considerable parallel middle body.

Step 3: Drawing and fairing the waterplanes:

It is now possible to draw in the waterplanes on the half-breadth plan. On the body plan the half-breadths of each waterplane at frame stations can be measured and transferred to the half-breadth plan. However, when the waterplane is drawn by connecting the points, an unfair curve will result. The waterplane must be faired by drawing a smooth curve through as many of the points as possible; the new offsets are taken back to the body plan. When these points are laid down, a new set of frame stations must be drawn (maintaining the proper sectional area), and the resulting offsets transferred back to the half-breadth plan. This process continues until the offsets used produce smooth frame stations and waterplanes.

Step 4: Drawing and fairing the buttocks:

The heights of buttocks on frame stations are indicated now on the body plan. Using these offsets, a series of points are made on the profile plan for each buttock. When curves are drawn through these points, however, the buttocks will be somewhat unfair. It is now necessary to fair these lines by drawing smooth curves through as many of the points as possible; the resulting offsets are transferred to the other two plans. The unfairness must then be worked out among the *three* plans until the offsets used produce smooth frame stations, waterplanes, and buttocks, with the desired sectional areas maintained.

Step 5: Using diagonals in the fairing of lines:

It would seem from the above description of how lines are drawn and faired that the process is complicated and difficult enough without adding to the problem. However, an additional step *is* usually made by using another line or set of lines—the diagonals. However, if accuracy is desired the use of diagonals in fairing the lines actually makes the process of fairing the lines easier.

The student should observe that the more accuracy desired, the closer the frame stations, waterlines, and buttocks should be spaced. We have already seen that since the form of the ship is the same through a great part of the length, we may increase accuracy by spacing the frame stations closer together only in the bow and stern sections where most fineness exists. However, we do not wish to space our stations, etc. any closer than we have to since the addition of each line means another line to be faired. So, a line or set of lines is passed through the area of greatest fineness. This requirement results, on the Body Plan, in a diagonal line passing from the centerline at some higher waterplane through the bilge area. This line may now be used to fair the other lines.

For example: The distance from the point where the diagonal cuts the centerline to the points (on the Body Plan) where the diagonal cuts the frame stations is measured and transferred to the Profile Plan where these offsets are measured up from the base line at each frame station. When a curve is drawn through these points, it is likely to be unfair. The offsets are then transferred back to the Body Plan; the frame stations readjusted, and the process continued until the curve of the bilge diagonal and the curves of the frame stations are both smooth and fair. The curve of the diagonal may also be transferred to the half-breadth plan and used in a similar fashion. When used in this manner, the diagonal is in its expanded or true form. However, the diagonal may be transferred to the Profile Plan in its projected form by measuring its height where it crosses the frame stations on the Body Plan; or transferred to the Half-Breadth Plan in still another projected form by measuring its half-breadth where it crosses the frame stations on the Body Plan.

No matter which form of the diagonal is used the purpose remains the same; that is, to reduce the work involved in fairing the lines by enabling stations, waterplanes, and buttocks to be spaced further apart than would be normally possible for a given degree of accuracy.

Tables of Offsets

After the lines have been drawn and faired by the designer, a *Table of Offsets is made.* All offsets necessary to reconstruct the lines are measured and made up in table form. For example, to reconstruct a frame station, the half-breadths on waterlines are measured on the Body Plan; or to reconstruct a waterline, half-breadths on frame stations are measured on the Half-Breadth Plan; or to reconstruct a buttock (or diagonal) heights on frame stations are measured on the Profile Plan.

When completed the table is known as *preliminary or designer's offsets.*

Use of Offset Tables: Offset Tables have two important areas of usefulness.

TABLE V

HALF - BREADTHS ON WATER LINES

FR.	2'-0"	4'-3"	6'-0"	9'-0"	12'-0"	14'-6"	18'-0"	21'-0"	24'-0"	27'-3"	32'-0"	34'-0"
C												
B												
A												0- 2-4+
0						0- 4-2	0- 6-1+	0- 7-5+	0- 3-2	0- 4-6	0- 1-1	0- 8-1
1					0- 2-6	0-10-5	1- 0-2	1- 1-5	0- 9-0	0-10-4+	1- 0-6	1- 2-0
2		0- 2-5	0- 5-0	0- 7-3	0- 9-2	1- 4-7	1- 6-4	1- 7-5	1- 2-7	1- 4-2	1- 6-4	1- 7-7
3	0- 2-5+	0- 7-7+	0-10-6	1- 1-4	1- 3-5	1-11-1	2- 0-6+	2- 1-7	1- 8-6+	1-10-2	2- 0-4	2- 2-1
4	0- 7-7+	1- 1-2	1- 4-2	1- 7-5	1- 9-6+	2- 5-2+	2- 6-7	2- 7-7+	2- 3-0	2- 4-3	2- 6-7	2- 8-5
5	1- 0-0+	1- 6-1+	1- 9-4+	2- 1-4+	2- 4-0	2-11-3+	3- 1-1	3- 2-1+	2- 9-1	2-10-4	3- 1-4	3- 3-1
6	1- 3-4	1-11-0+	2- 2-7	2- 7-3	2-10-0	3- 5-5+	3- 7-3+	3- 8-4+	3- 3-4	3- 4-7	3- 8-1	3- 9-7+
7	1- 6-5	2- 3-5+	2- 8-0	3- 1-0+	3- 4-0+	3-11-7	4- 1-7+	4- 3-1	3- 9-7+	3-11-4	4- 2-7	4- 4-7+
8	1- 9-5	2- 8-0	3- 1-0+	3- 6-7	3-10-1	4- 6-1+	4- 8-3	4- 9-6	4- 4-5	4- 6-2	4- 9-7+	5- 0-1
9	2- 0-5+	3- 0-1+	3- 6-0	4- 0-3	4- 4-1	5- 0-3	5- 2-7	5- 4-4	4-11-3	5- 1-1+	5- 5-1	5- 7-4
10	2- 3-4+	3- 4-1+	3-10-6	4- 5-7	4-10-0	5- 6-6	5- 9-5	5-11-2+	5- 6-1	5- 8-1	6- 0-6+	6- 3-0
11	2- 6-4	3- 8-2	4- 3-4	4-11-3	5- 4-1	6- 1-2	6- 4-3+	6- 6-3	6- 1-1	6- 3-4	6- 8-1+	6-11-0
12	2- 9-4	4- 0-2	4- 8-1	5- 4-6+	5-10-1	6- 7-6	6-11-2	7- 1-4	6- 8-3	6-10-6	7- 3-6+	7- 6-7
13	3- 0-1+	4- 4-1	5- 0-7	5-10-3	6- 4-3+	7- 3-2	7- 7-1+	7- 9-5	7- 3-3+	7- 6-2	7-11-3+	8- 2-4+
14	3- 3-2	4- 8-4+	5- 6-1	6- 4-7	6-11-3+	7-10-5	8- 3-0+	8- 5-6	7-11-6+	8- 2-6	8- 8-2+	8-11-4
15	3- 6-2	5- 1-0	5-11-3	6-11-1	7- 6-4	8- 6-3	8-11-0	9- 2-2	8- 8-2	8-11-3	9- 5-2	9- 8-5+
16	3- 9-3	5- 5-5	6- 4-5	7- 5-4	8- 1-5+	9- 2-1	9- 7-1	9-10-5	9- 5-0	9- 8-2+	10- 2-3	10- 5-7
17	4- 0-3	5-10-0+	6-10-0	7-11-6+	8- 8-7	9-10-0	10- 3-6	10- 7-1	10- 1-7	10- 5-1	10-11-4+	11- 3-2
18	4- 3-2	6- 2-5	7- 3-2	8- 6-3+	9- 4-2	10- 6-0+	11- 0-0	11- 3-7	10-10-4	11- 2-1+	11- 8-6	12- 0-5
19	4- 6-1	6- 7-0+	7- 8-5	9- 1-0	9-11-5	11- 2-0	11- 8-4	12- 0-4+	11- 7-2	11-11-1	12- 6-0	12-10-0
20	4- 9-0	6-11-7	8- 2-1+	9- 7-6	10- 7-2+	11-10-2	12- 5-0	12- 9-2	12- 4-1+	12- 8-1+	13- 3-2	13- 7-1+
21	4-11-7	7- 4-4+	8- 7-7	10- 2-5+	11- 2-7	12- 6-2	13- 1-4	13- 6-1	13- 0-7+	13- 5-2+	14- 0-4+	14- 4-6
22	5- 2-6	7- 9-3+	9- 1-4	10- 9-5	11-10-4	13- 2-4	13-10-0+	14- 3-0	13-10-0	14- 2-4	14-10-0	15- 2-1+
23	5- 5-6+	8- 2-3	9- 7-3	11- 4-5	12- 6-2+	13-10-4+	14- 6-5	14-11-6	14- 7-1	14-11-5+	15- 7-2+	15-11-4
24	5- 8-7	8- 7-3	10- 1-3	11-11-6	13- 2-1	14- 6-5			15- 4-1	15- 8-6+	16- 4-4	16- 8-6

TYPICAL PAGE—OFFSET TABLES

Table VI

HEIGHTS ON BUTTOCKS

FR.	1'-6"	3'-0"	6'-0"	9'-0"	12'-0"	15'-0"	18'-0"	21'-0"	24'-0"	27'-0"	30'-0"	33'-0"	FR.
C	57- 8-3	62- 5-4											C
B	50- 4-4	56- 4-3+	65- 0-1										B
A	45-10-0	52- 3-6	61- 0-1+										A
0	41-11-1	49- 2-0	58- 0-4	64-10-6+									0
1	37- 9-2+	46- 3-4	55- 5-2	62- 2-1									1
2	30-10-7	43- 6-0	53- 1-2	59- 9-4+									2
3	16- 6-2	40- 7-3	50-11-3	57- 8-0	63- 4-1								3
4	7- 3-2	36-10-4	48-10-4	55- 8-1	61- 3-5								4
5	4- 1-3	30- 0-1	46-10-3	53- 9-7+	59- 5-7	64- 6-1							5
6	2- 4-0+	15- 8-2	44- 9-5	52- 0-6+	57- 9-0	62- 9-4							6
7	1- 9-4	8- 2-5+	42- 7-6	50- 4-1	56- 1-1	61- 1-6							7
8		5- 7-3	40- 1-4	48- 8-0	54- 6-0	59- 7-1							8
9		4- 2-4	36- 9-0+	46-11-4	52-11-1	58- 0-5							9
10		3- 4-1+	31- 6-0	45- 2-1	51- 5-0	56- 6-5+							10
11		2- 9-3	22- 1-6	43- 2-6	49-10-7	55- 1-3+	59-10-5+						11
12		2- 4-2+	13- 4-6	40-11-6+	48- 4-3+	53- 8-0	58- 5-5						12
13		1-11-7+	9- 7-3+	38- 3-2	46- 9-2	52- 3-2	57- 1-2+						13
14		1- 8-2	7- 5-3	34- 2-4	44-10-4+	50- 8-1	55- 7-2						14
15		1- 5-6+	6- 1-4	27- 8-5	42-10-0	49- 0-7	54- 1-2+	58- 8-6					15
16		1- 3-7	5- 2-5	18- 7-7	40- 5-6	47- 5-0	52- 7-4	57- 3-7					16
17		1- 2-3	4- 6-2+	13- 3-7+	37- 6-5+	45- 8-5+	51- 1-5+	55-11-2+					17
18		1- 1-0	3-11-5	10- 6-3	33- 8-1+	43-10-7	49- 7-6	54- 6-7	59- 2-0				18
19		0-11-7+	3- 6-2	8- 8-5	27-11-5+	41-10-5+	48- 1-3	53- 2-2+	57-10-3+				19
20		0-10-7+	3- 1-7	7- 5-6	20- 7-0+	39- 6-7	46- 6-4	51- 9-6+	56- 7-2				20
21		0-10-1	2-10-0+	6- 6-4+	15- 4-4	36- 9-1	44-10-6	50- 5-0+	55- 4-2				21
22		0- 9-3	2- 6-6+	5- 9-7+	12- 5-2	33- 0-7	43- 2-0	49- 0-4	54- 1-2+	58-11-2			22
23		0- 8-6	2- 4-1	5- 2-3	10- 5-6+	27- 6-0	41- 3-2	47- 7-4	52-10-2	57- 9-5			23
24		0- 8-1	2- 2-0	4- 8-1	9- 0-6	22- 2-2	39- 0-7	46- 2-2	51- 7-2	56- 8-1			24
25		0- 7-5+	2- 0-0+	4- 2-6	7-11-5+	16- 6-3+	36- 3-4+	44- 8-0	50- 4-2	55- 6-6			25
26		0- 7-1	1-10-3	3-10-1+	7- 1-2	13- 6-4	32- 5-6	43- 0-0+	49- 1-3	54- 5-4			26
27		0- 6-5	1- 8-5	3- 6-2	6- 4-7	11- 6-5+	27- 3-2+	41- 2-1	47-10-0	53- 4-2+			27

TYPICAL PAGE—OFFSET TABLES

(1) *As a basis for use in ship's calculations:*

As we shall see in the Chapter on Ship's Calculations, offsets are used as the basic data of the Displacement Sheet where such vital hydrostatic data as the displacement, center of buoyancy, Tons per Inch Immersion and height of metacenters are calculated.

(2) *As the basic reference data used in ship construction:*

Obviously the form of the vessel as drawn by the designer on the Lines Plan must be translated into the actual form of a ship in the construction yard. Offset tables are used in the shipyard Mold Loft to lay down the ship's lines. From these lines, the templates (or patterns) for almost all ship's members are made.

Offset tables destined to be used in the Mold Loft have one very important difference from those meant for use in ship's calculations. The Body Plan, instead of showing frame stations or imaginary planes at uniform intervals along the length of the ship, shows *frame lines* or the actual appearance of the side frames of the vessel. Thus on such a Body Plan instead of some 21 frame stations, there may be 200 or more frame lines.

Offset tables, then, must show the offsets for these frame lines rather than the frame stations.

Drill in Drawing Ship's Lines

The lines to be drawn are for a vessel with LBP of 440 feet, beam of 62 feet, standard depth plus 10 feet, standard sheer, camber, and fullness. The vessel is a full scantling type with a bridge superstructure having class 1 doors forward and class 2 doors aft. The bridge is 88 feet long.

The object of the drill is to draw on all three plans of the Lines Drawing, the line of the upper deck using the fixed information given above as well as logical shiplike form where definite information is not given. The position of the load waterplane must be calculated from data above and using a copy of the "Load Line Regulations". Frame station #1 is drawn on the Body Plan; the load waterplane is drawn forward on the Half-breadth Plan; and the buttock which passes through the intersection of the LWL and FS #1 is drawn on the Sheer Plan. A bilge diagonal is drawn on the body plan and expanded to its true form on the Half-breadth Plan.

Steps in completing this drill are:

1. Lay off a sheer line in profile which is the correct depth above the base line at Station #10 (21 stations) and using standard sheer ordinates from the freeboard rules.
2. Calculate the summer draft and lay off the DLWL at this draft. (Use *Load Line Regulations*.)
3. Draw a logical bow and stern profile showing a raked bow and cruiser spoon stern with a stern post.
4. After drawing a centerline for the Half-breadth Plan, lay off the line of the upper deck with the proper half-breadth amidships, length as indicated by the sheer profile, and a logical curve forward and aft.
5. Lay off the midship section, superimposed on the sheer plan using proper half-breadth, height of deck line at the various stations as indicated by the height of these stations on the sheer plan, half-breadth of deck line at the various stations as indicated by the half-breadths at these stations on the Half-breadth Plan, no dead rise and a reasonable bilge radius. If the upper deck line as it now is drawn on the Body Plan is not reasonably fair, the line will have to be faired.
6. Lay off Frame Station #1 on the Body Plan with logical form. (Note that the upper and lower termini of the station have already been established.)

7. Lay off a logically formed load waterplane on the Half-breadth Plan. (Note that the forward terminus, the half-breadth at FS #1 and the half-breadth amidships have been established for this waterplane.)
8. Lay off a logically formed buttock which passes through the intersection of the DLWL and FS #1. (The latter intersection is the only point established on this buttock.)
9. Lay off bilge diagonals on the body plan which extend from the intersection of the centerline and DLWL, through and normal to the curve of the bilge amidships. Expand the diagonal to its true form on the half-breadth plan. (Points on this diagonal which have been established are: Forward and after termini, distance from centerline amidships, and distance from centerline at #1 FS.)

The Mold Loft

The Mold Loft is that place in a shipyard where the first steps in the construction of a ship take place. The loftsmen are in effect the middlemen between the designer and the shipwright.

Sun Oil Co.

Figure 72. Mold Loft at the Sun Shipbuilding & Dry Dock Co., Chester, Pa.

Appearance and Location of the Mold Loft: The mold loft is usually centrally located among the various fabrication shops, generally occupying the second floor of one of the larger shops.

It is a huge loft, since the lines of a ship must be laid down to full size on the floor of the loft and many ships may be under construction in the yard. (In a repair yard, the loft may be considerably smaller.) The loft must be well illuminated and therefore its sides are almost completely glassed in; also, it is well lighted by overhead lamps. The floor is made of wood.

U.S. Maritime Commission

Figure 73.   Guiding a travograph (oxy-acetylene cutting machine) along a steel shell plate. At opposite end of machine another workman guides the controlling arm along the grooved lines of a template. The steel plate seen here in foreground is thus cut exactly to pattern.

U.S. Maritime Commission

Figure 74.   Bending a frame on the Bending Slab. Information as to curvature of the frame and angle of bevel is provided by the Mold Loft.

Laying Down the Lines in the Mold Loft: After receiving the preliminary offsets from the designer, the loftsmen lay down the lines to full size on the mold loft floor using these offsets. First the usual "graph" is drawn. For example, in the Body Plan, a base line and centerline is drawn; then, waterlines and buttocks. Then from the Offset Tables half-breadths are used to obtain a series of points indicating the form of the frame lines. These points are connected, and a curve drawn through them, by means of a flexible wooden *batten*.

Now, the task of the loftsmen is not as easy as it seems, since the "blowing up" of the small scale offsets to full size means that any slight error by the designer in measuring the offsets from his plans results in a magnification of the error on the mold loft floor. Therefore, it is necessary for the Mold Loft to fair the lines once more. As we have seen, this is a tedious job.

When the lines have been faired, the new offsets are measured and made up into a new table or book. These offsets are known as *corrected or mold loft offsets*. A ship is built to these dimensions. If ships are to be mass produced, these offsets could be sent to other shipyards where the mold lofts there would not be obliged to go through the fairing process. The corrected offsets are sent by the mold loft to the shipyard drawing rooms where they are of assistance in making the detailed plans of structural members and are also sent to the fabrication shops where they may be consulted in checking on the dimensions of structural members.

Lifting templates from Ship's Lines: The process by which templates or patterns of the ship's plating and framing are made by reference to the lines as they are scribed in the mold loft floor is called *lifting templates*.

Templates are usually constructed of some light wood, but may also be made of heavy paper and other durable materials. In addition to conforming to the curvature of the member in question, templates will show such information as the location of rivet holes, and other openings, waterlines, buttocks, etc.

After completion, the templates are sent to the appropriate fabrication shop where they are used as patterns in cutting, shaping, bending, beveling, and punching ship's members.

The Pantograph: Sometimes it is possible to bypass the construction of templates by the mold loft. This is done by means of a pantograph or enlarging device, whereby a stylus on one end of the pantograph traces out the form of the member to be cut directly from the designers blueprint. Through a series of enlarging hinges a cutting torch is moved over the steel plate and cuts out the member to full size.

Due to the necessity for greater accuracy and control than can be provided by a pantograph, the latter has not made any deep inroads on the function of the Mold Loft.

Photographic methods of lofting: A recent innovation which shows great promise is a process of lofting and layout by an optical method. In this method, the designer's plans are drawn on dimensionally stable materials which are then photographed. The resulting glass negative can then be used to project a "picture" of the drawing down on the plate or workpiece to be fabricated. The layout is then center-punched and/or traced out with a paint brush.

The advantages of this system are readily apparent. The mold loft is almost completely eliminated. Bulky templates are replaced by glass negatives which can be stored in a filing cabinet. There is a considerable saving in time and money. Wasted material is brought to a minimum since structural parts can be laid out efficiently right on the drawing board.

U.S. Maritime Commission

Figure 75. A four hundred-ton joggling press in a knuckling operation.

QUESTIONS

1. Describe the function of the sectional-area curve in the process of drawing ship's lines.
2. What are the three plans comprising the Lines Drawing?
3. What lines are curved on the Body Plan? on the Profile Plan? on the Half-breadth Plan?
4. How are frame stations designated? Frame lines? Buttocks? Waterplanes?
5. What is the designation for offsets which give the vertical height of a point from the base line and for offsets which give the transverse distance of a point from the centerline?
6. Why is it necessary to use additional frame stations forward and aft?
7. What coordinates (offsets) establish the line of the upper deck on the Body Plan? Why is it necessary to fair this line?
8. Explain in detail how lines are faired on the three plans of the Lines Drawing.
9. What are the three forms of a diagonal?
10. How do diagonals make the work of fairing the lines easier?
11. Why is it necessary to fair the lines all over again in the Mold Loft?
12. What is the difference between frame stations and frame lines?
13. Describe a pantograph.

BIBLIOGRAPHY

Garyantes, H. F., *Handbook for Shipwrights,* McGraw-Hill Book Company, Inc., New York, 1944.

Rossell & Chapman, *Principles of Naval Architecture,* Vol. I, Society of Naval Architects and Marine Engineers, New York, 1942.

Comstock, J. P., *Introduction to Naval Architecture,* Simmons-Boardman Publishing Company, New York.
NOTE: For those students who are interested in the construction of ship models, an application of the subject of ship's lines, the following text is recommended:

Grimwood, V. R., *American Ship Models and How to Build Them,* W. W. Norton Company, Inc., New York, 1942.

D. Arnott, *Design and Construction of Steel Merchant Ships,* SNAME, New York, 1955.

Chapter 8

RIVETING AND WELDING

The hull and other portions of a ship's structure are composed of thousands of small members, each of which must be connected to another or several others in such a way as to form a structure capable of withstanding the tremendous stresses to which a large ship is subjected. The members of a large modern vessel are connected in two ways:—riveting and welding. Each of these methods is entirely different in its technique and the determination of which method of connection (or whether both methods are to be used) has an important bearing on the structural design, the strength, and seaworthiness of the vessel.

In considering the subjects of riveting and welding, no attempt will be made here to explain in detail the techniques involved in actually riveting and welding ship members. Our principal concern is the impact of these methods of connection on the design and operation of a ship and in particular, to study the impact of welding on ship construction. In order to discuss these subjects with intelligence, however, the student must have in his possession first certain basic knowledge relating to the subjects.

RIVETS AND RIVETING

It might well be stated at the outset lest the student consider time spent in studying the subject of riveting as wasted, that this method of connection still occupies a position of importance in the construction of modern ships. The completely all-welded ship, although not unknown, has been found lacking in at least one vital respect and ships being constructed today incorporate an appreciable percentage of riveting in their structure. The exact extent of riveting and the reasons therefor will be considered later in this chapter.

We shall consider the following aspects of the subject:

1) Rivet definitions and nomenclature.
2) Riveted plating and framing.
3) Preparation of the riveted member.
4) Riveting tools and procedure.
5) Making the riveted joint watertight.
6) Testing of rivets.
7) Replacing and maintaining rivets.
8) Riveting and welding combination.
9) Stresses on rivets.
10) American Bureau Rules.

Definitions and Nomenclature:

1. *Rivet Material:* Rivets are almost always made of mild steel, although high-tensile steel is used when high-tensile members are connected and occasionally wrought-iron rivets are used.

2. *Rivet Nomenclature:* (Figure 76). A rivet is made with a round *shank* with various types of *heads* at one end. Incidentally, a rivet is designated according to the type of head which it has. The other end of the rivet is the *point* which is formed when the rivet is driven. Rivets are specified according to their *diameter* (diameter of the shank); *head size* (diameter of the head); *length* (length of the shank); and the *grip,* or the length of the shank between head and point after rivet is driven. The grip represents the thickness of the members to be connected. That portion of the shank just below the head is called the *neck.* The neck is sometimes swelled or coned.

The rivet size used varies with the thickness of the plates to be connected. For merchant ship work, rivet sizes (diameters) will vary from about $5/8$ in. to $7/8$ in.

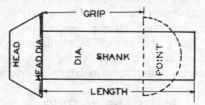

Figure 76. Rivet Nomenclature

3. *Types of rivets:* (Figure 77). The most widely used type of rivet in merchant work is the *pan head.* Also used are the *button head,* (or snap head) *countersunk,* and *steeple head types.* All these types may or may not have a coned neck. A special type rivet used to connect re-

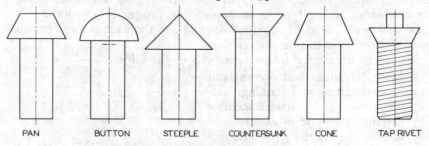

PAN   BUTTON   STEEPLE   COUNTERSUNK   CONE   TAP RIVET

Figure 77. Types of Rivets

latively thin plates to large members, or for use where the normal technique of riveting cannot be used due to the inaccessibility of the member, is the so-called *tap rivet.* The tap rivet is threaded and has a square head. The rivet is screwed in with a wrench and the head then chipped off.

4. *Riveting Systems:* (Figure 78). Members may be joined by a single row of rivets; or they may be double, treble, or quadruple riveted. The rivets in each row may be so located so as to be in line with each other in which case a *chain system* is used; or, a *staggered system* may be used. The distance between rivets in a row is known as the *pitch;* the distance between the rows as the *gage.*

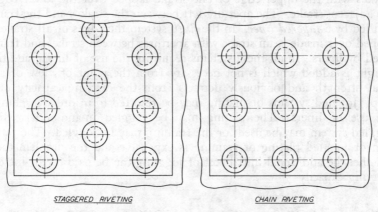

STAGGERED RIVETING   CHAIN RIVETING

Figure 78. Riveting Systems

5. *Riveted joints:* (Figure 79). It is apparent that a riveted joint must be formed by riveting through two (or more) layers of material. This can be done either by a *lap joint* where an edge of one plate is

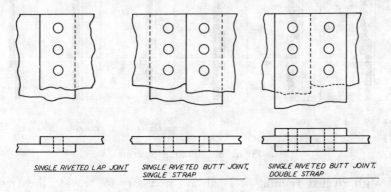

SINGLE RIVETED LAP JOINT   SINGLE RIVETED BUTT JOINT, SINGLE STRAP   SINGLE RIVETED BUTT JOINT, DOUBLE STRAP

Figure 79. Riveted Joints

lapped over the edge of the member to which it is to be connected; or by a *strap joint* where a third small plate is riveted over two plates butted together. A double-strap joint is formed when two small plates are used; one on one side and one on the other.

6. *Riveted plating and framing:* (Figure 80). There are several systems of plating which can be used where the joints must be riveted. The *in-and-out* plating system has alternately, inner strakes and outer strakes with the latter lapped over the edges of the former. This leaves an aperture between the outer strake and the framing which must be filled in by a small plate called a *parallel liner*. The *clinker* system uses a series of strakes with the upper edge of one strake lapped over the lower edge of the adjacent strake. The aperture left between the strakes and the framing is filled by a *tapered liner*. In the *flush* system the edges of all strakes are lapped over inside seam straps with apertures between strakes and framing filled by liners. In all these systems requiring the use of liners, additional weight is added which is not necessary from the point of view of structural strength and obviously detracts from the carrying capacity of the ship. Joggled systems of plating may be resorted to in order to eliminate the use of liners. The plating may be joggled in-and-out; a clinker joggled system may be used; or the framing may be joggled. The fabrication of joggled plating or framing is expensive and the problem then is whether the additional initial cost of joggling can be paid for by increased carrying capacity.

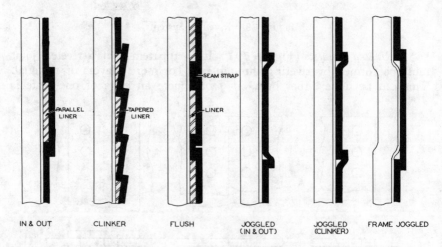

IN & OUT   CLINKER   FLUSH   JOGGLED   JOGGLED   FRAME JOGGLED
                                                  (IN & OUT)   (CLINKER)

Figure 80. Plating Systems

With riveted framing it is always necessary to provide the frames, beams, girders, etc. with a flange against which plating can be riveted. Or, where a deep web plate is to be riveted to plating, it is necessary to provide angle irons with one flange riveted to the web and one to the plating.

Briefly, in riveting two members together whether it be plate to plate, frame to frame, or frame to plate, it is always necessary to lap one member over the other in some way, or to provide a third connecting member.

Preparation of the Riveted Member: Without going into great detail, it might be apropos to outline the procedure of preparing members for riveting.

First, holes must be *punched* into which the rivets are to go. The diameter of the rivet hole must be about 1/16 in. larger than the diameter of the cold rivet in order to allow for expansion when the rivet is heated. Punching is usually done by machines which can punch one hole, or in some cases, dozens of holes, at one time.

Figure 81. Driving in the white hot point of a rivet in the deck of the S.S. America.

When the members are ready to be erected, they are taken to the building slip and bolted in place. *Bolting-up* consists of using enough bolts to secure the member in place in readiness for riveting. Sometimes it is necessary to line up the rivet holes or fair them up by using a tapered pin called a *drift pin,* although this is a dubious practice and reaming is preferable.

Holes, which could not be punched conveniently in the shop, are now *drilled* and all holes must be *reamed* to ensure smoothness. Where tap rivets are to be used, holes must be tapped. Where countersunk rivets are necessary or where coned neck rivets are used holes must be countersunk. Points of rivets are very frequently hammered into countersunk holes.

Riveting tools and Procedure: A very brief account of the actual process of riveting may be interesting and is of some value for our purposes.

U.S. Maritime Commission

Figure 82.   Bolt tighteners at work on new hull

Most riveting in American yards is done by pneumatic hammers, although some may be done by hand. In foreign yards, hand riveting still predominates. The riveter, who hammers up the point, works in conjunction with a *heater,* who heats the rivets in a portable forge, a *passer,* who transmits the heated rivet to the work, and a *holder-on,* who bucks up the head of the rivet while the riveter is working. The riveter uses a *riveting gun* which varies in size depending upon the size rivets used. The holder-on, who pushes the rivet into the hole, then holds it there with a holding-on tool of some sort. The latter may simply be a heavy hammer, or *dolly bar,* or a more complicated tool with special jigs for fitting the type rivet head used.

The point is formed by the riveter on the watertight side of the plating. A snap point may be formed, or the point may be nearly flush depending upon the importance of achieving flushness. In any case, it is important that the point be driven in so as to completely fill the rivet hole.

Making the Riveted Joint Watertight: Where a riveted joint, in addition to the necessity of being structurally sound, must be watertight, the joint must be calked. The calking tool, a chisel-like instrument, may be used pneumatically or by hand as in the case of the riveting tools. Calking consists of driving the material of one member against the material of the other member and, in effect, "welding" completely around the joint.

Of course, watertightness cannot be achieved without an eye to the proper spacing of rivets. In general, rivets should be close enough to the calked edge and to each other to prevent bulging of the edge. Rivet spacing varies with the nature of the joint, i.e., whether it is single, double, or treble riveted; but for watertight work is about 4 diameters generally. (This means that rivet centers are spaced a distance apart equal to four times the diameter of the rivet). For oiltight work, the rivet spacing must be less, say, by one diameter.

Sometimes it is necessary to supplement the calking by some sort of packing laid between the *faying surfaces* of the joint (those surfaces which bear against each other), although this is not an approved method of obtaining watertightness. The packing when used takes the form of felt or canvas soaked in red lead and is sometimes called a *stopwater.* For oiltight work the packing is also soaked in shellac and may then be called an *oilstop.* Sometimes a packing material may be gunned into an open joint in order to obtain tightness.

Calking, however, is the principal method by which riveted joints are made watertight and it is a highly important operation in the construction of a ship since superficial calking can very readily be opened up at sea where high stresses and vibration are encountered.

Testing of Rivets and Riveted Work: Calking is tested by the use of a knife blade with the inspector attempting to insert the blade into the joint.

Watertightness is tested by filling tanks to the highest level to which the contents may rise under service conditions. The riveted work may then be observed for signs of leaks. In dry cargo compartments, a stream of water from a hose is directed against the riveted work and an inspector on the other side of the work may then look for signs of leaks.

The presence of loose or cracked rivets can be detected by hammering the rivet, at the same time feeling the rivet. Looseness can usually be detected by this method.

When the vessel is drydocked, a started rivet is sometimes indicated by corrosion rings around the points. Where such rings are found, the rivet should be tested by tapping with a hammer.

Replacing and Maintaining Rivets: To remove a rivet, the rivet head must first be taken off and then the rivet can be driven out with a punch. The rivet head may be taken off by a pneumatic tool called a rivet buster which slices off the head or a cutting torch which burns it off.

A leaky rivet may sometimes be repaired by calking if it has not been corroded or eaten away to a serious extent. Even with a seriously corroded rivet it may not be necessary to replace it today since it can be built up by welding and then burnished to the proper shape with a riveting hammer.

Riveting and Welding Combination: Sometimes it is desirable to connect a member both by riveting and welding. In these cases, welding must be completed before the riveting commences. If the reverse order were adopted, the riveted joint might be sprung due to the tremendous heat and stresses induced by the welding process.

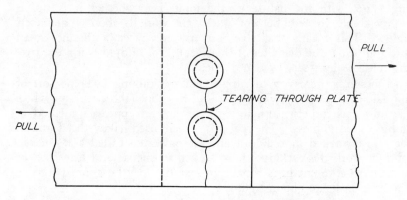

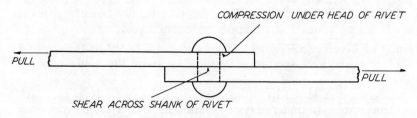

Figure 83. Stresses on a Riveted Joint

Stresses on Riveted Joints: (Figure 83). A riveted joint must be carefully designed to avoid the various types of failures which may occur when the joint or the rivet is subjected to the stresses of tension, compression, or shear.

Punching a row of rivet holes in a ship's member obviously creates a line of weakness relative to the solid plating. A plate may then fail by tearing along this line of weakness. Therefore rivets must not be spaced any closer together than is necessary to achieve proper connection and tightness.

When a strake or riveted plating is subjected to a tensile stress, the plates in the strake tend to pull apart and a shearing stress develops across the shank of the rivet. The size of the rivets used must be adequate to withstand this stress. Where the use of reasonably large rivets in a single row is not adequate to take this shearing load, multiple rows of rivets must be used. If the shearing stress does not result in the shearing of the rivet across its shank, it may cause the rivet head to pop off or the rivet to pull through the plate. The size of the rivet head must be adequate to resist this tendency.

If a riveted point is subjected to compressive stress the same dangers exist as for joints stressed in tension; that is, the rivets may shear or the rivet heads may be forced off.

Finally, when riveted joints are compressed or tensed, the plate may be torn. This would occur if the rivets were placed too close to the edge of the plate or if the plate were too thin. Edge distance should be about 1½ diameters; that is, the center of the rivet should be 1½ rivet diameters from the edge of the plate. The plate must be thick enough that the rivet would fail in shear before the plate is torn.

The *efficiency of a riveted joint* is arrived at by dividing the strength of riveted joint (determined by which of the various ways in which a joint can fail is the weakest) by the strength of the solid plate.

ABS Rules for Riveting: The American Bureau of Shipping specifies the sizes and spacing of rivets depending on the thickness of plates, the number of rows of rivets, the particular member to be riveted and so on, in a series of tables in the "Rules for Building and Classing steel Vessels".

More general requirements include:

1. *Liners* are to be of iron or steel and are to have breadths not less than 3½ times the diameter of the connecting rivets.

2. *Workmanship:* "Holes in two-ply work are to be punched from the faying surfaces; burr and other projections are to be carefully removed from all faying surfaces; the holes in three-ply and four-ply work are to be fair. The material is to be thoroughly bolted up (before riveting commences) with a sufficient number of service bolts to ensure close fitting. After the work is bolted, all unfair holes are to be reamed and re-countersunk and the size of the rivet suitably increased. Except where specially approved otherwise, rivet holes should be countersunk on the caulking side in watertight and oiltight work. Riveted work must be so closely plied up that an ordinary testing knife can not be inserted between the surfaces; rivets are to be finished with full points."

3. *"Caulking* in watertight work must be thorough; light or superficial caulking will not be accepted."

WELDING

The impact of welding on the construction of ships in the last twenty years has been overwhelming. It has happened so suddenly that one has difficulty in comprehending the vast changes in the processes of fabricating, erecting, and repairing ships. It has been, literally, a revolution in the science of ship construction.

In World War I welding amounted to nothing more than a repair tool of doubtful efficiency, and the research in welding induced by the war was almost halted at war's end. The use of welding in ship construction began to spread in the thirties, however, with the first all-welded U.S. merchant ship launched in 1930. It was World War II that caused the wide-spread use of welding with most of the T-2's and Liberties being completely welded. The birth of welding was not without pains, however, as we shall see; and those who saw the death of riveting were to find this "outmoded" method of connection still very much alive and useful.

In the following sections an attempt will be made to describe the various welding methods employed in ship construction; a necessarily brief account of the welding operations; and most important of all, a discussion of how welding has affected the construction of ships.

What is Welding?

Welding may be defined as the fusing of the edges of two pieces of metal after the edges have been heated to a molten state. This basic objective can be achieved in many ways. Forge welding, which is accomplished by heating the parts to be welded and then hammering the parts together, is an operation which has been in use for many years. In ship construction, forge welding was used to make the joints in forged members. This is not the type of welding which we are going to study.

Modern welding methods may be subdivided into two broad categories depending upon the principle resorted to in the particular method of welding.

These two principles are:

1. *Fusion welding,* which is accomplished by heating the metal to be welded to or above the melting point. A filler metal may or may not be used, but no pressure on the two parts to be united is required. (Soldering and brazing differ from welding technically even though similar techniques may be used, since they employ a softer metal in making the joint.)

2. *Pressure welding,* which is accomplished by heating the metal to be welded to a point below the melting point and then uniting the two parts by pressing them together. Forge welding may therefore be

considered as a form of pressure welding. Most modern methods involving the idea of pressure use the *resistance* principle, where the edges of the members to be welded are heated by an electric arc created by the resistance offered the current in crossing a gap between the members.

Welding Methods Employing the Fusion Process

There are three main methods of welding which employ the fusion process: *Electric-arc welding; gas welding;* and *thermit welding.*

Electric-arc Welding: The overwhelming majority of welded members of modern ships are welded by the use of some method employing the electric arc, and using the fusion principle.

Electric-arc welding may be done by hand with a welding electrode placed in a holder of some sort or it may be done by machine. The electrode may be covered or bare; a metallic electrode or a carbon electrode may be used.

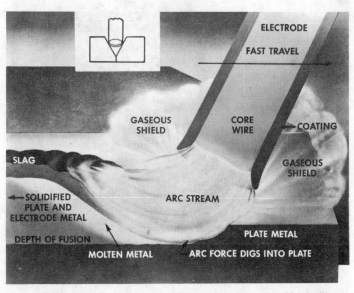

Lincoln Electric Company

Figure 84.   Artists conception of action in Electric-arc welding

The principle of electric-arc welding is relatively simple. An electrical circuit is established (See Figure 84) by connecting the electrode to a motor generator which provides direct current. (Alternating current is sometimes provided by a transformer.) The members to be welded are grounded and the ground connected to the negative terminal of the generator. Thus when the tip of the electrode is placed against the work, a flow of current is established. The arc is then "struck" by lifting the end of the electrode slightly from the metal. This "short circuit" creates resistance across the arc and causes the temperature to rise to many thousands of degrees, Fahrenheit, in some cases as high as 10,000°, although usually in the neighborhood of 6,000°. Both the base metal in the members to be welded and the filler metal melt, combining to form the *welding bead*, uniting the members.

Now, if a bare electrode is used, the weld is exposed to the air surrounding it. Oxygen in the air may convert elements of the base metal into oxides which form on the top of the weld as slag; nitrogen in the air makes the weld brittle. Therefore most electric arc welding is shielded from the air. In hand welding, the electrode is covered by a flux, which when heated, surrounds the weld with a protective veil of gas.

Figure 85.   Arc Welder at Work

A carbon electrode is usually used for joining cast iron. Since the electrode does not provide a filler metal, a rod of metal is held in the arc and melts into the weld. Carbon is absorbed by the cast iron during this process increasing the tensile strength of the iron.

Many companies have developed automatic welding machines which operate on the electric-arc principle. The most well known of these machine welders are the *Lincolnweld* and the *Unionmelt* welders. In this type of welding, a machine moves along a long joint automatically and feeds a bare-wire electrode mounted on a reel, into the work. The weld is shielded from the air by a granular substance (flux or melt) which flows over the weld completely shielding it from the air. When this machine is in use, no sparks or splutter usually associated with electric-arc welding can be seen. The granular substance is swept up by hand (or picked up by a vacuum device) and reused. Some of the melt fuses on top of the welding bead, but is easily knocked off, exposing a smooth,

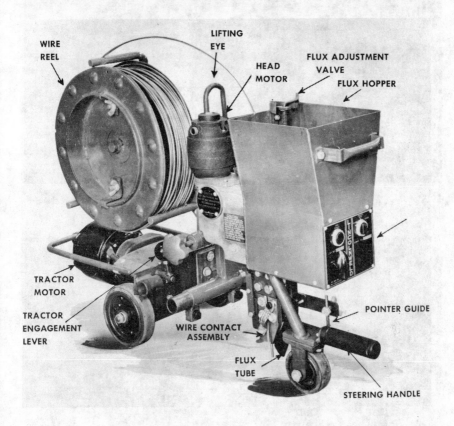

Lincoln Electric Company

Figure 86. Lincolnweld Machine Welder

reliable weld. Machine welding can be used to best advantage on long flat plating like deck seams. Where shell plating is assembled in panels off the ways, shell seams can and usually are machine welded. The difference between machine and hand welds is easily seen aboard ship, the hand weld being very rough in appearance. Machine welding can legitimately lay claim to a considerable portion of the credit for the rapidity with which ships were built in World War II.

Lincoln Electric Company

Figure 87. Lincolnweld Machine Welder at Work

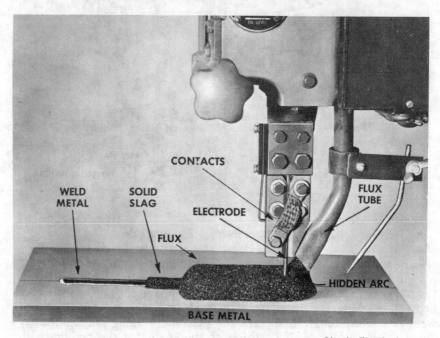

Lincoln Electric Company

Figure 88. Cut-away View of Lincolnweld Automatic Welding Operation.

Gas Welding: Gas welding is limited in its importance in ship construction, being used generally in certain high pressure piping where a sound weld is imperative. The gas torch is now used chiefly in cutting operations. The welding torch is useful as a repair tool for welding thin gauges of metals requiring low heat and has the advantage of being easily portable equipment.

The gases most frequently used are oxygen and acetylene which when combined into oxyacetylene, produce the fusing flame. Essentially, gas welding is a puddling process in which the metal of the joint is melted with a blowpipe and filler metal is provided by a rod held in the flame.

U.S. Maritime Commission

Figure 89.   Welding with an Oxy-acetylene Torch

The two gases are contained in separate cylinders with the oxygen under a pressure of some 2000 lbs. per sq. in. and the acetylene dissolved in acetone under a pressure of about 250 lbs. per sq. in. Each cylinder has a regulator to reduce the pressure of the gases to the working level. The working pressures vary from 1 to 10 lbs. per sq. in. depending on the thickness of plating to be welded. When propane is used instead of acetylene it is not necessary to have the gas dissolved in acetone.

The relative amounts of oxygen and acetylene reaching the blowpipe may be varied so as to produce a neutral, an oxidizing, or a carburizing flame. The most commonly used flame for welding operations is the neutral flame, achieved by approximately equal amounts of the two gases. Using more oxygen than acetylene produces an oxidizing flame which is generally used in preheating operations for flame cutting or in the welding of non-ferrous metals where it is desirable to oxidize impurities in the joint metal. By using an excess of acetylene, a carburizing flame is obtained which increases the rate of welding.

Thermit Welding: Thermit welding is used generally for the welding or repair of large and heavy steel castings or forgings and as far as ship

U.S. Maritime Commission

Figure 90. Thermit Welding a Stern Frame

construction is concerned is mainly limited to the welding of parts of the stern frame or the repair of the stern frame.

A stern frame is a huge casting (a Victory ship stern frame weighs about 38 tons, for example) and very few foundries in the country are equipped to handle such a job. Moreover, if the frame is cast as a unit, a major problem of transportation to the shipbuilding yard still exists. So, during World War II when thousands of stern frames had to be fabricated, thermit welding came into its own. The stern frames were cast in four or five sections with the work spread among many foundries, and then shipped to the yard where they were welded together by the Thermit process. There is no record to date of a complete failure of a thermit welded joint on a ship's stern frame.

The operation consists of positioning the sections of the stern frame to be joined; then building up a wax joint to the form desired. The joint is then enclosed in a large steel molding box and a refractory material, usually made of silica sand and plastic clay, is tamped into the box. Several pipes are led through the mold to the joint. Heating gates are used for preheating the joint, an operation taking some seven or eight hours. A pouring gate must, of course, be provided. Also "risers" lead out of the joint and provide an escape for the slag which, being lighter than the molten Thermit mixture floats to the top through the risers to a slag basin.

A crucible, lined with magnasite, a refractory material, is now loaded with the Thermit and positioned over the pouring gate. Thermit is a finely divided mixture of iron oxide and aluminum and until subjected to intense heat is quite inert. The thermit is fired by means of a special ignition powder (finely divided magnesium) and produces a chemical reaction. It takes about 30 seconds for the reaction, which is quite an impressive display of pyrotechnics, to produce the molten steel. The crucible is then tapped and the joint filled. After cooling, the metal in the gates can be chipped off. The built-up collar on a thermit weld is not there to add strength but rather to generate great heat at the center of the weld. The collar can be chipped off also if that is desirable.

Although Thermit welding is essentially a casting process, the joint can be compared to a forging since the grains of the metal are slurred instead of being arranged in lines as a normal casting. Therefore, the joint has a strength equivalent to a forged joint.

Welding Methods Employing Pressure

Welding methods employing an electric arc combined with the use of pressure to form the joint (resistance welding), obviously must be associated with some sort of machine or equipment for applying the pressure. Therefore resistance welding lends itself best to operations on small items (like tin cans) involving mass production. The only important application of the resistance principle to shipbuilding is found in stud welding.

Stud Welding: The major application of the resistance welding principle to ship construction is *Stud Welding*[1].

Stud welding has many shipbuilding uses including the securing of wood decking, securing cargo battens using hook studs, securing all types of insulation, securing cover plates of all kinds, and many other uses.

Inexperienced workers can be trained rapidly in the use of the stud welding equipment and can soon be completing 500 to 1000 welds daily. The manufacturers claim a saving of 75% in costs over previous methods of securing studs.

Welding Nomenclature and Welding Definitions: We have seen that in making a riveted connection, it is necessary to use at least two thicknesses of plating in the form of a lap or strap when connecting two plates; or a flanged angle when connecting framing to plating. In making the welded connection, these methods can be discarded. Welded joints take two basic forms: (when a fusion process is used):

1. *The butt weld* (Figure 92) is made by butting the two plates together leaving a proper gap between them and properly preparing the joint. The joint can then be fusion welded by laying the

---

[1] The following description of the operation of a Nelson Stud Welding Gun is quoted from the manufacturer's descriptive booklet.

"The fundamental operating principle of the Nelson Stud Welding Gun is to create and control an arc between the stud and the surface to which it is to be welded.

"The operator loads the gun and places it in the proper welding position, with the stud end and the spacer legs pressed firmly against the plate. From the moment the trigger is pulled, the entire weld cycle is automatic. The welding current is turned on and the stud is automatically lifted to create the arc, which burns a predetermined length of time. The lift of the stud is accomplished by a solenoid coil in the gun which is set into action by the flowing of the welding current through the coil when the trigger is pulled. The number of cycles the arc is allowed to burn is controlled by a pneumatic timing device which is built into the control unit.

"When the arcing period is completed, the timing device disconnects the welding current which trips the gun, thus forcing the end of the stud to be plunged into the molten metal. This completes the welding operation, after which the gun is removed from the stud and loaded for the next weld. The timer is adjustable and controls the operation of the gun in fractions of a second. The timer dial is calibrated in cycles and, when once set for a certain sized stud weld, repeats the same timing cycle for each weld. The gun operates from a 400 ampere D.C. generator, and uses straight polarity."

Figure 91.   Stud Welding

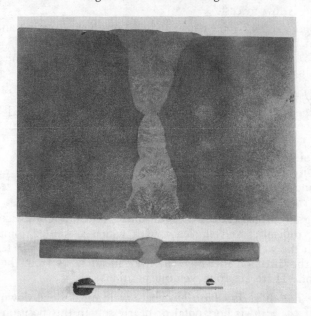

Figure 92.   Butt Welds: A one pass butt weld in 14 gage sheet steel, a sq. in.
2 pass butt weld in ½″ plate, and a multiple pass butt weld in 5″ plate.

welding bead down in the joint. If the joint is large the weld may have to be built up by laying a series of beads, each of such operations being known as a *"pass"*. It can be noted that both butts and seams of plating can be, and usually are, butt welded.

2. *The fillet weld* is made when two members are placed at right angles or nearly so, and the weld made at the corner of the angle. Most ship's framing today is welded to the plating by the use of *inverted angles* with the toe of the angle welded to the plating by a fillet weld. Two plates may be connected by lapping the edges of the plates and making fillet welds at both edges.

A welded connection may also be made by means of a *plug weld* where holes passing through two or more thicknesses of plate are filled with welding material. The plug weld is somewhat similar to a driven rivet.

Types of welded joints: When the edges of two plates are abutted in preparation for a butt weld, the joint must be prepared by proper beveling of the edges. The form and extent of the beveling depends on the thickness of the plates to be welded; the type of member welded (shell or bulkhead plating, etc.); and the type and extent of expected stress.

The *square butt joint,* where no beveling is needed, can be used on thin plating and is low in cost.

The *single vee butt joint* is usually used on thicker plating and is more costly than the square joint.

The *double vee butt joint* is used for very thick plating and for work which can be welded on both sides.

U butt joints, single and double, are used for high quality work.

The edged member in a fillet weld may also be beveled and such joints are: *Square tee joint, single or double bevel tee joints,* or *single or double J tee joints.*

A lap joint may have a single fillet or a double fillet.

Corner joints where the edges of two plates to be welded are located at right angles to each other may be welded as a *flush corner joint,* a *half-open corner joint,* or a *full-open corner joint.*

Welding Positions: Effect of Positioning on Ship Construction: The technique, difficulty, and efficiency with which a welded joint is made varies with the welding position used. Welding position is a term which relates to the direction in which the filler metal flows from the electrode to the joint. There are four welding positions:

1. *The Flat Welding Position* where welding is done downhand and the *face of the weld* is horizontal or nearly so. In this position the force of gravity aids in the flow of the small globules of molten filler metal across the electric arc.

2. *The Horizontal Welding Position* where the axis of the weld is horizontal or nearly so but the face of the weld lies in a surface which is vertical or nearly so.

3. *The Vertical Welding Position* where the axis of the weld is vertical or nearly so.

4. *The Overhead Welding Position* where the face of the weld is horizontal or nearly so, but where the flow of filler metal is vertically upwards, or nearly so, to the under side of the joint. Of course, the force of gravity works against the flow of filler metal in this position and makes the welding of a sound joint difficult, requiring special techniques.

Now, the extreme desirability of obtaining the flat welding position has had important effects on the way ships are fabricated. First, it has led to the devising of huge *positioning machines* which turn single members or large assemblies so that a flat welding position can be obtained on all joints. In the case of smaller vessels, entire hulls are placed in positioning equipment and turned so that even bottom plating can be welded in a flat position.

Secondly, it has encouraged the *sub-assembly* of members off the ways where more convenient welding positions can be used.

Also, the entire erection sequence of a ship is arranged with an eye to the achievement of easier welding positions. Many examples could be given of this: Formerly, the center vertical keel was connected to the flat plate keel on the ways and then the rider plate was connected to the CVK. If welded joints were used, it would mean that the overhead position would be necessary for the latter operation. So now the rider plate and CVK are assembled off the ways where a horizontal welding position can be used. Then the assembly is brought to the ship, turned over and the CVK welded to the keel.

It is difficult to underestimate the far-reaching consequences on the way that a ship is built, of the desirability and need for achieving the best possible welding position.

Welding Versus Riveting

The heading of this section suggests that a struggle for supremacy exists between the two methods of connecting ship members. The struggle is rather one-sided, however, with riveting running a poor second in almost every apparent aspect of the subject. Perhaps, a better analogy would be that of a cooperative effort with welding shouldering the major share of the burden and riveting coming through with assistance where welding falls down.

In this section we shall compare the two methods of connection and discuss their advantages and disadvantages:

Deadweight-Displacement Ratio: One of the major contributions which welding has made to the construction of ships is the appreciable reduction in the weight of hull steel necessary. This saving in weight can be added to the deadweight or carrying capacity of the ship and thus on a given displacement, the ratio between deadweight and displacement can be increased.

This saving in weight is due to the elimination of laps, straps, flanges, and the rivets themselves which are necessary in riveted construction. For example, a completely welded ship of about 5,000 tons light displacement will save some 600 or 700 tons of weight over the equivalent riveted ship.

Making a Watertight (or Oiltight) Joint: A sound welded joint is automatically watertight and requires no further operations after welding. A riveted joint, as we have seen, is very difficult to make watertight and must be caulked after riveting. When the ship is in operation, continuous repair is necessary as rivets and riveted joints work loose and start to leak.

Strength of Joint: There is no evidence to show that a welded joint is any stronger than a riveted joint if the latter is properly connected. Of course, the metal in a welded joint is stronger than the base metal and very few failures occur along the welded joint. But, the same thing can be said of the riveted joint, as far as failures are concerned. Cracks are apt to form in the plates proper rather than the joints in both welded and riveted construction.

Lincoln Electric Company

Figure 93. A weld test plate made to show that even sub-standard welds are strong. Even though this weld has external porosity, the plate broke rather than the weld when it was pulled in a testing machine.

Some claims have been made that a riveted joint is more flexible than a welded one and that a riveted ship is therefore stronger than a welded one. The consensus of opinion today is that this is an erroneous conception, since flexibility could be obtained only through the "slip" of rivets and no evidence is available to show that there is such rivet slip. Nor would rivet slip be desirable if it did exist.

The point here is that equal strength can be obtained in a welded joint with less material than a riveted joint.

Equipment and Personnel: Both riveting and welding operations require expensive equipment and trained personnel. The consideration of equipment, however, has acted to delay the advent of welding in some shipyards and in some countries, since a yard is loath to give up the large capital investment represented in their riveting equipment and lay-out. In the United States during World War II, many *new* yards and ways were constructed and welding equipment could be bought just as readily as riveting equipment. In Great Britain, for example, where few new yards were constructed, the change-over to welding has been slower.

Welding personnel can be trained faster than riveters and this was a vital factor in the War. Paradoxically, perhaps, it is more important for welders to do an efficient job than it is for riveters since a porous weld can lead to the formation of cracks which may mean the loss of a ship. Poor workmanship in riveted construction means only local trouble.

Ease of Construction and Repair: There are literally scores of ways in which welding has made the construction and repair of a ship easier and less costly operations. The items given below can be considered only as a partial listing. Riveting, as can be seen, still has its contribution to make:

1. Welding can be done just as easily at *night as by day.*

2. A welding yard is much more *quiet* than a riveting yard. This is not as insignificant a factor as it might appear to be on first sight. Studies made in various industrial establishments have shown that efficiency of personnel is an inverse ratio to the number of decibels of sound.

3. As to *temperature,* riveting seems to have the better of it, since welding cannot be done practically when the temperature is below 10°. Cold weather also seems to aggravate the tendency of welded construction to crack.

4. Welding can be done *under water.*

5. The absence of butts, straps, rivet points and so on in the shell of a vessel makes a smooth surface which *cuts down on frictional resistance* and increases speed proportionately.

6. Decks can be *sheathed* with wooden planking much more easily when a flush surface is available. In riveted decks, the planking must be cut to fit the unevenness of the riveted plating.

7. Side frames, in addition to the advantage derived from the elimination of the flange by which riveted angles are connected to plating, have the additional advantage of *eliminating the need for beveling* the flange to suit the change in curvature of the plating at the bow and stern. By glancing at the half-breadth plan of a vessel (Chap. 7), one can see that the *bevel angle* changes from waterline to waterline. In fabricating a riveted side frame, the flange of the angle which lies against the shell plating must, therefore, be beveled appropriately. This is an expensive, time-consuming operation. A welded side frame has the toe of an inverted angle welded to the shell and no beveling is necessary.

8. Where joints are relatively *inaccessible* welding can be done much more conveniently than riveting.

9. Where *studs* or bolts must be fitted, stud welding eliminates the need for drilling a hole through the plating and putting a nut on the other side.

10. Where the use of aluminum as a structural material for ships is concerned, progress in welding has been slow. However, a great deal has been learned and riveting of aluminum has now largely been replaced by welding and, in time, all such work probably will be welded. Special techniques and equipment must be used in welding aluminum and shipyards have been slow in converting.

11. The cost of *repairs*, always a headache to shipowners, has been diminished due to welding. In some ways, a welder can be compared to a carpenter. Steel plates can be cut with a torch to any odd shape desired; if the fit is not exact, it can be easily made so. Then the two plates can be welded. Contrast this procedure with the repair, say, of a riveted shell plate which has been badly pitted on one portion of the plate. The *entire plate* must be removed. To do this, the rivets must be punched out all around the plate and a new plate fabricated to the exact shape needed. In welding, the pitted area could be cut out and replaced.

12. Welding is not without its serious difficulties. The application of extremely high temperatures associated with welding, brings in its wake a tendency to *distortion* of the material surrounding the joint, high stresses placed on the material some of which may be left over after construction in the form of *"residual stresses"*, and a high susceptibility to the formation of *cracks*.

Early welded construction, before the development of techniques which have eliminated or reduced the difficulties, was characterized by the welding "wave" and resembled a housewife's washboard. The reason for welding distortion is not difficult to understand. When welding, a local area is heated to great temperatures. This heated area, attempting to expand freely, is prevented from doing so by the relatively cool area surrounding it. The steel is stretched beyond its yield point by the resulting stresses and permanent distortion results.

Now, the welding wave would be bad enough, but apparently the stresses associated with distortion are not completely relieved during and directly after the welding operation. Remaining unrelieved welding stresses, which have been called residual or "locked-up" stresses, accumulate, and although their exact role in whole cracking picture, is not known, it is generally agreed that they contribute to the formation and propagation of cracks when the ship is in service. When the vessel is subjected to sudden shocks such as those encountered in heavy weather, the residual stresses may be suddenly released, and assist in the formation of cracks.

Residual welding stresses, however, do not appear to be the main culprit in causing ship crackings. A welded ship, especially if poor workmanship exists, has more *"notches"* than a riveted ship. A notch is considered to be any discontinuity in the structure such as openings in plating. A faulty weld may be porous and this too, is a notch. Now, a plate or any member is easier to crack if it has a notch in it. This can be illustrated simply by pulling at a piece of notebook paper. The paper will withstand a relatively strong pull without ripping. But if a small notch is cut in one edge, the paper will rip with comparative ease at the notch.

U.S. Maritime Commission

Figure 94.   Burning the deck to remove buckles

With experience in welding, coupled with vast research into the problem, most of the difficulties associated with welding have been eliminated or reduced. The procedures developed in this direction, and the effect that they have had on ship design and construction will now be described:

Welding Technique

Workmanship: It is particularly important in welding that welds are made soundly. Obviously, the welder must be a good workman in order to accomplish this. Today, the personnel engaged in welding are subjected to very strict examinations and tests by the American Bureau and by the shipyard to ensure competency. Another factor in good workmanship, the tools used, is important too but is not part of the scope of this section. Suffice it to state that such factors as the size of the electrode used, electrode quality, preparation of the joint and current setting on the generator, must be carefully considered.

Lincoln Electric Company

Figure 95. A plate with welds made on it under varying conditions. "A" is a weld made with correct current, voltage and normal speed. "B" was made with current too low. "C" was made with current too high. "D" was made with arc voltage too low. "E" was made with arc voltage too high. "F" was made with the speed of travel too low and "G" was made with the speed of travel too high.

Proper Regulating and Securing: The distortion due to welding can be held down by proper regulation of the plates to be welded plus proper securing. These operations require considerable skill and experience in welding. For example, if the amount of shrinkage encountered in a particular operation is known, extra material may be provided; or the work may be so aligned that after welding the material will shrink and distort to the alignment actually desired; or, one force tending to distort may be balanced by another force tending to distort, and so on.

The use of such tools as *strongbacks* secure the members to be welded and hold down distortion. *Tack welds* are made to secure the members before the *production welding* commences.

Intermittent Welding: Where a watertight joint is unnecessary like the connection of beams to decks, or stiffeners to bulkheads, a continuous weld does not have to be made. Then the weld may be made intermittently by laying down a weld for a few inches, skipping a few inches and making another short pass, and so on. This reduces the heat generated and consequently reduces the tendency to distort.

The use of *serrated members* is related to "skip" welding. A serrated member is one which has a series of semi-circular cuts made in the edge of the plate or flange of the angle to be welded. When the edge of the member is then welded, intermittency is automatically obtained. Serrated members have the added advantage of reducing the weight of the members. Serrations are not commonly made in important strength members, especially longitudinal members, since it is important to maintain the effective cross-sectional area of such members. Transverse decks beams and bilge keels are two examples of members sometimes serrated.

Proper Sequence of Welding: The setting up of the sequence in which the various parts of a ship are welded is important. Here the services of a competent welding engineer are invaluable. This is a highly technical matter, but in general, it can be stated that welding in a given area should always progress *out* from some center rather than working in toward that center.

Pre-heat and Post-heat Treatment: In order to control the build-up and reduction of heat in the welding process, it is sometimes desirable to pre-heat or post-heat (or both) the joint. In this way, the extent of stress and distortion is held down. "The term *'stress relieving'* is sometimes applied to the elimination of internal stresses by slowly heating the steel structure to a temperature of approximately 1200° F. and allowing it to cool in a furnace. What happens in this case is merely an accelerated relief of the stresses which would occur in exactly the same way but in a very much longer time at atmospheric temperatures."[1] The term "stress relieving" is also used to describe a process resorted to *after* a ship has been constructed and it is desired to reduce the possibility of residual stresses. This process "making use of the principle of mechanical overstressing, has been adopted for 'stress relieving' many all-welded tankers. The process consists of heating the plate on both sides of the weld to about 400 degrees F. so that the metal adjacent to the weld expands. This stretches the weld metal which is sandwiched in between. When the plate contracts on cooling (aided by a water spray) the weld metal, having been stretched beyond its yield point, contracts elastically to a relatively low stress. The areas stress relieved are usually confined to the tank space and include butts and seams in the deck and bottom shell and seams only in the side shell."[2]

Peening: Peening consists of hammering a weld, usually with a pneumatic machine fitted with a round-nose tool. The objective of peening

---

[1] *Procedure Handbook of Arc Welding, Design, and Practice,* Lincoln Electric Company, Eighth Edition, 1945.
[2] H. G. Acker, "Highlights of Welded Ship Research", *Transactions of the Society of Naval Architects and Marine Engineers,* 1949.

is to assist in stress relieving. ABS specifies that when peening is necessary to relieve stress in important joints welded under restraint, it must
be done immediately after depositing and cleaning each pass of filler
metal. The first and last passes in butt welds are not ordinarily peened.

Todds Shipyard Corporation

Figure 96. A worker moves a stress relieving machine along the welded seams of
the deck of a T-2 tanker, to heat a six-inch strip on each side of the seam to 400
degree F., and immediately cools it off with a stream of water. This job was
performed on almost 9,000 feet of seams from the keel to the rail and along the
tanker's deck.

Inspection of Welding

As we have seen, it is extremely important that welds be of good quality and sound. A great deal of attention is paid, therefore, to the inspection of welds and various methods have been developed to ensure as far as is possible the making of sound welds. The following methods are now in use:

Visual Inspection: Most welding inspection takes the form of careful observation by qualified inspectors. Such factors as the size, shape, and appearance of the bead, presence of slag, undercut or overlap, will reveal to the experienced inspector signs of poor welds.

Todd Shipyard Corporation

Figure 97.   A side stress relieving machine on a dolly moves along a rail installed on the special staging erected along the length of the vessel.

Electro-Magnetic Method: In the *Magna-Flux* method the weldment is charged or magnetized. Then a fine powder of steel dust is sifted over the weld (before magnetizing). If a crack is present, the magnetism will pull the fine dust into it. Then a two pound air pressure (which is almost like a breadth in strength) is applied to blow off this dust thus revealing by the line of remaining dust, the presence of a crack. Or, cracks can be detected by sifting the powder on a piece of paper placed on the weld and observing the picture formed. Another somewhat similar method uses fluorescent powder under ultraviolet light.

Radiographic Inspection: A radiograph, or X-ray picture of the weld, can be made by the simple but expensive method of exposing a photographic film on one side of the weld to an X-ray tube on the other side. A porous weld will be indicated by darker spots on the film.

Radiographs can also be made using the Gamma ray method. Gamma rays emanate from radium and penetrate the weld more quickly than the X-ray and are used for inspecting heavy members where the X-ray would have to be exposed for too long a time or where the high power X-ray equipment is not available. Cobalt 60 is now being used as a substitute for radium.

Radiographic inspection, in addition to its obvious worth in discovering poor welds, has a psychological effect on welders which sometimes prevents the making of poor welds.

Use of the Stethoscope: If a welded joint is tapped softly with a hammer while an experienced inspector listens with a stethoscope, a difference in the sound will reveal the presence of a fault. The Sperry Company has developed a supersonic device along these lines.

"Destructive" Inspection Methods: The ABS requires, when a surveyor deems it necessary, that plugs are to be trepanned from the weld in order to determine its soundness; or parts of the weld may be flame-gouged for the same purpose. (Flame gouging is done by a oxy-acetylene torch using special nozzles.)

A Comparison of the Welded and Riveted Ship

The tremendous shipbuilding program of World War II put into high gear the movement toward the construction of all welded or nearly all welded vessels which had commenced in the thirties, even though experience with welding had been very limited. The urgency of the need for ships dictated the use of welding with its speed and ease of training new personnel. Early experience with these welded vessels, however, disclosed a dishearteningly high proportion of crackings and some complete failures of the hull girder.

The question was naturally raised in view of welded ship failures whether the concept of the welded ship was basically sound and if so, what were the causes and the possible corrective measures for fractures in welded construction.

Analysis of welded ship fractures and research by government, classification, and other agencies have yielded a fairly complete set of answers to these questions. One of the most comprehensive and rewarding of these efforts can be found in the report of a Board of Investigation convened by the Secretary of the Navy in 1943.[1] This report and others have established without question the basic soundness of the welded ship, but have also shown the need for more careful design, workmanship, and the use of some riveted seams.

Causes of Fractures in Welded Ships: One of the first theories advanced to explain welding failures was the idea of "locked-up stresses"

---

[1] *"The Design and Methods of Construction of Welded Steel Merchant Vessels"*, Final Report of a Board of Investigation, July 1946, hereinafter referred to as the Welding Investigation.

and "residual" stresses which when the ship was subjected to heavy weather or other sudden shocks would be released, suddenly leading to fractures. While "locked-up" stresses have not been completely eliminated as a factor in causing cracks, it has been shown that other factors are of greater importance. The role of "locked-up" stresses seems to be that of accentuating local concentrations of stress.

One point on which all researchers are agreed is that notches in the construction of welded vessels are a primary cause of cracks. The Welding Investigation showed that every one of the thousands of fractures investigated started in a notch. A notch may be created by a structural discontinuity such as a hatch corner, or cut in the sheer strake, or by faulty welds. A welded ship is more apt to have notches than a riveted ship due to the possibility of notches in faulty welds.

Another point in general agreement is that shipbuilding steel possessed a property which has been entitled *"notch sensitivity"*. This property is a form of brittleness and is due to the chemical composition of steel. The brittleness can be effected by the welding operation. Brittleness can also be increased by low temperatures. The Welding Investigation showed that a great majority of the welding casualties occurred in the winter time.

Causes of fractures can then be summed up in this way: Primary factors are notches and notch-sensitive steel; secondary factors are low temperatures, heavy weather and unusually high bending moments, and "locked-up" stresses acting in combination with the primary factors. It is also pertinent to observe that ships with riveted seams and riveted gunwale attachments did not suffer as many major fractures as ships with welded seams. This has been attributed to the fact that most cracks will not jump the gap between the riveted plates, whereas in welded ships there is nothing to stop the crack from propagating once it has started.

Corrective Measures for Welded Ships: The causes of fractures in welded ships suggest the corrective measures to be employed. The number of notches in a ship's structure can be reduced by good design, such as the elimination of unnecessary cuts and corners, and by good workmanship. Good workmanship is a function of careful welding engineering, careful training of welders, and careful inspection of welds.

The American Bureau of Shipping has made a start on the problem of notch-sensitive steel by specifying new chemical requirements for plates.[1]

"Stress relieving" is still considered beneficial.

All modern ships are being built with some riveted seams and with the gunwale riveted to the sheer strake. These riveted seams act as crack arrestors. Older ships are being fitted in a number of cases with special

---

[1] The new requirements (1948) specify steels of higher manganese content for all plates over ½ inch thick. For material over 1 inch thick, a specified amount of silicon is required; as well as a mill process which will produce a fine-grain structure. (Notch sensitivity increases with thickness of material.) In 1958, ABS approved an alternative method of proving notch toughness. This method utilizes tests on small specimens of the steel to be approved.

"crack arrestors" made by cutting a slit in the plating and riveting a strap over it.

Work is continuing on these problems.

Conclusions: In view of the fact that the disadvantages of welding are far outweighed by the advantages; and since the problem of fractures in welded ships has been largely overcome, it seems apparent that the nearly all welded ship is here to stay. The riveted ship has not been proved to be any "stronger" than the welded ship, nor has it been proven to be more "flexible".[1] In tests made on welded and riveted sister ships it has been found that no real differences exist in regard to bending moment stresses, and deflections.[2] The fact that riveted ships have laps, straps, etc. does not mean that these ships possess more strength than a welded ship, since the latter is designed with a moment of inertia and section modulus sufficient to withstand the designed stress.

QUESTIONS

1. When will:
   a) A tap rivet be used?
   b) Multiple rows of rivets be necessary?
   c) Liners be eliminated in riveted plating?
   d) A dolly bar be used?
   e) A drift pin be used?
   f) A rivet be hammered?
   g) Corrosion rings form around a rivet point?
   h) Rivet heads pop off?
   i) Rivets tear through the plate?
2. Describe a typical ship's rivet with respect to the following points:
   a) Material of which it is made
   b) Diameter
   c) Type of head
   d) Appearance on the watertight side
   e) Diameter of the rivet hole
   f) Rivet spacing (for watertight work).
3. A riveted ship is in drydock for repairs. Describe:
   a) The method for testing the watertightness of tanks and watertight bulkheads
   b) How a loose rivet may be detected in some cases
   c) How a rivet may be tested for looseness
   d) How a defective rivet is replaced
   e) How a defective riveted plate is replaced.
4. How are riveted joints made watertight?

---

[1] H. G. Acker, op. cit.
[2] "Structural Investigation in Still Water of the Tanker *Newcombia, Transactions* of the North East Coast Institution of Engineers and Shipbuilders, Vol. 63, April 1947 and *"Report of Hogging and Sagging Tests on All-Welded Tanker M.V. Neverita,* The Admiralty Ship Welding Committee, London, H.M. Stationery Office, 1946.

5. Describe the following shipyard procedures:
    a) Punching
    b) Bolting-up
    c) Reaming
    d) Drilling
    e) Tapping
    f) Driving in a rivet.
6. What are the elements which must be considered in the design of a riveted joint?
7. For what elements of the riveting process does the ABS show particular concern?
8. Differentiate among: Electric-arc welding; pressure welding; brazing; gas welding.
9. Define the terms: Bead, pass, fillet, melt, stud, peen, tack, notch, serration, trepanning, crack arrestor, stress relieving.
10. Describe in detail how the following elements of ship construction have been made easier by the advent of welding:
    a) Personnel and training.
    b) Fabrication of side frames.
    c) Fitting of bolts and studs.
    d) Sheathing of decks with wood planking.
    e) Connections at plate seams and butts.
    f) Obtaining watertight and oiltight joints.
    g) Pre-fabrication and sub-assembly.
11. What are the causes, primary and secondary, in the formation and propagation of cracks in welded ships? What can the ship's officer do to prevent and/or restrict the cracks?
12. Explain the importance of positioning in welded work. What effect has this had on the methods by which modern ships are constructed?
13. Why are almost all ships in the postwar period being built with many riveted seams in shell and deck plating?
14. Why is the gunwale bar an important ship's member?
15. In regard to Thermit welding:
    a) What are the materials of which Thermit is composed?
    b) What ship's member is commonly welded by the Thermit process?
    c) Why is a Thermit weld, although cast, analagous to a forged member?
16. What welding equipment is sometimes carried aboard ship?
17. What is the function of "melt" in the machine welding process?
18. What members are commonly welded "intermittently" on a ship? Why?
19. Explain the principle involved in each of the following methods of weld inspection:
    a) Magna-Flux
    b) Radiographic
    c) Stethoscope
    d) Trepanning.

BIBLIOGRAPHY

Lincoln Electric Company, *Procedure Handbooks of Arc Welding, Design, and Practice,* Eighth Edition, 1945.

H. G. Acker, "Highlights of Welded Ship Research", *Transactions of the Society of Naval Architects and Marine Engineers*, Vol. 57, 1949.

The Design and Methods of Construction of Welded Steel Merchant Vessels, Final Report of a Board of Investigation Convened by Order of the Secretary of the Navy, Government Printing Office, Washington, D. C., 1947.

"Structural Investigation in Still Water of the Tanker *"Newcombia"*, *Transactions of the North East Coast Institution of Engineers and Shipbuilders*, Vol. 63, April, 1947.

"Report of Hogging and Sagging Tests on All-Welded Tanker *M. V. Neverita"*, The Admiralty Ship Welding Committee, H. M. Stationery Office, London, 1946.

Jonassen, F., "A Summary of the Research Work Conducted under the Direction of the Ship Structure Committee", *Transactions of the Society of Naval Architects and Marine Engineers*, Vol. 57, 1949.

MacCutcheon, E. M., "Rivet Slip, Stress Distribution, and the Deflection of Ships' Hulls", *Transactions of the Society of Naval Architects and Marine Engineers*, Vol. 57, 1949.

Kennedy, H. E., "Notes on Welding and Welding Stresses", *Transactions of the Society of Naval Architects and Marine Engineers*, Vol. 53, 1945.

Rules for Building and Classing Steel Vessels, issued annually by the American Bureau of Shipping, New York.

Carmichael, A. W., *Practical Ship Production*, McGraw-Hill Book Company, Inc., New York, 1941.

Walton & Baird, *Steel Ships, Their Construction and Maintenance*, Charles Griffin and Company Limited, London, 1944.

D'Arcangelo, *A Guide to Sound Ship Structures*, Cornell Maritime Press, Inc., Cambridge, Md., 1964.

The Design and Methods of Construction of Welded Merchant Ships, U. S. Government Printing Office, 1956.

R. Smith, *Recent Developments in Shipyard Welding Practices*, SNAME Lakes and Rivers Section, Jan., 1960.

Chapter 9

TANKS, BILGES, AND PIPING SYSTEMS

Incorporated into the structure of all dry cargo vessels are a number of tanks which are utilized for the operation of the vessels and, in some cases, the carriage of cargo liquids. Serving these tanks and the drainage system of a vessel are the various piping systems.

Although the maintenance and operation of all hull systems is primarily the responsibility of the engine department, deck officers must be conversant with the location of the systems, the valves which control their operation, and the problems of operation. This knowledge of piping systems by the deck officers is highly desirable since he must, in many cases, give the orders for the operation of the piping systems. The deck officer is responsible for such things as:

1. Sounding of bilges and drain wells.

2. The vertical and longitudinal distribution of liquid weights.

3. Use of deck operated valves in case of emergencies such as flooding damage.

4. Use of "water on deck" for the fire system and deck and anchor wash connections.

5. Amount of fuel oil, feed water, salt water ballast, potable water, and cargo liquids to be loaded or discharged; and the place and time of loading and discharging.

Too many deck officers discharge these responsibilities without adequate knowledge of piping systems and the problems involved in their operation. The purpose of this chapter is to remedy this lack of knowledge.

Table VII lists the type of tanks found on most cargo vessels, the system which serves the tanks, and the pumps necessary for using the system. Most systems, although served customarily by one set of pipes and pumps, are usually arranged so that in the case of breakdowns of pumps or other emergencies, another or several different pumps and piping systems can be pressed into service for the particular suction or discharge desired.

The deck officer should be particularly acquainted with the following piping systems:

1. *The Bilge and Clean Ballast System:* The bilge system is designed to collect drains from compartments that cannot be drained overboard by gravity and to pump this bilge water overboard. The clean ballast system

Table VII
DRY CARGO SHIPS
TANKS, PIPING SYSTEMS, AND PUMPS

Type of Tank	Liquid carried	Piping System serving tank	Pump serving system	Function of System
Fore and after peak tanks	Salt water	Clean ballast system	Fire pump or fire and standby bilge pump	Trim, stability, immersion
	Fresh water	Clean ballast system	Washing wtr. pmp.	Washing water
	Liquid cargo	Independent pump at tank	Independent pmp.	Carry palm oil, etc.
Double bottom tanks	Fuel Oil	Fuel Oil transfer and oily ballast system	Fuel Oil transfer; general svc. pumps	Storage and transfer of Fuel Oil
	Salt water	Fuel Oil transfer and oily ballast system	General Svc. and Bilge & Ballast pump	Stability, trim, immersion
	Fresh water	Filling connections for loading water; evaporators	Feed pumps	Feed water; distilled and washing wtr.
Deep tanks	Fuel Oil	Fuel Oil transfer and oily ballast system	Fuel Oil transfer; Gen. Svc. pumps	Storage and transfer of Fuel Oil
	Salt water	Fuel Oil transfer and oily ballast system	Gen. svc.; bilge and ballast pumps	Stability, trim, immersion
	Liquid cargo	Independent line usually	Independent pump	Carry edible oils, etc.
Bilges or drain wells; Cofferdams	Drainage	Bilge system	Bilge and Ballast General Service Fire and standby blg.	Drain compartments not drained overboard by gravity
Settlers	Fuel Oil	Fuel Oil transfer system	F.O. Transfer and gen. service pumps	Settle wtr. and impurities from Fuel Oil
Potable wtr.	Drinking wtr.	Drinking wtr. system; evap.	Drinking wtr. pump	Store drinking wtr.
Lub. Oil tank	Lub. Oil			Store Lub. Oil.

is designed to load and discharge the fore and after peak tanks (and in some cases, one or more deep tanks) with clean salt water ballast. The purpose of the system is to maintain the proper trim, stability, and immersion of the vessel.

2. *The Fuel Oil and Oily Ballast System:* This system is arranged to store and transfer fuel oil so that a supply of clean oil can be maintained for the ship's fuel oil service system, and it is also arranged to transfer sea water so that the ship's tanks can be ballasted as required to maintain proper stability, trim, and immersion.

3. *The Fire System:* The fire system supplies sea water under pressure to all the fire stations, and to the deck and anchor wash connections.

4. *The Sanitary System:* This system supplies sea water to all the sanitary fixtures.

5. *The Washing Water System:* This system supplies fresh cold or hot water for all washing water fixtures on the vessel except those in the galley.

6. *The Drinking Water System:* This system supplies drinking water to the drinking fountains and outlets throughout the vessel including washing and culinary water to the galley.

7. *Auxiliary Steam System:* This system supplies steam to the vessel's heating system, hot water storage heater and galley, and deck machinery.

8. *Ship's Service Compressed Air System:* This system supplies air to the various service outlets for cleaning and for operating pneumatic tools.

Bilge and Clean Ballast Systems

All compartments on a vessel must be provided with some means for draining off liquids. These liquids can stem from damaged cargo, leakage through deck and side openings, cleaning and testing watertightness, and in some cases, condensation. Some compartments can be drained by *scuppers* which lead overboard and operate by gravity. Other compartments have deck *drains* which are connected by drain pipes to the bilges. In both of these cases, it is important to keep the drains from becoming clogged, and they should be checked frequently. On most merchant ships fore peak compartments including the chain locker drain to a sump located under the locker. The sump is then pumped out by an *eductor*. Eductors are generally connected by a line to the fire line and when the latter is operating the water in the sump is sucked up and ejected through the fire outlet. Sometimes, fore peak sumps are pumped out by hand. A sump is usually located in the after end of the shaft alley too.

There are two types of bilges. One type which is found more on older vessels is the side bilge arrangement. In this type the outboard strake of plating in the inner bottom is slanted down and connected normal to the bilge strake. This is a very efficient drainage system but has the disadvantage of reducing the protection offered by an inner bottom since vessels

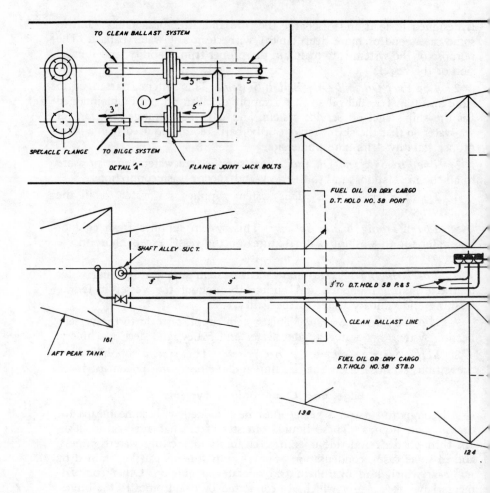

Figure 98.   Bilge and Clean Ballast System

are often breached in the bilge area. With side bilges the entire compartment is likely to be flooded although the ABS does specify limits on how far down on the bilge area the connection of margin plate can be made.

On most modern vessels the bilge or *drain well* has supplanted side bilges either entirely or in the fore part of the vessels. Drain wells are simply small "tanks" which project down from the inner bottom into the double bottom. At the top they are covered with plates and strainers which are flush with the inner bottom. The wells are usually located at the after end of compartments since it is much more likely that a vessel will be

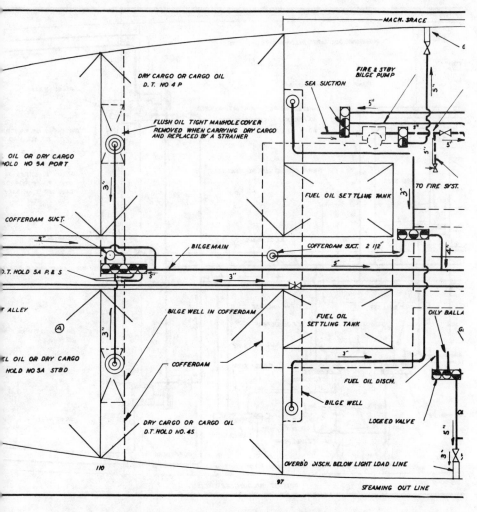

Figure 98. (*Continued on next page*)

trimmed by the stern than by the head. ABS specifies that the wells are not to extend downward more than necessary and in the case of passenger vessels they are not to be less than 18 inches from the outer shell except at the after end of the shaft alley where the well may extend to the shell. With these restrictions, the drain well system definitely offers greater protection from flooding, but sacrifices something in drainage efficiency. It should be noted that in the case of side bilges the lower layer of dunnage must be laid athwartships and in the case of drain wells, fore and aft.

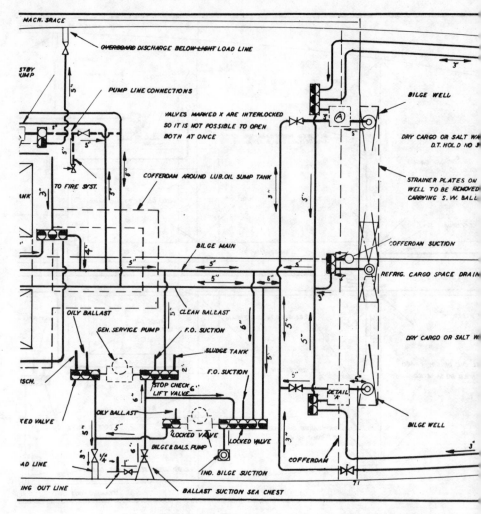

Figure 98. (*Continued on next page*)

Now, each bilge or well is connected by the bilge system to the pumps in the machinery space. The lines are led in various ways but the most commonly used system is as follows: The suction at each bilge is enclosed in· a *strum* or *rose box,* which minimizes the possibility of clogging the suction. In some cases it is necessary to have a valve at the suction. This valve is operated from deck by remote control through *reach rods* and is usually a stop check lift valve. The lift feature permits filling of a seized valve and is very important since the valve of course is inaccessible. This type of valve has three positions: open, check, and

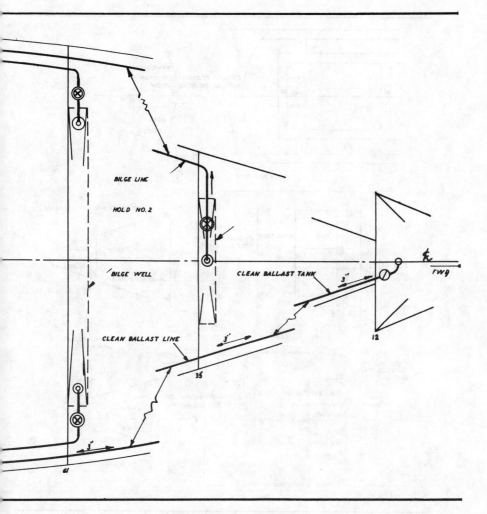

Figure 98. (*Concluded*)

closed. The ship's officer should be very familiar with the location and operation of every reach rod on his vessel since in case of damage to pipes amidships the reach rods forward and aft should be operated so as to close the valves and prevent flooding of forward and/or after compartments.[1]

Each bilge has a line which leads from the suction up to point above the inner bottom, then outboard where they are led under the wing brackets to manifolds on the machinery space bulkheads. In the machinery space all manifolds are connected to a *bilge main* which is led to the

[1] However, many vessels recently constructed have the bilge suction valve and the remote controls eliminated since the bilge piping is adequately protected by ducts or other means.

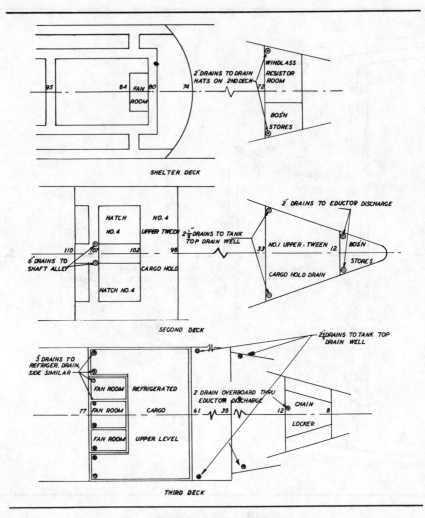

Figure 99.   Deck Drains to Bilge, etc.

pumps. Between the manifold and the pumps a *mud box* or basket strainer must be fitted. In order to take suction from any space the following valves must be opened: The proper manifold valve; the suction valve in the pump suction manifold; the overboard discharge valve in the pump suction manifold; and the valves at the bilge well (if any).

In addition to the normal drain well in the machinery space it is required that the main circulating pumps be fitted with direct suction connections provided with non-return valves. This *"bilge injection valve"* is a means of using the large capacity circulating pump to pump out

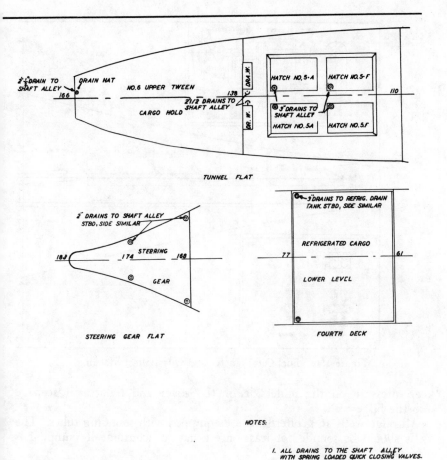

Figure 99.   (*Concluded*)

large quantities of water from the engine room in an emergency. The ABS requires that this direct bilge suction have a diameter of not less than two-thirds the diameter of the main sea inlet.

When cargo oil is carried in deep tanks, a manhole cover replaces the bilge strainer in the bilge well. Precautions should be taken to insure tightness of this cover. One method of doing this is to fill the well with water through the sounding tube after which any leaks around the covers can then be observed and stopped. Keeping the water in the well will

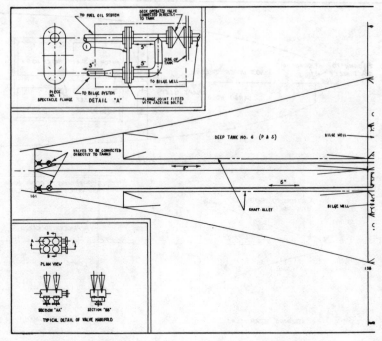

Figure 100.   Fuel Oil Transfer and Oily Ballast System.

keep pressure on the underside of the cover and reduce oil seepage into the bilge well.

All bilge wells and cofferdams are equipped with sounding tubes. The wells should be sounded at least once a day to determine if pumping is necessary.

ABS Rules Regarding Pumping Arrangements:

1. All vessels are to be provided with a satisfactory pumping plant capable of pumping from and draining any compartment when the vessel is on an even keel and either upright or listed five degrees. (For this purpose drain wells must be located fairly well outboard.)

2. Ocean-going vessels must have at least three power pumps connected to the bilge main. In the case of passenger vessels one of these pumps must be an emergency pump of a reliable submersible type with the source of power located above the bulkhead deck.

3. One of the three required pumps may be attached to the propelling unit; the other two must be independent (the required submersible pump being one of these). The necessary cocks and valves for controlling the bilge suctions in each compartment must be so arranged and oper-

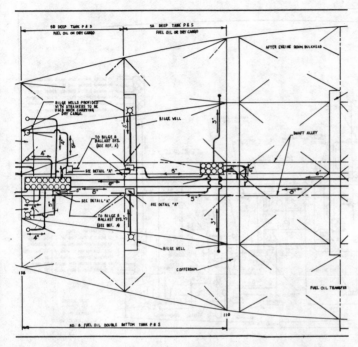

Figure 100. (*Continued on next page*)

ated from the bulkhead deck, that in the event of flooding, the emergency pump may be operated on any compartment.

4. No main suction piping should be less than $2\frac{1}{2}$ inches internal diameter. No branch piping need be more than 4 inches nor should it be less than 2 inches in diameter.

The Clean Ballast System: Clean ballast lines are led to the fore and after peak tanks and in some cases to deep tanks. The ballast lines are used for both filling and discharging so that transfer of ballast is not possible. If the deep tanks are adjacent to machinery space bulkheads the bilge line is utilized for clean ballast by blanking off the bilge system at the manifold. In this case when flooding a deep tank which may have been used for dry cargo it is a good idea to remove the strainer plates in the bilge well so as to prevent clogging of the strainer.

The ballast lines to the peaks must be, of course, run through the fore and after peak bulkheads. These bulkheads are vital to the watertight integrity of a vessel and special precautions are necessary here. ABS requires screw down valves operable from above the bulkhead deck. These control rods must be provided with an indicator to show whether the valve is open or closed. These valves should be closed except when filling or discharging the tanks.

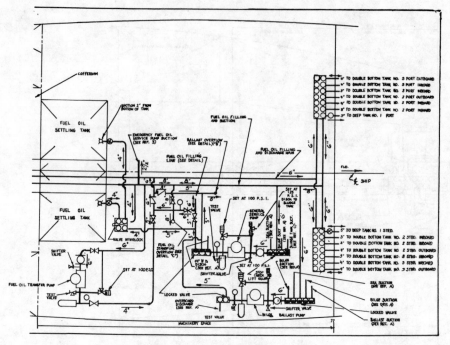

Figure 100. (*Continued on next page*)

The Fuel Oil and Oily Ballast System: Although this piping system primarily is an engineering responsibility and hence a detailed description of the system does not properly belong in this text, deck officers should have some knowledge of the problems which face the engineers, especially when fuel oil tanks are used for salt water ballast since this situation is one which has been in many cases a source of irritation between the deck and engine staffs.

Individual suctions are led to each double bottom and deep tank used for the storage of fuel oil. These lines are led through the double bottoms rather than above the inner bottom as was the case with bilge lines. The fuel oil lines are connected to manifolds in the engine room which in turn lead to fuel oil suction and discharge mains and thence to the fuel oil pumps. With this piping arrangement the following duties can be performed:

1. Storage and settling tanks can be filled from the outside through the fuel oil filling station.

2. Fuel oil or salt water ballast in any tank can be transferred to any other fuel oil tank or it can be pumped overboard.

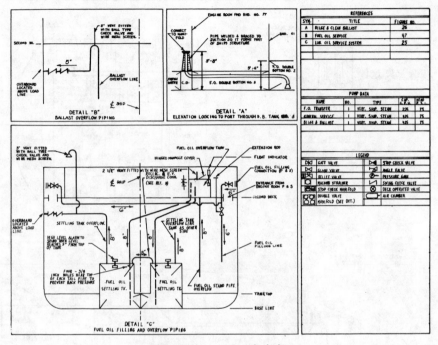

Figure 100. (*Concluded*)

3. Fuel oil tanks can be ballasted by sea water by gravity flooding or by means of the ship's pumps.

Normally fuel oil is transferred once each day at sea and once every two or three days in port to the settling tanks. In the operation of the system sea water is inevitably mixed to a greater or less degree with the oil. Most of this water can be removed in the settlers with careful operation by the engineers. However, deck officers should realize the troubles entailed by the ballasting of fuel oil tanks with sea water and should not request such ballasting unless necessary due to requirements of trim, stability or immersion. On the other hand, engine officers should cooperate with deck officers in maintaining the ship in the best possible condition of seaworthiness.

Sometimes deep tanks are designed to carry fuel oil or dry cargo. In this case the tanks are filled and discharged through the bilge wells in the tanks and means are provided for blanking off the bilge system when oil is carried and the fuel oil system when dry cargo is carried. When oil is carried the strainers in the bilge well should be removed. Of course extreme care must be taken when dry cargo is carried to see that the fuel oil system is blanked off.

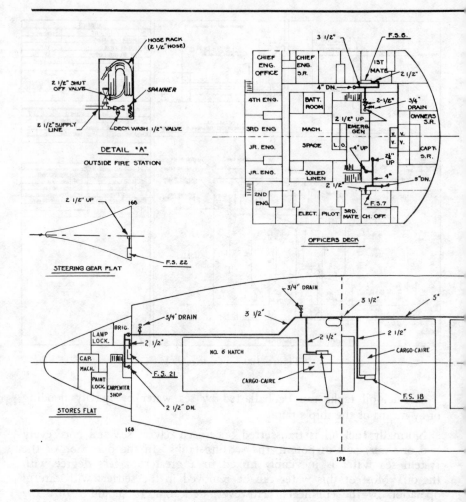

Figure 101. Fire System on Decks

ABS Rules Regarding Vent Pipes for Oil Tanks:

1. Tanks having a comparatively small surface, such as fuel oil settling tanks, need be fitted with only one vent pipe, while tanks having a comparatively large surface should be fitted with at least two vent pipes, one of which should be located at the highest part of the tank.

2. The diameter of each vent pipe should not be less than 2½ inches.

3. Where tanks are to be filled by pump pressure the aggregate area of the vents in the tank should be at least equal to the area of the filling line (unless other overflows are provided).

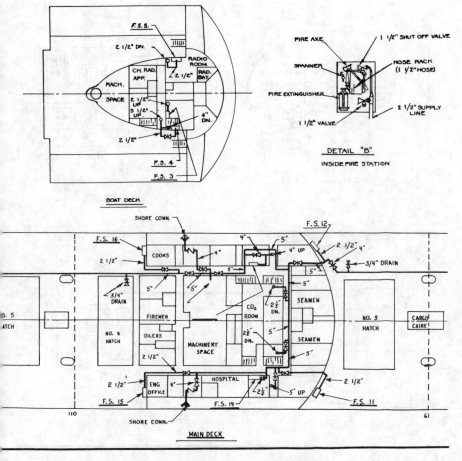

Figure 101. (*Continued on next page*)

4. All vent and overflow pipes should terminate by way of return bends (U bends); the height from the deck to the opening is to be at least 36 inches in wells on freeboard decks, and 18 inches on superstructure decks. Vent outlets should be fitted with corrosion-resistant wire gauze. Satisfactory means are to be provided for closing the opening of vent pipes in an emergency.

5. Vent pipes shall be led as direct as possible and the inclination in all cases shall not be less than 30° from the horizontal except where both ends are adequately drained to a tank.

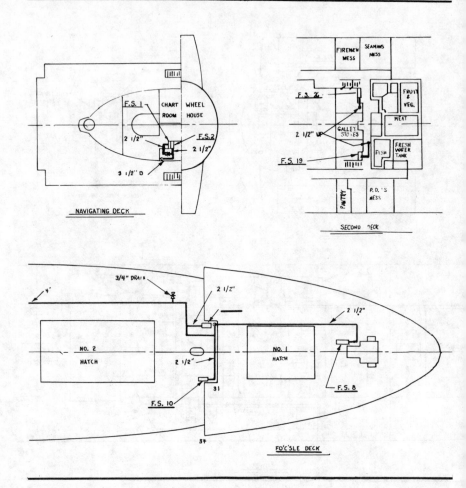

Figure 101. (*Concluded*)

Sounding pipes not less than 1½ inches in diameter shall be fitted to all tanks and hold compartments which are not at all times accessible. The pipes shall lead from within 2 inches of bottom of tank to the bulkhead deck, or other position always accessible. Where sounding pipes terminate below the bulkhead deck, they must be provided with a valve at the top. The upper end of sounding pipes terminating at a deck must be protected by a screw cap or plug. *Striking plates* must be provided under the sounding pipes to protect the hull plating from damage.

The Fire System: In this system, fire stations scattered strategically throughout the vessel are connected to the fire main in the machinery space and provided with sea water at a pressure of about 125 psi. Shore connections are usually provided on both sides of the upper deck for use by shoreside forces when the ship's pumps cannot be used.

Fire systems are arranged so that damaged sections or branches exposed to freezing conditions may be isolated for repairs or draining without shutting down the entire system. It is extremely important that outside lines liable to freeze be isolated and drained to maintain the system in a condition of readiness.

The Sanitary System: All water closets on a vessel are connected to the sanitary main which provides sea water under some 40 or 50 pounds pressure. The sanitary water pump takes suction from the sea through a strainer and a sanitary compression tank and thence to the sanitary main.

Sanitary discharges below the bulkhead deck must have means for preventing water from passing inboard. Either an automatic non-return valve with positive means of closing from above the bulkhead deck must be provided for or, two automatic non-return valves without such means may be provided with one storm valve at the vessel's side associated with another automatic valve in an accessible position above the deepest load line.

No valve attached to the skin of a vessel may be made of cast iron.

Washing Water System: The washing water system usually utilizes several tanks located in the double bottom and less usually the peak tanks are used for the carriage of fresh washing water. Fresh water both washing and drinking may be supplied by the ship's evaporators or taken aboard from shoreside sources.

Fresh water systems must be entirely independent of all other piping systems; all blank flanges, by-passes and other connections to any other system are illegal; and engineers are liable to loss of their license if any of these Public Health laws are violated.

There are two systems for supplying fresh water to the various outlets around a vessel. One is a gravity system which is found mainly on older vessels and the second is a pressure system which almost all newer vessels have.

In the gravity system a water pump in the machinery space pumps water to a gravity tank located somewhere high in the superstructure. The pump is run intermittently to fill the gravity tank, thus saving fuel. However, ship's personnel are sometimes inconvenienced when the tank is emptied. It is then necessary to notify the engine room to pump up the gravity tank. It is necessary to take freezing precautions in the winter time. The gravity tank is drained and by-passed and fresh water is supplied under pressure to the outlets.

In the pressure system a pressure tank is located in the machinery space. This tank is filled with compressed air in its upper portion and water in its lower portion. As water is pumped into the tank the air is further compressed until a set pressure is reached when the pump stops. This compression maintains pressure on the system until a minimum point is reached when the pump is then started again.

Hot water is supplied for this system via a storage type hot water heater and usually operates automatically under the control of a thermostatic valve.

The conservation of fresh water aboard ship is important for several reasons. First, if too much water is consumed the evaporators might not be able to maintain the supply and some sort of rationing will be necessary. Secondly, the evaporation of water (or the purchase of shoreside water) is expensive. For these reasons, faucets and taps aboard ship are usually self-closing to save water.

Drinking Water System: The drinking water (potable water) tank is usually located on the second deck in the interior of the ship. No drinking water tank may have a side common to the side of the ship due to danger of contamination by leakage. Drinking water is supplied to this system by a compression tank similar to the one in the washing water system (but smaller). The tank is fitted with deck filling connections located port and starboard and it may also be filled with distilled water from the evaporators.

Drinking and washing water systems are often combined.

Fresh water tanks should be cleaned and sterilized at least once a year. The procedure is usually as follows:

The tank is painted with a thin coating of cement. It is then sterilized by adding one pound of hypochlorite of lime to every 5000 gallons, circulating this water through the system, and then allowing the mixture to remain in the tank for 24 hours. The tank is then thoroughly rinsed until the chlorine taste is gone. If there is any doubt about the purity of the water in the tank, one tablespoon of tincture of iodine may be added to each 50 gallons of water.

Miscellaneous Piping Systems: There are several other piping systems on modern vessels in addition to the ones described above. However a description of these is beyond the scope of this text. Such systems as the auxiliary steam system and the ship's service compressed air system, however, should be traced out by the deck officer as well as the engineer officer; he should know the leads of all such lines, the location of and the operation of valves and outlets for these leads.

QUESTIONS

1. Draw a profile plan of a modern dry-cargo vessel showing and labeling all tanks. Under the name of the tank, indicate the type or types of liquid carried.
2. What ships' tanks are particularly important from the point of view of trim? from the point of view of stability?
3. Explain in detail the drainage system of a modern dry-cargo vessel with reference to:
   a) How all compartments and tanks drain to the bilges.

    b) The construction and operation of the bilge.

    c) How the bilges are connected to the pumps.

4. Compare a side bilge with a drain well installation. What are the advantages and disadvantages of each?

5. Define:
    a) Eductor
    b) Strum box
    c) Reach rod
    d) Mud box
    e) Bilge injection valve.

6. A ship is in collision and the entire side of #3 compartment is opened up. Explain what precaution should be taken in connection with the bilge and ballast lines leading forward.

7. What special emergency provisions for pumping out the machinery space are required for merchant vessels?

8. In the following loading situations involving a deep tank what provisions must be made in regard to the drain well? The deep tank is loaded with:
    a) Cargo oil
    b) Fuel oil
    c) Dry cargo
    d) Salt water ballast.

9. In regard to ABS Rules concerning pumping arrangements:
    a) How many power pumps must be connected to the bilge main?
    b) What is the character of the emergency pump required for passenger vessels?
    c) What is the minimum diameter of the bilge main? of branch piping?

10. What special precautions are required in regard to the ballast line leading through the forward collision bulkhead?

11. Seaworthiness of merchant vessels is often impaired by not fully utilizing the ballasting provisions provided by the designer. Discuss the problems involved.

12. What venting provisions are required for fuel oil tanks? In regard to:
    a) Number of vent pipes
    b) Aggregate area of vent pipes
    c) Construction of pipes above deck.

13. Explain how pressure is maintained at the washing water outlets in the gravity system and in the compression tank system.

14. How is a fresh water tank cleaned and sterilized?

BIBLIOGRAPHY

Walton & Baird, *Steel Ships, Their Construction and Maintenance,* Charles Griffin and Company Limited, London, 1944.

The following ships' plans:
    Piping Plan
    Capacity Plan
    Deck Plans

Information concerning piping can also be obtained from the Specifications for the Construction of ships.

Chapter 10

TURNING AND STEERING

Most mariners know in a general way the effects on a vessel when its rudder is put over; that is, they realize that an alteration of course and a reduction of speed occur; but very few understand in detail the many interesting and frequently practical reactions following a displacement of the rudder.

Let us first consider the kinematics of a vessel in a turn; that is, consider the motions of the vessel without reference to the forces which are causing them. Much of this subject is commonly included in a diagram of the turning circle. (Fig. 102)

The Turning Circle: Consider a vessel proceeding on a given course when the rudder is put to a given angle. The turning circle shows the path traversed by the center of gravity of the vessel. (G) It can be seen that the vessel undergoes a broadside movement *away* from the center of turning, in addition to the motion of rotation or change of heading. This gives the turning circle an "S" shaped path initially. The vessel then steadies down to a uniform motion around a circle with a motionless center. The distance that G moves on the original course from the time that the rudder is put over until the heading has been altered 90 degrees is called the *advance*. The distance that G moves in a direction at right angles to the original course in the same time is called the *transfer*. And the distance that G moves in a direction at right angles to the original course when the heading has been altered 180 degrees is called the tactical diameter. After the vessel has achieved true circular motion, the term *diameter of the turning circle* assumes significance. As the vessel turns in the circle its bow lies inside of the path which its center of gravity traverses and its stern lies outside of this path. The angle intercepted by the centerline of the vessel and a tangent to the turning circle at G is called the *drift angle.*

To an observer aboard ship during a turn, the vessel appears to pivot about a point which is well forward. This *pivoting point* is located approximately one-sixth of the length of the ship from the bow. The pivoting point can be located on a diagram of the turning circle by constructing a perpendicular from the center of the circle to the centerline of the ship. Let us consider the reason for this interesting fact: The instantaneous velocity of any point in a vessel making a turn is directed along the tangent to the circle at that point. Only at the pivoting point does this tangent correspond or lie parallel to the centerline. At all points

200

aft, the tangential force may be divided into two components with one component directed perpendicular to and *away* from the centerline; at all points forward, the tangential force may be divided into two components with one component directed perpendicular to and away (in the opposite direction from the after velocity component) from the centerline. (See Fig. 103)

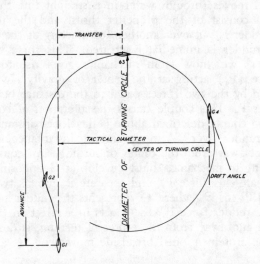

Figure 102. The Turning Circle

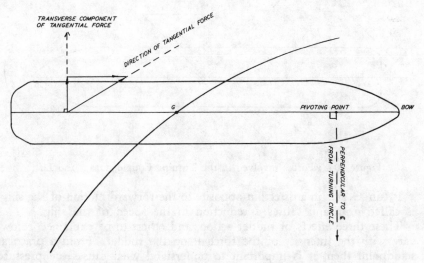

Figure 103. The Location of the Pivoting Point

In addition to these motions described above the vessel may heel to starboard or port. The reasons for heeling will be described below. Another motion, a change of trim may also occur, but since this reaction is negligible in large vessels, no explanation for this will be offered here.

It is now time to consider the *kinetics of steering;* that is, the motions related to the forces which cause them.

As a vessel moves through water in a straight line the forces acting on the vessel consist of the propeller thrust and the resisting forces. When the rudder is put over another force acting at the center of pressure of the rudder is immediately created. This force which we shall designate P, as we know from mechanics gives rise to an equal and opposite force (P_1) acting at the center of gravity. We now have a couple formed by the two forces equal to the distance between the lines of force times P. This couple causes the alteration of course.

The turning couple described above is developed instantaneously upon putting the rudder over. Also developing instantaneously is a broadside movement away from the center of turning. An equal and opposite force, according to mechanics, must develop at G opposing the force P_1. Let us designate this force P_2, and separate it into its two components: $P_2 \sin \Theta$ and $P_2 \cos \Theta$, where Θ represents the rudder angle. The component of the rudder force $P_2 \cos \Theta$ acts in a direction perpendicular to the centerline and away from the center of turning, is designated as *lift,* and causes the aforementioned broadside movement. (See Fig. 104)

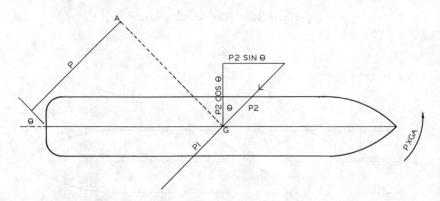

Figure 104. Forces involved in the Turning Couple; Drag, and Lift.

$P_2 \sin \Theta$ acts in a direction opposite to the forward motion of the ship, is called *drag* and causes a reduction in the speed of the ship.

These three effects of rudder action, and others to be explained below, vary with the intensity of the force P on the rudder. From a practical standpoint then, it is important to understand what causes the pressure on the rudder:

Pressure on the rudder varies: (1) as the *square* of the speed (2) directly with the angle of the rudder and (3) directly with the area of the rudder.

After the vessel has started to turn, a series of changes in the pressure distribution around the vessel's hull take place. (See Figure 105). As the result of the ship's rotation there is an increase in pressure on that side of the fore body nearest the center of turn and a decrease in pressure on the same side aft; while as a result of the forward motion of the ship, pressure has increased all along the opposite side. The pressure is no longer, in other words, balanced on either side of the centerline and the resultant of all pressure no longer is directed aft along the centerline but at an angle to the centerline, and at an unknown point (O) along the length of the vessel. This resultant force (which we will designate R) gives rise to an equal and opposite force R_1 acting at G. The couple formed by these two forces will aid the turning motion when 0 lies forward of

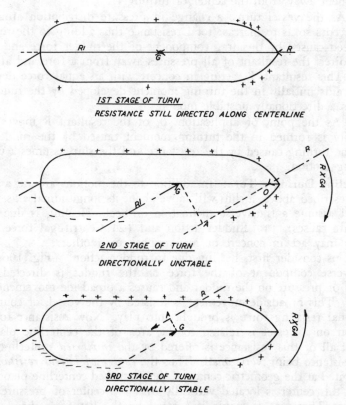

Figure 105. The Development of Uniform Turning Motion: When the moment "R x GA" is equal to the moment "P x GA" (See Figure 104), the forces tending to alter the vessel's heading are in equilibrium.

G and resist it when 0 lies aft of G. When the former is true a vessel is said to be *directionally unstable* and when the latter is true, *directionally stable*. Most vessels are directionally unstable at the beginning of a turn; that is, they tend to continue to rotate after the rudder is put amidships; however, after the ship has settled down to a uniform turning motion the moment of resistance must be equal to the turning moment of the rudder force. Therefore, the point 0 at which the pressure or resistance is applied must move aft of G until this equality of moments is achieved.

To recapitulate: The forces acting on a vessel during a turn may be divided into three stages.

1. The rudder force comes into play immediately upon the rudder being laid over. This rudder force acting in concert with an equal force developed at G causes a turning moment to be developed, while the thwartships component of the rudder force (lift) causes a broadside movement away from the center of turning.

2. As the vessel turns, a change in pressure distribution around the hull occurs so as to increase total resistance thus adding to the reduction in speed caused by the drag component of the rudder force and also so as to direct the resultant of all pressures away from a fore and aft direction. This resultant, R, acting in concert with an equal force developed at G, aids initially in the turning moment developed by the rudder and creates a directionally unstable motion.

3. As the point of application, 0, of the resultant R moves aft an equality is formed in the turning moment caused by the rudder force and the turning caused by the resistance and the ship assumes a uniform turning motion.

Heeling During a Turn: In addition to the motions around a vertical axis described above, a ship will move about its longitudinal axis; that is, it will assume a transverse inclination or heel. Heeling is due to two separate causes: (1) Rudder action and (2) Centrifugal force. These forces may act in concert or may oppose each other.

Let us consider first, heeling due to rudder action. (Fig. 106). The transverse component of the force on the rudder is directed at the center of pressure on the rudder and causes a broadside movement of the vessel. This broadside movement is resisted by the vessel, of course, and an equal resisting force is brought into play. Now resistance to lateral motion on a vessel is related to the area of the centerline plane and almost all of this resistance is offered by the *immersed* centerline plane, air resistance being very small. Thus the *center of lateral resistance* will be located at the geometric center of the immersed centerline plane. Generally this center is located vertically over the center of pressure on the rudder. Therefore a couple is formed by the lift force directed away from the center of turn, and the equal resisting force directed toward the center of turn, and the vessel will heel inwards until the heeling

moment is equal to the righting moment of the ship. The less the stability of the vessel, the greater the heel caused by this rudder action.
Of course, if the center of lateral resistance is vertically below the center
of pressure on the rudder, the heel will be outwards; and if, these two
points have the same vertical height, there will be no heel.

It can be seen that the heeling characteristics of a vessel can be changed
by arranging a given rudder area in different ways. For example, by
disposing the rudder area so as to create a long, narrow form the
center of pressure is raised.

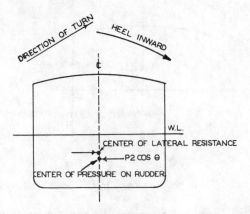

Figure 106.   The Development of Heel Due to Rudder Action.

Now let us consider heeling due to centrifugal force. (Fig. 107).
Centrifugal force acts through the center of gravity of the vessel and
in a direction opposite to the center of turn. As always a resisting force
must develop and since centrifugal force tends to push the vessel out
laterally, the resistance is concentrated at the center of lateral resistance.
These two equal forces acting in opposite directions create a heeling
moment or couple which will heel the vessel inwards or outwards
depending upon the vertical positions of G and the center of lateral
resistance. If G is above the center of lateral resistance, as it usually is
on a merchant ship, the vessel will heel outwards; if below, the vessel
will heel inwards.

Now, heeling due to rudder action occurs immediately upon laying
over the rudder; heeling due to centrifugal force occurs only after the
vessel has achieved a steady turning motion. Thus a merchant vessel
will usually heel inwards as soon as the rudder is put over, but as the
centrifugal force is applied, the heel will change until the vessel is
heeling outwards, since centrifugal force is usually greater than the rudder
action. A dangerous situation may develop if a vessel in a tender condition makes a sharp turn at high speed since the large heeling movement
due to centrifugal force is opposed by an equal righting moment only

after the vessel has assumed a large heel. This situation can be aggravated if, in alarm at the large heel, the mariner suddenly lays over the
rudder to the opposite side, since the heeling effect due to rudder action
which had been a steadying effect will now be acting to heel the vessel
to the same side to which she is already heeled. Vessels, principally small
vessels, may capsize after such a maneuver.

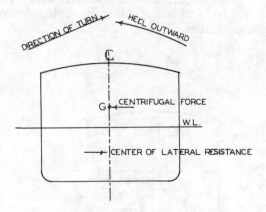

Figure 107.   The Development of Heel Due to Centrifugal Force.

Factors Which Influence Steering: In addition to those factors given
above, the following factors influencing steering may also be mentioned:

1. *Direction of the sea:* Steering in heavy weather is, of course, always
difficult, but with following seas the condition is aggravated. This difficulty may be traced to the fact that when waves are moving with the
vessel their impact upon the stern will be of longer duration than when
the waves are moving in a direction opposite to that of the vessel.

2. *Amount of deadwood:* Deadwood may be defined as the vertical
or nearly vertical surfaces of the hull at the stern. "Cutting away the
deadwood" would mean the redesign of stern hull form so as to make the
stern V-shaped. A large amount of deadwood at the stern will increase
the directional stability of a vessel and decrease the tendency of a vessel
to yaw in a heavy sea. This increase in directional stability is due to the
increased resistance offered by the relatively flat stern as it swings in a
turn. Cutting away the deadwood decreases this resistance and makes
it possible to reduce the tactical diameter of the vessel. Thus the amount
of deadwood provided at the stern must be a compromise between achieving a vessel which is steadier on her course and a vessel with a smaller
turning circle. With vessels like destroyers where maneuverability is an
important factor of design, cutting away of deadwood is marked.

3. *Direction of rotation of the propeller:* The ultimate effect on steering of propeller action is compounded of several individual effects. First,

assuming a right-handed propeller, the blades when making the lower half of their swing will, to put it in an untechnical sense, get a better "bite" and thus cause the stern to swing to starboard and the bow to port. This is especially true when a vessel is just starting from rest, and even more true if part of the screw is out of the water. Next, when a vessel is underway, the propeller is operating in the wake current, a current which moves in the same direction as the ship. The wake current is usually stronger at the surface,[1] and the propeller blades operating in the wake current have a tendency to push the stern to port and the bow to starboard. Finally, the propeller imparts a rotary motion to the propeller race which causes the race to strike the rudder at a small angle; i.e., from port to starboard in the upper half of the race, and from starboard to port in the lower half of the race. Since rudders are not usually symmetrical about their vertical center, a steering bias results.

Generally speaking, merchant vessels with right-handed screws carry a little right rudder to keep a straight course. Different effects, of course result with left-handed screws or twin-screw ships.

4. *Constriction of flow around hull:* When a vessel is operating in narrow channels, close to shoal water, or passing close to other vessels; in short, wherever a constriction of flow around the hull occurs, steering is effected. The reason lies in the increased velocity of constricted water and the consequent pressure changes. The theory behind this will be explained more fully in the section on resistance. For the present let it suffice to state that unsymmetrical pressure changes cause the bow to sheer away from the bank in a narrow channel and as mariners say, to "smell" shoal water. A knowledge of this phenomenon can be very helpful to the mariner. For example, let us say we are proceeding up a river in fog. If the vessel gets too close to the bank on either side the bow will tend to sheer away. The quartermaster will be made aware of this tendency by the necessity of carrying additional rudder and the vessel can then be directed away from the bank.

5. *Effectiveness of the rudder:* The effectiveness of the rudder is related to its size, its type, its position and the time required to put it over. These factors will now be considered.

Rudders and Their Characteristics

Rudders may be characterized by their area, aspect ratio, and shape. They may be of the single plate or of double-plate construction; they may be balanced, semi-balanced, or unbalanced; and they may have special features such as the contra-guide construction. Let us consider each of these characteristics in turn.

Rudder Area: In general, it may be stated that vessels requiring unusual maneuvering ability require larger rudders. The rudder area is usually

---

[1] See Chapter 16.

expressed as the ratio of rudder area to the product of length and draft (or to the area of the immersed centerline plane). A usual ratio for a cargo ship is about 0.015, while (to illustrate the need for larger rudders on some vessels) a usual ratio for a tugboat would be about 0.03 or 0.04.

Aspect Ratio: This ratio may be defined as the ratio of the "height" of the rudder to its "width". (Ratio of dimension across the flow when the rudder amidships to dimension in the direction of flow.) Pressure on a rudder is created by an increase in pressure on the upstream side of the rudder accompanied by a decrease in pressure on the downstream side. As the rudder turns, however, a "critical" angle is reached where eddying on the downstream side reduces the difference in pressure on the two rudder sides and thus the effectiveness of the rudder force. Now, the aspect ratio of a rudder affects this "critical" angle. Although the effects are complicated, it may be said that in general, the greater the aspect ratio the smaller the critical angle. However, the aspect ratio cannot be reduced indiscriminately since the initial force on the rudder before the critical angle is reached is greater for rudders of greater aspect ratio.

Shape of rudder: It has been found that, exclusive of aspect ratio, the shape of the rudder has little to do with its effectiveness. That is, the rudder may be rectangular or not without effecting efficiency.

Single Plate and Double Plate Rudders: (See Figures 108 and 109). Modern rudder design takes full advantage of the knowledge gained in the last several decades in regard to the reduction of resistance of stream-lined or airfoil shapes. Thus most rudders today are of double-plate construction with "teardrop" form. The maximum thickness of these rudders usually is found about 1/3 of the length from the leading edge. Another advantage of airfoil construction, better balancing character-istics, will be discussed below.

Double-plate construction, however, brings up a problem of water-tightness, since it is not desirable to have the inside of the rudder filled with water both from maintenance and weight viewpoints. Sometimes the inside is filled with a light wood to take care of this situation. However, with modern welded construction, the rudder can be made watertight. To aid in maintaining the inaccessible interior, the rudder is filled with a bitumastic material and then drained. Drain holes are provided for draining and testing when in drydock.

Balancing of Rudders: In order to turn the rudder the steering engine must exert a force equal to the couple formed by the pressure on the rudder acting through the distance from the turning axis to the center of pressure. If the turning axis were located at the center of pressure, the rudder could be turned with only that effort necessary to overcome friction. Unfortunately, the center of pressure shifts as the rudder is turned, moving from a point close to the leading edge of the rudder until, at a large angle of rudder it may be some 35 or 40 percent of the

Todd Shipyards, Corp.

Figure 108. Outmoded Single Plate Rudder. Notice *coupling* of rudder to *rudder stock; rudder arms;* connection by *pintles and gudgeons* to *stern frame.*

Cadet-Midshipmen R. W. Bullick and J. E. Hundt, Class of 1951,
U.S. Merchant Marine Academy

Figure 109. Double plate rudder.

length from the leading edge. Therefore, no rudder can be fully balanced for all rudder angles. A *balanced rudder,* so called, is commonly balanced for a rudder angle of about 15 degrees. This puts the rudder *stock* about one-quarter of the length from the leading edge. It should be observed that a full stern frame is not used when a balanced rudder is employed. The rudder post is not necessary.

U.S. Maritime Commission

Figure 110. Balanced, contra-guide rudder on a Liberty Ship

Now, a streamlined rudder lends itself to balancing better than a single plate rudder because the center of pressure does not shift as much and therefore reduces the force required to turn the rudder at angles other the 15 degrees mentioned above.

The term *semi-balanced rudder* is applied to the type of rudder commonly employed on a twin-screw vessel where most of the rudder is hinged on a body post by pintles and gudgeons, but a small portion of the rudder projects forward and under the body post. (See figure 111).

An *unbalanced rudder* or hinged rudder is attached to the rudder post of the stern frame and pivots around pintles and gudgeons. (See figure 112).

Sometimes a rudder is hung under the stern and is partially balanced. These types are called *spade rudders*.

U.S. Maritime Commission

Figure 111.   Semi-balanced Rudder

The Contra-Guide Rudder: The contra-guide rudder employs two sections, upper and lower, which are offset somewhat, one to starboard and one to port; thus the propeller race impinging on the offsets creates a force which may be divided into two components. One of these is a forward-acting component which, although small, is significant enough in terms of ship speed to make the construction of the rudder worthwhile. To aid in directing the flow of water around the rudder against the offsets in as efficient a manner as possible, the propeller post (the forward post of the stern frame) is sometimes offset too, but in a direction opposite to that of the rudder offset. For example, if the upper section of the rudder is offset to starboard, the upper section of the propeller post is offset to port. Contra-guide construction also helps to "straighten" out the propeller race and thus increase thrust.

Figure 112.   Unbalanced contraguide rudder.

QUESTIONS

1. Define:
   a) Advance
   b) Transfer
   c) Drift angle
   d) Tactical diameter
   e) Diameter of turning circle
   f) Pivoting point
2. The progress of what point in a ship is shown on a diagram of a turning circle?
3. Given a turning circle and the drift angle of a vessel traversing the circle, how can the pivoting point of the vessel be located? Explain why?
4. Differentiate between kinematics and kinetics of steering.
5. Explain why the force on a rudder causes:
   a) the development of a turning moment
   b) the development of a broadside movement away from the center of turn
   c) the development of "drag" reducing the vessel's speed
6. What is the most important component of pressure on the rudder?
7. Given a certain rudder area, explain how the shape of the rudder can alter the vessel's heeling characteristics.

8. Explain how a change in rudder area affects the vessel's turning moment, broadside movement, loss of speed, and heeling characteristics.

9. How does the extent and direction of a ship's resistance change when the vessel is in a turning circle?

10. A ship has assumed a uniform turning motion. Explain the equilibrium which exists among forces acting about the ship's longitudinal axis and the equilibrium which exists among the forces acting about the ship's vertical axis.

11. What is the relationship of the vertical positions of the center of lateral resistance and the center of rudder pressure when, due to rudder action, a ship:
    a) heels inward
    b) heels outward
    c) does not heel

12. What is the relationship of the vertical positions of the center of gravity and the center of lateral resistance when, due to centrifugal force, a ship:
    a) heels inward
    b) heels outward
    c) does not heel

13. Explain clearly how the heel caused by rudder action and centrifugal force is limited by the righting moment of the vessel, i.e., by the stability.

14. How is the hull form aft affected by maneuvering and steering requirements?

15. What are the three elements of propeller action which cause steering bias?

16. Two vessels are moving in a narrow channel, one up the channel, the other down. As the vessels pass each other close aboard, analyze the steering orders which might best be given in order to avoid the possibility of colliding. When:
    a) Bow is abreast of bow
    b) Ship is abreast of ship
    c) Stern is abreast of stern

17. How is rudder area expressed? How is the area of the rudder varied with maneuvering ability requirements?

18. With a given rudder area, the aspect ratio is made large. How does this affect the force on the rudder at small angles? How does it affect the "critical" angle?

19. Why are modern rudders generally of double-plate, streamlined construction?

20. How is the problem of watertightness and maintenance overcome in a modern double-plate rudder?

21. Define:
    a) Balanced rudder
    b) Semi-balanced rudder
    c) Unbalanced rudder
    d) Spade rudder
    e) Contra-guide rudder

22. Why are rudders sometimes "balanced"? What effect does the streamlined double-plate type of rudder have on the ease of balancing? Why?

BIBLIOGRAPHY

Rossell & Chapman, *Principles of Naval Architecture,* Vol. II, Society of Naval Architects and Marine Engineers, New York, 1942.

Davidson and Schiff, "Turning and Course-Keeping Qualities", *Transactions of the Society of Naval Architects and Marine Engineers,* Vol. 54, 1946.

Davidson, K. S. M., "On the Turning and Steering of Ships", *Transactions of the Society of Naval Architects and Marine Engineers,* Vol. 52, 1944.

Plummer, C. J., *Ship Handling in Narrow Channels,* Cornell Maritime Press, New York, 1945.

Pehrsson & Mende, *Design, Model Testing and Application of CP Bow Thrusters,* SNAME New York Section, Sept., 1960.

Gertler & Gover, *Handling Criteria for Surface Ships,* SNAME Chesapeake Section, May, 1959.

Chapter 11

LAUNCHING

A study of launching, although not directly associated with the objectives of this text, depicts an event so colorful and exciting that it is difficult to refrain from giving at least in outline form some account of this climax of ship construction. Too, the requirements of the launch have much to do with the way ships are built; the site of the shipyard and its slipways depend upon their relationship to launching; the incline on which a ship must be built (usually) complicates the techniques of ship erection. Previous to the launch the ship is just a hull number; after the launch it acquires a name, a personality if you will; it becomes a living, vital thing.

Consider for a moment the task which confronts the ship builder: Thousands upon thousands of tons of weight must be transferred from the shore to the water. The weight must be transferred quickly and safely. There can be no guess work or miscalculation or the consequences can be disastrous. Here, surely, is a subject which cannot fail to excite the interest and imagination of all who are concerned with ships.

Briefly, the task of launching a ship consists of shifting the weight of the ship from the supports of keel blocks, shores, and cribbing needed while construction proceeded, to a launching *cradle* which has been built up under the ship. The cradle, when released, then slides down ways extending into the water.

The problems associated with launching which will be considered are:

1. Declivity angles of ground, keel, and ways.
2. Construction of the launching ways.
3. Construction of the launching cradle.
4. Launching calculations.
5. Description of the launch.
6. Removal of the launching cradle.
7. Side launching.

Declivity Angles of Ground, Keel, and Ways

A ship must be constructed on an incline so that, when released, it can slide down launching ways into the water. Now, the angle of inclination or declivity angle of the ways must be somewhere around 0.5 to 0.7 inch per foot of length (depending on the size of the ship) in order to make this possible. It is apparent that the ground (the floor of the building slip) should be inclined so that the bow of the ship will not

215

rise to an excessive height above the ground. For example, if the ground were not inclined, the declivity angle of a 500 ft. keel being 0.7 and the keel at stern being 5 feet above the ground, then the keel at bow would be 34.2 feet above the ground. ($0.7 \times 500 = 350''$). Such a height would require an obviously excessive height of keel blocks, shoring and staging. Therefore it is customary for the ground to have a declivity of some $\frac{3}{8}$ in. or more to the foot.

The main support for the ship during construction consists of a line

Figure 113. The color and excitement of a launch is clearly seen here at the launching of the first Victory ship at the Oregon Shipbuilding Corp. Yard on January 12, 1944.

of keel blocks. The selection of a declivity angle for these blocks is a complicated and important task. The declivity angle of the keel blocks must be greater than that of the ground and usually varies from about 0.4 inch per foot to about 0.6 inch per foot. Various factors must be considered in arriving at the exact declivity angle of the keel blocks. First, the height of the keel blocks must be such as to give adequate head room and working conditions under the ship at all points along its length. Yet the declivity angle of the keel must not be too great or the bow will be too high. The distance between the keel and the launching ways must not be too great since the ways must be built close to the ground. Also, if this distance is too great, the extent of the distance which the bow will drop when it leaves the ways will be too great.

Finally, the declivity of the launching ways must be decided on. This question will be discussed more in detail below, but for the present it may be stated that the declivity should be sufficient to overcome the friction of the launching cradle on the ways without putting too much force on the releasing device which holds the ship on the ways in the interval of time between transfer of ship weight to the launching cradle and the release. If the declivity of the ways is too steep, it increases the problem of checking the run of the ship when it slides into the water. The type of ship has much to do with the declivity of the ways as indicated above. Generally, the larger the ship, the smaller the declivity selected.

To recapitulate: The building slip is constructed with a declivity, say, of 0.5 inch to the foot. The ship is constructed on keel blocks which have a steeper incline, say a declivity of 0.6 to the foot. Finally, when ready for launching, the ship is transferred from the keel blocks to launching ways with a still steeper incline, say a declivity of 0.7 inch to the foot. The height of the keel blocks will depend directly upon the required declivity of the ways.

Construction of the Launching Ways

Ships are launched by transfering the ship's weight from the keel blocks and other supports to a launching cradle which then slides down launching ways. These ways are known as *groundways*. In describing the construction of the groundways, the following points must be considered:

1. The number of ways.
2. The length and slope of the ways.
3. The spread and width of the ways.
4. Height of the ways.
5. Camber and cant of ways.
6. Description of the structure.
7. Launching lubricants.

Number of Ways: Almost all launchings are made with two groundways constructed equidistant from the keelblocks. This provides the necessary stability while on the ways and also gives sufficient bearing surface for the weight to be carried. In the Netherlands it is customary to launch vessels with the load concentrated on a centerline way with secondary ways outboard for stability.[1] Four ways were used to launch the gigantic *Iowa* class battleships built during the last war.

[1] Andrews, H. B., "Some Practical Aspects of Ship Launching", *Transactions of the Society of Naval Architects & Marine Engineers,* Vol. 54, 1946.

Length and Slope of the Ways: It is apparent that the groundways must be built out some way into the water. If the ways are not carried out far enough the vessel's stern is apt to drop as it reaches the ends of the ways and before the natural support provided by the buoyancy of the stern can prevent the vessel from tipping. On the other hand, extending the ways out a great distance under the water may not be feasible due to obstructions, and in any case, such construction is expensive and is difficult to maintain. Where there is a sufficient range of tide, the groundways are usually built out to the shore line at mean low water and the ship launched at high water. The state of the tide then becomes a matter of prime importance in launching calculations. It may be necessary to schedule the launching for the time of spring tides. It is customary to select a launching date when high water occurs about noon so that the necessary pre-launching tasks may be accomplished in the morning.

The importance of the slope of the groundways was mentioned above. The major factor determining the declivity angle of groundways is the frictional resistance of the launching lubricants. If the slope is too small, that component of the weight of the ship and cradle tending to force the ship down the ways may not be enough to overcome the friction of cradle against groundways. The coefficient of friction varies with the temperature, the pressure, and the type of launching lubricant used. The pressure, of course, depends upon the area of the ways exposed to the weight of the ship. Lubricants will be discussed below.

The Spread and Width of the Ways: The term "spread of the ways" relates to the distance between the two groundways. This spread will depend upon the breadth of the ship since the groundways are usually located about one-third the breadth of the ship apart. Thus for a ship with a beam of 60 feet, the ways would be located 10 feet from the centerline, with a spread of 20 feet.

The width of the ways depends primarily upon the pressure which will bear upon them. If the weight per square foot is too small, the ship may not be able to start, since the coefficient of friction is usually lowered by an increase in pressure. On the other hand, if the weight per square foot is too much, the lubricant can be squeezed out or burned, causing the ship to stick. Experience has dictated an average pressure somewhere between 2 and $2\frac{1}{2}$ tons of weight per square foot of groundway. This produces a width for most merchant ships of some two or three feet depending upon the weight.

Height of the Ways: As indicated above the groundways should not be built up to too great a height and the height and slope of the keel blocks are regulated with this in mind. Since the slope of the floor of the building slip is less than that of the ways usually, the ground ways will be higher at the bow than where they enter the water. The ways must be high enough so that when the ship enters the water and the stern is lifted by its buoyancy, the consequent pivoting of the ship at the bow will not cause the forefoot to strike the floor of the building slip. Therefore, the groundways are built up to a height of some two or three feet at the stern to a height of four or five feet at the bow.

Camber and Cant of the Ways: Groundways are sometimes given a longitudinal camber; that is, they are given a smaller declivity on the forward portion, and a steeper declivity on the after portion of the ways. The purpose of this camber is to reduce the distance which ways must be built out into the water. If the declivity is steeper at the outboard ends of the ways, more of the stern will be immersed as it enters the water and consequently more buoyancy will be achieved thus reducing the need for length of ways under water.

The tops of the groundways also may be given a slight inward cant. This decreases the possibility of the ship sliding transversely on the ways during the launching.

Groundway Structure: The groundways consist of blocks and timbers built up to the desired height and shored on their outboard sides to prevent capsizing when launching. (See Figure 114). The upper timber,

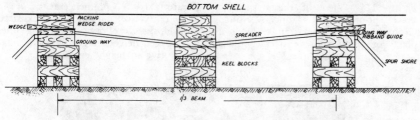

Figure 114. Structure of groundways, sliding ways, and keel blocks amidships.

upon which the launching lubricant will be spread, is carefully planed to a smooth finish. At the outboard edge of the top of the groundways a strip of wood called the ribband guide projects above the ways slightly and protects the lubricant after the timbers comprising the launching cradle are laid down on top of the groundways. It also helps to prevent the vessel from moving transversely on the ways while being launched.

Launching Lubricant: The lubrication which must be provided between groundways and cradle is applied in two coats. First, a *base coat* which must give a hard smooth surface is applied to the top of the groundways. *Grease irons,* which are small flat bars with the same thickness as the lubricant, are placed about 10 feet apart on the top of the groundways and the base coat applied between them. The grease irons prevent the lubricant from being squeezed out until the ship is ready for the launch. Just prior to the launch, they are removed. On top of the base coat, a *slip coat* is applied. The slip coat has the function of providing a lubri-

Maritime Reporter

U.S. Maritime Commission

Figure 115. View of the stern of a vessel prior to the launch. Notice: Groundways, ribband guide held in place by spur shores, after poppets, tricing lines.

Figure 116. Commencement of a launch. Notice: Groundways, capsized keel blocks, fore poppets, tricing lines to poppets, height of groundways, relative to height of workers.

American Export Lines

Figure 117. Launch of the S.S. Constitution. This is an excellent view of the size and complexity of the fore poppets necessary on a large passenger vessel.

U.S. Maritime Commission

Figure 118.   Fore end view—Vessel entering the water.

U.S. Maritime Commission

Figure 119.   Side view—Vessel entering water and about to pivot.

cant with a low coefficient of friction on top of the base coat, since
the base coat will not provide sufficient lubrication until its initial
resistance has been decreased by heat.

Launching lubricants today are generally commercially prepared mineral
base greases into which a great deal of careful research has been put,
although one hears now and again of such things as bananas being used
as launching lubrication.

U.S. Maritime Commission

Figure 120.   Using bananas as launching lubricant. Notice the size and number
of wedges used.

Construction of the Launching Cradle

The launching cradle consists of the *sliding ways, packing* timbers
built up from the sliding ways to the bottom plating, and fore and after
poppets. The sliding ways consist of timbers placed on top of the groundways. In between the sliding ways and the first layer of packing are
inserted wedges which are used to drive the packing up firmly against
the bottom plating and in the case of smaller ships, to lift the ship
off the keel blocks just prior to the launch. The first layer of packing
timber is called the *wedge rider*. (See Figure 114).

Forward and aft where the rise of the ship's bottom requires that the
cradle be built up to a rather large height, are located the poppets. The

poppets are constructed with vertical or nearly vertical timbers which are attached to the hull by brackets, tie rods, shores, and so on. The fore poppet is of particular importance since during the launch a good part of the ship's weight will be borne by this poppet when the ship pivots on its forefoot. The fore poppet must be constructed so that all of the pivoting pressure is not taken by the forward section of the poppet. One method of preventing this is to insert *crushing strips* of soft wood between horizontal layers of timbers built up under the vertical members of the poppet. These crushing strips are spaced farther apart at the forward end of the poppet. Thus when the pivoting pressure is thrown on the forward end of the poppet the strips will crush, gradually distributing the pressure evenly over the entire length of the poppet. Another method is to build into the poppet structure an arrangement something like the base of a rocking chair. This rocker-type fore poppet is fitted with steel rockers and the pivoting pressure is automatically equalized along the length of the poppet by a rocking movement.

Methods of securing the cradle to the ship vary. In some cases the sliding ways are joined by tie rods passing under the ship from one way to the other. Cables are usually attached to the sliding ways and led up on deck. These cables then hold the ways to the ship after launching. If the timbers comprising the launching cradle were free to shoot out from the ship when the latter is waterborne, damage to the hull may result. The extent to which the cradle is held together by lashings, bolts, etc., varies, and in some launchings some of the timbers in the cradle are free to float clear of the ship when launched.

The sliding ways usually extend about 80% of the ship's length.

Launching Calculations

It should be apparent from what has been stated above that launching a ship is an involved and highly technical matter. Arrangements can no longer be left solely in the hands of the shipbuilder. Very careful calculations must be made by the Naval Architect to ensure:

a. That the vessel will not tip about the ends of the ways and that way-end pressure will not cause structural damage to the bottom.

b. That the vessel will pivot on its fore poppet, but that the pivoting pressure will not be excessive.

c. That the vessel will possess transverse stability after launching. Ships have been known to slide down the ways and promptly capsize when waterborne.

Tipping and Pivoting: If the buoyancy of the stern as it slides into the water is not sufficient to lift the stern, the vessel will tip around the ends of the ways, an eventuality which cannot be tolerated as the way-end pressure would then be so excessive as to cause extensive damage to the ship's bottom. Therefore, as indicated above, the ways must be extended far enough out in the water to prevent this; or, sufficient camber must be given the ways; or the center of gravity of the ship must be brought far enough forward so that the moment of the ship's weight acting around the wayends is not greater than the moment of the ship's buoyancy around the wayends. (See Figure 121).

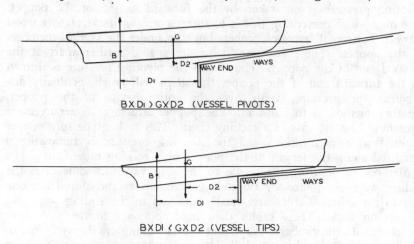

BXD₁ > GXD2 (VESSEL PIVOTS)

BXDI < GXD2 (VESSEL TIPS)

Figure 121. Launching calculations must ensure that the moment of the ship's buoyancy around the way ends must be greater than the moment of the ship's weight.

Now, as the stern lifts as it enters the water, all of the ship's weight which is not supported by the buoyancy of that portion of the vessel which is immersed, is thrown on the fore poppet and the vessel pivots on the poppet. One of the most important calculations is to ensure, first, that the vessel will pivot rather than tip, and second, that the pivoting pressure will not be excessive.

In order to investigate this problem, the Naval Architect must know at least approximately the longitudinal and vertical position of the ship's center of gravity when the ship is launched. Therefore a record of the weight and position of all members which are erected is kept as the ship is constructed and these data are used to calculate the position of G. The position of the center of buoyancy must also be known at every instant of the launch and since B is shifting constantly as an increasing portion of the ship's hull enters the water, these calculations must necessarily be extensive. A series of waterlines must be drawn and then by means of Bonjeans Curves (described in Chapter 13) the volume of displacement up to these waterlines can be calculated.

In Figure 121, the moment of the ship's buoyancy around the end of the ways (B × d), must always be greater than the moment of the ship's weight around the end of the ways (G $\times$ d') to prevent tipping. Ballasting of water tanks may be resorted to in order to shift the center of gravity to a point where the weight moment bears a proper relationship to the buoyancy moment. Another method of obtaining this relationship may be accomplished by attaching floats at the stern thus increasing the buoyancy moment.

U.S. Maritime Commission

Figure 122.   Use of a tank at the stern to increase buoyancy moment and ensure pivoting.

Whether or not a vessel will pivot depends upon the relationship of the moment of the weight of the ship acting around the fore poppet and the moment of the buoyancy of the ship acting around the same point. The latter moment is made greater than the former moment, so that the vessel will pivot. The pressure on the fore poppet while the vessel is pivoting is the difference between the total weight of the ship and buoyancy of the ship. This difference must be held to a minimum.

In many cases it is necessary to employ internal shoring, especially at the bow, to guard against excessive pressure on the ship's structure, either from way-end pressure or pivoting pressure.

Another calculation necessary is that for strength. Care must be taken not to launch the ship with a longitudinal weight distribution producing excessive bending and shearing moments, a situation which might occur with only part of the vessel's equipment and machinery installed. Also the pressures incident to the launch must be investigated to ensure an acceptable stress distribution along the hull girder.

Description of the Launch

A description of the launching of a ship includes the following items:

1. Pre-launching activities.
2. Releasing arrangements.
3. The problem of starting.
4. Checking arrangements.

Pre-Launching Activities: Several weeks before the date of the launch, the launching cradle is erected; the launching lubricants applied.

The extent to which the work of construction has been carried at the time of the launch varies, but usually about 80 or 85 percent of the total weight of the ship has been erected.

On the day of the launch, a thorough inspection of ways, cradle, and ship bottom is made. The outboard ends of the ways are lubricated after being thoroughly cleaned and dried. The underwater portion of the ways are checked to make sure that the ways are clear of all obstructions.

Checking arrangements, which will be described below, are completed.

Grease irons are removed and carefully accounted for.

The wedges between sliding ways and wedge riders are now driven in, in a series of rallies, thus driving the packing up firmly against the ship's bottom and taking some, if not all, of the weight of the ship off the keel blocks. All shores and cribbing is removed. The removal of the keel blocks is a difficult job since, in most cases, a tremendous weight still bears on the blocks. Various methods are used to remove the keel blocks. One method is to split the upper keel blocks; another method uses collapsible keel blocks filled with sand as the upper keel blocks. When the sides of the blocks are removed, the sand runs out.

After the keel blocks are collapsed, the weight of the ship has been transferred to the ways, and the ship is now ready to be launched, being held only by the releasing devices.

Releasing Arrangements:[1] One of the earliest and simplest releasing devices utilizes a few pieces of timber and rope lashing. A dog shore, or heavy beam, is laid at right angles to the ways on each side of the ship. A few feet out from the ways on the outboard side of the beam a pile is driven into the ground to act as a fulcrum. One end of the

---

[1] Information on releasing devices obtained from Andrews, H. B., *op. cit.*

beam is fitted against the sliding ways while at the other end rope lashings prevent the ship from moving until the lashings are cut.

A more customary method of release for ships of moderate weight is that which employs a steel *"sole plate"* at the forward end of each sliding way. These sole plates tie the sliding ways to the ground ways until the two plates are burned through simultaneously.

For larger ships, it is customary to use two or more hydraulic or mechanical *triggers*. The triggers operate through a series of levers, rams, and so on which can be released manually or electrically.

Starting Problems: The ship is christened by smashing a champagne bottle against the bow as the ship is released, and then usually, will start sliding down the ways immediately. However, it is possible that the ship may not start, in which case, a ram located under the launching platform can be brought into play to give the ship enough of a push to overcome inertia. There have been cases, however, where even more drastic methods have had to be used in order to start the ship and to keep it going.

Checking Arrangements:[1] The run of a ship after launching usually must be checked by one or more methods, although some building yards are situated so that a sufficient expanse of deep water is available and the kinetic energy of the ship can be dissipated entirely by the water resistance.

The simplest type of checking device utilizes a wooden mask secured at the stern at right angles to the centerline. This increases water resistance and reduces the distance the ship will travel. When the velocity of the ship has been sufficiently reduced, the ship's anchors may then be dropped.

Another more positive method employs rope stops. In this method, a series of chains with center sections of rope are secured to the ship and the shore. The rope lashings are so arranged that they will part one at a time, the ships speed being decreased each time the ropes part.

Still another method employs piles of chain made fast to the vessel with wire ropes. As the ship moves into the water the chains are dragged along the slipway.

Where the expanse of water available is very limited the ship may have to be *slewed*. Slewing methods involve the use of chain piles placed in the water and made fast to the stern by wire ropes. The piles are so located that when the ship is launched the stern will be slewed around by the resistance of the chains, thus diverting the vessel from its initial path.

Removal of the Cradle

After the launching, and before the ship can be taken to the outfitting pier, the launching cradle must be removed. Methods of accomplishing this vary. In some cases, the cradle is removed at the outfitting pier with

---

[1] See Andrews, H. B., *op. cit.*

divers releasing the underwater fastenings and cranes removing them. In other cases, the ship is put in a flooded drydock, the cradle is hauled to the bottom of the dock by means of tricing lines, and the ship is then removed from the dock. This method leaves the cradle essentially intact and ready for the launching of another ship. In still another method, the cradle is secured to the end of a pier and the ship is backed off the cradle.

U.S. Maritime Commission

Figure 123.   Checking the run of a vessel.

Side Launchings

In inland waterways where the expanse of water available is extremely limited, it is the practice to launch vessels sideways. One of the advantages of this type of launching is that the ship is built on an even keel.

In side launchings, two ways are obviously not sufficient; and the groundways are spaced some 10 to 15 feet apart for the entire length of the ship. Declivity angles must be greater, being about 1½ inches per foot.

A special problem associated with side launchings is the stability of the ship since the ship must take a severe heel when launched.

Figure 124.   Side Launching.

229

QUESTIONS

1. With reference to the declivity angles of launching ways, floor of the building slip, and keel blocks, explain the connection of the following factors:
   a) Working room under the vessel during construction.
   b) Starting and keeping the vessel moving down the ways.
   c) Height of keel blocks, cribbing, ways, etc., at the bow.
   d) Height of launching ways.
   e) Pivoting.
   f) Tipping.
   g) Drop of bow when ship leaves ways.
   h) Releasing.
   i) Checking.
   j) Size of ship.
2. What methods are used to prevent the vessel from sliding transversely on the ways during the launch?
3. Define:
   a) Spread of the ways.
   b) Pivoting.
   c) Tipping.
   d) Base coat and slip coat.
   e) Grease iron.
   f) Ribband guide.
   g) Poppets.
   h) Wedge rider.
   i) Sole plate.
4. Describe the construction of groundways with regard to:
   a) Spread.
   b) Length.
   c) Width.
   d) Height.
   e) Camber and cant.
5. Describe the construction of the launching cradle with regard to:
   a) Sliding ways.
   b) Packing timbers.
   c) Poppets.
6. Describe the method of distributing pivoting pressure on the fore poppet by the method involving:
   a) Crushing strips.
   b) Rockers.
7. Describe the following methods of ensuring that the moment of buoyancy around the way ends will be greater than the moment of ship's weight around way ends:
   a) Use of ballast.
   b) Use of floats at stern.
   c) Length of ways into water.
   d) Camber of ways.
8. What is the purpose of driving in wedges between sliding ways and wedge rider?

9. What methods are used to remove the top timbers of the keel blocks?
10. How are vessels customarily released at the start of the launch?
11. Describe the following methods of checking the run of a vessel after launching:
    a) Wooden mask at stern.
    b) Rope stops.
    c) Chain drags.
    d) Slewing.
12. How do side launchings differ from stern launchings?
13. Problem Illustrating Launching Calculations:

    A vessel as launched weighs 5000 tons, is 500 feet in length, and is launched on ways with a declivity of 5/8" to the foot. In the table data are given for six positions of the center of gravity of the ship from the way-ends, each position being 100 feet apart. The symbol I stands for inshore of way-ends; the symbol O for offshore of way-ends.

    The ways are built out into the water 250 feet. G is assumed to be amidships; fore poppet assumed 250 feet forward of G.

	1	2	3	4	5	6
Buoyancy in tons	500	1000	2000	3000	4000	5000
C.B. from way-ends, ft.	100I	50I	0.0	100-0	180-0	200-0
C.G. from way-ends, ft.	300I	200I	100I	0.0	100-0	200-0

1. What is the weight on the groundways at point 1?
2. What is the weight on the groundways at point 3?
3. At what point, if any, will the vessel tip? (If W x d' is greater than B x d, the vessel will tip)
4. Between what two points does ship start to pivot? (Pivoting starts when buoyancy moment *around fore poppet* is greater than weight moment around fore poppet)
5. What is the pressure on the fore poppet at point 5? at point 6?
6. Will the vessel "drop" off the way-ends or float off? How much shorter would the way-ends have to be for the vessel to "drop"?
7. If pivoting pressure is too high what can be done about it?
    a) Shift C.G. aft or forward?
    b) Lengthen or shorten ways?
    c) Increase or decrease declivity angle?
    d) Provide tanks at stern?
8. Answer questions 1-6 above if ways are shortened 50', 100', 150'.
    Note: Problem can be illustrated by drawing ways on board and using profile of vessel to show movement of G and B relative to way-ends.

BIBLIOGRAPHY

Andrews and Nickerson, "Some Practical Aspects of Ship Launching", *Transactions of the Society of Naval Architects and Marine Engineers*, Vol. 54, 1946.

Chantry, A., "Launching of U.S.S. 'New Jersey' and U.S.S. 'Wisconsin' ", *Transactions of the Society of Naval Architects and Marine Engineers,* Vol. 52, 1944.

Hancock, C., "The Equipment and Methods Used in Operating the Newport News Hydraulic Laboratory", *Transactions of the Society of Naval Architects and Marine Engineers,* Vol. 56, 1948.

Fahey, J. H., "Side-launching on the Great Lakes", *Transactions of the Society of Naval Architects and Marine Engineers,* Vol. 50, 1942.

Rossell & Chapman, *Principles of Naval Architecture,* Society of Naval Architects, and Marine Engineers, New York, 1942.

Walton & Baird, *Steel Ships, Their Construction and Maintenance,* Charles Griffin and Company, Limited, London, 1944.

Garyantes, H., *Handbook for Shipwrights,* McGraw-Hill Book Company, New York, 1944.

J. Surgenor, *Side Launching,* SNAME Pacific Northwest Section, May, 1955.

Chapter 12

DRYDOCKING

All large vessels must be drydocked intermittently, the interval between dockings varying with the circumstances. The operation of exposing the underwater portion of a large ship so that routine inspection, maintenance, and repair can be carried on, is very important and very expensive. The construction and maintenance of drydocking facilities represents a large fraction of the total investment of a ship repair yard. Therefore, every effort is made to keep to a minimum the time that a ship actually spends in the dock. Dockage fees are usually assessed on the basis of gross tonnage which is rather surprising when one considers the inability of registered tonnage to reflect either the size or weight of a vessel.[1]

Drydocking installations for large ships may consist of a *Graving Dock* or a *Floating Drydock*. The construction and operation of these types will be explained in detail below. Smaller vessels can also be brought out of the water by means of a *Marine Railway*. This installation consists of an inclined ramp fitted with rails, usually, on which a cradle or carriage can be moved by means of wire rope or chains led to a winch or other form of power. The cradle is run down the ramp into the water; the vessel is then positioned and secured to the cradle, and hauled up the ramp.

Of course, a ship's bottom can be exposed by beaching or *"careening"*, but in these days of huge ships and highly developed technology, this ancient method of "drydocking" is hardly desirable or feasible.

THE GRAVING DOCK [2]

Essentially, a graving dock is a large basin most of which lies below the water level at high tide. (See fig. 129). A tremendous excavation job, in addition to extensive piling and concrete work, is necessary and this type of dock is, therefore very expensive. For example, the Boston Commonwealth Dry Dock, constructed by the State of Massachusetts is 1204 feet in length, 147 feet in breadth at the top and 139 feet at the bottom; the walls are 56 feet high with draft over the sill of thirty-five feet at mean low water and forty-five feet at high tide; 380,000 yards of earth and 85,000 yards of rock had to be excavated; 115,000 yards of concrete

---

[1] The fees have, in the past, ranged from ten to twelve cents per ton.
[2] The term "graving" derives from the root *"grave"*, to carve. A dock carved out, hence a graving dock.

233

Cadet-Midshipman R. M. Marshall, Class of 1951, U.S. Merchant Marine Academy

Figure 125.   A 500 ton capacity Marine Railway

234

were used for walls and bottom.[1] Due to the costly nature of graving docks very few commercial yards can afford them and they are constructed mainly by the U. S. Navy.

The principle of the graving dock is very simple. The entrance to the dock is closed by a *caisson* or gate. The dock is then flooded by gravity, the caisson floated or swung away and the ship brought into the dock. After closing the entrance with the caisson, the dock is pumped out and the ship settles down on the blocks which have been prepared for it. (See figure 131)

The Caisson Gate: A caisson, as the derivation of the word would indicate, is essentially a box-like structure. It is, in effect, a separate vessel with keel, framing, and shell plating. Caissons are usually of the floating type but they may be hinged at one side and swung open or hinged at both sides and swung open like a lock gate. In earlier days of shipbuilding caissons were built exclusively of wood. Later, with the construction of larger docks, iron and finally steel has been used. Modern caissons are now all welded.

The floating type caisson is sunk by opening valves which admit the water. It is capable of self-pumping for raising.

When closing the dock entrance, the caisson gate is sunk onto the sill, a bar on the bottom and sides of the gate coming up against a strip of material, say, rubber, along the walls and sill of the entrance. Watertightness is maintained by the water pressure against the outside face of the caisson.

Some graving docks are built so that the caisson can be moved to different positions, thus lengthening or shortening the dock. Also, some graving docks can be divided into two separate chambers which can be pumped independently so that two or more vessels can be accommodated at the same time.

THE FLOATING DRYDOCK

Basically, the floating drydock consists of a pontoon or series of connected pontoons. The pontoons can be flooded or pumped out, thus raising or lowering the entire structure. The pontoons must possess enough buoyancy to support not only the weight of the dock itself but also the weight of the vessel to be lifted by the dock. To obtain this buoyancy, most floating docks have a "U" shaped form open at both ends with side walls projecting up from the water on either side.

Floating drydocks are classed as sectional type when they are formed by a series of separate units and as trough type when they are constructed as a continuous, rigid structure. They may be constructed of wood or steel or a combination of these materials. During World War II, some docks were built of concrete.

---

[1] MacElwee, *Port Development*, page 206.

Although most floating docks can be moved about to where there is a need for their services, it is customary to locate them more or less permanently at some particular site in a shipyard. There is, therefore, a problem involved in selecting a site where enough depth of water exists or can be provided by dredging; where cranes and other shipyard equipment can be conveniently provided; and where men and material can be efficiently channeled through the fabrication and other shops of the yard.

Todd Shipyards, Inc.

Figure 126.　General View of floating drydocks.

Pumping facilities, in these shipyard docks, consist of a shoreside central pumping control station which is connected by piping to each of the separate pontoons and to each of the several tanks which make up a pontoon. In addition, each pontoon has separate controls which offer more flexibility in the operation of the dock. A floating dock, therefore, can be inclined longitudinally and transversely to accommodate ships in listing or out-of-trim conditions, although this is not a desirable method of docking a ship and is avoided wherever possible.

During World War II, the U. S. Navy found it necessary to embark on a large drydock construction program.[1] In addition to the non-military type; that is, the customary graving dock or floating dock permanently stationed at shipyards and depending on shoreside supply of power, and other facilities, the Navy built a great number of strictly military type floating docks. The latter docks were constructed as mobile, completely self-contained plants, being provided with power, various shops, crew's quarters, anti-aircraft guns, and other facilities. These docks were con-

---

[1] For a good account of the U.S. Navy Dry Dock program, see Comdr. W. Ammann, USNR, "U.S. Navy Floating Dry Docks", *Journal of the American Society of Naval Engineers,* May, 1946.

Cadet-Midshipmen P. J. Isbensen and H. Fry,
Class of 1951, U.S. Merchant Marine Academy

Figure 127.   Two general views of floating drydock.

Cadet-Midshipmen P. J. Isbensen and H. Fry,
Class of 1951, U.S. Merchant Marine Academy
Figure 127A.   Close-up of a bilge block and a keel block.

Figure 128. The ARD-18, built in 1944, is 492 feet in length, has an inside width of 59 feet, a 20′ 9″ draft over blocks and a 33′-3″ draft when submerged. The vessel has twin rudders which insure effective steering ability while under tow at sea.

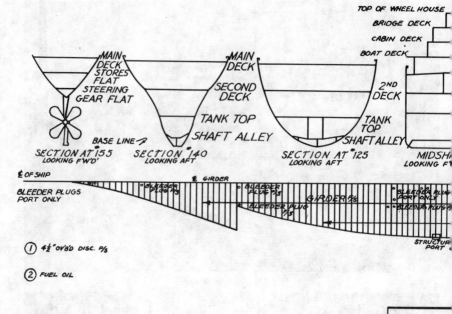

U. S. Maritime Commission

Figure 128A. Drydocking Plan of a Victory Ship.

structed with a usual ship's bow to facilitate towing. Steering mechanisms were provided.

Briefly, the Navy type docks consisted of:

1. The AFD, Auxiliary Floating Dry Dock with a lifting capacity of up to 1,900 long tons.

2. The ARD, Auxiliary Repair Dock with a lifting capacity of some 4,000 tons. This vessel has a stern gate which makes it unnecessary to raise itself high out of the water.

3. The ARDC, Auxiliary Repair Dock Concrete, with a 28 ton capacity.

4. The YFD, Yard Floating Dock, with many types of docks with lifts ranging from 1,000 tons to 18,000 tons.

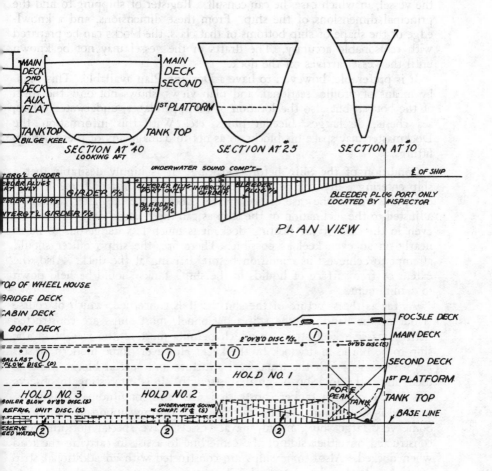

5. Steel sectional docks of three types; AFDB (Auxiliary Floating Dock, large) with capacities over 30,000 tons; AFDM (10,000–30,000); and AFDL (under 10,000).

Docking a Vessel

The procedures followed in docking a vessel both in the graving and floating types are very similar and for the most part can be described together. Where procedures differ, it will be indicated below.

The Docking Plan: Before a ship can be docked, it is apparent that some information must be available to the Dockmaster who is in charge of docking operations. The extent of the information may vary. In some isolated cases, the Dockmaster may be provided only with the name of the vessel, in which case, he can consult a Register of shipping to find the principal dimensions of the ship. From these dimensions, and a knowledge of the shape of ship bottoms of that class, the blocks can be prepared with resasonable accuracy. The drafts of the vessel may not be known until the vessel arrives off the dock.

It is preferable, however, to have a Docking Plan available. This Plan, by means of profile, sectional, and plan views, shows not only the form of the bottom but also the location of all appendages, underwater valves, sea chests, discharges, bleeder plugs, etc. With this information, the Dockmaster may space his blocks so as not to damage any of these bottom fittings.

Condition of the Ship before Docking: It is highly desirable that a ship entering a drydock be on an even keel with no list or trim. This is especially true in the case of the graving dock, since the latter cannot be adjusted to the inclination of the ship as can the floating dock. However, even in the case of the floating dock, it is much less dangerous to be as nearly on an even keel as possible. Therefore, the ship's officer should attempt to achieve this condition before arriving at the dock. Also, the extent of free surface of liquids in the ship's tanks should be held down to a minimum.

As far as the structure of the ship itself is concerned, which of course is out of the hands of the ship's personnel, most ships are constructed with a massive keel structure which permits most of the weight of the ship to be borne in drydock by the keel. However, some modern vessels have dispensed with the usual keel structure and special blocks must be used under the location of greatest strength. It is interesting to observe that in the modern tanker constructed with two longitudinal bulkheads, the keel is still retained for the purpose of affording support in a drydock. Some very large ships, mainly naval vessels, have special docking keels constructed on either side of the centerline to assist in carrying the load when docked. Also, some ships are constructed with an additional strip of steel under the flat plate keel. This *rubbing strip* protects the flat plate keel when docking and is also a protection against damage when grounding.

Preparation of the Drydock: The blocks which support the ship when in dock consist of: *Keel Blocks,* which are arranged along the centerline of the dock at a convenient height. A record is usually kept of the location of keel blocks so that the keel plates not taken care of in one docking can be taken care of in the next docking. *Bilge Blocks,* which can be pulled in to the bilge area of the bottom by an endless block and tackle arrangement. These blocks must ride on tracks of some sort so that they can be easily hauled in and out by the men on top of the side walls. As indicated above, other blocks must be placed, in some cases, under certain other vital areas. All blocks must be placed so as not to damage, or interfere with the work on, underwater fittings. Special arrangement of blocks to accommodate a damaged and listing ship will be discussed below.

Docking the Ship: As the ship approaches the dock it has been flooded; in the case of the graving dock, the caisson gate has been removed and in the case of the floating dock, the tanks have been flooded and the dock immersed to the proper level. Lines from the ship are sent out to the men stationed on the side walls. After this the ship is controlled entirely by the dock force and the ship is now worked into the dock.

Todd Shipyards, Inc.

Figure 129. Preparation of a Graving Dock.

The ship must now be positioned exactly in the fore and aft location and the transverse location planned for her by the Dockmaster. This is accomplished by various means in different docks. Usually, at the forward end of the dock where the dockmaster is stationed, a set of two long poles or battens indicates the centerline of the keel blocks. The Dockmaster lines up the battens and the bow of the ship by giving orders over a telephone hook-up or a loud speaker. At the stern, the ship is centered over the keel blocks, in some cases, by the use of long poles which are thrust out from the side walls to the ship. When the offset on each pole is the same, the ship is centered. A small boat may be used with a worker manipulating a long pole to check the position of the ship in reference to the blocks. The fore-and-aft position of the ship may be spotted by hanging a line over the bow. When this line reaches a predetermined point, the ship is stopped and made fast.

Now, the dock is pumped out and the ship sinks toward the blocks (graving dock) or the blocks move up toward the ship (floating dock). A crucial point in drydocking is reached when the weight of the ship begins to be borne by the blocks. At this time the center of gravity of the

Todd Shipyards, Inc.

Figure 130. Flooding a Graving Dock.

vessel, in effect, starts to rise since every ton of pressure at the keel blocks is equivalent to the discharge of a ton of the ship's weight at the keel. If the center of gravity rises above the metacenter before the bilge blocks are hauled into place, the ship will list over and may slide off the keel blocks. Therefore the Dockmaster must carefully observe the depth of water in the dock as compared with the draft of the ship to see when the ship's weight begins to be borne by the keel blocks. The bilge blocks are then hauled in by the men stationed on the side walls.

With vessels with a large amount of deadrise, bilge blocks may not be feasible to use. In this case, wale shores are placed on either side of the ship wedging her against the side walls. In some drydocks, mainly foreign ones, wale shores are used in addition to bilge blocks.

Todd. Shipyards, Inc.

Figure 131. Workers at steam winches prepare to pull caisson gate out of way to permit entrance of vessel.

Figure 132. Removal of caisson gate.   Todd. Shipyards, Inc.

Figure 133. Vessel enters Graving Dock.

Figure 134. Another view of vessel entering Graving Dock.

Todd Shipyards, Inc.

Figure 135. Vessel being worked into dock.

Todd Shipyards, Inc.

Figure 136. Positioning a vessel in dock.

When the bilge blocks are in place, the dock may be completely pumped out, leaving the vessel "high and dry".

Docking a Damaged Ship: It is in handling damaged ships that dry-docking men must display the greatest skill and ingenuity. We cannot cover the interesting drydockings which have occurred in recent years in the limited space of this text. However, it might be well to indicate some of the hazards involved.

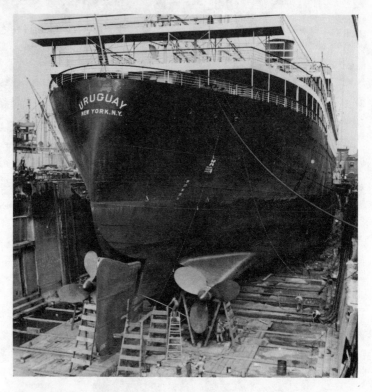

Todd Shipyards, Inc.

Figure 137.   Vessel Docked—Work begins.

Let us assume a situation where the ship has been damaged below the waterline and a compartment or several compartments are open to the sea, with a consequent severe list. A floating dock can be adjusted so that the angle of list on both dock and ship is the same. However, when the weight of the ship begins to be borne by the blocks, the ship may slide off the keel blocks unless carefully shored. Now as the water level recedes on the ship, the water will pour out of the holes in the ship and the ship will heel over the other way. It is obvious that the dock must be skillfully operated to prevent disaster. And with the great number of

Figure 138. Employment of wale shores and blocking in a foreign dock.

Figure 139. This view illustrates the difficulty of docking a damaged vessel.

separate tanks in the floating dock, each one of which must be controlled separately, one can see the need for experienced hands on the valves and a skilled Dockmaster.

It is necessary in the case of damaged ships to send a diver down before the ship gets in the dock to ascertain the exact extent of damage. This knowledge is vital to the preparation for, and operation of, the drydock.

Advantages and Disadvantages of Floating and Graving Docks

Although there are many similarities in the floating type dock and the graving dock, there are many more dissimilarities. The latter will emerge in the discussion which follows on the advantages and disadvantages of the two types.

Initial Cost: This is the single most important factor determining whether or not one or the other type of dock will be constructed. The initial cost of the graving dock is much greater than that of the floating dock. This fact accounts for the overwhelmingly greater number of floating docks used by commercial yards.

Upkeep: The graving dock seems to have the better of it here. Very little upkeep is required for the concrete construction of the graving dock. The floating dock, on the other hand, especially if it is made of steel, or a composite of wood and steel, is especially susceptible to damage, corrosion, rotting, marine growth and teredoes, etc.

A greater number of personnel is required to man the pumping stations on the floating type.

The site of the floating dock may have to be dredged from time to time in order to keep the required depth of water.

On the other hand, the graving dock accumulates a mass of mud on the dock floor which has to be cleaned off by men with buckets and shovels. The mud on a floating dock is pretty much removed every time the dock is sunk.

Mobility: There is, of course, no comparison here. The floating dock can be easily moved if that is desirable. This is especially true of the self-contained Navy docks.

Speed of Docking: A ship can be docked much quicker in a floating dock than in the graving dock, primarily due to the lesser pumping requirements.

Size of Ships Which Can Be Handled: Very few floating docks can handle the really large passenger liners and naval vessels. However, as was remarked above, the Navy has built floating docks capable of lifting 100,000 tons. Also, floating docks have a flexibility of size which cannot be achieved by the graving dock. Due to the sectional construction of floating docks, sections may be added or removed in many docks so that the size of the dock is adjusted to the size of the ship. The Navy type floating docks have sections which are completely alike making for a very flexible operation.

Weather Conditions: One of the major drawbacks of the floating type dock is it's exposed position. With high winds and rough water, the dock of course is effected making it very dangerous and difficult to dock a ship and very uncomfortable and difficult to proceed with work when the ship is in the dock. These problems are not found at all in the protected basin of a graving dock.

Danger of Stresses on the Ship: Another danger which must be carefully avoided on a floating dock is the possibility that the buoyancy of one section may vary slightly from that of others thus creating greater loads on the more buoyant sections and consequently creating stresses on the ship due to the difference of load along the length of the ship. This danger is not present on the stable floor of a graving dock.

Deck Officer's Duties in Drydocking

In addition to the obvious assistance which the ship's officers must provide to the port engineer and port superintendent in specifying and inspecting repairs while in dock, the deck officers should keep in mind the following items:

Drydock Report: Most steamship companies require the ship's personnel to make a Drydocking Report on a prepared form. This report may include:

1. All important times such as time of entering and leaving dock; time of beginning and finishing the painting of bottom, and so on.

2. Condition of all underwater structure and fittings at the time of drydocking with a list of all work done.

3. A detailed Paint Report with information as to condition of paint at various locations, quantity of grass and barnacles found, location and number plates scaled, number of coats of paint and amount of paint used, weather and temperatures during painting, etc.

Maintenance Book: Most ships keep a record of all maintenance work done on the ship. For example, the location and number of plates scaled and painted so that an efficient rotation system for this work can be maintained.

Fire Lines: Since water cannot be pumped while the ship is in dock, the ship's fire lines are led out to shoreside outlets. If the mate wants to keep his white fire hose in good shape it would be sensible to cover it securely with dunnage or other protection.

Shifting of Weights: It is very important that the Dockmaster be informed of all prospective shifts of weight aboard the ship since the location of blocks depend on the weight location aboard the ship when docked. If, for example, weight is shifted outboard without informing the Dockmaster, the ship will list when undocked and may lead to damage to ship and/or dock. It is necessary to test tanks for watertightness by filling them with water while in dock. Once, again, the Dockmaster should be notified.

Engineers' Duties in Drydocking

Preparation for Docking: Vessel should be put on an even keel by shifting of ballast. The atmospheric exhaust valve should be checked to make certain that it is not jammed.

Entering Drydock: As soon as the ship is in the dock and before the main injection is out of the water, all auxiliary exhausts should be put on atmosphere. Pumps like the feed and fuel oil service and the generator may be left running unless the plant is to be completely shut down.

When the exhaust is on atmosphere, the main and auxiliary condenser will be shut down. In shutting down the condenser, the discharge from the circulator to the condenser is shut if one is fitted; then the circulator is stopped. This assures the condenser being left full of water. If it is left empty, the packing will dry out and may cause leaks when put back in service. If no discharge valve is fitted to the circulator, the pump is secured and the main injection left open so that water will drain out and permit work to be done on the injection valve.

All other pumps using sea suction should be shut down including the auxiliary circulator, sanitary, and cooling water.

In Dock: If shore current is to be used and it is alternating current, all motor switches, room fans, and so on, should be pulled since ship's current is usually direct. The switches on the switch board should be checked for proper arrangement and the generator secured.

All toilets must be locked for obvious reasons.

The boiler or evaporator must never be blown down without permission and adequate warning to the men on the dock. And of course, the main engine should never be turned over without warning to all personnel.

Un-docking: All skin valves should be checked to see that they have been replaced and the bonnets tightened. Those valves, normally closed at sea, should be closed before undocking.

A check should be made to see that all electrical leads to the dock have been disconnected.

As soon as the ship is in the water, the auxiliary circulator should be started. Exhaust steam is put into the auxiliary condenser and atmosphere exhaust shut. Other salt water pumps such as sanitary and cooling are started.

All skin valves should be examined for possible leaks. And all work which has been done on hull, piping, and machinery should be examined as soon as possible.

Work Done While in Drydock

It is obvious that only such work which cannot be done at any other time should be done while actually in drydock. Due to the tremendous expense of docking, the work to be done must be carefully planned and carried out.

Docking a New Ship: Due to the possibility of mill scale corrosion and corrosion due to stray currents when building, a new ship should be docked at frequent intervals during the first year or two after launching.[1] This is especially true if the shipbuilding steel has not had sufficient weathering time to remove the mill scale. (Rapid construction of war-built ships led to aggravated mill scale corrosion.) New ships should be docked at three-month intervals, preferably, and not more than six-month intervals and the mill scale removed or thoroughly painted over.

ABS Surveys: The American Bureau of Shipping requires that, at the Special Periodical Surveys, the ship is to be placed in drydock. At that time the "keel, stem, stern frame or stern post and outside plating are to be cleaned and afterward examined and recoated where necessary. Load line marks are to be checked and re-cut or painted as required". Also, the rudder must be examined, lifted when required and the gudgeons re-bushed. All tanks are tested under a head of water. All shell openings are inspected. The chain cables must be ranged and examined and at this time they may be cleaned, and the markings renewed. At the later surveys (#3 and subsequent), shell plating may be drilled to test for excessive corrosion. The ABS requires that the tail shaft be drawn at least once every three years.

Work Usually Performed in Drydock: In addition to the work mentioned above, the following jobs are done, if necessary, in drydock:

1. Bottom plating is cleaned by scaling, sand-blasting, pickling or other method.

2. Bottom plating is painted with anti-corrosive and anti-fouling coats. Boot-topping is painted.

3. Loose or badly corroded rivets are cut out and redriven.

4. Leaky seams and rivets are caulked.

5. Underwater stuffing boxes are repacked.

6. Zinc, steel, or Scandinavian iron protecting plates are renewed.

7. The bilge keel, usually a trouble spot, is inspected and repaired.

8. Draft marks may be conveniently recut or painted.

9. Propeller pitch is checked.

10. All skin valves are examined and if necessary, ground in, repacked and rejointed.

11. All sea strainers are cleaned. The steam lines to sea chests may be overhauled at this time.

---

[1] A good account on corrosion of new ship bottoms appears in the paper by Paul Ffield, "Some Aspects of Ship Bottom Corrosion", *Transactions of the Society of Naval Architects and Marine Eng.*, 1950.

12. When tail shaft is drawn the engineers should check to see that all water service lines and the like are not damaged and are properly replaced. Shaft liners are tested for evidence of wear or looseness. The propeller, shaft keys, and hub are inspected for cracks and damage. New stern gland packing is installed.

13. Bleeder plugs in all tanks below the waterline and adjacent to the shell may be opened to drain the tanks.

14. Major repair and construction jobs ranging from the replacement of shell plating to the complete operation of the construction of a ship.

Cadet-Midshipman O. D. Garcia, Class of 1952, U.S. Merchant Marine Academy

Cadet-Midshipman R. M. McCormick, Class of 1952, U.S. Merchant Marine Academy

Figure 140. Washing down the hull before painting.

Figure 141. Painting a hull in a floating drydock.

QUESTIONS

1. Define:
   a) Marine Railway
   b) Careen
   c) Caisson Gate
   d) Trough type dock
   e) Sectional type dock
   f) Rubbing strip
   g) Wale shores
2. How is it possible to accommodate two or more vessels in the same graving dock?
3. How does the method used in docking a listed or trimmed ship in a floating dock differ from that necessary in a graving dock?
4. What is the maximum lifting capacity of the Navy type docks?

5. What information is available on a Docking Plan? If a Docking Plan is not available, how does the Dockmaster proceed in preparing the dock?
6. What can ship's officers do to prepare the ship properly for docking?
7. Describe the structural arrangements necessary solely for meeting the stresses of drydocking.
8. What methods do Dockmasters use to assure themselves that when blocks and bottom meet, the vessel is properly positioned?
9. When do the most critical moments occur in drydocking?
10. Compare the floating drydock with the graving dock with regard to the following:
   a) Initial cost
   b) Upkeep
   c) Mobility
   d) Speed of Docking
   e) Size of ship which can be handled
   f) Weather conditions
   g) Structural stresses on ship
11. Describe a typical Drydock Report.
12. Why must a shift of weight aboard a ship in dock be cleared with the Dockmaster?
13. When entering a drydock what is the procedure in shutting down the condenser?
14. What pumps must be shut down when entering drydock?
15. When in dock, what precautions must be taken in regard to:
   a) Electric current
   b) Toilets
   c) Blowing down boiler or evaporator.
   d) Fire hose.
16. Why is a new ship commonly docked at more frequent intervals than an old ship?
17. List the jobs usually performed when a vessel is in dock.

BIBLIOGRAPHY

Rules for Building and Classing Steel Vessels, issued annually by the American Bureau of Shipping.

Ammann, W., "U.S. Navy Floating Dry Docks", *Journal of the American Society of Naval Engineers,* May 1946.

MacElwee, *Port Development,* McGraw-Hill Book Company, New York, 1924.

Seibert, E. C., "Composite Concrete and Timber Blocking for Dry Docks", *Transactions of the Society of Naval Architects and Marine Engineers,* Vol. 45, 1937.

Donnelly, W. T., "Floating Drydocks in the United States", *Transactions of the Society of Naval Architects and Marine Engineers,* Vol. 18, 1910.

"Stresses in Dry Docks", *Dock and Harbour Authority,* April and May, 1945.

P. Grandall, *Characteristics and Relative Merits of Railway and Floating Drydocks,* SNAME Philadelphia Section, Jan., 1958.

P. Brinck, *The Floating Drydock,* SNAME Pacific Northwest Section, Jan., 1954.

Chapter 13

SHIP'S CALCULATIONS

Ship's calculations, involving as they do the complex form of a floating body, do not lend themselves to the simple rules of arithmetic and geometry. A new set of rules and principles must be learned by the student in naval architecture.[1] The most important of these are the rules for finding the area of curvilinear figures and the volume of forms with curvature. In ship's calculations this consists of finding the area of waterplanes and sections and the volume of the molded form of the hull up to various waterplanes.

Although there are many Rules used by Naval Architects in this connection, this text will concentrate on the two most practical and most frequently used Rules—The Trapezoidal Rule and Simpson's First Rule.

Rules for Integration

The Trapezoidal Rule: Consider Figure 142: A base line is established and a series of equally spaced ordinates (y_0, y_1, y_2, etc.) are erected at right angles to the base line. The problem is to integrate the area under the curved line and above the base line, that is, find the total area bound by these lines. If the top of each ordinate is joined, a series of trapezoids is formed. If the sum of the areas of each individual trapezoid is now found, this will be a reasonable approximation of the area we are looking for.

Let us do this (keeping in mind that the area of a trapezoid is equal to one-half the sum of the bases times the altitude.) Let "s" be the equal distance between ordinates or in this case the altitude of each trapezoid.

$$A = \tfrac{1}{2}(y_0 + y_1)s + \tfrac{1}{2}(y_1 + y_2)s \ldots \ldots + \tfrac{1}{2}(y_{n-1} + y_n)s$$

This formula can be simplified considerably since s is a common factor and one-half of each ordinate except the first and the last must be totaled. Simplifying then:

---

[1] The scope of this section on ship's calculation is fixed by these considerations: (1) Simple rules of mensuration such as those for the area of rectangles, triangles and trapezoids and the volume of rectangular and cylindrical shapes belong properly to texts on arithmetic and geometry. (2) A text for ship's officers does not require, in some cases the detailed study necessary for a text in Naval Architecture. However, proper application of ship's calculations does require in many cases, a comprehensive knowledge of the theory underlying the use of information provided the ship by its designer. (3) The operating practices relating to ship's stability and trim will not be presented here since they have been given in a companion text. (La Dage & Van Gemert, *Stability and Trim for the Ship's Officer*.) However, certain theoretical background relating to these subjects will be included.

$$A = s(\tfrac{1}{2}y_0 + y_1 + y_2 \ldots\ldots + y_{n-1} + \tfrac{1}{2}y_n) \text{ (The Trapezoidal Rule)}$$

The work involved in using the Trapezoidal Rule can be done efficiently by a form similar to the following:

Ordinate	Multiplier	Function of Area
y_0	$\tfrac{1}{2}$	
y_1	1	
y_2	1	
y_3	1	
..	1	
y_n	$\tfrac{1}{2}$	

$$A = \text{Sum } F(a) \times s$$

Total F(a) _____

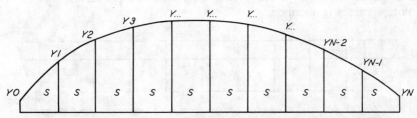

EQUALLY SPACED ORDINATES ARE ERECTED ON A BASELINE IN ORDER TO CALCULATE THE AREA OF A CURVILINEAR FIGURE BY MEANS OF RULES OF INTEGRATION.

Figure 142

It should be noted that *any* number of ordinates may be used in the Trapezoidal Rule. The number does not have to be an odd number as will be the case with Simpson's First Rule. Accuracy depends upon the number used however, since chances for error are reduced as the number of ordinates is increased.

By this time the student perhaps has noted the resemblance of the layout in Figure 142: to the system of laying out frame stations in the Lines Drawing. This is not a coincidence. The designer deliberately constructs the Lines Drawing in this way so that the value of ordinates (in this case, half-breadths of waterplanes) can be measured from the Lines, made up in the form of a Table of Offsets, and used for the calculations of areas of waterplanes and sections.

Now, if planes are established an equal distance apart, the areas of the planes may be considered ordinates in the Rule and "run through" to find the volume enclosed between the first and last plane. The work involved may be laid out as follows:

Area	Multiplier	Function of Volume
y_0	$\frac{1}{2}$	
y_1	1	
y_2	1	
..	1	
y_n	$\frac{1}{2}$	

$$V = \text{Sum } F(v) \times s$$

Total $F(v)$ _____

In applying these principles to the calculation of the volume of displacement of a vessel up to a certain waterplane, either the areas of waterplanes or the areas of sections at the frame stations may be used. However, since a vessel is symmetrical about its centerline, it is only necessary to calculate half-areas of waterplanes or sections and use these to find one-half of the volume. The full volume can then be obtained easily by multiplying by two. Once again, the closer the planes are spaced the more accuracy is obtained.

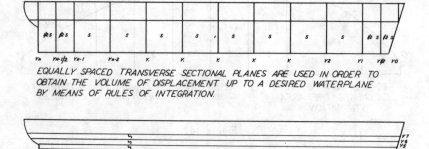

EQUALLY SPACED TRANSVERSE SECTIONAL PLANES ARE USED IN ORDER TO OBTAIN THE VOLUME OF DISPLACEMENT UP TO A DESIRED WATERPLANE BY MEANS OF RULES OF INTEGRATION.

EQUALLY SPACED WATERPLANES ARE USED IN ORDER TO OBTAIN THE VOLUME OF DISPLACEMENT OF A VESSEL UP TO A DESIRED WATERPLANE BY MEANS OF RULES OF INTEGRATION.

Figure 143

Simpson's First Rule: It can be shown both analytically and mathematically that the area of a curvilinear figure such as the one in Figure 142: can be found by the following rule. Theoretically, the curve must be that of a parabola of the second or third order, but practically, accuracy can be obtained for any curve by the use of sufficient ordinates. In general, Simpson's Rule is more accurate than the trapezoidal rule and should be used wherever possible.

$$A = s/3 \ (y_0 + 4y_1 + 2y_2 + 4y_3 \ldots \ldots + 4y_{n-1} + y_n)$$

It should be noted that in Simpson's Rule, an odd number of ordinates must be used. (It is for this reason that an odd number of frame stations is used in the Lines Drawing.) The appropriate form for use with Simpson's Rule would then be:

Ordinate	Multiplier	Function of Area
y_0	1	
y_1	4	$A = s/3 \times \text{sum } F(a)$
y_2	2	
y_3	4	
..	.	
y_{n-1}	4	
y_n	1	

Total $F(a)$ _____

It should be stressed that in Simpson's Rule, the first and last multipliers are 1; the second and the next to the last multipliers are 4.

Simpson's Rule can be used also to find volume in the same manner as described above for the Trapezoidal Rule. The form would then be:

Area	Multiplier	Function of Volume
y_0	1	
y_1	4	$V = s/3 \times \text{Sum } F(v)$
y_2	2	
y_3	4	
..	.	
y_{n-1}	4	
y_n	1	

Total $F(v)$ _____

Use of Half-Multipliers and Half-Spaced Ordinates: The work involved in using the forms given above for Simpson's Rule can be reduced by the use of half-multipliers; that is, divide the normal Simpson's multipliers in two making them $\frac{1}{2}$,2,1,2, etc. This reduces the arithmetic considerably and is especially time-saving when a problem involving a great number of ordinates or planes is worked on. Since all components of the Function of Area or Volume are then halved, it is necessary to multiply the total $F(a)$ or $F(v)$ by two.

It has been mentioned that accuracy can be increased by the use of additional ordinates. Now, in the case of a ship's form where very little change takes place throughout the midship section, accuracy can be increased by using half-spaced (or quarter-spaced) ordinates forward and aft where the greatest change in form occurs. The use of half-spaced ordinates will, of course, necessitate a change in the Simpson's multipliers, since what we have in effect is three separate integrations; that is, one forward, one amidships, and one aft. The combination of these three separate problems into one causes the Simpson's multipliers to become: (if two additional ordinates are used forward and aft):

$\frac{1}{2}$ 2 1 2 $1\frac{1}{2}$ 4 2 . . . . . . 2 4 $1\frac{1}{2}$ 2 1 2 $\frac{1}{2}$

(and if one additional ordinate is used forward and aft):

$\frac{1}{2}$ 2 $1\frac{1}{2}$ 4 2 4 2 . . . . . . 2 4 2 4 $1\frac{1}{2}$ 2 $\frac{1}{2}$

If both of these methods is resorted to (if one additional ordinate is used forward and aft), the necessary form would appear as:

Ordinate or Plane	Multiplier	Function of Area or Volume	
y_0	$\frac{1}{4}$		
$y_{1/2}$	1		
y_1	$\frac{3}{4}$	$A = \dfrac{2s}{3} \times \text{Sum F(a)}$	
y_2	2		
. .	.		
y_{n-2}		$V = \dfrac{2s}{3} \times \text{Sum F(v)}$	
y_{n-1}	$\frac{3}{4}$		
$y_{-n1/2}$	1		
y_n	$\frac{1}{4}$		

Total F(a) or F(v) _____

To recapitulate: Simpson's First Rule (and the Trapezoidal Rule where the number of ordinates is even) can be used to find the areas of curvilinear figures such as half-waterplanes and half-sections; it can be used to find the areas of sections through a tank. With these areas, the volume of displacement of a vessel up to any desired waterplane can be found; or the volumetric capacity of a tank or compartment may be found. Problems at the end of this chapter will illustrate these situations.

Mechanical Integration: Integration of areas can be done mechanically by means of an instrument called a *planimeter*. Since this instrument is not commonly available to ship's officers and is not needed for the type of problem the latter usually is concerned with, a detailed description of the instrument will not be given here. However, the operation of a planimeter consists of tracing the perimeter of the figure whose area is desired with a pointer. A guage which is set at zero at the start of the operation automatically indicates the area after the figure has been completely traced. Thus a quick approximation of the area of a figure may be obtained. However, even Naval Architects do not use a planimeter for all integration, since a check on work can be more positively accomplished if the work is laid out in forms similar to the ones illustrated above for Simpson's Rule. The planimeter is invaluable for preliminary work on the Lines Drawing and other drawings.

THE CALCULATION AND USE OF HYDROSTATIC VALUES

Hydrostatic values are those values which involve the *underwater* form of a vessel. Furthermore since they are static values, it is to be understood that they are calculated for a ship *on an even keel* (with no trim or list) and with a straight waterline. Of course, a ship at sea will not have a straight waterline, but the hydrostatic values calculated for the latter case will reasonably approximate the values for a ship in waves. If, however, the vessel is trimmed, *all* hydrostatic values calculated for a vessel on an even keel are in error. The error for some hydrostatic values is not of a practical extent and may safely be ignored; other hydrostatic values, as will be shown, may be appreciably and practically in error, and in these cases, a correction is in order.

Hydrostatic values, then, are calculated by the designer and made up in the form of curves which are provided to the ship operator and the ship's officer. They are called variously:

1. Hydrostatic Curves
2. Curves of Form
3. Displacement and other Curves.

Hydrostatic values are also made up in the form of scales and tables. One important example is the *Deadweight Scale*.

One further point concerning hydrostatic values must be emphasized: Since these values are determined by the underwater form of a vessel *and nothing else,* they are not affected by any changes *within* a vessel. Therefore a set of hydrostatic curves for one Liberty ship, for example, is valid for any other Liberty ship, since the underwater form of all Liberties is the same. In this connection it should be noted that the vertical and longitudinal positions of the center of gravity of a vessel are *not* hydrostatic values and can, of course, be affected by changes within a vessel.

We shall now consider in turn each of the many hydrostatic values which have an important bearing on the operation of a merchant ship.

Calculation of Displacement

Displacement is one of the most important hydrostatic values which must be calculated. This value and the others to be considered below involve considerable arithmetical work. The work is commonly done on a series of forms known as the *Displacement Sheet*.[1] However, before we

---

[1] In the calculations to follow, the student will be referred to the Displacement Sheet for a model used at the United States Merchant Marine Academy. The name of the model is *Miss Calculation*. It is to be noted that units of inches and pounds are necessary for the model instead of the customary feet and tons for a full scale ship. Two of the many sheets required for the calculation of hydrostatic values are reproduced. (Tables VIII & IX). The first sheet shows the layout for calculating sectional areas at the 12″ waterplane and the second sheet, the layout for the calculation of the hydrostatic values listed at the head of the various columns, also for the 12″ draft.

enter upon these extensive calculations, it is important to have an exact understanding of what displacement is.

What is Displacement? Displacement is commonly defined as the weight of that volume of water displaced by a vessel. This principle was first stated by Archimedes. It may be stated in another way by showing that the weight of a floating body which attempts to move vertically down towards the center of the earth through the body's center of gravity must be opposed by an equal buoyant force moving vertically upwards through the center of buoyancy. Now, buoyant force is merely the sum of all vertically acting pressure on the underwater form. Pressure in turn is determined principally by the density of the liquid involved, and the depth of the liquid. For example, at a depth of 1 foot, the pressure in salt water will be 64 pounds per square foot; at a depth of 2 feet, 2×64 pounds per square foot, etc. If we calculate the sum of such vertically acting pressure around the underwater form of a vessel, we would have the total buoyant force and therefore the total displacement or weight of the vessel. However, it is not necessary to make such a difficult calculation, since the displacement is equal to the weight of the volume of water displaced. This may be proved by considering the displacement of a simple barge form with the dimensions as indicated in Figure 144. The objective is to show that the weight of salt water displaced is equal to the sum of all forces acting vertically upwards.

1. $\text{Displacement} = \dfrac{50 \times 20 \times 10}{35} = 285.7 \text{ tons}$

2. $\begin{array}{l} \text{Total Pressure} \\ \text{of Buoyancy} \end{array} = \dfrac{50 \times 20 \times 64 \times 10}{2240} = 285.7 \text{ tons}$

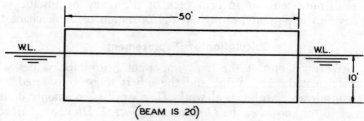

(BEAM IS 20')

Figure 144

In step 1., the total volume of displacement is calculated by finding the product of length, beam, and draft. Then since 1 ton of salt water occupies 35 cubic feet, the tons displacement is found by dividing volume of displacement by 35. (If fresh water were involved we would divide by 36.)

In step 2., pressure is acting vertically upwards only on the bottom of the barge. Pressure on either side is the same and has no upward effect. The area of the bottom of the barge is found by the product of length and beam. This area in square feet is multiplied by the pressure per square foot or (10 x 64) pounds. (If fresh water were involved the pressure would be found by multiplying the draft by 62.5 pounds.) Pounds are converted to tons by dividing by 2240, the number of pounds in a long ton.

Thus it is shown that buoyant force is provided by the depth of liquid and not by the amount of liquid around the ship. A ship will float as long as there is a layer of liquid around the hull, regardless of the thickness of that layer. For example, if a vessel were put in a drydock which has a form approximately the same as that of the vessel, the latter could float in, say, an inch of water. See Figure 145.

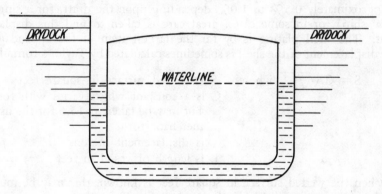

Figure 145. A vessel will float as long as its hull is submerged, regardless of the amount of water.

Calculation of Volume of Displacement (molded): In calculating the volume of displacement, the first step is to calculate the area of equally spaced sections or waterplanes. In order to do this, we need half-breadths on waterplanes. This information is readily available to the designer from the Table of Offsets. Now, it must be remembered that the Table of Offsets was compiled by measuring the offsets on the Lines Plan. The drawings of the Lines Plan are of the *molded form* of the vessel. Therefore, the displacement calculated by the use of these offsets will be a *molded displacement*. This will not include the displacement of such items as the shell plating, rudder, bilge keels, etc. The displacement of all these items which are designated collectively as the *appendages* must be done separately and the appendage displacement added to the molded displacement to obtain the *total displacement*.

On Table VIII, are listed the calculations for finding the half-sectional areas at all frame stations, including two half-spaced stations. Half-breadths are run through Simpson's Rule to find the half-areas. If a planimeter were available these areas could be found by use of this instrument.

Then, on Table IX, which is that part of the Displacement Sheet necessary for finding hydrostatic values at the load waterline, the half-areas are listed in that block of the Sheet designated "Displacement". The areas are run through Simpson's Rule to find the total Function of Volume or Sum_1. Sum_1 is multiplied by s/3 for the Rule and 2 since half-areas were used to find volume of displacement. Molded displacement in terms of weight can then be found by dividing by the appropriate figure for weight per cubic unit.

Appendage Displacement: Calculation of Wetted Surface: The calculation of the displacement of all appendages may be treated by some designers as simply some percentage of the molded displacement (a figure of approximately 0.5% to 1.0% depending upon the draft, for a single-screw ship), or in some cases, great care is taken to find this displacement. The shell plating is by far the largest item of the appendages. The displacement of the shell is sometimes calculated by Taylor's formula:[1]

$$S = C \sqrt{\triangle L}$$ where: S is wetted surface in square feet
C is a constant which varies with form, but may be taken as 15.6 for the usual merchant form
$\triangle$ is displacement in tons
L is length of vessel in feet

When the wetted surface in square feet is known, this may be multiplied by the mean thickness of the shell to obtain the volume of displacement of the shell. The formula may be used by ship's officers to obtain the amount of paint needed to cover the bottom or any part of the bottom or sides—the boottopping, for example.

However, wetted surface can be calculated with more exactness than afforded by Taylor approximation. These methods are considered beyond the scope of this text.[2]

Change of Volume of Displacement with Density of Water: When a vessel enters fresh water from salt water the draft will increase due to the lesser density of fresh water. The displacement in tons will, of course, remain the same but the volume of displacement will increase. The volume in salt water (tons displacement $\times$ 35) will increase to a new volume (tons displacement $\times$ 35.9).

---

[1] Admiral D. W. Taylor, *"The Speed and Power of Ships"*, U.S. Government Printing Office, 1943, pages 18-23.
[2] For a more exact method see: Rossell & Chapman, *Principles of Naval Architecture*, Vol. I, page 44.

TABLE VIII

SECTIONAL AREAS AT 12" WATERPLANE—MISS CALCULATION

WL	½ HB	SM	F(a)	1 HB	SM	F(a)	2 HB	SM	F(a)	3, 4, 5, 6 HB	SM	F(a)
BL	0.50	1		0.50	1		6.12	1		12.40	1	
2"	2.02	4		4.86	4		11.88	4		16.18	4	
4"	2.50	2		5.94	2		12.92	2		16.98	2	
6"	2.72	4		6.38	4		13.48	4		17.06	4	
8"	2.87	2		6.63	2		13.83	2		17.06	2	
10"	3.02	4		6.78	4		14.08	4		17.06	4	
12"	3.14	1		6.95	1		14.26	1		17.06	1	
Sum												

WL	7 HB	SM	F(a)	8 HB	SM	F(a).	9 HB	SM	F(a)	9½ HB	SM	F(a)
BL	7.20	1		2.60	1		0.42	1		0.42	1	
2"	13.56	4		8.18	4		2.65	4		1.02	4	
4"	14.85	2		9.77	2		3.65	2		1.38	2	
6"	15.60	4		10.94	4		4.20	4		1.62	4	
8"	16.17	2		12.00	2		4.74	2		1.77	2	
10"	16.46	4		12.80	4		5.44	4		2.04	4	
12"	16.70	1		13.54	1		6.62	1		2.90	1	
Sum												

NOTE: ½ Sectional Area at 0 Station (FP) is zero.
½ Sectional Area at Station 10 (AP) is 5.04 sq. in.

265

TABLE IX

CURVES OF FORM CALCULATIONS FOR TV MISS CALCULATIONS

Sta.	DISPLACEMENT			LONG C. B.		Awp & TPI			C. F. & LBM				Trans. BM		
	Half Sta. Area	SM	F(v)	Arm	Moments	HB	SM	F(a)	Arm	$F(a) \times$ Arm (Arm)	$F(a) \times$ Arm² (Arm)	Arm²	HB³	SM	Product
FP		½		5			½		5	5				½		
½		2		4½			2		4½	4½				2		
1		1½		4			1½		4	4				1½		
2		4		3			4		3	3				4		
3		2		2			2		2	2				2		
4		4		1			4		1	1				4		
5		2		Fwd			2		Fwd	0				2		
6		4		1			4		1	1				4		
7		2		2			2		2	2				2		
8		4		3			4		3	3				4		
9		1½		4			1½		4	4				1½		
9½		2		4½			2		4½	4½				2		
10		½		5			½		5	5				½		
	Sum₁			Aft Sum₂			Sum₃		Aft Sum₄		Sum₅		Sum₆		

Cubic in. disp.
Pounds Dis:
b:

LCB
m
l

Awp
PPI
p

C.F.
I about amid:
I about C.F.
L.B.M.

Trans: BM:
Decrease in disp. per inch trim by stern:
Moment to trim 1"

More permanent change increases of volume, however, is the increase draft... See Figure 172. This dimensible draft can be calculated by

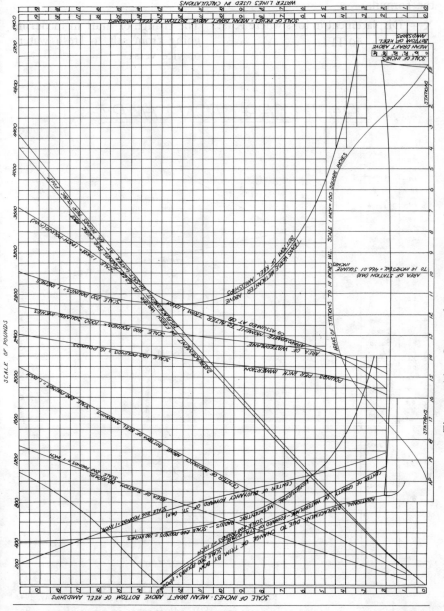

Figure 146. Curve of Form—*Miss Calculation*.

More pertinent than the increase of volume, however, is the increase in draft. (See figure 147). This change in draft can be calculated by the formula:

$$X = \frac{\text{Displacement in tons}}{40 \text{ TPI}} \text{ where X is:}$$

The change of draft in inches in going from salt to fresh water, or vice versa

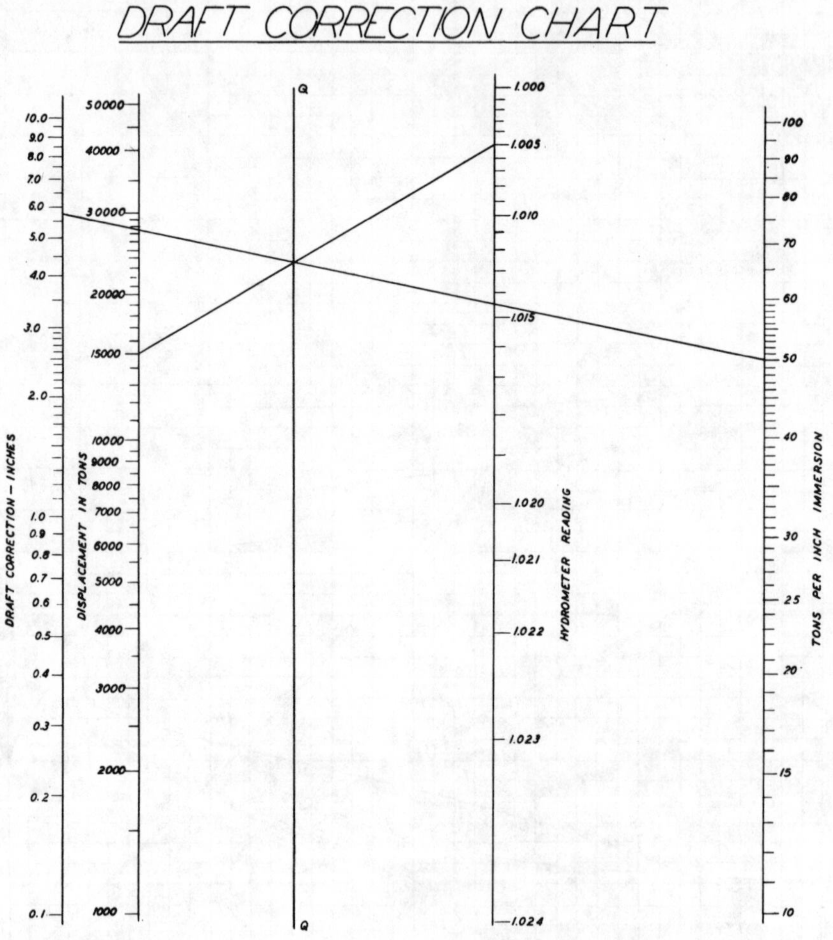

DRAFT CORRECTION CHART

A. R. Anderson, *Marine Engineering & Shipping Review*, May, 1942

Figure. 147. To find increase in draft from S.W. draft when in water of any other density, connect displacement and density; then connect TPI with "Q" line, and extend to correction line.

When going from water of one density to water of any other density either of these formulas may be used:

1. Draft varies inversely with the density:[1]

$$\text{That is: } \frac{D}{D'} = \frac{S.G'}{S.G.}$$

2. $$X = \frac{\text{Displacement} \times \text{Change in S.G.}}{\text{TPI}}$$

Plotting of the Displacement Curves: When total displacement has been calculated at sufficient drafts, a curve of displacement in tons (S.W.) is plotted against a scale of tons and draft in feet. It is also customary to plot a curve of displacement in tons (F.W.).

Displacement when Trimmed: As mentioned above, when a vessel is trimmed all hydrostatic values given on the Curves are in error. Displacement is such an important ship characteristic, however, that an accurate displacement is usually desirable. This can be obtained approximately by the use of a correcting curve usually included with the Hydrostatic Curves. The curve will be described below. However, even this correction is not sufficiently accurate for some purposes and another method must be employed. This method utilizes a set of sectional area curves called Bonjean's Curves.

Bonjean's Curves are constructed by using a profile plan showing all frame stations. The Bonjean's Curves then consist of sectional area curves drawn at each frame station. The sectional area is plotted, with any convenient scale representing area in square feet, horizontally out from the frame station, for a sufficient number of drafts to obtain a fair curve. Thus, if the sectional area at any frame station up to any draft is required the distance from the frame station out to the curve is measured, and the accompanying scale consulted to find the sectional area in square feet. (See Figures 148 and 149).

Now, if the displacement in any trimmed condition is desired, the trimmed waterline is drawn on the profile; the sectional area at each frame station ascertained by the Bonjean Curves; and these areas run through Simpson's Rule to obtain the correct displacement.

Bonjean's Curves are especially valuable for such calculations as those for launching where the underwater form during launching undergoes constant change.

Coefficients of Form

The four most frequently used coefficients of form are:

---

[1] The density of liquid is measured by its specific gravity. S.G. aboard ship may be obtained by use of a hydrometer and for salt water is around 1.026. Pure fresh water has a S.G. of 1.000 which when considered in relation to the figure of 62.355 lbs. of FW per cubic foot, produces a figure of 64 lbs. per cu. ft. for salt water; 35.9 cu. ft. to a ton of fresh water and 35 cu. ft. to the ton of salt water.

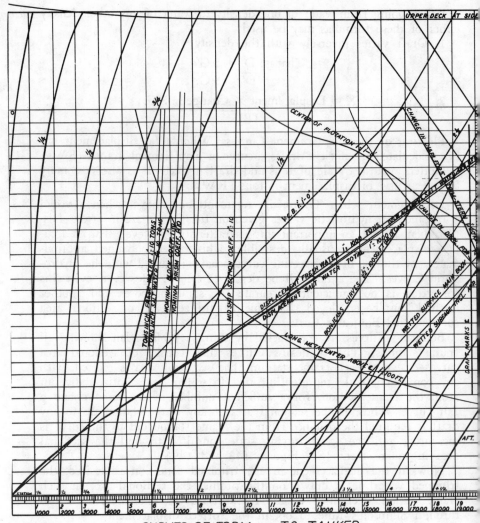

CURVES OF FORM — T2 TANKER

Figure 148

1. The Block coefficient (b).
2. The Midship Section (or maximum section) coefficient (m).
3. The Prismatic (or longitudinal) coefficient (l).
4. The Waterplane Coefficient (p).

Curves for these coefficients are usually included on the Hydrostatic Curves.

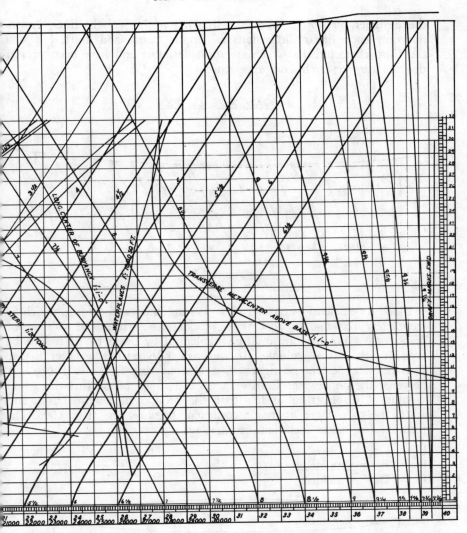

Coefficients of form are among the most important "yardsticks" or scales by which research on the effect of ship form on such operating characteristics as resistance, stability, and trim can be facilitated. For example, a series of models can be made with, say, various midship section coefficients. These models can then be tested in a towing tank to discover the effect of varying this particular form characteristic. Researchers have by this method been able to prepare graphs and tables demonstrating how ship performance varies with form. Thus the designer, *before* he starts the drawing of his vessel's lines, knows not only such linear dimensions as length, beam, and draft, but also the form characteristics which are most desirable and have been proven desirable by research and experience.

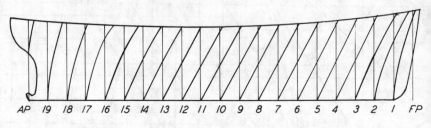

Figure 149

Block Coefficient: Consider first a ship underwater form which is completely rectangular; that is, a block form. Here, the volume of displacement obtained by multiplying length by beam by draft will be equal to the actual volume. If we wished to relate the latter to the former by a percentage figure it is obvious that figure is 100%. If however the underwater form of a vessel is fined off so that the actual volume of displacement is less than the product of length, beam, and draft, the percentage figure or coefficient becomes less than 100. The formula for block coefficient is now readily seen to be:

L = LBP
B = Beam (molded)
H = Draft (molded)

$$b = \frac{V}{L \times B \times H} \quad \text{where:}$$

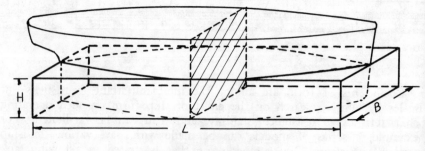

BLOCK COEFFICIENT

Figure 150. The Block Coefficient relates the underwater form of a vessel to a block having the length, beam, and draft of the vessel.

All coefficients of form must be related to a particular draft. The coefficients appearing in the list of "Principal Dimensions and Characteristics," however, are usually given for the load draft. For modern merchant ships the block coefficient, at load draft, varies from about 0.65 to 0.75 depending upon, mainly, speed (although there are many other form characteristics which are of importance in determining speed).

In drawing the curve of block coefficient, the designer usually uses the same length and beam; that is, LBP and molded beam. This, of course, is true only for merchant ships where beam remains the same throughout the operating range of drafts. Then the products of this length and beam and a series of drafts are divided into the volume of displacement at the various drafts to obtain values of block coefficient. Since most merchant ships have finer forms at the lighter drafts than at load drafts, the curve generally shows the block coefficient to increase with draft.

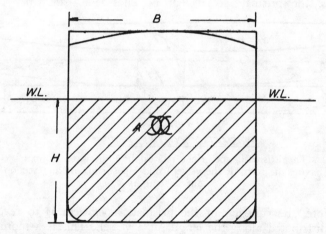

Figure 151.   The midship (or maximum) section coefficient relates the area of the midship section to a rectangle having the beam and draft of the section.

The Midship Section Coefficient: On most vessels, the midship section area is equal to or greater than the area at any other section. If, however, some other section is of maximum area, the latter is used to obtain the maximum section coefficient.

The coefficient relates the actual area of the midship section to a rectangle having the beam and draft of the section. On a barge, the coefficient would be 1.0. Most merchant vessels have extremely high values of midship section coefficient at all drafts due to the almost completely rectangular nature of the section. The only fineness occurs at the bilge. The coefficient, at load draft is around 0.99. At the light draft, it may be about 0.96. The formula for midship section coefficient is:

$$m = \frac{\text{Area of Midship Section}}{B \times H}$$

It is possible for the midship section coefficient to have a value greater than 1.0 if the hull amidships has a blister or bulge below the waterline. Model basin experiments have shown that such a form is helpful in dampening rolling without an appreciable increase in resistance.

The Prismatic Coefficient: Consider a form where the sectional form at every point of the length is the same as the form at the maximum section. This shape may, although it is something of a misnomer, be considered as having the form of a prism. Now, if we relate the actual form of the vessel to this "prism" we obtain a very interesting and important coefficient. If the actual form were the same as the form of the "prism," it would indicate that, forward and aft of amidships, there is no fining off of form. If the form, forward and aft is finer than that amidships, the prismatic coefficient becomes less than 1.0.

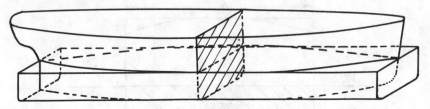

PRISMATIC COEFFICIENT

Figure 152. The Prismatic coefficient relates the underwater form of a vessel to a "prism" having the form of the vessel's midship (or maximum) section throughout its length.

Therefore, the function of the prismatic coefficient is to reveal how form is distributed along the length of a vessel. This is a more precise definition of form than that offered by the block coefficient. The formula for this coefficient is:

$$l = \frac{V}{L \times \text{Area of Midship Section}}$$

The prismatic coefficient has an important relationship to speed; and, in general, the lower the coefficient, the greater the speed which can be obtained on a given power. However, in some high ranges of speed a greater coefficient may produce better resistance characteristics. In the Chapter on Resistance this subject will be covered more fully.

It is sometimes desirable to use forward and after prismatic coefficients. In this case the coefficient is calculated by dividing the volume of displacement forward and aft of amidships by the product of L/2 and area of midship section.

The prismatic coefficient is related to the block coefficient and the midship section coefficient: $1 = b/m$

This may be proven as follows:

$$b = \dfrac{\dfrac{V}{L \times B \times H}}{\dfrac{A\,\text{⊠}}{B \times H}} = \dfrac{V}{L \times A\,\text{⊠}} = 1$$

For merchant vessels, the prismatic will be only of slightly greater value than the block coefficient. The reason for this can be seen when it is realized that in the case of the prismatic coefficient the figure produced by multiplying the area of the midship section by the length is almost a block due to the almost completely rectangular nature of the midship section.

The Waterplane Coefficient: This coefficient relates the actual area of waterplane to a rectangle having the length and beam of the waterplane. The formula for the waterplane coefficient is:

$$p = \dfrac{Awp}{L \times B}$$

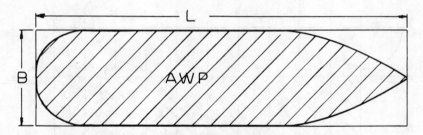

Figure 153. The waterplane coefficient relates the area of a waterplane to a rectangle having the length and beam of the waterplane.

The form of the waterplane is of great importance to such operating characteristics as stability and the coefficient is very useful in these connections.

Like the other coefficients of form, the waterplane coefficient generally increases with draft. For the load draft, p varies from about 0.7 to 0.8.

Centers of Areas and Volumes

Three very important hydrostatic values are:

1. The *geometric* center of gravity of the underwater form, expressed in terms of distance from amidships (or in some cases from the forward

or after perpendicular). This point is also known as the *center of buoyancy;* in this case the longitudinal position of the center of buoyancy (LCB).

2. The center of buoyancy expressed in terms of distance from the keel or baseline. In this case the value desired is the vertical position of the center of buoyancy. (VCB or KB).

3. The *geometric* center of gravity of waterplanes, expressed in terms of distance from amidships. This point is also known as the *center of flotation* or *tipping center,* and is the point around which a vessel trims.

The method used to calculate such geometric centers as these is similar for each center. (As well as for the calculation of the center of gravity of a mass.) The following statement of this method should be carefully noted by the student:

> Moments of area, volume, or weight are taken about some selected baseline or plane. The sum of the moments is divided by the total area, volume, or weight (as the case may be) to obtain the position of the center of area, volume, or mass from the selected base. (If the base is taken somewhere between the extremities of the form, the *net* moment is divided by the total area, volume, or mass.)

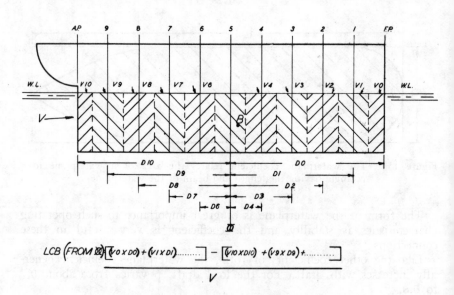

Figure 154. The Calculation of LCB.

Longitudinal Center of Buoyancy (LCB): It is now time to consider the displacement sheet method of calculating the longitudinal position of the center of buoyancy in terms of distance from the midship section.

The theory is this: Wedges of volume, the center of each wedge being taken at the frame station, are multiplied by their distance from amidships. These moments, forward and aft, are compared and a net moment obtained. This must be divided by the total volume of displacement to obtain LCB forward or aft of amidships.

However, on the displacement sheet, in order to make the arithmetical work easier, functions of volume instead of actual volume are multiplied by functions of distance from the midship section instead of actual distance. (The functions of distance may be seen to be the actual distances divided by the frame station spacing, s.) The net moment obtained (Sum_2) is then a function of the true net moment. To restore it to true value it must be multiplied by $2s/3$ (since each function of volume is multiplied by $2s/3$ to obtain true displacement) and s (since each function of distance must be multiplied by s to obtain actual distance). The multiplier of Sum_2 is then arrived at by:

$$Sum_2 \times \frac{2s/3 \times s}{Sum_1 \times 2s/3} \text{ or } Sum_2 \times \frac{s}{Sum_1} = LCB \text{ (from amidships)}$$

It should be observed that $Sum_1 \times 2s/3$ is equal to the volume of displacement. Thus we are dividing the true net moment by the true volume of displacement which produces our desired LCB from amidships.

Tons Per Inch Immersion (TPI): If weight is loaded or discharged from a vessel, the draft increases or decreases. Aboard ship it is important to know how this change of displacement affects draft. The hydrostatic value called "Tons per inch Immersion" offers a quick method of finding this change of draft, since TPI stands for the number of tons required to change the draft of the vessel by one inch.

To find the value of TPI at any draft it is necessary to find the weight of that layer of displacement one inch thick, which is added or removed as weight is loaded or discharged. If we find this weight it will represent the difference in displacement between the two drafts one inch apart, or it will represent TPI.

Now, if we find the area of the waterplane at that draft, (which is the next step on the displacement sheet) by running half-breadths through Simpson's Rule, it is a simple matter to find the volume of an inch thick layer at that waterplane. The volume of a *one foot* thick layer will be equal in cubic feet to the area of the waterplane in square feet. Dividing this figure by 12 will give the volume of a *one inch* thick layer in cubic feet. The weight of this one inch thick layer can then be found for salt water by dividing the volume by 35. Therefore the forula for finding TPI is:

$$TPI = \frac{Awp}{12 \times 35} \text{ or } \frac{Awp}{420} \text{ (Salt water)}$$

$$TPI = \frac{Awp}{12 \times 36} \text{ or } \frac{Awp}{432} \text{ (Fresh water)}$$

In practice, TPI is found by the designer and made up into a hydro-static curve for only salt water since the error involved in using a salt water TPI when in fresh water is negligible.

Center of Flotation: The center of flotation, or tipping center, is the geometric center of a waterplane. As such, the method used to calculate the longitudinal position of this point is the same as given above for finding the center of any area, volume, or mass.

The waterplane is divided up into a number of separate areas with a frame station being the center of each area. The moment of each area from amidships is found; the forward moments added and the after moments added; and the resulting net moment divided by the total area of the waterplane to find the center of flotation from amidships.

To facilitate the work on the displacement sheet, functions of area instead of actual areas are used since these are already available from the work involved in calculating the area of the waterplane in the preceding block of the displacement sheet. Also, functions of distance from amid-ships are used in the same way as in the calculation for LCB.

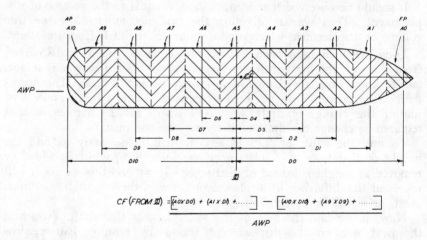

Figure 155. The Calculation of the geometric center of gravity of a waterplane (Center of Flotation).

The Sum_4 is then multiplied by $2s/3$ (to restore functions of area to true area) and s (since each lever arm, or distance from amidships, must be multiplied by s to obtain true distance from amidships). The product of this multiplication is then divided by $Sum_3 \times 2s/3$ (since this is equivalent to total area of the waterplane): The multiplier of Sum_4 is then:

$$Sum_4 \times \frac{2s/3 \times s}{Sum_3 \times 2s/3} \quad \text{or} \quad Sum_4 \times \frac{s}{Sum_3} = \text{C.F. from amidships}$$

Height of Metacenter Above Keel (KM)

An important hydrostatic value, needed for the calculation of GM, is the height of the transverse metacenter above the keel. Needed in some trim calculations is the height of the longitudinal metacenter above the keel. As has already been indicated, a detailed study of stability and trim calculations will not be given in this text. However, in order to have some idea of the meaning of the displacement sheet calculations involving KM, a short explanation of metacenter is given below:

When a vessel heels to a small angle, the center of gravity (G) may be assumed to be a fixed point. But the center of buoyancy (B) moves toward the immersed side in the arc of a circle. The line of force through B after this small inclination will intersect the original line of force through B when the ship was erect, at a point we call the metacenter (M). Now, if G is located below this point, it is clear that the couple formed by the downward force through G and the upward force through B will tend to right the vessel; if, however, G is located above M, the couple created will cause the vessel to heel to a greater angle. It is evident that M is an important point since a vessel must be loaded so that the center of gravity will be below M.

Now, the distance from the keel to M can be considered to be divided into two separate values—the distance from the keel to the center of buoyancy (KB) and the distance from the center of buoyancy to the metacenter (BM). KB or VCB can be calculated as indicated above for any geometric center. BM is called the metacentric radius, since it is a radius of that circle which has M for its center and the movement of B for small angles as an arc of that circle. BM can be shown to be equal to the moment of inertia of the waterplane divided by the volume of displacement:

$$BM = I/V$$

Longitudinally, KM has a much greater value than transversely due to the much greater moment of inertia of the waterplane longitudinally, thus giving a much greater BM. KB is the same, of course, in both cases.

Longitudinal BM: We may now observe the displacement sheet calculations necessary to obtain the longitudinal metacentric radius. The principal calculation here is that of the moment of inertia of the waterplane about a transverse axis through the center of gravity of the waterplane. The calculation of I is similar to that described in the Chapter on Strength; this is, areas, the center of each being at the various frame stations, are multiplied by the *square* of their distances from amidships. (Amidships is assumed to be the location of the axis of the waterplane initially; a correction for the distance between amidships and the center of gravity of the waterplane is then necessary.) The sum of these moments will be the moment of inertia of the waterplane. It should be noted that *all* moments, forward and aft, are added.

On the displacement sheet, functions of area instead of actual area are multiplied by the square of the lever arms to obtain the moments. Therefore the Sum_5 must be multiplied by $2s/3$ (to restore functions of area to true area) and s^2 (to restore lever arms to actual distance in feet). The multiplier of Sum_5 is then:

$$Sum_5 \times 2s/3 \times s^2 \ or \ Sum_5 \times 2s^3/3$$

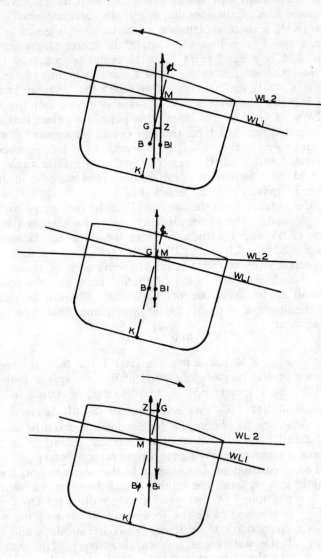

Figure 156. The Relationship of transverse KM to initial stability.

To find I about the true axis; that is, the axis through the center of gravity of the waterplane instead of an axis through the midship section, the following rule is used:

The moment of inertia of the waterplane area about the midship axis is reduced by the product of the waterplane area and the square of the distance from the center of gravity of the waterplane to the midship section.

On the displacement sheet, the distance from CG of waterplane to amidships has already been computed as well as the area of the waterplane. The correction to I may then be readily made.

Longitudinal BM can then be calculated by dividing this corrected I by the volume of displacement (which is available from the first block of the displacement sheet), since BM = I/V.

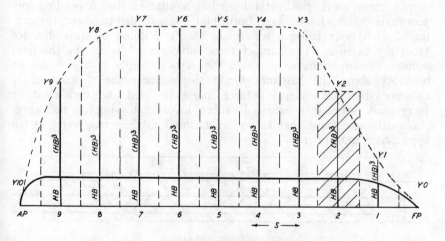

TO FIND I = FIND AREA OF LARGE FIGURE BY SIMPSONS RULE THIS
IS EQUAL TO THREE TIMES THE SUM OF THE MOMENTS
OF INERTIA OF EACH RECTANGLE $\boxed{S \times (HB)^3}$. DIVIDE BY
3 TO OBTAIN I AROUND ONE SIDE OF CENTERLINE. MULTIPLY
BY 2 TO OBTAIN TOTAL I.

Figure 157.   Calculation of Moment of Inertia of Waterplane around centerline.

Transverse BM: The theory of calculating transverse BM is similar to that for longitudinal BM. However, the axis around which moments are taken is now the centerline of the waterplane and we do not have the waterplane divided up into convenient longitudinal "stations" as we did transversely. Another method of finding transverse I must be used.

Consider the waterplane divided into a series of rectangles on either side of the centerline, each rectangle having a length equal to the distance between frame stations (s); each having its center at a frame station; and each having a breadth equal to the half-breadth on the frame station.

Now we know that the moment of inertia of a rectangle *taken around one edge* is: $LB^3/3$. It would be possible then, by using this formula to calculate the I of each one of these rectangles on *both* sides of the centerline; total all of these individual I's; and obtain the moment of inertia of the waterplane about its centerline axis.

On the displacement sheet, it is simpler to "add them up" by using Simpson's Rule, however. We consider each frame station to have a half-breadth equal to the half-breadth cubed and find the "area" under this curve. The multiplier of Sum_6 is then obtained by the product of s/3 (for Simpson's Rule; 1/3 for the inertia formula ($LB^3/3$); and 2, (since we used half-breadths instead of full breadths):

$$Sum_6 \times s/3 \times 1/3 \times 2 \text{ or } Sum_6 \times 2s/9$$

After obtaining the transverse moment of inertia, it is divided by the volume of displacement to obtain transverse BM.

Calculation of VCB and KM: Although the calculations necessary to obtain the vertical height of the center of buoyancy are not given on this displacement sheet, the method used is similar to that of finding any geometric center. In this case, horizontal layers of displacement, the center of each layer being a waterplane, are multiplied by their distance from the baseline. The sum of these moments is divided by the total volume of displacement to obtain the vertical height of the center of buoyancy above the baseline. On a displacement sheet, functions of volume rather than actual volume might be used and multiplied by lever arms rather than actual distances, in order to simplify the work. As usual these functional values are restored to their true value by an appropriate multiplier.

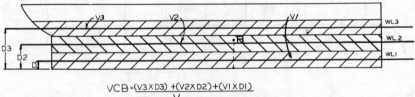

$$VCB = \frac{(V3 \times D3) + (V2 \times D2) + (V1 \times D1)}{V}$$

Figure 158.   Calculation of VCB.

Now, when VCB has been calculated, KM, both longitudinally and transversely, may be obtained easily by adding to VCB, the longitudinal BM to obtain longitudinal KM, and the transverse BM to obtain transverse KM. When the KM's for a sufficient number of drafts have been calculated, curves for these two values are included on the Curves of Form.

Change in displacement for one foot trim by the stern: As was mentioned above, when a vessel is in a trimmed condition the displacement as read from the mean draft obtained, is in error. This can be seen by reference to Figure 159 where a vessel, trimming around a center of flotation forward of amidships, has a mean draft as obtained from the forward and after draft readings which is greater than the true (even keel) mean draft. In this case, a subtractive correction is necessary. If the ship were trimmed by the head instead of the stern, an additive correction would be necessary. Also, if the center of flotation were aft of amidships, the necessary corrections to displacement would be reversed from the above condition.

In the following proof of the formula for finding this correction it should be noted that the object is to find the number of inches difference between the two mean drafts; that is, the mean draft obtained from the draft marks and the even keel draft. Since each inch difference in these drafts represents a layer of displacement one inch thick, the correction to displacement is found by multiplying the number of inches (or fraction thereof) by the "tons per inch immersion."

PROOF: Change in Displacement for 1' Trim by Stern =

$$\frac{\text{Tons per inch} \times 12 \times (\text{CG of WP from amidships})}{\text{LWL}}$$

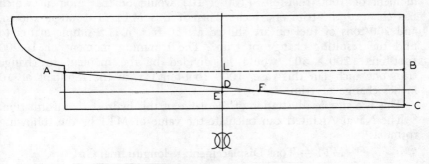

Figure 159.   The mean draft of a trimmed vessel is not the even keel draft unless the center of flotation is amidships.

1. Triangles ABC and DEF are similar.

2. $\dfrac{AB}{EF} = \dfrac{BC}{DE}$ where BC is considered to be 1 foot (the trim)

3. $AB \times DE = EF$

4. $DE = \dfrac{EF}{AB}$

5. Correction to displacement = $DE \times 12 \times TPI$

6. $DE = \dfrac{\text{Correction}}{12 \times TPI}$

7. Correction $= \dfrac{EF}{12 \times TPI}$ (Substituting in (4) $\dfrac{EF}{AB}$

8. Correction $= \dfrac{EF \times 12 \times TPI}{AB}$

9. Correction $= \dfrac{TPI \times 12 \times (CG \text{ of WP from amidships})}{LWL}$

For model:

Notice that in step 5 above, it would not be necessary to multiply DE by 12 since DE would already be in inches. Formula for model would then be:

$$\text{Change in displacement for } 1'' \text{ trim by the stern} = \dfrac{PPI \times CG \text{ of WP from amidships}}{LWL}$$

Moment to change trim one inch (MT1 or ITM): Suppose that for a vessel at a certain draft 100 tons are shifted longitudinally 10 feet and it is observed that the vessel changes its trim one inch. The trimming moment of 1000 foot-tons (100×10) would be that moment which has changed the trim one inch. Then if this MT1 of 1000 is known, and 200 tons of fuel oil are shifted aft 50 feet, it is a simple matter to find the resulting change of trim. The trimming moment of 10,000 foot-tons (200×50) would be divided by the moment to change trim one inch (in this case, 1000 foot-tons) with the resultant of 10 inches change of trim.

This is a simple illustration of the value of this hydrostatic information. The Naval Architect can calculate the value of MT1 by the following formula:[1]

$$MT1 = \dfrac{\text{Tons Displacement} \times \text{longitudinal GM}}{12 \times \text{Length}}$$

For the model displacement sheet, the formula is:

$$MT1 = \dfrac{\text{Pounds Displacement} \times \text{Longitudinal GM}}{L}$$

It is customary in the above formulas to use BM instead of GM since the latter is a variable for any given draft. However, the relative difference between the two values is very small and BM can be used with negligible error.

The Deadweight Scale: Unfortunately, the Curves of Form are very rarely found aboard merchant ships. However, certain hydrostatic infor-

---

[1] The proof for this formula and detailed information on the use of MT1 is given in Chapter 8, La Dage & Van Gemert, *Stability and Trim for the Ship's Officer.*

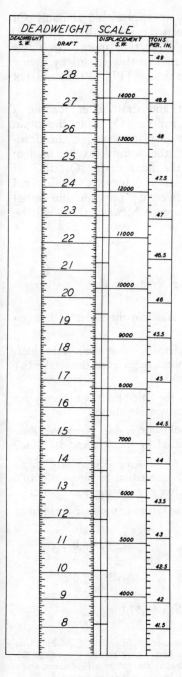

Figure 160.

mation considered particularly important is made up in the form of scales and placed on the *Capacity Plan*. The Capacity Plan *is* found on all merchant ships.

The hydrostatic information most commonly given in this form includes:

1. Displacement (in salt water).
2. Tons per inch immersion.
3. Moment to change trim one inch (sometimes omitted).
4. Deadweight.

Due to the inclusion of the latter value, the name given this form of information is the Deadweight Scale.

The Deadweight Scale is constructed by first laying out a vertical scale of drafts. The corresponding displacement, TPI, and MT1 values are then placed on vertical scales adjoining the draft scale. Remembering that deadweight is the weight of cargo, fuel, stores, oil, etc., aboard, it is apparent that at light displacement, deadweight will be zero. As displacement increases by units, say, of 100 tons, deadweight increases the same amount. Therefore, light displacement plus the total deadweight is equal to the load displacement.

The TPI figure should never be used for a large change of mean draft; that is, to find the change of draft after loading or discharging weight over, say, 1000 tons; or to find the number of tons necessary to increase or decrease draft, say, two feet. The reason for this is fairly obvious: Suppose that in picking off TPI, an error of 0.1 ton results. Now if only 10 or 20 inches of draft is involved, the error is only 1 or 2 tons of displacement. Suppose, however, that 100 or 200 inches of draft were involved; the error then is 10 or 20 tons, an appreciable amount. Of course, in picking off a TPI, a mean between the initial draft and final draft should be used whenever the change of draft is more than a few inches. One might lay down a rule of thumb in this regard by saying that whenever it is important to pick off a *mean* TPI, TPI should not be used.

How, then does one find displacement and draft after loading a great amount of weight? The method is simple: Opposite the mean draft for the initial condition, pick off the displacement (or the dead-weight); then, add to this displacement, the weight to be loaded; opposite the new displacement, pick off the final draft. Or, if it is desired to know the number of tons to load to achieve a certain final draft: Pick off the displacement (or deadweight) opposite the initial draft and the final desired draft. The difference between them will be the number of tons to load.[1]

QUESTIONS

1. How many ordinates are necessary in using Simpson's Rule? the Trape-zoidal Rule?

2. What relationship does the number of ordinates in the Rules of Integra-tion have to the number of equal intervals?

3. If the area of a waterplane is to be calculated by Simpson's Rule, half-breadths being multiplied by halved multipliers, what must the total F(a) be multiplied by to obtain area?

4. From what source does the designer obtain the half-breadths necessary for calculating the areas of waterplanes and transverse sections?

5. Why, when finding the area under a parabolic curve, does Simpson's Rule produce an answer in excess of that produced by the Trapezoidal Rule?

6. Explain why, with reference to the task of drawing and fairing ship's lines, it is better to increase the accuracy of integration by Simpson's Rule by adding ordinates only at the fore and after ends of the waterplanes.

7. Find the area in square feet of a vessels waterplane if the half-breadths at frame stations are as follows: (LBP = 400')

F.P.:	1.0 feet	#4:	28.0 feet	#8:	26.0 feet
#1:	22.0 "	#5:	28.0 "	#9:	20.0 "
#2:	28.0 "	#6:	28.0 "	AP:	7.0 "
#3:	28.0 "	#7:	28.0 "		

ANS: 19,520

---

[1] A recent progressive development has been the issuance of improved Capacity Plans by the firm of George Sharpe. These Plans include, among other things, the values for transverse KM on the Deadweight Scale. It is hoped that in the future all merchant ships will have Deadweight Scales with this very important hydrostatic value included.

8. A ship with a length of 500 feet and with half-sectional areas in square feet as follows is floating in salt water. Find her displacement in tons.

FP: 0   #4: 720   #8: 460
#1:   45   #5: 800   #9: 210
#2: 370   #6: 740   AP: 60
#3: 550   #7: 630

ANS: 12,933 tons

9. The areas of a vessel's waterplanes in square feet are: 2000, 2000, 1600, 1250, and 300. The common interval between them is 1.5 feet. Find the displacement in tons of the vessel in salt water neglecting the small portion below the lowest waterplane.

ANS: 264.3 tons

10. The floors in #1 D.B. tank on a certain vessel are spaced 2 feet apart. Find the capacity of the tank in tons of salt water if the half-breadths on every fourth floor measured at the base line, at the 2' W.L., and the 4' W.L. are:

	Forwardmost Floor	Second Floor	Third Floor	Fourth and aftermost floors
B.L.	2.0	4.0	12.0	15.0
2' W.L.	10.0	15.0	21.0	23.0
4' W.L.	18.0	24.0	24.5	25.0

ANS: 133.4 tons

11. A fore peak tank is 15 feet deep. Half-breadths are measured on three waterplanes at frames as follows: (Frame spacing is 2.0 feet)

Frame	Bottom W.P.	Middle W.P.	Top W.P.
#2			0.0
3		0.0	1.0
4	0.0	1.0	2.4
5	0.5	2.0	4.0
6	1.6	3.0	5.2
7	2.6	4.0	6.6
8	4.0	6.0	8.4

Find the capacity of the tank in tons of salt water. Use the trapezoidal rules to find the areas of waterplanes; use Simpson's Rule with half-multipliers to find volume.

ANS: 23.5 tons

12. Which one of the following alterations to a vessel would necessitate drawing up new hydrostatic curves? Why?
a) Adding ballast of a permanent nature in the double bottoms.
b) Building additional superstructure on the weather deck.
c) Converting a cargo space to reefer space.
d) Adding a "blister" on either side of vessel amidships.

13. Why is it sometimes necessary to correct the hydrostatic values obtained by using the mean draft of a vessel in a trimmed condition.

14. Buoyancy, or vertically upward pressure, is a function of what two factors?

15. What is the pressure per square inch at a depth of 50 feet in salt water?

ANS: 22.22 lbs.

16. If the weight of a cubic foot of fresh water is 62.4 lbs., what is the pressure per square foot at a depth of 100 feet in water of 1.013 density?

ANS: 6320 lbs.

17. Prove the validity of Archimedes Principle by showing that the total vertically upwards pressure of a barge with a length of 80 feet, beam of 30 feet and draft of 20 feet, is equal to the weight of the water displaced by the barge.

18. Define:
    a) Molded displacement
    b) Appendage displacement
    c) Specific gravity

19. The Victory ship (LBP —436.5 ft.) has a displacement of 4543 tons, light. Her load displacement is 15,200 tons. Find her wetted surface at (a) light draft (b) load draft and find (c) the area of her boot topping.

ANS: (a) 21,969.5 sq. ft.; (b) 40,182.5 sq. ft.; (c) 18,213.0 sq. ft.

20. A vessel has a displacement of 11,200 tons at a certain draft. What will be her change of draft when she enters fresh water from salt water if her TPI is 40.0?

ANS: 7 inches, increase.

21. Using the theory that draft varies inversely with density, what will be the new draft of a merchant vessel in water of 1.020 S.G., if her draft were 22 feet in fresh water?

ANS: 21' 06.8"

22. A vessel at a certain draft has a displacement of 15,000 tons and a TPI of 49.5. What will be the change of draft in inches when she goes from salt water to water of 1.006 density?

ANS: 6.06 in., increase.

23. A landing boat, which weighs 50 tons is lowered over the side by ship's gear, until 700 cubic feet of salt water is displaced by the boat. At this point, what is the reduction in the ship's displacement?

ANS: 20 tons

24. Describe the construction and use of Bonjean's Curves

25. An empty barge 50 feet in length, 20 feet in beam, and 10 feet in depth is floating in sea water at a draft of 5 feet. If the barge has five water-tight compartments of equal length, and one is damaged and flooded, what will be the new draft of the barge?

ANS: 6' 03"

26. Bilge keels are to be fitted to a ship whose TPI is 48. The estimated weight of the bilge keels is 36 tons and the volume they occupy is 840 cubic feet. What will be the increase in draft due to fitting these keels?

ANS: ¼ in.

27. The displacement of a barge form vessel floating light in sea water at a draft of 5 feet forward and 6 feet aft is desired. Her length is 100 feet; beam, 20 feet. When loaded the vessel draws 12 feet of water forward and aft. What is the deadweight?

ANS: 314.3 tons
371.4 tons

28. In finding volume of displacement on a displacement sheet areas of half-sections are run through Simpson's Rule using half-multipliers. There are 21 frame stations over a length of 460 feet. What multiplier is needed to convert F(V) to volume of displacement in cubic feet? to tons displacement (SW)?

ANS: 30.667 — 0.8762

29. In general, how do coefficients of form vary with:
    a) Increase in draft
    b) The type of vessel with regard to speed

30. What, exactly, is a coefficient of form and what is its function?

31. Given that length is 450 feet, beam is 60 feet, draft is 20 feet, prismatic coefficient is 0.82 and midship section coefficient is 0.95, calculate the displacement of the vessel in salt water.

ANS: 12,019 tons

32. A vessel has the following characteristics: Length, 400 ft.; Beam, 50 feet; draft, 27′ 06″; Depth, 34 feet; midship section coefficient, 0.96; longitudinal coefficient, 0.78; waterplane area, 16,400 square feet. Calculate the displacement in salt water, and the waterplane coefficient.

ANS: 11,767 tons—0.82

33. What is the prismatic coefficient of a vessel with the following characteristics? Length, 420 feet; beam, 50 feet, draft, 25 feet; midship section coefficient, 0.91; tons displacement, 12,000.

ANS: 0.88

34. A vessel has the following dimensions and characteristics: Length, 400 feet; beam, 50 feet, draft, 28 feet; area of midship section, 1260 square feet; block coefficient, 0.75. Calculate the midship section and longitudinal coefficients.

ANS: 0.90 — 0.83

35. Information relating to the positions of two longitudinal centers are commonly included on a set of Curves of Form. What are they?

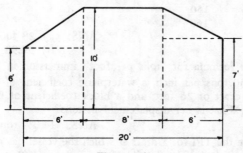

Figure 161.

36. For Figure 161 find the geometric center of gravity with reference to:
    a) The left hand side of the figure.
    b) The baseline of the figure.

ANS: a) 10.13 feet; b) 4.55 feet

37. What is a synonym for (a) geometric center of underwater form (b) geometric center of gravity of a waterplane?

38. If volume of displacement in cubic feet is known and functions of volume at frame stations are known $F(V)$ being obtained from the displacement block where half-areas were run thru Simpson's Rule using half-multipliers) and then suppose the functions of volume to be multiplied by the distance in feet from the after perpendicular, find the multiplier necessary to convert the sum of the moments to LCB from AP.

ANS: $4s/3V$

39. On the displacement sheet, how does one tell whether LCB is forward or aft of amidships?

40. Given a vessel with a length between perpendiculars of 120 feet and one-half areas at frame stations as follows, calculate (a) Volume of displacement (b) LCB from amidships. Note: Use same form as in text with $\frac{1}{2}$ multipliers.

Station	$\frac{1}{2}$ Areas	Station	$\frac{1}{2}$ Areas
0	0 sq. ft.	5	140 sq. ft.
1	70	6	140
2	90	7	80
3	120	8	60
4	140		

ANS: a) 24,400 cu. ft.
b) 3.93 ft. aft of amid.

41. Given a vessel with a length between perpendiculars of 120 feet and $\frac{1}{2}$ areas at frame stations as follows, calculate (a) Volume of displacement (b) LCB from AP. Note: Use form similar to one in text, but with $\frac{1}{2}$ Simpsons multipliers.

Station	$\frac{1}{2}$ Areas	Station	$\frac{1}{2}$ Areas
0	0 sq. ft.	5	160 sq. ft.
1	60	6	160
2	120	7	110
3	150	8	40
4	160		

ANS: a) 28,400 cu. ft.
b) 54.93 feet

42. What is the formula for "tons per foot" immersion in S.W.?

43. A ship of 50 tons per inch, a waterplane coefficient of 0.8, a length of 400 feet, a draft of 26 feet, and a block coefficient of 0.72 is sailing in salt water. What is her displacement in tons?

ANS: 14,039 tons

44. Approximate the TPI for a draft at which the vessel has a waterplane area of 2000 square feet. The density of the water is 1.013.

ANS: 4.7 tons

45. A ship whose draft changes 5 inches in passing from salt water to fresh water has a displacement of 6000 tons, a length of 300 feet and a beam of 50 feet. What is her waterplane coefficient?

ANS: 0.84

46. Given a vessel with a length between perpendiculars of 160 feet and half-breadths on frame stations as follows, calculate (a) area of waterplane (b) TPI (c) C.ofF. from amidships. Note: Use same form as in text, but with one-half Simpsons multipliers.

Station	½ Breadths	Station	½ Breadths
0	0 ft.	5	10 ft.
1	7	6	10
2	9	7	9
3	10	8	6
4	10		

ANS: a) 2773.3 sq. ft.; b) 6.6 tons; c) 5.0 feet aft of amid.

47. Suppose that F(A) at frame stations are multiplied by distance in feet from the forward perpendicular, the F(A) being obtained by running half-breadths through Simpsons Rule using half-multipliers. The area of the waterplane is known. Find the multiplier necessary to convert the sum of the moments to the distance of the center of flotation from forward perpendicular.

ANS: 4s/3 Awp

48. Supply symbols for the following values:
a) Height of metacenter above keel.
b) Height of metacenter above center of gravity.
c) Metacentric radius.
d) Height of center of buoyancy above keel.

49. Show, by means of a sketch why the relationship between the vertical positions of G and M control the initial stability of a vessel.

50. With the data supplied in Ques. 46 and using the same form as shown in the text, compute the moment of inertia of the waterplane about its transverse axis through (a) the midship section and (b) the center of flotation.

ANS: a) 4,821,333 ft.^{4}; b) 4,752,001 ft.^{4}

51. Explain why the correction to I about amidships is always applied subtractively to obtain I about center of flotation.

52. With the data supplied in Ques. 46 and using the same form as shown in the text, compute the transverse moment of inertia of the waterplane, I.

ANS: 79,831 ft.^{4}

53. Suppose, in computing transverse BM, the cubes of half-breadths are multiplied by half Simpson's multipliers and the sum of the resulting moments is obtained. What multiplier is needed to convert this sum to BM if volume of displacement (V) is known?

ANS: 4s/9V

54. It is desired to compute the transverse moment of inertia of the waterplane by the same method described in the text but using the formula for moment of inertia of a rectangle about its neutral axis — LB^3/12. What changes will be necessary in the form and what will be the multiplier for the sum of the moments?

ANS: s/36

55. For the data in Ques. 46, find the change in displacement (a) for one foot trim by the stern (b) for 3 feet trim by the stern (c) 2 feet trim by the head.

ANS: a) plus 2.4 tons
      b) plus 7.2 tons
      c) minus 4.8 tons

56. The displacement as read from the mean draft of a vessel with a trim of 2 feet 6 inches by the stern is 20 tons less than the true displacement. If LWL is 400 feet and TPI is 50 tons, find the distance forward or aft of amidships of the center of flotation.

ANS: 5.33 feet aft.

57. At load draft, center of flotation lies aft of amidships. If a maximum number of tons is to be loaded without submerging the applicable load line, should the vessel be trimmed by the head or stern? Why?

58. If, in calculating VCB, $\frac{1}{2}$ waterplane areas spaced 6 feet apart are run through Simpson's Rule, using $\frac{1}{2}$ multipliers to find F(V) and these F(V)'s are multiplied by arms instead of actual distances from the baseline, what is the multiplier necessary to convert the sum of the moments to VCB? V, the volume of displacement is known.

ANS: 144/3V

59. If tons displacement are 12,000, longitudinal BM, 400 feet, and length, 400 feet, find MTI.

ANS: 1000 ft. tons.

60. A vessel has a trim of 3 feet by the stern. The correction to displacement for one foot trim by the stern is a plus 8 tons. TPI is 48 and the mean draft as read from the draft marks forward and aft is 20 feet 4 inches. (a) Is center of flotation forward or aft of amidships? (b) What is the even keel draft for this vessel (with the same displacement)?

ANS: a) Aft
      b) 20′ 4½″

Chapter 14

THE SHIP IN WAVES

The action of a ship in waves is a fascinating, but extremely complex study. No one can predict with exactitude the behavior of a vessel subjected to the forces of wind and weather. Nevertheless, it is possible to study the various motions of a vessel in waves and how these motions are effected by the hull design, the condition of loading, and the characteristics of the waves themselves.

The principal motions of a vessel in waves are:

1. *Rolling* or motion about the vessel's longitudinal axis.
2. *Pitching* or motion about the vessel's transverse axis.
3. *Yawing* or motion about the vessel's vertical axis.
4. *Heaving* or vertical bodily motion of the vessel.
5. *Sway,* or *lateral,* side-to-side bodily motion.
6. *Surge,* or longitudinal bodily motion.

In addition, there are such motions as *lurching* which may be defined as an abnormal, deep, and sometimes sudden roll; and *slamming* which results from a combination of heaving and the forward motion of the vessel and is characterized by a jarring impact of the seas on the bottom of the vessel around the second compartment from the stem.

Some of these motions are related to each other; others are entirely independent motions. All or most of the motions, however, occur simultaneously and have their effect on the efficient operation of a ship. Although the mariner does not possess complete control over these motions, there *is* much that he can do to diminish the motions or alleviate their effects.

Before considering these various motions of a ship in waves, it is necessary to consider the nature of the waves themselves.

The Nature of Ocean Waves

All men who go to sea or intend to go to sea, should be interested in the nature of ocean waves. What *are* waves? How are they propagated? How about their length, their velocity, their height and period? And how do these wave characteristics effect the motions of a vessel and its operation? The answers to these questions are of great practical value to mariners. Let us consider, in turn, the elements which create ocean waves.

Wave Motion: To understand the manner in which waves are formed, we must first observe the behavior of individual water particles. The latter are found to revolve in a circle. At the crest of a wave these particles are moving in the direction of wave travel; and in the trough, they are moving in a direction opposite to the wave travel. At intermediate points of the wave profile, the particles move as indicated in Figure 162. This interesting orbital motion of water particles in a wave can be seen and felt very clearly when surf bathing.

In Figure 162 it is assumed that the wave travel is from left to right. The water particles composing the wave are then moving clockwise, each particle in its own circle. If we draw 13 circles and let the sum of their diameters represent the length of a wave from crest to crest, the manner in which the wave profile is formed can be easily seen. At the crest, the particles are moving horizontally to the right. In the next circle to the right, the particles are nearing the top of *their* circle, and their movement is partially vertical. In circle number 4, the particles are moving vertically upwards; in circle number 7, the particles are moving horizontally but in a direction opposite to the travel of the wave; and in circle number 10, the particles are moving vertically downwards. If a curve is drawn through the points on each circle which represent the position of the water particles at those points, the wave profile has been drawn.

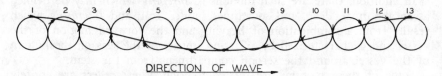

DIRECTION OF WAVE

Figure 162.   The orbital motion of water particles create a wave form.

The curve drawn results in a *trochoid* form. Therefore, this theoretical wave which corresponds very closely with the form of actual waves which have been observed, is called a *trochoidal wave*. The wave profile may be relatively flat or steep depending upon the ratio of wave length to wave height. The limiting form of a trochoid is called a cycloid. The latter form is developed when a point on the perimeter of a circle is traced as the circle is rolled along a straight line. In all ship calculations which require a wave form to be used, Naval Architects accept the trochoidal wave (with length-height ratio = 20) as reasonably approximating actual conditions. We have seen, for example, that in strength calculations, the ship is "suspended" on the crest of a trochoidal wave, and the resulting stresses calculated.

The orbital motion of water particles described above, exists not only near the surface but also extends some distance down from the surface. However, the diameter of the circles decreases with depth and therefore the form of the sub-surfaces becomes flatter as the depth of water increases. (See Figure 163).

Effect of waves on ship's speed: Consider the case of a ship heading into waves. When the crest of a wave strikes the ship's bow, the increased height of water will of course increase the ships resistance merely from the point of view of increased pressure in this area. But also, it should be noted that the orbital motion of the water at the crest is such that the water is moving horizontally in a direction opposite to the direction of ship travel. Now, of course the water in the trough further aft along the ship's length is moving with the ship, but this water is not able to

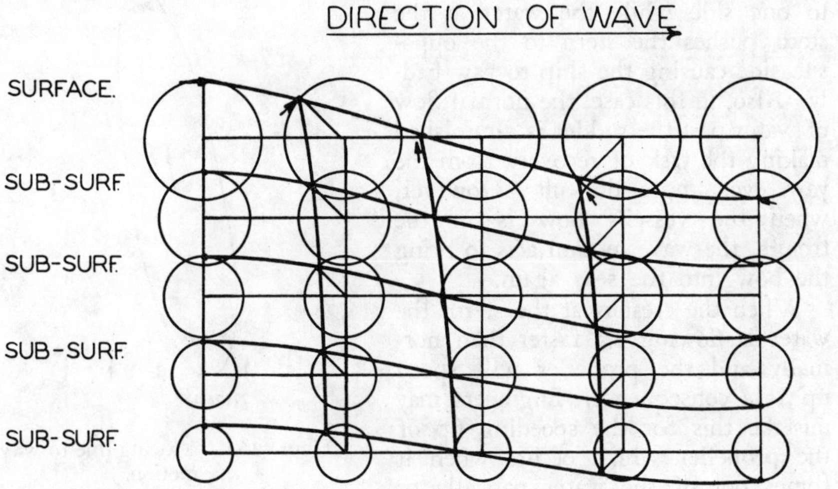

Figure 163. Cross section of wave showing how the orbital motion of water particles create not only the surface of the wave, but also the sub-surfaces. The latter become flatter due to the reduction in diameter of the circle in which the water particles revolve.

exert as much effect as the water at the bow due to the fact that there is no place for it to "push". Also, the depth of the water is less. If a trough occurs at the stern, the benefit which might accrue from the forward push here is more than counterbalanced by the disadvantage of decreased forward-acting pressure.

A person on a surfboard may take advantage of the orbital motion of waves to ride a crest into the beach. Let the board lag behind the crest, however, and its rider will quickly find himself dislodged from his precarious perch. A small boat traveling with the waves will make more progress when the crest sweeps by than when it is in the trough. A small boat lying alongside a dock or ship is in a dangerous situation when acted upon by the waves, since the crest will throw the boat against the side; the trough will bring it away; and then the next crest will once again cause the boat to crash against the side. And so it goes: numerous examples could be cited of the effect of orbital water motion.

Yawing due to wave motion: Steering can be tremendously effected by wave motion. Consider for example, a ship operating in waves of lengths roughly double the length of the ship. In this case, the water at the bow and stern is traveling in opposite directions. Now, if the bow falls off even slightly into the crest of a wave, the water at the bow pushes the bow to one side while the water at the stern pushes the stern to the opposite side causing the ship to yaw badly. Also, in this case, the normal flow of water past the rudder is diminished making the task of recovery from the yaw even more difficult. However, when the vessel's bow is in the trough, the wave motion acts to bring the bow into the seas again.

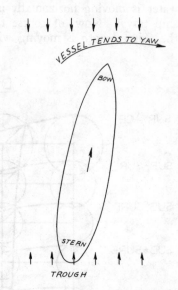

When the crest is at the stern, the water is flowing aft faster than normally and the propeller will speed up as a consequence. Engineers may mistake this for the speeding up of the propeller which occurs when it comes out of the water partially or

Figure 164.   Yawing due to wave motion.

completely. Engine revolutions should be reduced in the lattter case, but not the former.

Wave Characteristics: From the mathematical conception of the trochoidal wave and also from some empirical formulas derived from observation it is possible to predict certain wave characteristics. In this section we shall investigate the following:

Length of wave, speed of wave, wave period, orbital velocity of water at the surface, and the height of the wave. Most of these characteristics are interrelated and can be easily calculated by simple formulas.

The *length of a wave* is defined as the distance in feet between successive crests. The formula for length is:

$$L = 5.12T^2 \quad \text{where: } L \text{ is the length of wave in feet}$$
$$\text{or} \qquad\qquad\quad T \text{ is the wave period in seconds}$$
$$L = 0.557V^2 \quad\quad V \text{ is the speed of the wave in knots}$$

Observations at sea for many years by competent observers bring out the fact that ocean waves are normally several hundred feet in length. Waves over 500 or 600 feet in length are· rare and would only be encountered in a severe storm, although waves of over 1000 feet have been recorded.

From the formulas for wave length it can be seen that length, period, and speed of waves depend upon each other; that length varies as the square of both the wave period and wave velocity.

The *speed of a wave* is defined as the speed, say, of the crest in knots and must not be confused with the orbital velocity of water. The formulas for wave speed are:

$$V = 3.03T$$
or
$$V = 1.34 \sqrt{L}$$

The *wave period* is defined as the time in seconds for successive crests to pass a fixed point. The formulas for wave period are:

$$T = 0.442 \sqrt{L}$$
or
$$T = 0.33 \ V$$

From the formulas for wave speed and period, it should be noted that the speed and period of waves vary directly with each other and that both speed and period vary as the square root of the length.

The relationships among length, speed, and period of waves can, perhaps, be best demonstrated by a tabular listing such as the following:

Length of wave, feet:	100	200	300	400	500	600	700
Speed of wave, knots:	13.4	19.0	23.2	26.8	30.0	32.8	35.4
Wave period, seconds:	4.4	6.3	7.7	8.8	9.9	10.8	11.7

The *height of a wave* can not be predicted reliably from the wave's length, speed, or velocity since wave height is related to the wind force, the "fetch" of open water over which the wind is free to blow, and the wind duration. However, observers have suggested that the height of waves in feet will generally approximate one-half to two-thirds the wind velocity in knots. Other observers relate wave height to the "fetch" as well as the wind velocity.

It should be noted that wave heights are commonly exaggerated by some mariners. This is due to the transverse or longitudinal inclination from which the observer measures the height. However, it should be noted that if two wave systems exist with waves of different lengths moving in the same direction, at one point the crest of one wave will be superposed on the crest of another causing a considerable increase in height.

Wave Propagation: Consider first the water surface to be perfectly smooth. Then as a light wind blows over the surface slight irregularities are raised. The flow of air over these irregularities rapidly builds them up into waves. The pressure on the windward side of the waves presses down, while the resulting defect of pressure on the leeward side causes the wave surface to be raised. As long as the wind velocity is greater than the wave velocity, the wave will continue to increase in length, velocity, and period.

It should be noted that the propagation of waves is not due to wind "friction" on the water surface as was once believed to be the case.

Shallow Water Waves: Due to the restriction of water depth, the circular orbit of deep water particles becomes more nearly elliptical. The wave length decreases and the speed of the wave becomes smaller; however, the height increases, the trough bcomes wider, and the crests steep and sharp, making the going rough for small boats.

It is interesting to note that the number of waves per minute to pass a fixed point at sea is the same number of these waves which will break on the shore in a minute. This is due to the reduction in wave length as well as wave speed, the wave period remaining the same in shallow water as it is in deep water. The observer on a beach therefore can use the deep water formula for wave period to find the length and velocity of the ocean waves which have caused the shallow water waves.

Rolling

A ship's design, no matter how well conceived and carefully brought to completion, cannot be properly utilized unless the operating officer is aware of the purpose of the design and its limitations. This point is illustrated vividly in that portion of the design which concerns the vessel's stability. The designer can only produce a vessel with proper stability for an average condition, and as any ship's officer knows, the variations in loading conditions of a dry cargo vessel can be extreme. The action of this type of vessel in a seaway, therefore, is dependent to no small degree upon the judgment of those persons who are responsible for the loading of cargo and the disposition of fuel and solid and liquid ballast. "Those persons" include the Master and by delegation, his subordinate officers.

The purpose of this section is to acquaint the student in as untechnical language as possible of some of the practical considerations open to him in attempting to obtain as easy a motion as possible for his vessel. We will ignore the effect of the form of his vessel since the officer cannot alter it. However, it is well to remember that most of the rolling characteristics of a vessel are due to her design and the inevitable seas in which she operates. When a vessel moves among waves, she will roll and the control of the ship's officer over this rolling can only be partial.

If a normal form merchant vessel were caused to roll in *still water* it would be found that her rolling period, that is, the time required for the vessel to roll from starboard to port and back to starboard, would be approximated by the following relationship:

$$T = \frac{.44 \ B}{\sqrt{GM}}$$

where: T is the rolling period in seconds

B is the beam of the ship in feet

GM is the metacentric height in ft.

This still water rolling period is know as the *natural rolling period*. In a seaway a vessel will attempt to roll in her natural period and over a period of time the average rolling time will be very close to the natural period. The ship's officer is interested in the rolling period since a rapid period means an uncomfortable ship, as well as a possible cause of damage to topside structure and gear. Also, a slowly rolling vessel, although comfortable, has poor stability and seas are able to wash more freely over her decks. GM bears a direct relationship to rolling period as indicated in the formula. A large GM indicates a stiff ship with fast rolling. A small GM indicates a tender ship with slow rolling.

The ship's officer is also interested in the angle or amplitude of rolling. Rolling to moderate angles does not increase the period of rolling but merely increases angular velocity. However, if the amplitude of roll is great the period of roll will increase somewhat.

Although waves are usually very irregular, occasionally wind blowing steadily over a great expanse of ocean may cause the period of the waves to be regular. The *wave period* can be defined as the time required for successive crests to pass a fixed point. However, the ship's officer is interested in the *apparent period*, that is; the time required for successive crests to strike his vessel. The apparent period is equal to the wave period only when the ship is at right angles to the waves. When the apparent period is the same as the natural period of a vessel, heavy synchronized rolling can be expected.

Our problem now resolves itself into two questions and their answers: (1) What are the factors affecting *period* of roll? (2) What are the factors affecting *amplitude* of roll?

Factors affecting period of roll: As far as the ship's officer is concerned control of rolling period depends primarily on the metacentric height (GM). If a vessel is loaded or ballasted so as to have a very low center of gravity, the chances are that GM will be very large. However, the draft of the vessel has a great deal to do with the position of M, thus the value of GM. The metacenter in the usual form merchant vessel is very high at the lighter drafts, but moves down rapidly with increase of draft. At the lesser drafts, then more weight must be loaded in the upper decks of a ship if GM is not to be increased to the point where rapid, uncomfortable rolling would occur.

Another factor which controls the period of roll is the distribution of the heavier weights transversely and vertically away from the center of gyration. The rolling period formula assumes that the cargo is loaded homogeneously. This is not always the case. If weights are "winged out" or loaded high and low, the result is similar to that of a man trying to balance on a tightrope. The longer the pole which he uses to assist himself, the easier it is for him to achieve an easy balance. Also, if he placed weights on the end of the pole balance would be even more easily achieved. Thus, an increase in the *"mass moment of inertia"* or *"radius of gyration"* increases the period of roll for a vessel. However, in many cases it may be impractical to load or ballast in this fashion.

It may be well at this point to answer the question: "What is a proper GM for my vessel"? The figure, 5% of the beam is often cited as a good GM for a dry cargo vessel at load draft. However, this figure is a maximum and a vessel will be perfectly safe and a great deal more comfortable at a somewhat lower figure. For example, a vessel with a 60 foot beam would require a 3 foot GM using the 5% of beam figure. This would produce a rolling period of about 15.3 seconds. This is satisfactory but not ideal. A 2 foot GM with a resultant rolling period of about 18.7 seconds would be better for the *load draft*. However, at lighter drafts where the righting force is reduced by a reduction in displacement, a GM of 5% of the beam is preferable. In the final analysis, the best GM for a given vessel and a given draft can only be arrived at by experience with that vessel.

Factors affecting amplitude of roll: The amplitude of roll is even less susceptible of control by the ship's officer than the period of roll, since one of the most important factors involved is the wave slope. The wave slope depends upon the length and height of the wave, which in turn, depends upon the duration, velocity, and "fetch" of the wind, and the depth of the water. Nevertheless, some control does exist and should be considered.

At sea, a very stiff ship (one with a large GM) will *tend* to assume the angle of the wave slope and therefore will undergo large amplitudes of roll in heavy weather. Couple this with the rapid angular velocity of the stiff ship and one has a thoroughly uncomfortable and dangerously stressed vessel. On the other hand, a very tender ship will not respond quickly to the seas, thus permitting them to sweep up and over the weather decks. Obviously, this is as undesirable as large amplitudes of roll. It must be emphasized though, that the condition of a ship which is rolling violently cannot necessarily (and probably will not be) improved by increasing stability (GM). The ideal condition seems to be as small a GM as will permit of reasonable safety in a damaged condition (or listed condition due to a reasonable weight shift). Recommended once more is a GM somewhat less than 5% of the beam.

Another factor affecting amplitudes of roll is the disposition of the heavier weights transversely and vertically. "Winging out" weights or placing them high and low in the vessel, results in *greater* amplitudes of roll. Conversely, concentrating the heavier weights along the center line would decrease the amplitude of roll. Thus, to obtain an increase in period of roll by increasing the radius of gyration, one must accept the undesirable increase in amplitude of roll. Theoretically, it would appear that a moderate GM coupled with a moderate radius of gyration would produce optimum rolling climate since the moderate GM would offer a large period of roll while the moderate radius of gyration would prevent excessive amplitudes of roll.

A very important factor determining amplitude of roll is the relation between the natural period of the ship and the apparent period of the waves. If these periods synchronize, violent rolling can occur regardless of other factors. However, in studies made at model basins it has been found that probability of synchronism decreases as GM decreases. A natural period of 20 seconds would very rarely produce synchronized rolling while a period of say, 12 seconds, would lend itself very well to customary apparent periods. Of course, it is possible to reduce or eliminate synchronous rolling by an alteration of course or speed, but this solution may not be a desirable one.

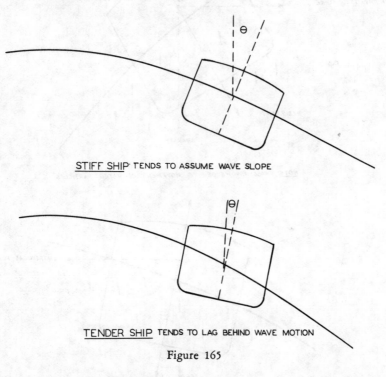

STIFF SHIP TENDS TO ASSUME WAVE SLOPE

TENDER SHIP TENDS TO LAG BEHIND WAVE MOTION

Figure 165

It should be pointed out if synchronism *did* occur when a vessel was very tender, extremely dangerous amplitudes of roll might occur. In this case, it might be desirable to increase the GM by ballasting.

Also to be noted on the debit side of small GM's is the fact that in spite of the steadier motion of a vessel with a small GM, the vessel is more apt to lurch occasionally. Sometimes the deliberate creation of free surface in order to reduce the GM is suggested. This method will undoubtedly increase the period of roll, but also will increase the tendency to lurch. Once again, experience with a particular vessel is the best answer to all alternatives.

The Virtual Upright Position

The customary conception of the development of righting arms and moments as a vessel heels must be modified to some extent when con-

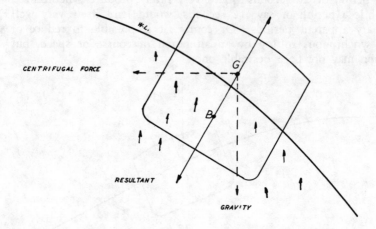

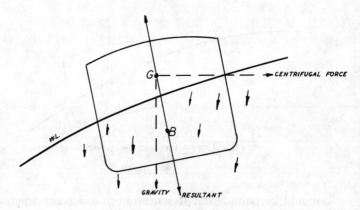

Figure 166. The Virtual Upright position.

sidering a vessel moving in a seaway. Ordinarily it is assumed that as a vessel heels, the center of buoyancy moves to the low side thereby creating a couple with the forces of buoyancy and weight as the forces and the righting arm as the arm of the couple. The motion of the water in which the vessel is immersed modifies this concept.

First, it must be remembered that water in a wave is moving in an orbital path. Thus the water (and the ship in it) is affected by centrifugal force in addition to the force of gravity. The two latter forces may be considered as components of a resultant force which acts through the center of gravity of the vessel. For example, consider a vessel on the leeward slope of a wave. All the water particles around the vessel are moving approximately vertically upwards. However, the centrifugal force is directed out along the radius of the circle in which the water is moving. Thus the centrifugal force component is directed , in this case, approximately horizontally toward the oncoming crest of the wave. The resultant force will then act down along the centerline of the vessel (and not vertically down toward the center of the earth). Meanwhile, the center of buoyancy has not moved to the low side since the waterline is at right angles to the centerline and buoyancy has not been shifted to the low side. The orbital motion of the water particles has also disturbed the normal (still water) upward pressure distribution and results in the force of buoyancy being directed vertically upwards along the centerline of the vessel instead of vertically upwards from the center of the earth.

In this situation, then, the lines of force through G and B are not separated even though the ship is heeled. No righting arm or moment exists. The vessel is in a "virtual upright" position. Righting arms and moments will be developed as the vessel swings away from the virtual upright position to port or starboard. Therefore in a seaway, a vessel attempts to return to the virtual upright position, not the actual upright position. Perhaps the student can understand more clearly now why a stiff ship tends to assume the wave slope angle.

Virtual Displacement: The righting moment of a vessel acting in a seaway is modified not only by changes in the development of righting arms but also by a virtual change in the displacement (weight) of the vessel. The apparent weight of any body moving vertically upwards or downwards is greater or less than its actual weight depending upon the direction of movement, up or down. Since the water in a wave (and the ship) is "heavier" in the trough and "lighter" in a crest, the virtual weight of a vessel is reduced when on the crest and increased when in the trough of a sea.

This phenomenon has interesting applications, especially for small boats. Consider a sail boat, heeled over to an angle where the righting force exactly balances the inclining force of the wind. When the boat is on a crest, its weight is decreased in effect, thus decreasing the righting moment. In order to obtain equilibrium again the boat will have to heel over further until the righting moment has once again achieved equality with the heeling moment. If the boat does not possess this reserve of stability, it will capsize.

Clinometer Error

If the ship's officer uses a clinometer to obtain amplitudes of roll, he is cautioned that unless the clinometer is mounted at the axis of roll (approximately at the waterline) it will show an angle of roll considerably in error. This is due to the fact that the point of support for the pendulum is undergoing acceleration to a degree which varies with the height of the clinometer above the waterline and the period of roll. If the clinometer is placed in the wheelhouse, for example, it will indicate an angle in excess of the true one. Preferably, the clinometer should be located in the

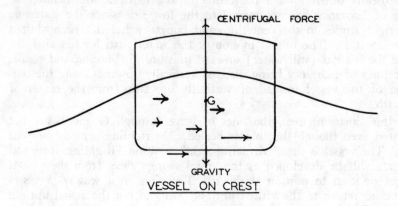

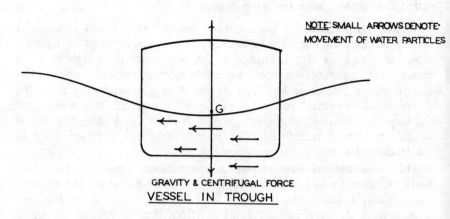

Figure 167. When a vessel is on a crest, the centrifugal force developed by the orbital motion of water particles is opposed to the force of gravity and the displacement is virtually less; when in the trough, centrifugal force combines with gravity to increase the displacement of the vessel virtually.

engine room. However, some clinometers are adjusted for this angular acceleration.

Anti-rolling Devices

Many devices have been designed to reduce the amplitude of ship's rolls, and in some cases to increase the period of roll. The principal factor leading to dangerous and uncomfortable rolling is the angular acceleration, so that reducing the amplitude of roll does not in itself lead to a more comfortable and seaworthy ship. Conversely, if the period of roll can be increased, this will improve rolling characteristics even though the amplitude is not decreased. Let us consider some of the anti-rolling devices which have been developed and analyze their advantages and disadvantages. In this connection, it should be noted it is not beneficial to eliminate rolling entirely since the yielding of a vessel to the tremendous pounding of the seas is a necessary characteristic of a seaworthy vessel. Too much success in dampening rolling may result in serious shocks and structural damage.

Bilge Keels: The installation of fins or "keels" at or near the turn of the bilge has been known to be beneficial for many years. Froude was the first, however, to show their effectiveness experimentally, around 1870. Since then almost all large vessels have been fitted with bilge keels. Longitudinally, bilge keels extend from 25% to 75% of the length and vary in depth from less than a foot to about three feet. Although the effectiveness of the bilge keel increases with depth, practical considerations limit keel depths. These considerations include the necessity of keeping the keels within the extreme depth and breadth of the vessel; difficulties in drydocking; necessity of limiting the stress on the plating of the keel and thus reducing the probability of leakage where the keel is attached to the hull; and increase in hull resistance and the consequent loss of speed or increase in horsepower.

Bilge keels derive their roll quenching abilities by setting in motion a mass of water which is carried along by the vessel, thus increasing virtually the mass moment of inertia of the vessel. The eddying of water behind the keel results in a loss of energy which otherwise would go into an increase in the amplitude of roll. Also, not only do the normal pressures increase on the leading side of the keels, but the reduction of velocity of water on the following sides lead to an increase in pressure with components acting around the axis of rotation of the ship in a direction opposite to the ship's rotation.

Bilge keels increase in effectiveness with amplitude of roll producing greater periods of roll than would otherwise exist at these angles of roll. However, the principle purpose of bilge keels is to reduce the amplitude of roll. They increase the period of roll only slightly, normally.

Bilge keels also increase in effectiveness with speed of the vessel. Another factor influencing the effectiveness of bilge keels is the mass moment of inertia of the vessel. (The less the mass moment of inertia, the greater the effectiveness.)

Experiments with different forms of bilge keels have shown that discontinuous keels are more effective than continuous keels.

Modern practice dictates the installation of bilge keels along the streamlines in the vicinity of the bilge. This prevents cross-flow across the keels and a consequent increase in resistance. With this practice, bilge keel resistance is almost entirely frictional and is thus held within acceptable limits.

Anti-rolling tanks: Considerable attention has been given in the past to the use of anti-rolling tanks, and various types of installations have been made with varying degrees of success. Experimental work in this field is continuing.

Early anti-rolling tanks (around 1874) took the form of simply creating free surface in tanks located in the upper decks of the ship. These so-called "water chambers" operate, obviously by reducing the stability of the ship and may be dangerous in some situations, especially if the period of the water in the tank and the period of roll of the ship get into synchronism. For these reasons, this type of tank was abandoned.

Progress in anti-rolling tanks since then may be divided into two directions: Non-activated tanks and activated tanks. The non-activated tanks are usually some application of the U-tube principle with horizontal ducts and vertical ducts. In these non-activated tanks, the water can only move "downhill", the theory being that as the ship rolls the water will move to the low side, achieving its maximum heeling moment when the ship starts to roll back to the other side, thus creating a moment which acts in opposition to the direction of roll. In these tanks care must be taken to provide proper dimensions to the ducts and also proper venting at the top of the vertical ducts.

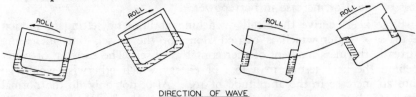

DIRECTION OF WAVE

Figure 168. Two types of non-activated anti-rolling tanks.

Another form of non-activated tank has long (about 180 feet) narrow tanks located around amidships with approximately half of the tank above the load waterline and half below the waterline. The tanks are open to the sea at the bottom and vented at the top. Thus, as the ship rolls the tank on the low side fills up and as the ship rolls back the full or almost full tank creates a heeling moment in opposition to the direction of roll.

In the 1960's, a non-activated installation called "Flume Stabilization" has been remarkably successful and has been installed on many vessels.

Activated anti-rolling tanks have used various methods to obtain a more precise control over the movement of water in U-tube arrangements. One method is by the use of air compression, with a gyroscope controlling an air compressor which varies the air pressure on either side of the tank, thus controlling the amount of water on each side of the ship. More recently, the U. S. Navy has been experimenting with anti-rolling tanks where pumps operate to move water through the ducts in such a way as to create heeling moments which oppose the roll of the ship.

Anti-rolling Fins: Anti-rolling fins have been considered for use in dampening ship rolling since before the turn of the century, and recently the Denny-Brown fins which were developed about this time have been improved and are creating a great deal of interest. In the U. S., the Sperry Company has developed somewhat similar fins, the principal difference being that the Sperry "Gyrofin" folds back into a recess in the hull.

Figure 169

Anti-rolling fins are rudder-like in appearance; project out from the side amidships just above the bilge keel. In the new Denny-Brown installation they are retractable so that they can be withdrawn into a pocket in the ship when they are not in use. The fins operate by creating a couple opposing the roll of the ship. For example, if the ship rolls to starboard the fins are angled so that the forward side of the star fin is pointing diagonally upwards and the port fin is pointing diagonally downwards. Then, the forward motion of the ship causes the water to exert an upward force on the starboard fin and a downward force on the port fin. This couple tends to roll the ship to port and thus is an offset to the starboard roll. The movement of the fins are controlled by sensitive gyroscopes.

These anti-rolling fins have proved highly successful and it is possible that their use may be wide-spread in the future. However, there are disadvantages connected with their use, one of the principal disadvantages

Figure 170

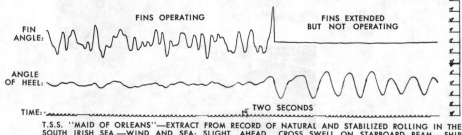

T.S.S. "MAID OF ORLEANS"—EXTRACT FROM RECORD OF NATURAL AND STABILIZED ROLLING IN THE SOUTH IRISH SEA.—WIND AND SEA: SLIGHT, AHEAD. CROSS SWELL ON STARBOARD BEAM.—SHIP SPEED: 21 KNOTS.

Figure 171

being the increase in resistance. Another is the fact that speed is essential to their operation and thus their effectiveness varies with the ship's speed.

Gyroscopic Stabilizers: Gyro stabilizers have been installed on many vessels, most of them being yachts. However, the largest installation was on the S.S. *Conte di Savoia,* where three rotors weighing 344 tons were used. This installation was successful in reducing rolling, but it is doubtful whether the use of such stabilizers will spread due to the high cost of purchasing and operating, as well as the loss of deadweight and space.

QUESTIONS

1. Identify the six principal motions of a vessel in waves.
2. Explain how the orbital motion of water particles results in the formation of the wave profile. What causes the water particles to move in an orbital path?
3. Describe the effect of orbital motion of sea water on the speed of ships.
4. How does the orbital motion of sea water contribute to the tendency of a ship to yaw?
5. An observer on a vessel heading at right angles to the seas, observes the wave period to be 10 seconds. What is the length and speed of the waves?

> ANS: Length: 512 feet
> Speed: 30.3 knots

6. Your vessel is at sea and the wind has been blowing with an estimated velocity of 60 knots for some time. What would be a fair estimate of the height of the waves?

> ANS: Between 30 and 40 feet.

7. Describe the process by which ocean waves are propagated and show how this process contributes to the orbital motion of the water in the waves.
8. An observer on a beach notices that waves are breaking on the shore at intervals of about 9 seconds. What estimate could the observer make about conditions at sea which have caused these waves?
9. What are the advantages and disadvantages of operating a merchant vessel with a large GM? with a small GM?
10. Explain how variations in the mass moment of inertia of a vessel will affect its rolling characteristics.
11. A vessel at sea is rolling rapidly and to great amplitudes. Wing ballast tanks in the upper tween decks are filled with salt water. How will this action affect the rolling of the vessel?
12. A vessel is loaded vertically so as to produce a small GM. Discuss the effect of loading this vessel transversely so as to concentrate a good percentage of the total deadweight around the centerline of the vessel.
13. Explain why, in general, it is better to operate a merchant vessel with a reasonably small GM than a large GM. Under what conditions would it be wise to increase the GM?
14. Make a sketch showing the virtual upright position of a vessel on the windward slope of an ocean wave.
15. Make a sketch showing the virtual upright position of a vessel on the crest of a wave. By referring to your sketch, show that the virtual displacement of the vessel is less than its actual displacement.
16. Why are the angles of inclination reported by many ship's officers apt to be in error?

17. How does the effectiveness of a bilge keel vary with:
    a) The amplitude of roll
    b) Speed of the vessel
    c) Continuity of the keel.
18. Describe the forces acting around the bilge keels of a vessel rolling in a seaway.
19. What is the theory behind the roll quenching abilities of all anti-rolling tanks?
20. What are the advantages and disadvantages of anti-rolling fins?
21. Describe the theory of anti-rolling fins.
22. What are the factors which prohibit the widespread use of gyroscopic stabilizers?

BIBLIOGRAPHY

Bigelow & Edmondson, "Wind Waves at Sea: Breakers and Surf", U.S. Navy Department, Hydrographic Office, H.O. Pub. No. 602, Washington, D.C., 1947.

Rossell & Chapman, *Principles of Naval Architecture,* Vol. II, Society of Naval Architects and Marine Engineers, New York, 1942.

Walton, *Know Your Own Ship,* Charles Griffin and Company, Ltd., London, 1942.

Browning, F. H., "The Action of Ocean Waves", *United States Naval Institute Proceedings,* December, 1945.

Abell, T., *Stability and Seaworthiness of Ships,* The University Press of Liverpool, Ltd., Hodder and Stoughton, Ltd., London, 1926.

Introduction to Ship Design and Damage Control, U.S. Naval Academy, Department of Marine Engineering, 1948 (not published).

Taylor, D. W., *The Speed and Power of Ships,* U.S. Maritime Administration, U.S. Government Printing Office, Washington, 1943.

Comstock, J. P., *Introduction to Naval Architecture,* Simmons-Boardman Publishing Corporation, New York.

Sperry, E. A., "Gyro Ship Stabilizers in Service", *Transactions of the Society of Naval Architects and Marine Engineers,* Vol. 25, 1917. "Active Type of Stabilizing Gyro", *Transactions,* Vol. 20, 1912.

Lidgerwood Industries Inc., "A New Ship Stabilizing Device", *Motorship,* March, 1950.

Robb, A. M., *Studies of Naval Architecture—Strength and Rolling,* Charles Griffin & Co., Ltd., London, 1927.

Chalmers, T. W., *The Automatic Stabilization of Ships,* Chapman & Hall, Ltd., London, 1931.

J. Vasta, *Roll Stabilization by Means of Passive Tanks,* SNAME Transactions, Vol. 69, 1961.

H. McVey, *Anti-roll Fin Stabilizers,* SNAME Philadelphia Section, March 1959.

N. Jasper, *Statistical Distribution Patterns of Ocean Waves and Wave-induced Ship Stresses and Motions with Engineering Applications,* SNAME Transactions, Vol. 64, 1956.

Frahm, "Results of Trials of the Anti-Rolling Tanks at Sea", *Engineering,* Vol. 91, London, 1911.

Weinblum and St. Denis, "On the Motions of Ships at Sea", *Transactions of the Society of Naval Architects and Marine Engineers,* Vol. 58, 1950.

Niedermair, J. C., "Further Developments in the Stability and Rolling of Ships", *Transactions of the Society of Naval Architects and Marine Engineers,* Vol. 44, 1936. "Rolling of the S.S. *Conte di Savoia, "Transactions,* Vol. 44, 1936. (Discussion) "Use of Models in Study of Rolling of Ships", *Transactions,* Vol. 46, 1938. (Discussion)

Serat, M. E., "Effect of Form on Roll", *Transactions of the Society of Naval Architects and Marine Engineers,* Vol. 41, 1933. "New Studies of Ship Motion", *Transactions,* Vol. 43, 1935. (Discussion)

Note: The interested student will find many other papers on Ocean Waves and Rolling in the *Transactions of the Society of Naval Architects and Marine Engineers* and the British Society, *The Institution of Naval Architects.* Especially recommended in the latter Transactions are the papers of J. L. Kent.

Chapter 15

RESISTANCE AND POWERING

The student is about to enter one of the most interesting, yet one of the most involved subjects in the science of Naval Architecture. Resistance and powering considerations are the most important factors in determining the form of a ship's hull and are therefore worthy of attention by the men who man and operate ships.

The theories of resistance and powering, which form part of the subject of *Hydrodynamics* are presented to prospective ship's officers and operators with the following points in mind:

1. These theories have important *practical* applications which ship's personnel will find useful in improving the efficiency of operation and seaworthiness.

2. Inevitably some ship's officers take up positions of responsibility within the shoreside organization of steamship companies. Here, they will be concerned with the design of new ships. It is well that they understand the language of the ship designer when the various factors of design are being discussed.

3. The well-rounded ship's officer should understand the design of the ship on which he spends a good part of his life, even though some of his understanding may not have any "dollars and cents" applications.

Before entering on the subject of resistance and powering proper, it is necessary to consider the fundamental theories of Hydrodynamics which underly the development of our subject. These theories include:

1. *The nature of ocean waves.* This subject has already been considered in a previous chapter.

2. *Bernoulli's Theorem* relating to water pressure and velocity.

3. *Stream lines and flow lines.*

4. *Ship Wave Patterns.*

Hydrodynamic Principles Relating to Resistance

Bernoulli's Theorem: This widely known and widely applicable theorem, insofar as it relates to our problem here, can be stated very simply:

When a fluid is in motion, the pressure of the fluid varies inversely with the velocity.

312

The classical illustration of this principle shows that with flow of a fluid through a pipe the pressure decreases as the diameter of the pipe decreases due to the consequent increase of velocity.

A practical shipboard application of the principle was noted in the Chapter on Steering where it was shown that a ship proceeding in a narrow channel will, as it approaches a bank, will sheer away from the bank. This was traced to the constriction of flow between the bank and the ship, with the lesser constriction occurring forward. With a constriction of flow, velocity increases, and pressure drops. Therefore with the greater pressure forward, the bow swings away from the bank. But it should be remembered that the ship as a whole moves in toward the bank.

When two ships are passing each other close aboard, especially when one ship is overtaking the other, there is a pronounced constriction of flow between them. Velocity of flow increases, pressure drops and the ships are forced together. Most mariners are aware of this phenomenon, but are not aware of its causes, simply attributing it to "suction".

When vessels proceed in shallow water a constriction of flow occurs under their bottoms. With the usual pattern of velocity increase and pressure decrease, the vessel "drops" into the decreased pressure trough and may very well ground. Danger of grounding obviously increases with speed, and since most ships operate with trims by the stern, the constriction of flow is greatest there and the increase of draft is consequently greatest at the stern. Mariners sometimes call this squat.[1]

Stream and Flow Lines around ship's hulls: The term "stream line" relates to line of flow taken by fluid around a body immersed in the fluid. The line of flow taken will be the same whether the body is moving through the fluid, or the fluid is flowing about a stationary body.

We shall confine our discussion of stream lines here to flow of water about a ship's form. Of particular interest is the pressure pattern about a ship's hull as it moves through water, since this is directly related to our subject of resistance. In the following discussion, velocity of water around the hull is always considered in its relation to velocity of the undisturbed stream lines at some distance away from the ship.

Forward of the bow, at the bow, and for a short distance abaft the bow, a diagram showing stream lines around the moving ship would reveal a wider distance between the lines than for the lines of undisturbed flow. This means a reduction of velocity and a considerable increase in pressure around the bow. We can entitle this *"impact pressure"*.

For most of the remaining length of the hull, the diagram reveals the stream lines closer together than for the lines of undisturbed flow. This is caused by the constriction of flow around the ship. The velocity

---

[1] See page 331 for another definition of squat.

increases and the pressure decreases, thus causing a "defect" of pressure over most of the ship's length.

Around the stern however, the stream lines separate again. The indicated decrease in velocity may be easily traced to the closing in of the water around the stern, a customary characteristic of stream line flow. With decrease of velocity, pressure increases around the stern, not reaching, however, anywhere near the extent of pressure increase forward. Now increase of pressure forward can only oppose the progress of the vessel, while increase of pressure aft can only act in a forward direction thus assisting the progress of the vessel. One of the principal components of ship resistance, that caused by waves, can be stated simply as the algebraic sum of the aftward acting forward pressure and the forward acting after pressure.

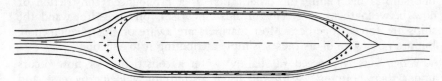

Figure 172.   Stream lines around vessel in motion. Pressures relative to normal hydrostatic pressures increase forward and aft; decrease amidships.

Flow lines under and around the hull of any particular vessel can be located by techniques developed in model basins. A model is towed and a marking fluid of some sort is ejected from a hole in the bottom forward. Smears will then mark the lines of flow. Admiral Taylor in his *"Speed and Power of Ships"* states that in this connection "their most notable feature is the remarkably strong tendency of the water to dive under the fore body, as it were. In fact, it seems as if the water near the surface forward dives down and crowds away from the hull the water through which the fore part has passed, while aft the water rising up crowds away from the hull the water which was in contact with it near the surface amidships".

The location of lines of flow around ship's hulls has important practical bearing on resistance. For example, bilge keels on modern vessels are located along the lines of flow in the bilge area in accordance with model basin experiments. With no cross flow across the keels, resistance of the keels is held to a minimum.

Ship Wave Patterns: As a ship moves through water, the bow sets up a wave which in turn results in a wave train extending out from, and aft along the length of the ship. The crests of these waves have two components:

1. *Diverging components:* These components could be seen most clearly if one were in an airplane looking down on a ship underway. They extend out from the ship at an angle of some 20 degrees.

2. *Transverse components:* These components can be seen most clearly on a ship underway from the side. They extend aft along the length of the ship with the heights of the waves gradually decreasing with distance from the bow.

Lord Kelvin, in 1906, defined mathematically the form and heights of the diverging and transverse crests. The exact figures in this connection need not concern us here. However, Kelvin showed that the crests reach their maximum heights at the originating point of the disturbance (the bow) and at the cusps (where the transverse components intersect the diverging components). At these points, breaking water is apt to be found.

Most important, the length of Kelvin's waves can be found by use of the trochoidal wave formula for speed and length, substituting speed of ship for speed of wave. This formula was given in the section on "The Ship in Waves". The length of the bow waves has an important bearing on resistance as we shall see later.

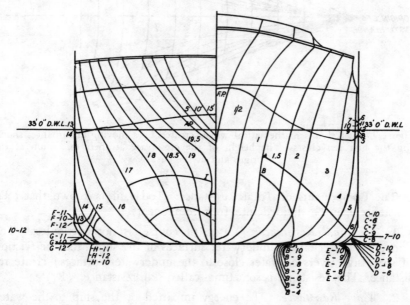

De Luce & Budd, "The Design of a Class of 28,000 Ton Tankers",
Oct. 1949 meeting of New England Section of SNAME

Figure 173.   Body Plan of Supertanker showing Wave Profile and Flow Lines for a speed of 16½ knots.

RESISTANCE OF SHIPS

With our study of necessary preliminaries out of the way, we may now turn to the study of our subject, proper:—Resistance offered to the forward progress of ships.

From Newton's laws of motion we know that a body in uniform motion tends to remain in a state of motion unless acted on by an unbalanced force. From this, we may deduce the important fact that the propelling force of a ship must be exactly balanced by the opposing force of resistance. Thus, if we can obtain the resistance of a vessel for a given speed, we know the propelling force required for that speed and can ascertain our powering needs. How, then, can the total resistance (R_t) of a vessel be obtained?

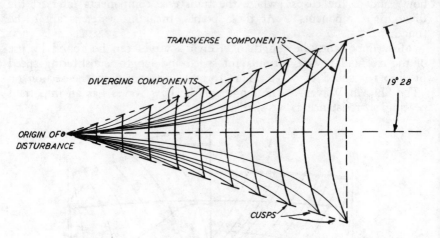

Figure 174. Kelvin's mathematical waves created by a moving disturbance, showing the first ten crests. The height of the crests are at their maximum at the origin and at the cusps.

The Components of Total Resistance: Today, it is known that total resistance may be divided into four components:

1. *Frictional Resistance:* Water, of course, is not frictionless. The friction of water on the underwater surfaces of the ship (and the friction of successive layers of water close to the underwater surfaces) create resistance. This resistance is sometimes called skin resistance. (R_f)

2. *Wave Resistance:* The energy imparted by the ship to the water about it creates and maintains waves. Energy so consumed represents a loss of propelling force or an increase in resistance due to wave-making. (R_w)

3. *Eddy Resistance:* Unless properly streamlined, ship appendages such as the stern post, propeller struts, and so on, leave behind them a swirling, eddying mass of water. The loss of energy represented here is designated as eddy resistance. It is usually a very small part of total resistance.

U.S. Maritime Commission

Figure 175.   Notice diverging componts of bow waves.

U.S. Maritime Commission

Figure 176.   In this photo, the diverging and transverse components of the bow waves can be seen clearly.

4. *Air Resistance:* Although water resistance provides the overwhelmingly greater portion of total resistance, that portion of a vessel above the water does offer some resistance which may in certain cases become appreciable. Air resistance too, can be divided into frictional, wave, and eddy components.

Although total resistance can be subdivided into the four components given above, it is customary and convenient as we shall see to lump all resistance except frictional into one category—*Residual Resistance.* Almost all of residual resistance (R_r) consists of wave resistance.

The Work of William Froude: If it were desirable, the total resistance of a vessel could be obtained by towing the vessel and measuring the force on the towing line. For this reason, total resistance is sometimes called *towrope resistance.* Obviously, this method is not feasible for routine work. The resistance of a vessel must be calculated before it is constructed. The answer lies in the proper use of models. The techniques used in modern towing tanks, surprisingly enough, are only some three-quarters of a century old. Before that time, the resistance and hence the powering needs and the computation of speed was empirical in nature, based principally on the performance of similar ships.

The name of William Froude is connected with the research in ship resistance which has enabled model basins to function. Before Froude, the nature of ship resistance was not known as tidily as indicated in the preceding section.

Froude constructed a 300 foot tank in his garden and experimented with the towing of models. His experiments led to a conclusion which, though it seems simple enough today, at that time was a brilliant and bold analysis. The development of his analysis is indicated briefly:

First, Froude towed models of different sizes but of geometric similarity at "corresponding speeds", that is, at the same speed-length ratio.[1] Froude then plotted speed-length ratio against resistance in terms of pounds of resistance per pound of displacement on a graph. For two models of different size but of geometric similarity, the curves of total resistance in these terms might have appeared something like the curves in Figure 177.

It is apparent immediately from these resistance curves that the total resistance of the larger model cannot be predicted from the performance of the smaller model; that is, *total resistance of vessels does not follow the law of comparison.* If the resistance of vessels varied directly with their displacement, then the two curves above would coincide since the curves are not plotted directly against pounds of resistance but pounds per pound of. displacement. (Rt/Disp.)

---

[1] Speed-length ratio is defined as the speed in knots divided by the square root of the length. Thus the speed of 20 knots for a 400 foot ship "corresponds" to a speed of 4 knots for a 16 foot model. (Since the speed-length ratio of the ship is 1.0: 1 $= V/4$ and V, the speed of the model is 4 knots.)

Froude noted this, but in addition noted that although the two curves did not coincide, they were similar in that the humps and hollows on each curve occurred at the same speed-length ratio. This observation led directly to a bold assumption:

Total resistance must be composed of two components, one of which must follow the law of comparison. Now, this fitted in with Froude's observation of wave trains generated by models of different size towed at the same speed-length ratio. The wave trains were mathematically similar. *Wave resistance (and residual resistance, for all practical purposes) must follow the law of comparison.* Frictional resistance does not.

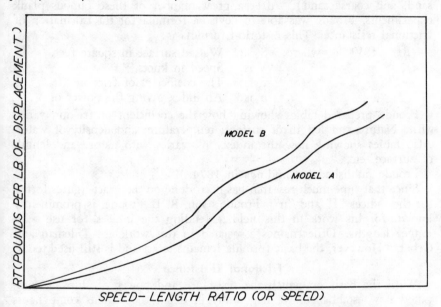

Figure 177. From these total resistance curves can be deduced the fact that wave-making resistance follows the Law of Comparison.

It remained only for Froude to isolate frictional resistance from total resistance and the science of the model basin would be born. For with a formula devised with which the frictional resistance of any size ship could be computed, a model could be towed, and the resistance of a ship of similar form computed. The method can be outlined as follows:

Find: Rt   (of model, by towing)
          Rf   (of model, by formula)
          Rr   (of model, subtracting Rf from Rt)
          Rr   (of ship, by law of comparison)
          Rf   (of ship, by formula)
          Rt   (of ship, by adding Rr and Rf)

One can only imagine the elation of William Froude when the implications of his discovery became clear. However, the isolation of frictional resistance and the devising of a formula therefor still remained. This problem was met by towing thin planks (3/16" x 19", of various lengths up to 50 feet) of the same wetted surface as the model. These planks could not create waves or eddies, would not have any air resistance since they were towed just under the surface. Therefore all measured resistance would have to be frictional. To establish the effect of nature of wetted surface on frictional resistance, Froude coated his planks with various substances. (Varnish, paraffin, tinfoil, calico, fine sand, medium sand, and coarse sand). After a great number of these famous plank experiments, Froude was able to devise a formula for the calculation of frictional resistance. This historical formula is:

$$Rf = fSV^n$$ where: S is: Wetted surface in square feet.

V is: Speed in knots.

f is: The coefficient of friction.

n is: An index giving the power of V.

Froude prepared tables showing how the coefficient of friction varies with: Nature and length of surface; temperature; and density of water. Also tables showing how the index "n" varies with nature and length of surface, etc.

Froude published his findings in 1874.

Since that time much research has been done on the exact figures to use for the indices "f" and "n". Froude's son, R. E. Froude, is prominently known for his work in this field, extending the indices for use with longer lengths. Other names associated in this work are Tideman and Gebers. However, the basic formula remains intact and is still used today.

Frictional Resistance

With the basis on which the resistance and power of ships is computed now established, we may study in detail the various components of total resistance and see how the design and operation of vessels is effected.

What is Frictional Resistance? The wetted surface of a vessel underway carries along with it, with no slip, the water layer actually adjacent to the surface. However, the infinitesimal layers outboard travel at diminishing speeds until the water at a short distance out from the hull is undisturbed. Since these infinitesimal layers are all moving at different speeds, it is evident that fluid shearing stresses must exist between them. It is the sum of all this fluid shear that we call frictional resistance. The water moving with the ship (and quite apparent to observers aboard ship) is known as the *boundary layer*.

Factors Which Determine the Extent of Frictional Resistance:

1. *Amount of wetted surface:* As we have seen in Froude's formula frictional resistance varies directly with the amount of wetted surface.

This leads to the interesting observation that the form of a vessel's hull does not effect frictional resistance. The one exception to this is the length of the vessel since, for a given displacement, the greater the length, the greater the wetted surface. This fact may be seen from Taylor's formula for wetted surface where S = C x square root of (displacement x length).

2. *Nature of wetted surface: Effect of fouling.* Froude first demonstrated quantitatively the effect of nature of wetted surface on skin resistance by using different substances on his planks. As far as a ship is concerned, the nature of wetted surface is related primarily to the degree of fouling although the existence of the laps, straps, and rivet heads of riveted construction adds considerably to resistance. We shall not dwell here on the well known effect of fouling except to state that skin resistance may be increased as much as four or five times over the clean condition. The necessity for frequent drydockings and the concern shown for the type of anti-fouling paint used is evident.

It should be pointed out, however, that skin resistance is only part of total resistance thus an increase in skin resistance does not represent the same percentage increase in total resistance. For a slow speed ship, frictional resistance may be as much as 90% of total resistance, with the percentage decreasing with speed. It is rare that frictional resistance is less than 50% of total resistance.

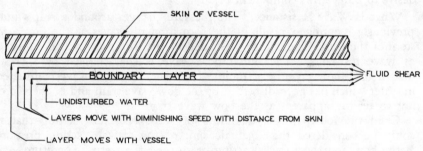

Figure 178

3. *Speed:* As seen in Froude's formula, the effect of speed on skin resistance varies to the power "n". This power is usually around 1.83 (Tideman's figure). That is, skin resistance varies as almost the square of the speed, and is therefore one of the most important factors determining skin resistance.

4. *Density:* Skin resistance varies directly with the density of the water in which the ship is moving. Since the variation of density is relatively small, this factor is of minor importance.

5. *Viscosity and Temperature:* Skin resistance varies directly with viscosity, a minor factor. Temperature is presumed to effect viscosity,

therefore skin resistance also varies with temperature. Admiral Taylor cites tests which indicate that with a 10°F. variation of temperature, skin resistance varies 1½ to 2 percent. (Resistance increasing with decrease of temperature).

6. *Type of flow:* There has been some concern shown about the accuracy of model basin work where models are towed under conditions of *laminar flow.* (Smooth, even flow lines of still water testing). As a result, some work has been done in the direction of creating *turbulent flow,* to simulate more exactly conditions at sea.

It should be observed that little can be done by the ship designer about frictional resistance, except to attempt a more accurate calculation of its extent. The latter task is important since the accuracy of model basin determination of ship horsepower depends upon the accuracy of the frictional resistance calculated. An error in this produces an error in the deduced residual resistance of the model which is magnified when the model's resistance is expanded to that of the ship's.

Wave Resistance

We have noted that wave resistance is an important component of total resistance, its importance varying with the speed-length ratio. Almost all research in resistance is done with the objective of reducing wave resistance and the hull form of ships is dictated to a great degree by the desire to reduce this component of Rt.

What is Wave Resistance: The pressure changes around a ship's hull previously mentioned result in the formation of waves at the bow *and* stern of the ship. The energy dissipated by the ship thereby is designated as wave resistance. The initial bow wave is characterized by a crest; that of the stern wave, by a trough. However, the stern wave is initiated in water which has been disturbed by the bow wave train and is, therefore, not so readily apparent as the bow wave train.

Cited previously was a definition of wave resistance stating that it could be considered the algebraic sum of the aftward acting pressure at the bow and the forward acting pressure at the stern. Therefore, one of the objectives of hull design is to decrease the wave profile forward and increase it aft. Now, we have seen that the bow wave train stretches aft in a series of crests and troughs with the wave heights gradually diminishing, the wave length remaining a constant and susceptible of calculation by the trochoidal wave formula for length and speed. It follows then that, depending upon the speed of the ship, either a crest or a trough of the bow wave train will appear at the stern. An increase in speed will increase the length of the bow waves and result in moving the crest aft of the stern and replacing it with a trough, or vice versa. From the point of view of wave resistance, *it is better to have a crest of the bow wave train at the stern than a trough* since this increases the water level at the stern and hence increases the forward acting pressures at the stern. This means that, *all other things equal,* the designed speed of a ship should be such that the resulting bow wave train will produce a crest at the stern. The value of this can be seen clearly if a wave resistance curve is plotted with coordinates of wave resistance and speed. Notice in Figure 179 the humps and hollows of the curve. Consider the advantages of a speed which lands on the hollow of the curve rather than a hump. At a relatively small cost in increased wave resistance, a relatively large increase in speed can be obtained.

On the other hand, if a speed which lands on a hollow is being considered for an increase which will land the desired speed on a hump, this increase in speed will result in a disproportionate increase in resistance and will tend to discourage this type of speed increase.

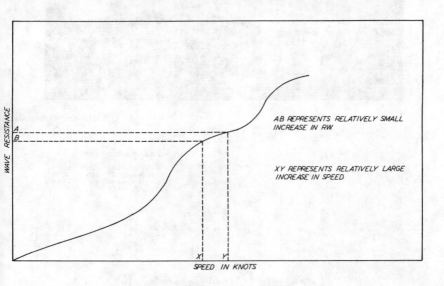

Figure 179

It must not be supposed however, that this consideration (desirability of selecting a speed which will result in a crest of the bow wave system landing at the stern) is all-important. There are many other considerations in hull design which must be considered. One or more of these (propulsive efficiency, for example) may dictate a speed which will produce a trough of the bow wave system at the stern. But designers always give careful attention to this point.

In a latter section of this Chapter, we shall consider how the various characteristics of modern hull form are arrived at by their relationship to minimum wave-making resistance.

Figure 180. Bow wave.

Figure 181. The fact that a crest appears at the stern indicates that the vessel is probably being operated at or near its optimum speed-length ratio.

Eddy Resistance

The basic causes of eddy resistance are not difficult to understand. The eddying of water behind blunt appendages is easily seen to represent a reduction of energy which might otherwise have been used to drive the ship. Therefore, it is necessary to streamline all such appendages. For example, the importance of reducing the gap between the stern post and rudder (or placing fairwater plates between them) is now recognized by all ship designers.

An interesting application of the theory of eddy resistance is seen in the resistance of lapped plates on riveted ships. The question is: Should the plates be lapped so that the butt faces forward (giving rise to increased frictional resistance) or aft (giving rise to eddy resistance)? Experiments on this question in model basins have shown that the increase in eddy resistance is more important than the increase in frictional resistance and therefore it is better for butts to face forward. This is especially true if the edges of the butts are rounded.

Air Resistance

Although air resistance is generally considered to be an insignificant portion of total resistance it can, under high wind velocity conditions, assume great significance. Ship designers therefore have given some attention to the possibility of reducing the wave component of air resistance. Considerable difficulties arise in this connection. First, the maximum air resistance is not encountered with the wind directly ahead, but when it is at some angle with the centerline. Since this is true, the advantages of streamlining superstructure in a fore and aft direction become less desirable and ridiculous in any other direction. Second, the expense involved in such streamlining is very apt to outweigh any savings encountered in a reduction of resistance. It is fair to say that, where such streamlining is used in modern ships it is probably there for appearances sake.

Air resistance is apt to add to total resistance indirectly when the rudder must be kept over under certain wind conditions in order to make the desired course.

Admiral Taylor cites figures indicating that air resistance in still air amounts to $1\frac{1}{2}$ or 2% of water resistance and the possibility of air resistance amounting to some 24% of water resistance with a relative wind of 30 knots.

RESISTANCE AND POWERING CONSIDERATIONS IN HULL DESIGN

One of the elements that enters into the design of a ship's hull is the resistance created by the form of the hull. As we have seen, total resistance is determined by a combination of frictional and residual resistances. The former is established principally by the extent of wetted surface and the speed and is, therefore, not susceptible of reduction by good hull design to any appreciable extent. Residual resistance, however, (which is mainly wave-making resistance) can be influenced considerably by varying the hull form. The objective of design in this direction is to so combine the bow and stern wave trains and the pressures which accompany them (as well as pressure changes emanating from other elements of hull form) so as to produce minimum resistance. It must be remembered, however, that resistance is only one element of hull design and the demands of other elements such as stability, cargo capacity, and propulsive efficiency may force a compromise in form that will result in higher wave-making resistances than might be obtained if only the one design factor were considered.

Much of the progress made in the direction of reduction of residual resistance by proper hull form has been due to the work of the model basins. A great number of forms arranged in series and "families" have and are being towed in these basins to determine the best proper hull form for reducing resistance.

Various elements of hull form will now be considered and the results of experimentation and experience in this regard reported on:

Form of hull forward and aft: It has been recognized for many years that, in general, the form of the forward sections should be of U shape and the form of after sections of V shape. This results forward in relatively narrow waterlines at the deeper drafts and a good proportion of the displacement under the waterline; and aft in full waterlines at the deeper drafts with most of the displacement at these drafts. The practical

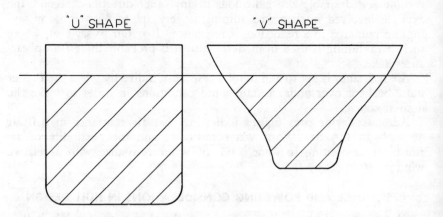

Figure 182. With the hatched areas being equal, it is apparent that a "V" shaped bow section is obtained by increasing the waterline breadth. In the "U" shaped bow, the displacement is moved down where it is less apt to raise a large bow wave.

application of these theories can be seen by glancing at the body plan of modern ships. The shape of the waterplanes forward and aft depend upon the longitudinal coefficient, and the sectional area curve. These, in turn, will vary with desired speed as discussed below. This general rule

Cadet-Midshipmen R. W. Bullick and J. E. Hundt, Class of 1951,
U.S. Merchant Marine Academy

Figure 183. Bulbous bow.

of U-shape sections forward and V shape sections aft may be varied in some cases to give greater propulsive efficiency, especially for slow speed merchant types.

The Bulbous Bow. At certain speed-length ratios it is possible to obtain reductions in residuary resistance by fitting bulbs at the under-

water section of the bow. These bulbs are roughly triangular in section
with a rather flat base at keel level and the apex somewhere near the
load waterline. The purpose of a bulbous bow is to so combine the
wave systems generated by the bow, stern, and bulb that the net effect
will produce less wave-making than would result in a form without the
bulb. For merchant types of vessels little advantage can be derived from
a bulb until a speed-length ratio of about 0.8 is reached. Bulbs can
then be effective in the range of speed-length ratios from 0.8 to 1.0,
although in the latter part of this range, the bulbs may have to be so
large that the bulb may have serious disadvantages in heavy seas. Somewhere between 10 and 30 percent of the residuary resistance may be
saved in this range of speed-length ratios with resulting savings of 3
to 18 percent of total resistance. However, there is some feeling that
careful design of the bow, and selection of the prismatic coefficient is
preferable to introduction of such a peculiarity of form as a bulbous bow.[1]

Effect of trim on resistance: Since trim changes the shape of the underwater form of a vessel, especially at the ends, some effect on resistance
is to be expected. However, model basin experiments have indicated
that the effect is almost negligible. For most vessels a slight trim by the
stern will be beneficial when proceeding at full speed, but the gain
is not sufficient to dictate such a trim apart from other considerations such
as improvement of steering characteristics and immersion of the propeller.[2]

Effect of midship section coefficient: Given a certain midship section
area, a merchant type vessel will actually find it of some slight benefit
to have a full midship section with high coefficients. Even with high
speed vessels, small midship section coefficients do not result in any
appreciable reduction of residuary resistance. These observations relate
only to the shape of the midship section and not to its size.[3]

Effect of length on resistance: As has been demonstrated the speed-
length ratio, $V/\sqrt{L}$, is a major factor in the determination of total
resistance. Thus, for a given speed, an increase of length will, in general, result in decreased total resistance. For example, it is quite possible
for a 400 ft. ship to have as much resistance as a 700 ft. ship of geometric
similarity at a very high speed.[1] The effect of length on frictional resistance is to increase the resistance as the $\sqrt{L}$, while residual resistance is
reduced considerably with increase of length, displacement remaining
constant. It is possible, therefore, for a given displacement and speed
to arrive at a length which will reduce resistance to a minimum. Unfortunately the length for minimum resistance is usually undesirable from
other important considerations and a shorter length must be selected.

---

[1] Rossell & Chapman, *"Principals of Naval Architecture"*, Vol. II, page 106.
[2] Taylor, *Speed and Power of Ships*, pages 56-57.
[3] Ibid, page 57.

The Beam-Draft Ratio: With a given midship section area, it has been shown by many model basin experiments that a broad and shallow form will create more resistance than a narrow and deep form, with wave-making resistance varying as the square of the beam. It is interesting to note that stability considerations which dictate a broad form for increasing stability are opposed directly to resistance considerations. The beam-draft ratio therefore represents, among other factors, a compromise between resistance and stability considerations.

Midship section area compared with ends: (Effect of varying prismatic coefficient). Fine ends in comparison with full midship section; that is, a low prismatic coefficient, results in most case in a considerable reduction of residual resistance, and is a factor of great importance. However, for very slow ships with, say, speed-length ratios of less than 0.6, large prismatic coefficients may be used without any appreciable effect on residual resistance. This is due, of course, to the relative lack of wave-making in a slow ship. As speed is increased, low prismatic coefficients become very desirable.

However, a point can be reached where an *increase* of prismatic coefficient will result in a *decrease* of residual resistance. The speed-length ratio required to reach this point varies with the displacement but will be in the vicinity of 1.1 or 1.2. Admiral Taylor explains this phenomenon by the statement: "At moderate speeds, the ends do the bulk of the wave making and the fine ends make much less wave disturbance than the full ends. Hence, the enormous advantage of fine ends at these speeds. But at high speeds, the whole body of the ship takes part in the wave making, and the smaller the midship section, the less the wave making."[2]

Effect of displacement-length ratio on resistance: It can be shown that the displacement of a vessel varies as the cube of its linear dimensions. Therefore:

$$\frac{\text{Displacement of vessel A}}{\text{Displacement of vessel B}} = \frac{(\text{Length of vessel A})^3}{(\text{Length of vessel B})^3}$$

where: vessels A and B have the same geometric form with different displacements.

Then: Displacement divided by L^3 is a ratio *which does not change with size*. If this ratio is to be conveniently used as a measure of the displacement on a given length, however, it is helpful to use a function of L^3 since this would produce a ratio which would be unwieldy. Therefore, the displacement-length ratio is taken to be displacement divided by $(L/100)^3$.

---

1 Rossell & Chapman, op. cit., pages 90-91.
2 Taylor, op. cit., page 58.

Suppose the displacement of some vessel to be 5000 tons on a length of 300 feet. What would be the displacement of a similar ship 600 feet in length?

$$\frac{5000}{X} = \frac{3^3}{6^3} \text{ and } X = 40,000 \text{ tons}$$

The significance of any given displacement-length ratio may be seen if it is remembered that the ratio is the displacement of a similar vessel 100 feet in length.

The displacement-length ratio, that is displacement divided by 1/100th of the length cubed, is a measure of the fullness of a vessel for a given length, so what is desired here is an indication of how total resistance varies with different displacement-length ratios at varying speed-length ratios. Within the merchant ship range of speed-length ratios; that is, up to a ratio of 1.0, the residual resistance *per ton* is almost the same for all reasonable displacement-length ratios. Therefore, the total residual resistance will vary directly with the displacement in this range. This can be accounted for by observing that wavemaking for these speeds is determined more by the form of the extreme ends than by the middle-body fullness. Frictional resistance, too, for a given speed, will vary only as the square root of displacement. These relationships can be taken advantage of in the merchant ship designs to obtain middle-body fullness with minor effect on resistance. As we have seen, however, this fullness must not be accompanied by an increase in the prismatic coefficient since this will have a pronounced effect on resistance.[1] At higher speed-length ratios, however, increases of displacement-length ratio do result in disproportionate increases in resistance.

Extent and position of parallel middle body: Vessels which can employ any profitable length of parallel middle body must have, of necessity, limited speed, since high speed-length ratios must be associated with low prismatic coefficients. Experiments have shown that parallel middle bodies of any appreciable length cannot be employed on vessels with speed-length ratios over 0.8.[2] Below this ratio, however, the optimum length of parallel middle body will vary with the prismatic coefficient and the speed-length ratio. As we have seen above, the displacement-length ratio is not a factor in this range of speeds. Experiments at the Washington towing tank[3] produced the following results in this connection:

---

[1] Taylor, op. cit., page 63 and Rossell & Chapman, op. cit. pages 94-97.
[2] Rossell & Chapman, op. cit., pages 99-100.
[3] Ibid., page 100.

Prismatic Coefficient	Optimum parallel length
0.68	12 per cent
0.74	24 per cent
0.80	32 per cent

Optimum parallel lengths were found to be a little greater for speed-length ratios of about 0.70 and a little less for both higher and lower speed-length ratios. These optimum lengths produced varying reductions in resistance from corresponding Standard Series forms.

In practice, the length of parallel middle body may and usually is, greater than the optimum length for resistance in order to achieve more and convenient cargo space.

Studies on the longitudinal position of the center of parallel length seem to indicate that for slow speed ships this center should be somewhat forward of amidships so as to obtain a long relatively fine after body for the slow speed ships. For most cargo types, therefore, the longitudinal position of the center of buoyancy is seen to be forward of amidships. For vessels requiring more speed, the entrance becomes of greater relative importance than the run and the center of buoyancy is moved aft.

The Effect of Speed on Draft and Trim

The effect of speed on draft and trim, although not a practical consideration for displacement-type vessels, is interesting to note, and is related to the pressure changes, previously mentioned to exist around the hull of a vessel underway.

It will be remembered that, due to the defect of pressure over most of the ship's length, the vessel will settle into this trough of decreased pressure; that is, the draft will increase. The greater the speed, the greater the increase in draft will be, at least, that is, until speed is such that a speed-length ratio of about 2.0 is reached when the stern remains at about the same level and the bow continues to rise.

The change in trim is mainly due to the magnitude of the bow wave. At lower speed-length ratios, the change of trim is very small since the bow wave has not assumed significant proportions. Beyond a speed-length ratio of about 1.0 a series of changes in trim may occur with trim by the stern being replaced by trim by the head and so on. This can be traced to the fact that as speed increases, the bow wave train places crests and troughs at the stern alternately, thus alternately forcing the stern up and down. This alternation in trim that occurs sometimes in speed-length ratios from about 1.0 to 1.2 is known as *perturbation*. After the speed-length ratio of 1.2 is surpassed, the bow wave has become so large that only one crest and one trough exist, with the trough located at the stern. The stern slips into this trough and a sudden and very marked change of trim occurs with the stern going down rapidly and the bow moving up rapidly. This condition is known as *squat*. Above a speed-length ratio of 1.2, the stern will settle until about a 1.8 speed-length ratio is reached. The stern will then level off, with the bow continuing to rise. For displacement type vessels however, the level of the vessel will never exceed its level in still water. Planing type vessels however, may rise bodily.[1]

The Effect of Shallow Water on Resistance

This is a matter of academic interest to most ship operators since in shallow water, a vessel is apt to be operated at reduced speeds where the increase in resistance would not be a practical matter. However, the reason for increase in resistance in shallow water over that experienced for the same speed in deep water is easily seen to be due to the increased pressures caused by the restriction of flow downward at the bow, thus increasing the impact pressure.

The effect of shallow water on resistance does have a practical bearing on the selection of a trial course. Authorities differ on just what depth of water is necessary to eliminate all shallow water effects for a ship of given length and speed, but all agree that several hundred feet of water is necessary.

Resistance Under Sea Conditions

The resistance of vessels is computed for the still water conditions of the model basin and the model basin results are checked on the standardization trials in relatively still water. It is fairly obvious that a ship at sea in rough water, rolling and pitching, will encounter more resistance than in still water.

The effect of rolling on resistance does not appear to be as great as one might suppose, although a significant increase does occur. The real culprit in this situation is pitching. When the period of encounter of the waves coincides with the pitching period of the vessel, violent pitching occurs and a considerable increase in resistance results. In addition to the loss of speed due to increase of resistance there are of course other factors which may dictate a deliberate decrease of speed. When the ship starts to pound too heavily, or seas start coming over the bow; when danger of excessive propeller racing occurs, prudent ship masters reduce revolutions. The effect of sea conditions on powering provisions will be discussed below.

CALCULATION OF SHIP HORSEPOWERS

The first and most important step in obtaining the effective horsepower necessary to drive a given ship at a given speed is to obtain the total resistance of the ship at this speed. This can be done, as we have seen, by estimating, using the performance of a similar or nearly

---

[1] See Taylor, op. cit., pages 72-74, for a more detailed description of the effect of speed on draft and trim.

similar ship as a guide. This is a very approximate method. The accurate method is the one employed in model basins; the method made possible by Froude's experiments. However, a third method exists which offers fairly accurate results and is used by almost all designers for preliminary estimations of power. This method utilizes the famous *Taylor's Standard Series*. The "Standard Series" is a series of charts embodying the results of towing a series of models of many different forms, thereby enabling the residual resistance per ton of displacement to be calculated and plotted on the graphs. The designer need only know four variables to use the Series: Beam-draft ratio, speed-length ratio, prismatic coefficient, and displacement-length ratio. These four variables define the form of a ship very closely. When residual resistance per ton of displacement is found from the series, it is multiplied by displacement to obtain the residual resistance of the ship. Froude's formula is then used to obtain the frictional resistance of the ship, and the two added, to obtain total resistance in pounds. This total resistance however is the total for a *bare hull*. Since a ship has appendages such as propeller, rudder, propeller struts, etc., the Rt for the bare hull must be increased by some percentage to account for resistance of appendages. A figure of 2% to 3% is usually used (for single screw ships). For twin screw ships the increase in resistance may be between 10% and 12% and for quadruple screw ships, the increase may be as high as 25%. This accounts for the reluctance of many designers to use multiple screws. The tendency in modern ships is definitely to use a single screw.

Another thing to keep in mind is that the model basin and trial trip predictions of horsepower needs is for relatively calm water and a clean bottom. The horsepower necessary to maintain a given speed over a period of time under average sea conditions must be increased about 15% over that of model basin results.

It should be noted that the Standard Series method of computing total resistance is based also on the use of models, and varies only from the method of actually towing a model of the ship in question, in the accuracy with which the Series variables define the form of the ship.

Conversion of total resistance to effective horsepower: As previously stated, for any given speed, the propelling force of a ship must be exactly equal to the opposing force of resistance. Now, ship's power is expressed in terms of horsepower, so it is necessary for us to convert propelling force in pounds (total resistance in pounds) to horsepower.

Since 1 H.P. = 33,000 foot pounds of work per minute and

$$H.P. = \frac{(\text{force in pounds}) \times (\text{speed in feet per min.})}{33,000}$$

Then: $$EHP = \frac{(\text{Resistance in pounds}) \times (\text{Speed in knots})}{325.7}$$

EHP, or effective horsepower, then is the power, expressed in terms of horsepower, needed to drive a ship with a given total resistance in pounds at a given speed, exclusive of all losses in efficiency due to transmission of power from the engines.

PHP, or propeller horsepower, is the power which must be delivered to the propeller in order to obtain the desired EHP. Since propulsive efficiency (EHP/PHP) can never be 100%, PHP must be greater than EHP.

SHP, or shaft horsepower, is measured as close to the propeller as possible (just forward of the after collision bulkhead) and must be greater than PHP due to losses occasioned by torque and friction in the tail shaft. The term "propulsive coefficient" is obtained by dividing EHP by SHP. Steam turbine engines are rated in terms of SHP.

BHP, or brake horsepower, is measured at the crankshaft coupling by a device called a brake. It is greater than SHP due to losses occasioned by torque and friction in the main shafting.

Steam reciprocating engines are usually rated in terms of IHP, or indicated horsepower, the power within the engines. Internal combustion engines may be rated in terms of IHP or BHP.

QUESTIONS

1. Look up the definition of "Hydrodynamics" in a good dictionary.
2. Two vessels are passing each other port to port and close aboard. Explain how the vessels will tend to move when (a) the bows are abeam of each other (b) the vessels are abeam of each other (c) the sterns are abeam of each other. In view of these facts what steering orders might be desirable.
3. Explain the logic of the saying that a ship can "smell" shoal water.
4. How do you explain the fact that a ship underway has a mean draft greater than the mean draft when not underway?
5. Explain how the normal pressures around a ship in undisturbed water are affected when the ship is making way through the water?
6. Define wave-making resistance in terms of pressures forward and aft.
7. To what do you attribute the defect of pressure along most of the length of a vessel underway?
8. What are the general characteristics of a crest in Kelvin's wave group?
9. How can the length of the transverse waves thrown up by a ship's bow be calculated?
10. Why is the propelling force of a vessel always exactly equal to the opposing force of resistance? What is the practical significance of this fact?
11. What are the four components of total resistance?
12. If a vessel has a length of 441 feet and a speed of 16 knots, what is the "corresponding" speed of a model 25 feet long?

ANS: 3.8 knots

13. Outline the logic by which Froude proved that the resistance of a ship can be predicted by towing a geometrically similar model.

14. How did Froude arrive at the conclusion that residual resistance of geometrically similar vessels follows the law of comparison?

15. How did Froude isolate frictional resistance from total resistance?

16. State Froude's formula for frictional resistance and explain the meaning of each symbol in the formula.

17. What is the "boundary layer"?

18. Explain why the longer of two ships with the same displacement will have a greater wetted surface.

19. How does frictional resistance vary with (a) nature of wetted surface (b) amount of wetted surface (c) speed (d) density of fluid (e) viscosity (f) type of flow (g) temperature.

20. When a bow wave results in a crest at the stern, what effect does this have on resistance? Why?

21. When a bow wave results in a trough at the stern, what effect does this have on resistance? Why?

22. Show by means of a curve of wave-making resistance plotted against speed why it is beneficial to have a crest of the bow wave system located at the stern.

23. Describe the role of eddy resistance in the total resistance picture.

24. Describe the role of air resistance in the total resistance picture.

25. If a U shaped form is used forward what does this mean in terms of (a) waterline breadth in comparison with a V shaped form of the same area (b) disposition of displacement at this section in comparison with a V shaped form of the same area?

26. What is the purpose of a bulbous bow? How is this purpose accomplished?

27. Describe the effect on resistance of the following:
    a) Length
    b) Beam-draft ratio
    c) Trim
    d) Midship section *form.*
    e) Midship section *area.*
    f) Displacement-length ratio.

28. The displacement of a certain vessel is 3000 tons. The vessel has a length of 200 feet. What would the displacement of a similarly formed vessel 500 feet in length be?

    ANS: 46,875 tons

29. What is the effect on resistance of a long parallel middle body on a slow speed ship? How should parallel middle body be disposed about amidships on merchant ships? Why?

30. Describe the effects on draft and trim as a vessel's speed-length ratio increases.

31. Define: a) perturbation
            b) squat

32. Describe the effects on resistance of:
    a) shallow water
    b) rolling
    c) pitching

33. Outline the method for obtaining EHP by the use of Taylor's Standard Series.
34. Define: EHP, PHP, SHP, BHP, IHP.
35. A vessel has a shaft horsepower of 10,000 at its designed speed of 32.57 knots. Its propulsive coefficient is 0.80. What is the total resistance in pounds at this speed?

ANS: 80,000 pounds

36. Find the effective horsepower necessary to drive a 15,000 ton vessel at 20 knots if:
   a) Residual resistance per ton of displacement is 4.2 lbs.
   b) Frictional resistance per ton of displacement is 5.6 lbs.

ANS: 9027

BIBLIOGRAPHY

Taylor, D. W., *"Speed and Power of Ships"*, U.S. Government Printing Office, Washington, D.C., 1943.

Rossell and Chapman, *"Principles of Naval Architecture"*, Society of Naval Architects and Marine Engineers, New York, 1942.

Comstock, J. P., *Introduction to Naval Architecture,* Simmons-Boardman Publishing Company, New York.

H. Saunders, *Hydrodynamics in Ship Design*, SNAME, 1957.

Note: For good reference material on resistance and its relationship to hull form, the student is directed to those *Transactions* of professional marine societies and Marine Periodicals where the papers are concerned with the design of new vessels.

Chapter 16

PROPELLERS AND PROPULSION

Although the subject of propulsion and the design of propellers lie properly in the field of marine engineering, there are many aspects of the subjects which are of concern to the naval architect and of interest and practical use to the ship's officer. It is with these aspects that we shall be concerned in this chapter.

Modern sea-going vessels are almost universally propelled by screw propellers. Other methods of propulsion will not be discussed.

Theory of the Screw Propeller: Since the screw propeller was first used for practical propulsion of ships (around 1800), numerous theories have been advanced for its action. A detailed study of these theories lies outside the scope of this text. However, if we remain in the physical rather than the mathematical analysis of propeller action, it can be stated that propellers develop a propulsive thrust by accelerating the water in which they act. The propeller works as a pump, driving a stream of water aft. The reaction of this stream upon the surrounding water produces the thrust imparted to the ship.

Propeller Definitions

To understand the action of a propeller and study the propulsive efficiency of a vessel, it is necessary to know certain fundamental definitions of propeller nomenclature and propulsion.

First, a screw propeller has two or more *blades* projecting from a hub. The hub, in turn, is keyed to the propeller shaft. Propellers may be of the *solid* type, where the hub and blades are cast as a unit; or, of the detachable type, where the blades are cast separately and bolted to the hub. Although detachable propellers have the advantage of easy replacement of damaged blades, a saving in weight and a more reliable wheel is had when a solid type is used; and with progress in casting, eliminating previous difficulties, most modern propellers are of the solid type. Where detachable blades are used, they are connected with methods of changing the pitch of the blades. (The term pitch will be explained below.)

When a propeller turns clockwise when viewed from aft, it is designated a *right-handed propeller;* when counter-clockwise, a *left-handed propeller.* Single screws are right-handed. With twin screws, it is usual to have them turning in opposite directions; and in this case they may be *in-turning* or *out-turning* screws.

The *face of the blade* is the after surface and may be considered to be the working surface of the blades since it drives the water astern. The *back of the blade* (the forward surface) is the surface opposite the face. When the blades are turning an increase in pressure develops on the blade face. However, a decrease in pressure, greater than the increase on the face, develops on the back of the blades thus indicating that the greater part of the propeller thrust is contributed by the back. That edge of a blade which cuts the water first when going ahead is called the *leading edge*. Opposite the leading edge is the *following edge*. The blade *tip* is the point furthest from the hub; the blade is connected to the hub at its *root*.

The face of a blade is of helicoidal form ;or developed from such a form. A helicoidal surface is defined as the surface generated by a line

Bethlehem Steel Company

Figure 184. One of the largest propellers ever made in the U.S., this huge "wheel" was designed and manufactured by Bethlehem Steel for the new American Export Lines passenger vessels. This propeller has a finished weight of almost 55,000 pounds, diameter of 19 feet 6 inches, and length at hub of 4 feet 9½ inches. The fairwater cap seated on the hub, weighs about a ton and has a height of more than 6 feet. The small four-bladed propeller at the right was manufactured for an Army tug and weighs about 1,000 pounds and has a diameter of 6 feet.

Figure 185.   One of the propellers on the S.S. America.

Figure 186.   Liberty ship propeller.

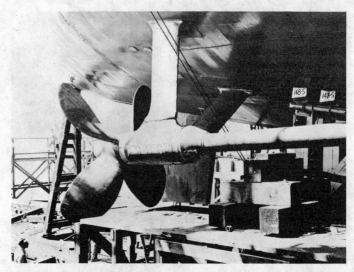

U.S. Maritime Commission

Figure 187. Starboard propeller and strut of an S4-SE2-BE1.

Bethlehem Steel Company

Figure 188. This 28,000-ton tanker propeller manufactured by Bethlehem Steel Company's Staten Island Propeller Shop has a diameter of 19 feet 8 inches and weighs about 53,500 pounds.

Bethlehem Steel Company

Figure 189. General view of the Propeller Shop at Bethlehem Steel Company's Staten Island Yard.

Bethlehem Steel Company

Figure 190. Pouring 30,000 pound propeller. Metal is poured first into a large basin adjoining mold and when filled enters mold at bottom of hub through sprue made up of tiles.

at an angle with an axis which revolves about this axis at a uniform angular rate and also advances along the axis at a uniform linear speed. A screw having such blade surfaces is a true screw.

Suppose now we consider some small elementary area at some point on the face of a blade. The distance that this area would advance axially in one revolution if it were connected to the axis by some rigid radius and advanced without slip would be the pitch of the blade at that point. Now, with a blade of helicoidal surface, any small area on the blade

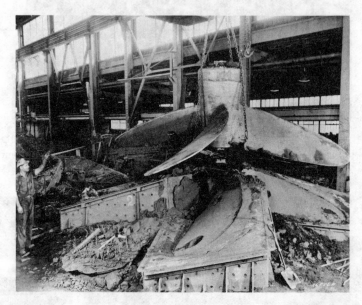

Bethlehem Steel Company

Figure 191. Lifting the rough casting for a Liberty ship propeller from the mold. After this operation, the casting is finished machined, losing about 15 per cent of its rough weight in the process.

would advance the same distance even if each area were acting separately and not as an integral blade. A true screw, then, has *uniform pitch.* A propeller, however, may be constructed with *variable pitch,* where each small area, if revolving on its own fixed radius, would advance a different distance in one revolution from the others. Of course, the distance that the propeller as a unit advances in one revolution when acting in a nut will be determined by the *mean pitch* and the latter is then designated as the pitch of the propeller. Variable pitch propellers may have *radially increasing* (or decreasing) pitch where the pitch increases (or decreases) with distance from the hub; or *axially increasing* (or decreasing) pitch where the pitch increases (or decreases) with distance from the leading edge.

The pitch of any small area on the face of a blade is determined by the angle which the small area makes with a plane perpendicular to the axis. This angle is called the *pitch angle*. The pitch angle of the blade as a unit is the mean of all such pitch angles. It should be apparent then, that the pitch of every point of a blade or the pitch of the propeller, can be changed by twisting the blades in a plane parallel to the plane of the axis. *Adjustable pitch propellers* are constructed with detachable blades capable of being twisted when the ship is in drydock. *Controllable pitch propellers* are constructed with detachable blades capable of being twisted by a hub mechanism controlled from within the ship. With controllable pitch, the ship's officers can change the pitch to suit the particular condition under which their vessel is operating. Such propellers are particularly valuable in vessels like tugboats where the thrust requirements vary widely. However, many ocean-going vessels, particularly Scandinavian vessels, are now equipped with controllable pitch propellers. Considerable controversy exists as to whether the advantages of such propellers outweigh the disadvantages.

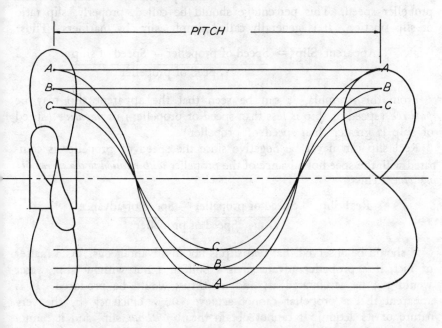

Figure 192. Illustrated are three points on a blade of uniform pitch. Each point travels the same distance in one revolution, i.e., each has the same pitch even if disassociated from the propeller. Point C, for example, makes up for its lesser radius by a greater pitch angle and travels the same distance as Point A with its greater radius (but smaller pitch angle).

The diameter of the circle swept by the blade tips is the *propeller diameter*. The area of this circle is the *disc area*. The *projected area* of a propeller is the area of projection of the propeller on a plane at right angles to the axis. The *developed area* is the total actual area of the faces of all blades.

Blades may be raked forward or aft of the vertical, the angle formed between the blade and a perpendicular to the axis being designated as the *rake angle*.

Propeller Slip: Theoretically, a propeller will advance in one revolution a distance equal to the pitch. Since water is not a solid medium, the actual distance will vary from the theoretical distance by the amount of slip. However, we must differentiate between the terms *real slip* and *apparent slip*.

We have, in effect, defined slip as the difference between the speed of the propeller and the speed of the ship. It is customary, however, to characterize slip as the ratio between the slip and the speed of the propeller; that is, to express it as a fraction or percentage of the theoretical propeller speed. This percentage should be called, properly, slip ratio or slip fraction. It is generally called simply, slip, by mariners. Thus:

$$\text{Apparent Slip} = \frac{\text{Speed of propeller} - \text{Speed of ship}}{\text{Speed of propeller}}$$

From this formula, it can be seen that the apparent slip may be *positive* (speed of ship is less than speed of propeller) or *negative* (speed of ship is greater than speed of propeller).

Real slip can never be negative since the speed of propeller is compared with the speed of advance of the propeller *with relation to the surrounding water*. Thus:

$$\text{Real Slip} = \frac{\text{Speed of propeller} - \text{Speed of advance}}{\text{Speed of propeller}}$$

It should be observed that real slip is not disadvantageous. As a matter of fact, if a propeller advanced as a bolt in a nut without slip, water would not be accelerated aft and no thrust would be produced. It is apparent that a propeller cannot achieve 100% efficiency, by the very nature of its action. It cannot obtain thrust *without* slip, and it cannot achieve perfect efficiency *with* slip.

Wake Current: The term wake is used by mariners to designate the swirling mass of water trailing aft of, and caused by, the propeller. The Naval Architect does not so define it.

Wake or wake current is the motion of the water immediately surrounding the ship's hull relative to undisturbed water. So defined it may be considered a stream of water flowing in the same direction as the ship is moving. The propeller, then, is operating in water flowing forward and not in undisturbed water. This fact has very important bearings on propulsion and will be discussed below in some detail. (See Figure 193).

Wake current may be divided into three components:

1. *Frictional Wake:* As we have seen above, the friction of the ship's hull on surrounding water particles causes the particles to be dragged along with the ship to some extent. The further aft along the ship, the greater is the intensity of frictional wake.

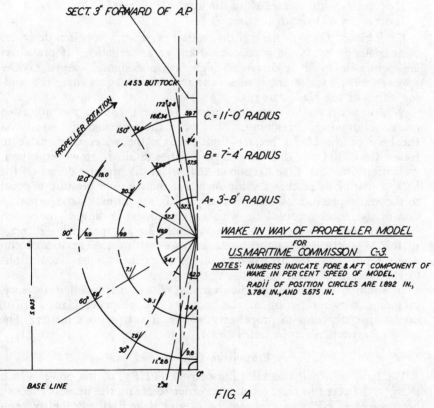

U.S. Maritime Commission

Figure 193. The influence of wake current on propulsion is shown here vividly by indicating the great and varying speeds of the current around a propeller. Pointed up also, is the need for varying pitch to suit the varying wake current.

2. *Streamline Wake:* As the .vessel moves through the water it is obvious that a vacuum cannot be left behind it; water must fill in around the stern. In so doing it must move forward, that is, in the direction of the ship.

3. *Wave Wake:* If the crest of a wave occurs at the stern, the water particles in the wave are all moving, at this stage of their orbital path, in the direction of the ship. In this case, wave wake adds to the other components of wake current. If a trough of a wave occurs at the stern, the reverse is true and wave wake is then an offset to the other two components. It is possible, due to wave wake, for the wake current to flow aft (to be negative rather than positive). However, this would only occur with extremely high speed vessels.

At the stern the intensity of the wake current varies as follows:

It decreases with distance out from the centerline.

It decreases with distance aft of the stern.

It decreases with depth of water.

Cavitation: One of the major headaches which propeller designers must contend with is the phenomenon known as cavitation. If propellers are poorly designed or driven at higher than designed speeds, cavities appear on the back of the blades (and to a lesser degree along the leading edges of the blade face).

When cavitation first became known (around 1894), the suggested causes followed this reasoning: That when the reduction of pressure on the back of the blades became high enough, the water was unable to follow the blades, and the formation of cavities resulted. However, experimentation since that time has shown that when the pressure defect on the back of the blade reaches a value such that the absolute pressure is equal to the vapor pressure of the water, a partial vacuum exists and vaporization of the water occurs along with a conventional boiling of the water.

When cavitation occurs, it is accompanied by an appreciable increase in R.P.M. without a commensurate increase in thrust. The loss of efficiency results from the diversion of energy (propeller torque) from thrust to the boiling of water.

In addition to the obvious disadvantage of loss of propeller efficiency, cavitation causes a pitting of the backs of the propeller blades. Also, cavitation contributes to propeller vibration, a very serious matter. The noise of cavitation can be heard clearly at the stern.

Propulsive Efficiency

We have seen that propeller horsepower (PHP), or the power which must be delivered to the propeller in order to obtain the desired effective horsepower (EHP), must always be greater than EHP. Propulsive efficiency can, therefore, be measured by the ratio EHP/PHP. It is desirable to increase this ratio as much as possible. In this section, we shall investigate the factors which contribute to propulsive efficiency.

Propulsive efficiency is determined by two main factors: (1) Propeller efficiency and (2) Hull efficiency. Thus:

$$\frac{EHP}{PHP} = Ep \times Eh$$

Propeller efficiency is a function of the design of the propeller itself. Since propeller design lies beyond the scope of this text, we shall not pursue the subject further except to repeat, that by the very nature of propeller action, it is impossible to achieve 100% efficiency. Good propeller design, however, can increase propeller efficiency and is of vital importance.

Hull Efficiency: If a propeller were mounted on a shaft projecting from the bow of a vessel and were far enough forward of the bow to be out of the field of pressure changes which surround a ship underway, the efficiency of the propulsion would be determined entirely by the propeller efficiency.[1] A propeller mounted in its conventional location at the stern acts *on* the hull, and in turn is acted *upon* by the hull. The combination of these two actions effects the propulsive efficiency of a vessel. The latter action is called *wake gain;* the former, *thrust deduction.*

We have seen that the propeller acts in the wake current and therefore has a speed of advance relative to the water surrounding it, which is less than the propeller speed relative to undisturbed water. This represents a gain in propulsive efficiency, which is called wake gain. In order to avoid a long and technical explanation of wake gain, let us just say that the propeller is able to get a better "bite" on the more slowly moving water of the wake current than it would if it were operating in the undisturbed water. If the student now refers to the formula for real slip it can be seen that when the speed of advance of the propeller relative to the wake current is decreased (when the intensity of the wake increases), the real slip increases, illustrating once more that real slip is not disadvantageous.

However, the gain contributed to propulsive efficiency by reason of wake current is largely lost due to thrust deduction. As indicated above, thrust deduction occurs due to action of the screw on the hull. It can be explained as follows:

The propeller acts by drawing water through the propeller disk. This creates a "suction" on the stern which reduces the water pressure around the stern. We know that pressure at the stern is beneficial from the point of view of resistance, since pressure at the stern can only act forward and thus help to push the ship forward. If the forward-acting pressure at the stern is reduced due to propeller action, this represents in effect, an *augmentation of resistance,* and thrust deduction is so characterized.

---

[1] Such an arrangement is resorted to in model basins and is called an "open water test".

Summarizing, hull efficiency consists of two main factors, wake gain and thrust deduction. But gain in efficiency due to wake is cancelled out by thrust deduction. Moreover, changes in hull design which act to increase wake intensity usually also increase thrust deduction. For example, if the lines at the stern are made fuller to increase the wake current, this exposes more of the stern to propeller suction and increases resistance. However, this does not mean that the hull designer can forget the effect of the hull on propulsive efficiency. By careful attention to details of the hull design at the stern, the designer can maximize the wake gain and minimize thrust deduction. E_h can and is made greater than unity.

Relative Rotative Efficiency: The propulsive efficiency of a vessel, in addition to propeller efficiency and hull efficiency, is affected by one more relatively minor factor. The wake current is not a flow of uniform intensity. The flow about the propeller varies from hub to tip in all directions. A propeller acting in undisturbed water would not have such a confused flow of water about it. It has been shown that the relation existing between thrust and torque in an open water test is altered when the propeller is acting in a wake current. This ratio of thrust to torque can be found in a model basin for both self-propelled and open water tests. Then these two ratios are compared to establish a ratio called the relative rotative efficiency (E_r.) Values of E_r are very close to 100% and may be a few percentage points below or above unity.

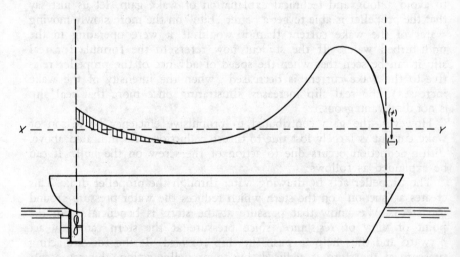

Figure 194. In this illustration of the meaning of "thrust deduction", the line XY represents the normal hydrostatic pressures around a ship. The solid line shows the change of pressures (plus and minus) around a ship underway. The hatched-in area indicates the reduction of pressures at the stern due to the operation of the propeller with a consequent "augmentation of resistance".

Our formula for propulsive efficiency should appear then as:

$$\frac{EHP}{PHP} = E_p \times E_h \times E_r$$

Before leaving the subject of propulsive efficiency, it would be well to remember that the propulsive coefficient EHP/SHP also includes losses in transmission of power by the tail shaft.

FACTORS EFFECTING PROPELLER PERFORMANCE

It is proposed in this section to consider briefly and as simply as possible these factors affecting propeller performance.

1. The number of blades.
2. Location of the propeller.
3. Number of screws.
4. Material used.
5. Contra-propellers.
6. Pitch (Pitch ratio).

There are, of course, many more factors affecting propeller performance. These include shape of blades, blade thickness and areas, size of hub, rake of blades, shaft obliquity, and the like. But these bear directly on highly technical features of propeller design and cannot be discussed here.

Number of Blades: The number of blades which a ship's propeller has may be an extremely important decision. In practice, for larger vessels, the choice generally lies between the three and four bladed propellers. For small craft, two blades are very efficient but for large vessels produce too much vibration. The five bladed propeller has been proposed with great enthusiasm by some people as a means of eliminating vibration, but it appears to be less efficient in most cases than the four or three bladed propeller.[1] The three bladed propeller appears to be preferred wherever it is possible to be used. However, most merchant vessels have four bladed propellers due to limitations of propeller diameter and the possibility of excessive vibration. Warships usually can use three bladed propellers efficiently because of their high speed.

Location of the Propeller: From the point of view of wake gain, a single propeller would be located on the centerline, as close to the water surface and as near to the hull as possible. From the point of view of thrust deduction, however, it would be placed as far aft as possible. In practice, neither of these considerations is of primary importance. The practical considerations of space to fit the required propeller diameter

---

[1] In an effort to eliminate tail shaft failures on the Liberty ship, a *six* bladed propeller was installed on the S.S. Megalohari in December, 1951 (See figure 194A).

and adequate tip clearance are of more importance. Especially important are the clearances around the propeller. If the tips of the blades get too close to the hull, excessive vibration will result. The propeller must be far enough aft of the propeller post for the water coming in from both sides to come together before entering the propeller disc.

Maryland Drydock

Figure 194A. Six Bladed propeller installed on Greek Liberty Ship "MEGALOHARI"

Number of Screws: Admiral Taylor states that "if there is no limit to diameter and revolutions, there is no question that the single screw should be the most efficient."[1] In general, if a single screw can absorb efficiently the power required, it is used. And in this connection it might be pointed out that much of the loss of efficiency in a propeller is represented by the energy involved in the propeller race; therefore, the larger the diameter and the smaller the number of revolutions, the better, since this results in giving a slow motion to a large mass of water rather than a rapid motion to a small mass of water. The need for reduction gears in turbines is clearly indicated by this fact.

[1]Taylor, *Speed and Power of Ships*, page 142.

When multiple screws are used the reason may be due to one or more of the following factors:

1. A single propeller cannot absorb all the power required (due perhaps to limitations on propeller diameter).

2. Decreased probability of a complete breakdown due to loss or damage of the single propeller. This is especially important in warships and passenger vessels.

3. More maneuvering power.

When twin screws are used, they are generally of the out-turning type. This is related to the fact that the wake current is apparently stronger around outturning screws when horizontal webs are used on the propeller bossings (as they usually are).[1] The problem of bossings on multiple screw ships is an important one since they tend to create a confused wake and lead to disturbing hull vibrations caused by the propeller, acting in this wake.

Material Used in the Construction of Propellers: Most propellers are constructed of manganese bronze since such propellers are tough, corrosion-resistant, and can be highly polished. For small harbor craft cast iron blades may be used since they will break off when an obstacle is struck instead of damaging shafting and machinery. Although cast iron propellers are cheap they corrode rapidly with a consequent reduction of efficiency. The condition of the surfaces of propeller blades is a very important factor in propeller efficiency. If the highly polished surfaces of new bronze propellers could be made to stay that way, upwards of a 10% increase in efficiency could be obtained.

Contra-Propellers: The term contra-propeller relates to the offsetting of appendages forward or aft of the propeller in such a way as to "straighten" out the propeller race and recover some of the energy which is lost in the rotative movement of the water passing through the propeller disc. In practice, this means the offsetting and streamlining of the rudder post, propeller post, or both.

The use of contra-propellers accounts for some of the increase in propulsive efficiency displayed by modern vessels.

Pitch: Where variable pitch propellers are used, it is generally provided so as to take advantage of the changing intensity of wake current around the propeller. For example, in discussing the design of the propeller on the 30,000 ton tanker, *Atlantic Seaman*, Dr. L. M. Goldsmith commented that the propeller has "pitch increasing over the blade length from root toward the tip to suit the variation in wake section behind the ship's hull, thus increasing efficiency."[2]

Pitch is usually expressed in terms of its relationship to propeller diameter and when so used is called the *pitch ratio*. For merchant ships, pitch

---

[1] Rossell & Chapman, *Principles of Naval Architecture*, Vol. II page 143.
[2] L. M. Goldsmith, "Engineering of a 30,000-ton Super-tanker", *Marine Engineering and Shipping Review*, January, 1951.

Bethlehem Steel Company
Figure 195. Technicians check the pitch of a propeller with a pitchometer.

U.S. Maritime Commission
Figure 196. Using a pitchometer in a shipyard.

ratios are somewhere in the neighborhood of 1.0. For highly loaded propellers such as those used on tugboats, a finer pitch is required and the pitch ratios range down to 0.6. For high speed propellers, a more coarse pitch is appropriate and a pitch ratio as high as 2.0 may be used.[1]

Since the pitch ratio is so intimately connected with propeller efficiency some designers prefer the built-up type of propeller with detachable blades where pitch adjustments can be made when desirable. However, as mentioned above, most propellers today are of the solid type. Reference has also been made to the controllable-pitch propeller.

The pitch of a propeller can be measured mechanically by means of a *pitchometer*,[2] or it can be obtained by the following means:

The propeller is set so that one blade is horizontal. A line weighted at both ends is looped over the edge of the blade at the widest section and allowed to hang clear of the opposite edge. The widest section is generally about one-third the distance from the tip to the root, and the mean pitch is usually found to be at this location. The following distances are then measured: (1) The horizontal distance between the lines, (2) the width of the blade and (3) the radius of the pitch circle which is the distance from the center of the hub to the point of measurement on the blade. With these measurements, pitch can be easily found. The diagram in Figure 198 can be used to keep the method in mind. In the diagram:

$$\text{Pitch (DE)} = \frac{AD \times BC}{AC}$$

where: AD is the circumference of pitch circle
   BC is the amount forward edge leads after edge axially
   AB is the width of the blade
   AC is the amount forward edge leads after edge in the direction of rotation.

Example Pitch Problem: In drydock the pitch of a propeller blade is to be ascertained. By hanging a line over the blade at its widest section, which is 6 feet out from the hub center, it is found that the forward edge is 20 inches in axial advance of the after edge. The width of the blade is 44 inches.

1. Circumference of pitch circle: $2 \times 6' \times 12 \times 3.1416 = 452.39''$

2. Amount forward edge leads after: Sq. rt. of $44^2 - 20^2 = 39.2''$

$$\text{Pitch} = \frac{452.39 \times 20}{39.2} = 230.81'' \text{ or } 19.23 \text{ feet}$$

---

[1] Rossell & Chapman, op. cit., page 157.
[2] Pitch can also be obtained by means of a set of templates, constructed to show the curvature of the blade at every 0.1 or 0.2 radius. This method is widely used by the U.S. Navy.

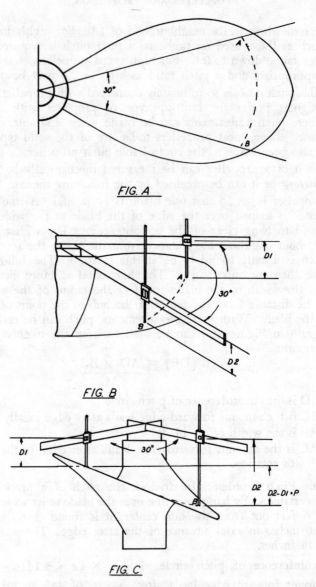

FIG. A

FIG. B

FIG. C

Figure 197. The pitchometer consists of an arm pivoted on the center of the hub, and an adjustable rod fixed at right angles to the arm. In using the pitchometer, the rod is set at the radius for which the pitch is to be obtained. Two measurements are taken with the calibrated rod (d_1 and d_2) at points 15 degrees on either side of the centerline of the blade. The difference in these distances in inches is the pitch in feet. This follows when it is realized that pitch is the axial advance of a small area in a revolution of 360 degrees. On the pitchometer the axial advance is 1/12 of a revolution, and ($d_2 - d_1$) is 1/12 of the pitch if measured in feet but equal to the pitch if measured in inches.

354

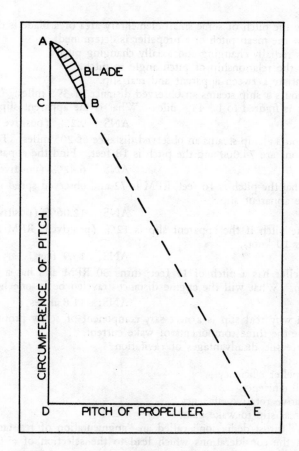

.Figure 198. Diagram illustrating the theory of obtaining the pitch of a propeller
by hanging a line over the blade.

QUESTIONS

1. How do screw propellers develop their propulsive thrust?
2. Define the following parts of a screw propeller:
   - a) Blade
   - b) Hub
   - c) Face
   - d) Back
   - e) Working surface
   - f) Leading edge
   - g) Following edge
   - h) Tip
   - i) Root
3. What are the considerations which lead to the selection of a solid propeller or one with detachable blades?
4. Explain why the back of a blade contributes more thrust than the face.
5. Differentiate:
   - a) Uniform pitch
   - b) Variable pitch
   - c) Adjustable pitch
   - d) Controllable pitch

6. Explain:
   a) How the pitch of some small elementary area of a blade is determined.
   b) How the mean pitch of a propeller is determined.
7. What is radially changing and axially changing pitch?
8. Explain the relationship of pitch angle to pitch.
9. Differentiate between apparent and real slip.
10. In 24 hours a ship steams an observed distance of 395 miles. The engine distance is figured to be 435 miles. What is the apparent slip?

ANS: 9.2% (positive)

11. In 12 hours a ship steams an observed distance of 205 miles. Total engine revolutions are 74,000 and the pitch is 18 feet. Find the apparent slip.

ANS: 6.42% (positive)

12. Given that the pitch is 16 feet, RPM is 72 and observed speed is 10 knots, find the apparent slip.

ANS: 12.06% (positive)

13. Find the pitch if the apparent slip is 12% (positive), RPM are 72 and speed is 10 knots.

ANS: 15.9 feet

14. A propeller has a pitch of 17 feet, turns 80 RPM and has a 12% positive slip. What will the engine distance traveled be in one hour.

ANS: 11.8 miles

15. Explain why real slip is a necessary component of screw propulsion.
16. Describe the three components of wake current.
17. What are the disadvantages of cavitation?
18. Describe:
    a) Propeller efficiency
    b) Hull efficiency
    c) Relative rotative efficiency
19. Relate real slip to wake gain.
20. Why is "thrust deduction" called an "augmentation of resistance"?
21. Explain the considerations which lead to the selection of a four bladed propeller for merchant vessels.
22. What are the important considerations in locating a propeller?
23. What are the advantages and disadvantages of multiple screws?
24. What does the term "contra-propeller" mean?
25. When is a propeller of coarse pitch, and when is one of fine pitch, appropriate?
26. Name three methods of checking the pitch of a propeller.
27. Explain the theory of the pitchometer.
28. Find the pitch of a propeller if the radius of the pitch circle is 6 feet, distance from forward edge to after edge is 24 inches, and distance from leading edge to following edge is 36 inches.

ANS: 25.13 feet

29. Find the pitch of a propeller if the diameter of the pitch circle is 14 feet, width of blade is 6.2 feet and forward edge is 2 feet in advance of after edge.

ANS: 15 feet

30. Find the radius of the pitch circle if the width of the blade is 6 feet, pitch is 18 feet and distance forward edge leads after edge is 2.2 feet.

ANS: 7.265 feet

BIBLIOGRAPHY

Taylor, D. W., *The Speed and Power of Ships,* U.S. Government Printing Office, Washington, D.C., 1943.

Rossell & Chapman, *Principles of Naval Architecture,* Vol. II, Society of Naval Architects and Marine Engineers, New York, 1942.

The following papers from the *Transactions of the Society of Naval Architects and Marine Engineers* are recommended for further study by interested students:

Schoenherr, K, "Recent Developments in Propeller Design", Vol. 42, 1934.

Lewis, F. M., "Propeller Vibration", Vol. 43, 1935.

Thau, W. E., "Propeller and Propelling Machinery: Maneuvering Characteristics During Stopping and Reversing", Vol. 45, 1937.

Towne, S. H., "Propeller Manufacture", Vol. 51, 1943.

Rupp, L. A., "Controllable-pitch Propellers", Vol. 56, 1948.

Couch & St. Denis, "Comparison of Power Performances of Ten 600-foot single-screw Tankers Hulls as Predicted From Model Tests", Vol. 56, 1948.

Hill, J. G., "The Design of Propellers," Vol. 57, 1949.

F. Lewis, *Propeller Vibration Forces,* Vol. 71, 1963.

Venning & Haberman, *Supercavitating Propeller Performance,* Vol. 70, 1962.

L. Troost, *A Simplified Method for Preliminary Powering of Single Screw Merchant Ships,* Vol. 65, 1957.

P. Wennberg, *Controllable Pitch Propellers,* Gulf Section, May, 1960.

Chapter 17

SHIP TRIALS

After launching and outfitting, a vessel and all of its equipment is submitted to a series of exhaustive trials. Speed relative to horsepower and RPM is tested; fuel oil consumption is checked; propulsion and other machinery is observed under severe operating conditions; equipment, such as anchor and steering gear is tested.

The building contract between owners and builders has specified certain requirements in regard to the performance of the vessel and its equipment. Certain government agencies such as the Maritime Administration, the Navy Department, the Public Health Service, and the Coast Guard Marine Inspection Division must also be satisfied that the vessel meets their peculiar requirements. The Trial Trips are, therefore, a time of great anxiety for builders and owners alike. In some cases, a bonus may be earned by the builder if speed and/or fuel oil consumption requirements are bettered; and, of course, penalties may be incurred for below-par performance.

The results of the Trial Trips are usually incorporated in a Trial Trip Report of some kind.[1] The information contained in these reports is then available to operating personnel and can be of great assistance in indicating the characteristics and capabilities of their vessel.

Although ship's officers rarely have the opportunity to participate in the activities of the trial trips since the construction of new ships in peace time is limited, it is felt that, since the results of the Trial Trips have such an important bearing on the operation of a vessel and since ship's officers are required to use trial trip reports, its will be in accord with the purposes of this text to explain at least in outline form, the purposes and activities of ship trials.

Types of Ship Trials

The various types of ship trials may be classified as follows:
1. Dock and Builder's Trials.
2. Standardization Trial.
3. Endurance and Fuel Economy Trials.
4. Maneuvering Trials.
5. Test of Steering Gear.

---

[1] When a vessel is built for the U.S. Maritime Administration, this agency issues the *"Report of Progressive Speed, Maneuvering, Endurance, and Fuel Economy Trials"*. This trial trip booklet, in addition to giving the results of all trials, contains a great amount of information relating to the ship and can be of great value to the ship's officer.

6. Test of Anchor Gear.

7. Miscellaneous Equipment Tests.

Each of these trials and tests will now be described.

Dock and Builder's Trials: It is only natural that the builder of the vessel, who is responsible for the performance of the vessel to a great degree, should want to test the vessel before the start of the Official Trials. These "private" trials take the form of *dock trials,* where propulsion machinery will be turned over and other equipment tested right at the dock and a *builder's sea trial* where the ship will make a short trip in deep water for further brief trials of all machinery and equipment. In many cases, shortcomings can be detected on these trials and rectified before the official trials.

Standardization Trial: One of the most important of the Official Trials is the standardization trial where the ship makes a series of runs over a measured mile course to collect data which are used in the drawing of speed and horsepower; and speed and RPM curves. As we have noted, the building contract specifies that a certain speed be reached for given RPM and horsepower, on a given displacement.

Now, speed is pretty much a function of ship form and it is the Naval Architect who is most vitally concerned with this aspect of ship performance. In these days of scientific model basins, however, the speed and horsepower curve can be drawn before the trials by the towing tank people, and the official trials amount to a check, albeit a very important check, on these predicted results. We have seen in the Chapters on Resistance and Powering and Propellers and Propulsion that the prediction of EHP and SHP is a well developed technique, and indeed, there are many who prefer the results of the model basin work to the data and curves gathered on the Standardization runs.

Conducting a Standardization Trial offers many knotty problems. Some of these are:

1. Condition of ship at the time of the Trial.

2. Obtaining the proper displacement and making the calculations associated with displacement.

3. The use of a good Trial Course; weather conditions.

4. Timing on the measured mile runs.

5. Trial Equipment.

1. *Condition of the ship at the time of the Trial:* Since the standardization trial amounts to a check on model basin results, the ship must operate under conditions obtaining in a basin. This means that the ship's bottom and propeller must be clean and new. Therefore the ship must be drydocked just prior to the trials. It means that the displacement of the ship on trials must be equivalent to the displacement of the model when towed. And it also means that the sea conditions must not be too rough since the model basin obviously cannot simulate heavy seas.

2. *The problem of displacement.* A new ship sometimes cannot be easily loaded to the deep drafts required for the trial runs. Special trunks may have to be built in the holds so that the holds may be flooded. Free surface must be guarded against in this case. Also, since the ship must

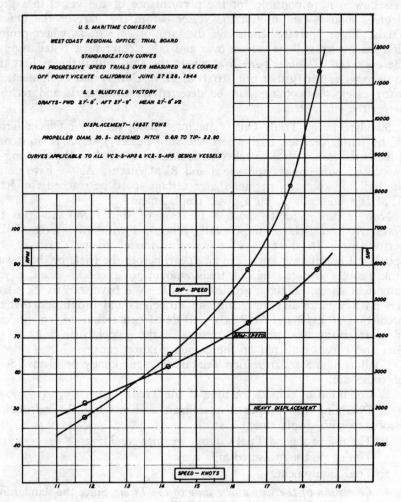

Figure 199

proceed to the Trial Course, a voyage sometimes of hundreds of miles, the displacement must be arranged to be reduced to the proper figure by consumption of fuel oil and so on as the ship proceeds to the Course.

We have also seen in a previous chapter that the computation of the exact displacement is not an easy task. First the drafts must be exactly ascertained. A correction must then be made to the mean draft for trim, deflection of the hull, and for variation in the location of draft marks from the perpendiculars.

3. *The Trial Course:* A good Trial Course must have as many as possible of the following requirements:

a. The depth of water must be such that the resistance of the ship is not affected. Some complicated formulas are available for figuring this proper depth, but a good estimate is a depth in feet about 20 times the draft of the ship.

b. Since a measured mile is marked by shore beacons, the course must be fairly close to the shore. This requires deep water close into land—an unusual situation.

c. *Sea Conditions:* The Course should be protected as much as is possible from heavy seas. Tides and currents, although always present should be as unviolent and regular as possible, and further should run parallel or nearly parallel with the course.

d. *Isolation from Sea Lanes:* Obviously, trials should not be interrupted by traffic across the course.

In the United States, one of the best Trial Courses is located at Rockland, Maine. Although this Course is not ideal it is as good as can be gotten. It's principal drawbacks are the great distance from most shipyards and the poor weather conditions in the winter.

4. *Timing on the measured mile runs:* Obtaining the speed by running over a mile course and clocking the elapsed time is not as easy a task as might be supposed. Let us consider the various ways in which a ship might obtain an accurate indication of her speed:

Suppose only *one run* is made over the mile course. This, obviously will not give accurate results, since some tide and/or current will always exist and will affect the speed of the ship to an unknown degree.

Well, then, how about *two runs,* one with the tide and one against it? Would not the addition to speed provided on the run with the tide be offset by the reduction of speed on the run against the tide? The answer to this question would be "yes" if no change in tide velocity occurred between the two runs, but since we cannot assume this, the answer must be "no". For example, if the true speed of the vessel were 10 knots and the tide velocity were 2 knots on the first run and 1 knot on the second run, the speeds obtained would be:

1st Run: 12 knots
2nd Run: 9 knots

Average Speed: 10.5 knots (or an error of 0.5 knot).

We come then to *three runs.* Suppose the tide velocity to be 3 knots on the first run (with the tide); 2 knots on the second run and 1 knot on the third run. Then, our speeds would be:

1st Run: 13 knots

2nd Run: 8 knots
3rd Run: 11 knots

Average Speed: 10.67 knots (an error of 0.67 knot).

This method too, fails to produce an accurate speed. Suppose, however, we obtain the mean of the first two runs and the mean of the second two runs and then get a "mean of the means":

Mean of 1st and 2nd Runs: 10.5 knots
Mean of 2nd and 3rd Runs: 9.5 knots

Average Speed: 10.0 knots (the correct speed)

This, then, is the answer to the problem. The reason why a correct speed is obtained lies in the double weight attached to the middle run. The error resulting from averaging the first two runs indicates a greater speed than the vessel actually makes through the water. The error resulting from averaging the last two runs indicates a lesser speed. Obtaining the mean of the means eliminates the error by offsetting the plus error with an equal minus error. It should be observed, however, that an exact speed would not be obtained by this method if the tide velocity varied erratically, although the error resulting would be small unless the change of tide velocity were extremely erratic. Better results can be obtained if five runs are made and a series of means obtained. As a matter of fact, five runs *are* made sometimes to obtain speed for the high-power run.

5. *Trial Equipment:* The following trial equipment must be placed aboard. *Revolution counters* are attached to the shaft so that a very accurate measurement of RPM on the mile runs can be obtained. *Torsion meters,* which measure the shaft horsepower are also attached to the shaft. To obtain the exact time required to make a mile run, an elaborate system of timing is used. *Stop watches* are held by deck observers. When they are started they actuate *contact makers* which are operated electrically. The contact makers can then do several jobs depending on the type of installation. They can start the revolution counters; they can start a *chronograph,* a timing machine which indicates by means of a broken line drawn on waxed paper, the elapsed time for the mile run.

To warn and notify all data collectors, a *system of bells, lights, or both* is set up and at the start and finish of the measured mile run, this system serves to indicate the exact times at which data taking should commence and end.

An *anemometer* which indicates wind speed is placed high up on the mast, and through an electrical system, automatically indicates wind velocity at every second of the time the vessel is on the mile run. After the standardization runs are over, this information is used to adjust the speeds computed.

Fuel oil meters, which are very carefully calibrated before and after the trials, are connected to the fuel oil lines.

Endurance and Fuel Economy Trials: The term *endurance trial* relates to the testing of engines, boilers, and other machinery while on a deep sea run of several hours duration. The performance of all machinery is observed on this run.

The fuel economy trial is usually run concurrently with the endurance trial, and its purpose, of course, is to establish the fuel oil consumption for a given condition. For example, the specifications for the *S.S. America,* regarding this were: [1]

"The computed overall fuel consumption for all purposes not to exceed .634 lbs. per shaft horsepower output per hour of main propelling machinery when developing 34,000 S.H.P. average at a displacement of about 28,826 tons, based on fuel of 18,500 B.T.U. calorific value per lb.

"The contract provides for a deduction from the contract price if the total fuel oil consumption exceeds 917.6 pounds per nautical mile while developing 34,000 S.H.P., the speed to be as determined by the standardization trials. It also provides that a premium shall be paid if the fuel oil consumption is less that 917.6 pounds per nautical mile while developing 34,000 S.H.P.

"An economy trial of six hours duration was made. The average values of the data recorded during this trial are as follows:

Displacement—tons approximate	28,860
R.P.M.	127.80
S.H.P.	34,709
Speed—knots from stand. curve	23.65
Fuel oil consumption, #/SHP/hr.	.5845
Fuel oil consumption, #/naut. mile	857.9

It should be observed that fuel oil consumption actually is not based on weight but on the number of B.T.U.'s, 18,500 B.T.U. being the equivalent of one pound of fuel oil. Therefore, it is customary to take samples of the fuel oil which are then sent to the Bureau of Standards for analysis. The consumption of fuel oil in pounds is then corrected up or down depending on whether B.T.U. content is greater or less than 18,500. Of course, the practical engineer does not think much about this sort of correction. He is interested in how much fuel oil is needed to operate the vessel at a certain speed.

Maneuvering Trials: Maneuvering trials consist of right and left turning circles, emergency astern and emergency ahead tests (crash stops), and the Z-Maneuver.

---

[1] *Report of Trials* for the S.S. America.

Average values for typical single screw cargo vessels with right handed propellers are: [1]

Turning Circle (See Chap. 10)	Left:	Right:
Advance ....3.3 lengths	3.9 lengths
Transfer ....2.4 lengths	2.4 lengths
Tactical Diameter ....5.1 lengths	5.3 lengths
Final Diameter ....4.0 lengths	4.3 lengths

Z-Maneuver (See below for explanation)
At 10 knots......................4 minutes, 20 seconds
At full speed ....3 minutes
Emergency stop (See below)
Turbine propulsion ....4 minutes; 7 lengths
Diesel propulsion ....3 minutes; 5.5 lengths

Note: Diesel and reciprocating plants are superior to turbines since the power of the latter astern is limited by the power of the astern turbine.

Turning circle definitions were given in Chapter 10 and will not be covered here. However, the turning circle track is usually plotted by means of stadimeter ranges and bearings, on some stationary object such as a buoy. (Figure 200.) Recently, in the Trials of the S.S. Independence, the track was obtained by means of radar ranges and bearings of a buoy. On this trial an attempt was also made to trace the pattern of the wake as it appeared on the radar scope and although the wake did produce a sharp pattern on the screen, other difficulties precluded the use of this method. The method appears to have possibilities; perhaps in conjunction with photographing the screen. While on the subject of electronics, it might be well to mention that some thought is being given to the possibility of eliminating the necessity of taking a vessel to a measured mile course for standardization runs, by the use of Shoran. The fixes obtained by Shoran are thought to be accurate enough for the purpose and would permit the runs to be made at any point off the coast. It would also permit running in a straight line and picking off any number of measured miles along that line. This would eliminate all the time consuming maneuvering required to get on the measured course before each individual run.[2] Another modern development which may eliminate the need for measured mile courses is the Raydist system which the new liner, the S.S. United States used on her trials in May, 1952. The Raydist system operates by placing two small buoys with their Raydist equipment in the water. The buoy equipment of each sends out impulses which are received on another set of apparatus installed on

---

[1] E. V. Lewis, "Functions of a Ship: Steering and Maneuvering", The Log, January, 1950.

[2] Information on Trials of the S.S. Independence taken from a Report by Cadet-Midshipman G. A. Quick, Class of June, 1951, United States Merchant Marine Academy.

the ship. The ship may then move in any direction from the buoy and a measurement possibly as accurate as one part in 5000 can be made of a given distance. The system may displace the method of sighting objects on land to measure the speed. Emergency ahead and astern tests can also be facilitated by measuring the head and stern reaches by means of the Raydist equipment.

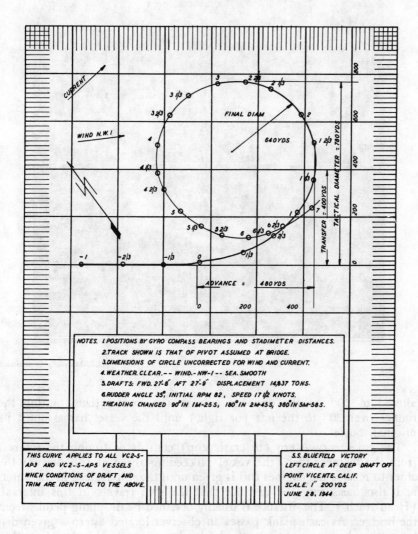

NOTES. 1.POSITIONS BY GYRO COMPASS BEARINGS AND STADIMETER DISTANCES.
2.TRACK SHOWN IS THAT OF PIVOT ASSUMED AT BRIDGE.
3.DIMENSIONS OF CIRCLE UNCORRECTED FOR WIND AND CURRENT.
4.WEATHER. CLEAR. -- WIND.- NW-1 -- SEA. SMOOTH
5.DRAFTS: FWD. 27-6" AFT 27-9" DISPLACEMENT 14,837 TONS.
6.RUDDER ANGLE 35°, INITIAL RPM 82, SPEED 17 1/2 KNOTS.
7.HEADING CHANGED 90° IN 1M-25S, 180° IN 2M-45S, 360° IN 5M-58S.

THIS CURVE APPLIES TO ALL VC2-S-AP3 AND VC2-S-AP5 VESSELS WHEN CONDITIONS OF DRAFT AND TRIM ARE IDENTICAL TO THE ABOVE.

S.S. BLUEFIELD VICTORY LEFT CIRCLE AT DEEP DRAFT OFF POINT VICENTE. CALIF.
SCALE. 1" 200 YDS
JUNE 28, 1944

U.S. Maritime Commission

Figure 200

The Z-maneuver consists of making a zig-zag or Z course, the time for completing the zig-zag being then considered to represent the maneuvering ability of the vessel. More precisely, the maneuver is accomplished by putting the rudder over 20° to the left (or right) and holding it there until the course has been altered 20°; then, putting the rudder over 20° to the right (or left) and holding it there until the course has been

U.S. Maritime Commission

Figure 201

altered to 20° on the opposite side of the course; then, putting the rudder over 20° to the left (or right) until the vessel has assumed its original course.

The emergency astern (or crash stop) consists of timing the interval from the moment that (the vessel proceeding ahead at full power) the order to reverse the engines full is given until the ship is dead in the water, and also measuring the distance that the ship travels in this interval. (Head reach.) The distance is usually obtained by dropping planks from the bridge. As each plank passes an observer located astern a given distance, the observer signals to the bridge by raising his hand and another plank is dropped. The number of planks dropped multiplied by the

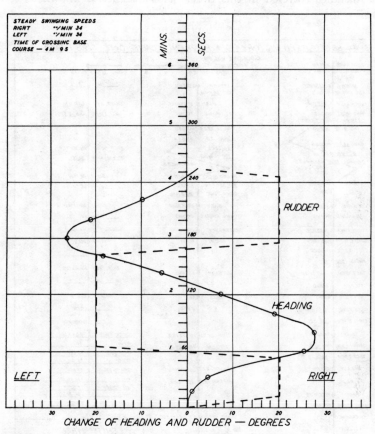

U.S. Maritime Commission

Figure 202

367

distance from bridge to after observer is adjudged to be the head reach.
The emergency ahead test is conducted in the same way and produces
the time that it takes to stop the vessel when it is proceeding full astern
and the distance traveled in this time. This distance is known as stern

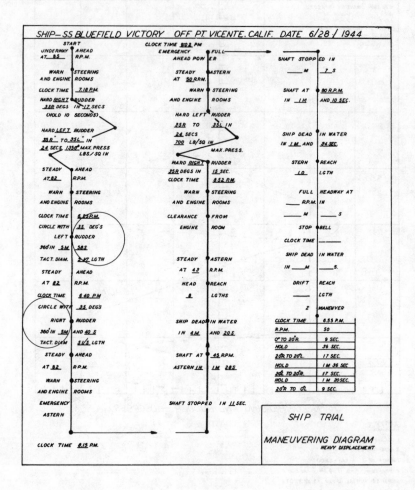

U.S. Maritime Commission

Figure 203

reach. The importance of head and stern reach to ship's officers and
pilots is obvious.

Steering Gear Test: The nature of the steering gear test may be
best described perhaps by quoting from the ABS Rules on these required
tests:

"All vessels, excluding certain towing barges, are to be provided with effective means for steering which shall be capable of putting the rudder from hard over to hard over in 30 seconds with the vessel running ahead at the designed maximum sea speed. In addition, they are to be provided with effective auxiliary means for actuating the rudder through an independent tiller, or its equivalent, designed to put the rudder from 15° over to 15° over in 60 seconds with the vessel running ahead at half the designed sea speed, or seven knots, whichever is the greater."

During these trials the draft aft must be sufficient to immerse the rudder completely or almost completely. The maximum steady oil pressure in the ram should also be measured.

Anchor Gear Tests: The tests on the anchor windlass are usually conducted along the lines recommended by the *Code on Maneuvering and Special Trials and Tests* (1950) issued by the Society of Naval Architects and Marine Engineers. The Code states:

"This test should be conducted in at least 35 fathoms of water (or other depth as agreed to). The ship shall be brought to a standstill and headed into the wind before commencing this test. The test usually consists of the following:

(1) Lower both anchors simultaneously under control of the electric motor and electric motor brake; to a depth of 30 fathoms, stopping and starting at 5 fathom intervals, or as agreed to.

(2) Hoist both anchors simultaneously until clear of water. House each anchor into hawsepipe independently.

(3) Disengage one wildcat. Let that anchor go "by the run" under control of hand brake, to a depth of 30 fathoms, stopping and starting at 15 fathoms or other agreed interval. Stop anchor and secure by means of riding stopper.

(4) Repeat (3) for second anchor.

(5) Repeat (2).

The chain speed, that is, the time required to hoist the 30 fathoms is specified to be around 5 fathoms per minute.

Miscellaneous Equipment Tests: At one time or another after the completion of the ship, all equipment must be tested. Many of these tests are made during the official trials. Equipment tested will include:

1. All deck machinery such as capstans, windlasses, etc.

2. Navigation equipment including gyro compasses and gyro-pilot, radio direction finder, fathometer, etc.

3. Boats and boat-handling equipment.

4. Fire protecting devices.

QUESTIONS

1. Explain briefly the purpose and nature of the following types of trials:
a) Dock and Builders

b) Standardization
c) Endurance
d) Fuel Economy
e) Steering and Anchor Gear

2. Describe the procedure necessary for making up a Speed and Power curve on the Standardization Trial.
3. Outline the requirements necessary for properly conducting the following elements of the Standardization Trial:
   a) Condition of the ship at the time of the trial.
   b) Loading the vessel to the exact displacement required.
   c) The Trial Course
   d) Timing on the mile runs.
   e) Equipment needed.
4. Suppose that a vessel making three runs over a measured mile course (1st and 3rd with the tide; 2nd against the tide) finds that its observed speed are: 17.2, 13.7, and 16.2 knots, respectively. What is the true speed of the vessel.

ANS: 15.2 knots

5. Explain why it is better to make a series of five runs over a measured mile course when extreme accuracy is desired.
6. What are two methods of expressing fuel oil consumption?
7. Why are samples of fuel oil gathered while on the Economy run and sent to the Bureau of Standards for analysis?
8. Explain how the following maneuvering characteristics of a vessel are obtained on the Trial Trip:
   a) Advance, transfer, tactical and final diameter.
   b) Head reach and stern reach.
9. Describe the required steering gear test.
10. Describe the required anchor gear test.
11. What type of equipment aboard a ship must be tested prior to putting the vessel in service?

BIBLIOGRAPHY

The following Codes on Trials prepared by the Society of Naval Architects and Marine Engineers:

Standardization Trials Code, 1949.

Economy and Endurance Trials Code, 1950.

Code on Maneuvering and Special Trials and Tests, 1950.

Taylor, D. W., The Speed and Power of Ships, U.S. Government Printing Office, 1943.

Rossell & Chapman, Principles of Naval Architecture, Vol. I, Society of Naval Architects and Marine Engnieers, New York, 1942.

Baker, Introduction to Steel Shipbuilding, McGraw-Hill Book Company, Inc., 2nd Ed., New York, 1953.

Report of Progressive Speed, Maneuvering, Endurance, and Fuel Economy Trials, for all vessels for which Trials are conducted by the U.S. Maritime Administration.

H. Saunders, Hydrodynamics in Ship Design, SNAME, 1957.

INDEX

Administration of Load Line Acts, 73
of Tonnage measurement, 34
Advance, 200
After perpendicular, definition of, 1, 136
Aluminum, use of, 12
welding of, 170
American Bureau of Shipping, History of, 53
organization of, 54
publications, 55
functions, 55
rules on strength, 55, 97, 177
on riveting and welding, 155, 172, 176
on piping, 190, 194
on drydocking, 253
on Trials, 368
Amplitude of roll, 300
Anchor gear trial, 369
Anti-rolling tanks, 306
fins, 307
devices, 305
Appendage displacement, 263
resistance, 333
Archimedes Principle, 262
Aspect ratio of rudder, 208
Augmentation of resistance, 347

Balanced rudder, 208
Ballasting, in structural tests, 123
Base line, location of, 1, 135
Beam (See Breadths)
Beam—theory of strength, 108
Bending moment, curve of, 114
formulas for beams, 100
Bernoulli's Theorem, 312
Bilge blocks, 242, 244
keels, 305, 253, 173, 314
well, 184
Bilges, sounding of, 190
side, 183
suction on, 186
injection valve for, 188
Bilge & ballast system, 183
Block coefficient, relationship to free board, 70, 76, 78
determination and use of, 272
Body Plan, 135, 136, 315
Bonjean's Curves, Definition of, 269
use of in launching calculations, 224
use of in strength calculations, 116
use of in displacement calculations, 269
Boot—topping, painting of, 253
calculation of area of, 264
Bows, types of, 9

Brake horsepower, 334
Breadth(s), Extreme, 3
molded, 3
by ABS, 3
registered, 3, 35
effect of on resistance, 329
Builder's trial, 359
Bulbous bow, 10, 327
Buoyancy, curve of, 112, 116
reserve, 69, 70
volume of, 263
center of, vertical, 282
center of, longitudinal, 276
in launching, 224
Butt, joint and strap, 149
weld, 166
Buttock, definition of, 1
drawing of, 137

Caisson gate for graving dock, 235
Calculations, tonnage, 45
freeboard, 78
strength, 77, 100, 104, 106, 125, 126
launching, 223
integration, area & volume, 256
displacement, 261
wetted surface, 264
density, 264
coefficients of form, 269
centers of area & volume, 275
tons per inch, 277
height of metacenter, 279
metacentric radius, 279, 281
change in displacement due to trim, 282
moment to change trim one inch, 284
wave characteristics, 296
resistance & powering, 330, 332
timing on trials, 361
Calking, 153
Camber, definition of, 3
straight & knuckled, 3
relationship to freeboard, 69
of launching ways, 219
Car Carriers, 29
Careening, 233
Cavitation, 346
Centerline plane, definition of, 1
Center of Buoyancy, vertical, 282
longitudinal, 276
optimum position for speed, 331
Center of gravity, calculation of for ship, 116, 276
for girder, 104
for waterplane, 278
Center of lateral resistance, 204

Certificate(s) of Admeasurement, 35, 38
  ABS, 56, 59, 60, 61
  International Load Line, 58, 74
Centrifugal force, effect on heel during
  turn, 205
  effect on motion of sea water, 295, 203
Checking arrangements in launching, 227
Chemical tanker, 32
Classification, history of, 52
  relationship to government, 54
  publications, 55
  effect on ship design, 58
Classification system, Maritime Administra-
  tion, 13
Clean ballast system, 183
Clinometer error, 304
Clipper bow, 10
Coefficients, of form, 269
  speed—length, 318
  displacement—length, 329
Concentration of stress, 118
Conditions of assignment, 76
Continuity in strength, 118
Contra—guide rudder, 211
Contra—propeller, 351
Corrugated plating, 12
Counter stern, 11
Cracks in welded ships, 170, 176
  arrestors, 177
Cradle, launching, 222
Crash stops, 366
Cruiser stern, types of, 11
  effect of on waterline length, 10
"C" type ships, 18
Curves, of form, 261, 267, 270
  strength, 110
  resistance, 319, 323
  speed & power, 359

Dead rise, 4
Deadweight, definition of, 5
  scale, 285
Deadweight—displacement ratio, 12
Deadwood, effect of, 206
Deck, upper to hull, 39
  freeboard, 73
  strength, 119
  sheathing of, 169
Declivity angles of launching ways, 215
Deductible spaces, definition of, 42
Density of water, effect on load lines, 72
  effect on draft, 264
  effect on resistance, 321
Depth, definition of, 3
  molded, 3
  relationship to freeboard, 70, 76
  relationship to strength, 103, 128
Designer's load waterplane, 136, 141
Diagonals, use of, 137
Diesels, 12
Directional stability, 204

Displacement, tonnage, 5, 262
  calculation of, 263
  appendage, 264
  change of with density, 264
  when trimmed, 269, 282
  virtual, in waves, 303
  on trial run, 360
  sheet, 261
Displacement—length ratio, 329
Docking, Plan, 241
  Description of, 243
  of damaged ships, 248
  deck officer's duties in, 251
  engineer's duties in, 252
Dock trial, 359
Double bottoms, tanks & piping, 182, 192
  treatment of in tonnage measurement, 37
Draft, definition of, 3
  molded, 3
  effect of speed on, 333, 360
Drag, 202
Drinking water system, 182, 198
Drydocking, fees, 48
  work performed, 253
  deck officer's duties, 251
  engineer's duties, 252
  report, 251
Drydocks, types of, 233
  graving, 233
  floating, 235
  marine railway, 233, 234
  U.S. Navy, 236

Eddy resistance, 325
Eductor, 183
Effective, length, 2
  horsepower, 333
Electric—arc welding, 157
Electrodes, 157
Endurance trial, 363
Entrance, definition of, 5
  effect of on speed, 326, 329
Equipment, tonnage, 7
  tests, 369
Excess of hatchways, 42
Exempted spaces, definition of, 39

Fabrication, Shops, 143
  of riveted side frames, 144, 169
Fairing lines, 135
Fees, tonnage, 48
  ABS, 54
Fetch, 297
Fillet weld, 166
Fire system, 194
Flare, 3
Floating drydock, description of, 235
  U.S. Navy types, 236
  advantages & disadvantages, 250
Flow, lines of, 313
  laminar & turbulent, 322
Fluted plating, 13

Forecastle head, requirements for, 81, 86
    desirability of, 77
Forge welding, 156
Form, coefficient, 269
Forward perpendicular, 1
Fouling, effect of, 320, 321
Frame, stations, 1
    lines, 141
    modulus, 125
Freeboard, definition of, 73
    history of, 67
    technical background of, 68
    marks, 79
    administration of, 73
    determination of, 73
    calculations, 78
    for steamers, 73
    for timber deck cargoes, 81
    for tankers, 84
    for Great Lake vessels, 86
    for passenger ships, 87
Fresh water, weight of, 269
    allowance, 80
    tanks, 182, 197
    piping systems, 197
Frictional resistance, 320
    Froude's formula for, 320
    factors which determine, 320
Froude, William, work of, 318
Fuel Economy trial, 363
Fuel oil & oily ballast system, 192
Full—scantling ship, 20
Funnels, types of, 12
    umbrella for, 12
Fusion welding, 156

Gamma-ray weld inspection, 176
Gas turbine, 12
Gas welding, 161
Girth, 4
Graving dock, description of, 233
    caisson gate for, 235
    advantages & disadvantages, 250
Great Lakes vessels, 31
    calculation of freeboard for, 86
Gross Registered Tonnage, 36
Groundways, 215
Gyroscopic stabilizers, 308

Half-breadth, Plan, 136
    offsets, 138
Head reach, 366
Heat treatments, 173
Heaving, 293
Heel, during turn, 204
Height, of waves, 297
    offsets, 138
    of platform, 69
History, of tonnage, 34
    of classification, 52
    of freeboard regulation, 67
Hog Islander, 15

Horsepower, calculation of, 332
    types of, 333
Hull efficiency, 347
Hull form, effect of on freeboard, 69
    effect of on resistance, 312
    effect of on stability, 69, 279
    drawing of, 135
    effect of on turning & steering, 203
    effect of on propulsion, 347
Hull girder, 108
Hydrostatic curves, 261, 267, 270

Included spaces, 36
Indicated horsepower, 334
    in power tonnage, 6
Integration, rules of, 256
International Load Line Certificate, 58, 74
International Load Line Conference, 68

Joints, riveted, 149
    welded, 166

Keel blocks, in drydocking, 242
    in construction, 216
Kelvin's waves, 315
Kinematics of turning, 200
Kinetics of turning, 202
Knuckle, 10
Knuckled camber, 3

Launching problems, in declivity angles, 215
    in construction of ways, 217
    in construction of cradle, 222
    in calculations, 223
    in releasing, 226
    in checking, 227
    in removal of cradle, 227
    in side launching, 228
Length, relationship of to freeboard, 70
    relationship of to strength, 100, 111, 125
    relationship of to stability, 279
    relationship of to resistance, 318, 329
Length, over-all, 2
    between perpendiculars, 2
    on the load waterline, 2
    effective, 2
    registered, 2, 35
    tonnage, 2
    of waves,
Liberty ship, 17
Lift, 202
Light and air space, 39, 46
Lines drawing, definition of, 1
    preliminary work for, 131
    theory of, 134
    drawing of, 135
    fairing of, 135
    use of diagonals in, 137
    use of in mold loft, 142
Lines Plan (See Lines drawing), 131
Lloyd's Register, 52

Load, definition of, 95
    curve, 112
Loading forms, for strength, 126
Load Lines (See Freeboard also),
    Acts of 1929 and 1935, 68
Load Line Regulations, administration of,
    73
    assigning authority, 73
    enforcement of, 73
Load waterline, definition of, 1, 79
    designer's, 1
Locked-up stresses, 170
Longitudinal dimensions, 2
    length-over-all, 2
    length between perpendiculars, 2
    length on the load waterline, 2
    effective length, 2
    registered length, 2, 35
    tonnage length, 2
Lubricant, for launching, 219
Lurching, 293

Machinery space, deduction, 43
Machine welding, 158
Magna-flux weld inspection, 175
Maneuvering trials, 363
Marine Document, 35
Marine Railway, 233, 234
Measured mile, 361
Measurement tonnage (See Register ton-
    nage)
Meierform bow, 9, 10
Metacenter, height of longitudinally, 279
    height of transversely, 279
Metacentric height, description of, 279
    proper, 300
Metacentric radius, transverse, 281
    longitudinal, 279
Middle body, parallel, 4
    scantlings for, 119
Midship section, location of, 1
    Plan, 120
    coefficient, 273
    effect of on resistance, 328, 329
Mild steel, ultimate strength of, 97
    as material for rivets, 148
Minimum freeboard, 73
Model basins, 318, 319
Modulus, section, 105
    of elasticity, 95
    frame, 125
Molded, length, 2
    breadth, 3
    depth, 3
Molded dimensions, definition of, 2
Molded surface, 1
Mold loft, 142
Moment of inertia, of structural shapes, 102
    of ship, mass, 300
    of waterplane, transverse, 281
    of waterplane, longitudinal, 279
Moorsom system, 34

Motion, of ship in waves, 293, 296, 298
    of waves, 293

Net register tonnage, 42
Neutral axis, 100
    calculation of, 103
Nomenclature, of rivets, 148
    of plating, 150
    of propellers, 337
    of welds, 164
    of rudders, 207
Notch, sensitivity, 171

Ocean waves (See waves)
Offsets, table of, 138, 140
    use of, 141
Open superstructure, tonnage treatment, 40
    freeboard treatment, 77
Orbital motion of water, 294
    effect on ship's speed, 295
    effect on yawing, 296
    in causing virtual upright position and
        virtual displacement, 302
Ore carriers, 31
Oxy-acetylene welding, 161

Painting, in drydock, 251, 253
Panama Canal tonnage, 49
Pantograph, 143
Parallel middle body, 4
    effect of on resistance, 330
Passenger accommodation exemption, 39
Passenger ships, types of, 26
Peening, 173
Period, of rolling, 299
    of waves, 297
Perpendiculars, forward & after, 1
Perturbation, 331
Piping system, bilge & clean ballast, 183
    fuel oil & oil ballast, 192
    fire, 196
    sanitary, 197
    washing water, 197
    drinking water, 198
    auxiliary steam, 198
    compressed air, 198
Pitch, definition of, 342
    of rivets, 149
    types of, 342
    problems, 353
Pitching, definition of, 293
    effect of on resistance, 332
Pivoting, in launching, 223
Pivoting point, 200
Planimeter, 260
Plan, midship section, 120
    lines, 131
    body, 136
    half-breadth, 136
    profile, 135
    drydocking, 241
    piping, 184, 188, 190, 194

Plating, scantlings of, 119
  systems, 150
Plimsoll marks, 67
Plug, weld, 166
  bleeding, 240, 242, 254
Plumb bow, 9
Poppets, 222
Positions, welding. 166
Power, types of, 334
  method of calculating, 333
  tonnage, 6
Pressure welding, 156
Prismatic coefficient, use of, 329
  calculation of, 274
Profile, plan, 135
Propeller, horsepower, 334
  theory of screw, 337
  definitions, 337
  slip, 344
  cavitation of, 346
  factors effecting performance of, 349
  contra, 351
  pitch of, 342
Propeller rotation, effect of on steering, 207
Properties of metals, 95
  elastic limit, 95
  yield point, 97
  modulus of elasticity, 95
  ultimate strength, 97
  ductility, 97
  hardness, 98
  toughness, 98
  fatigue strength, 98
Propulsive efficiency, 346
Pumping arrangements, aboard ship, 182
  in drydock, 235, 236
Pumps, requirements for, 190

Radiographic inspection, 175
Radius, of gyration, 299
  metacentric, 279, 281
Raked bow, 9
Reach rods, 186
Refrigerated vessel, 28
Register tonnage, definition of, 35
  history of, 34
  Gross, 35
  Net, 42
  calculations for, 45
  Miscellaneous information on, 48
Relative rotative efficiency, 348
Releasing arrangements, in launching, 226
Reserve buoyancy, in freeboard, 69, 70
Residual resistance, 318
Residual welding stresses,
Resistance, frictional, 320
  wave, 322
  eddy, 325
  air, 325
  effect of on hull design, 325
  effect of shallow water on, 332

under sea conditions, 332
  conversion of to horsepower, 333
Resistance welding, 157
Rigging, changes in, 11
Rivets & riveting, definitions of, 148
  plating & framing, 150
  preparation for, 151
  tools & procedure, 152
  making watertight, 153
  testing of, 153
  replacing & maintaining, 154
  combined with welding, 154
  stresses on, 154
  ABS Rules for, 155
Rolling, factors affecting period of, 299
  factors affecting ampliture of, 300
  devices to dampen, 305
  effect of on resistance, 332
Rose box, 186
Rudder characteristics, 207
Run, definition of, 5
  effect of on resistance, 326
  effect of on propulsion, 347
  effect of on steering, 206

Salt water, weight of, 269
Sanitary system, 197
Scantlings, definition of, 93
  of ground tackle, 7
  midship & end, 119
Scuppers, 183
Seasonal & zonal lines, 79
Sectional areas, curve of, 134
  calculation of, 256
Section modulus, calculation of, 105
  required in freeboard regulations, 125
Sequence welding, 173
Serrated members, 173
Shaft, tail, 253, 334
  horsepower, 334
Shallow water, waves,
  resistance, 332
Shear, stress, 94
  curve, 113
Sheer, definition of, 3
  relationship to freeboard, 70, 76
  plan, 135
Shelter deck ship, 20
Shelter deck space, 41
Ships, types of, 15
Side launching, 228
Simpson's Rule, 258
Slamming, 293
Slewing, in launching, 227
Sliding ways, 222
Slip, 344
Sounding, of bilges, 190
Spade rudder, 211
Special Passenger Accommodation exemption, 39
Speed, of waves, 297
  and power, 332

relationship to length, 318
trials, 359
Speed-length ratio, 318
  effect on resistance of, 333
  effect of on draft and trim, 331
Spoon bow, 9
Squat, 331
Stability, directional, 204
Stability, transverse, 279
  relationship to freeboard, 69
  relationship to heel during turn, 205
  problem of in side launching, 228
Standardization trial, 359
Steam turbines, 12
Steering, factors influencing, 206
Steering gear trial, 368
Stern post, 1, 209
Stern reach, 367
Sterns, types of, 10
Stethoscope, 176
Straight camber, 3
Straps, butt & seam, 149
  for strengthening, 178
Strength, relationship of to freeboard, 69,
  125
  of materials, 93
  tensile, 94
  compressive, 94
  shearing, 94, 123
  ultimate, 97
  relationship of to moment of inertia, 102
  relationship of to section modulus, 105
  equation, 105
  curves, 110
  calculations, 106
  of riveted and welded joints, 154, 178
  launching calculations for, 223, 225, 226
  considerations in docking, 242, 251
Strength of materials, definitions of, 93
Stress, tensile, 94
  compressive, 94
  shear, 94
  on a loaded beam, 98
  hogging and sagging, 109
  bending, 109
  local, 107
  structural, 108
  on rivets, 154
  relieving, 173, 174
Stress-strain diagram, 95
Strum box, 186
Stud welding, 164
Subdivision, load lines, 87
  relationship of to freeboard, 69
Suez canal tonnage, 49
Superstructure, open, 40
  definition of, 70
  relationship of to freeboard, 40
  stresses in, 119, 124
Surge, 293
Sway, 293
Synchronous rolling, 301

Tail shaft, requirements on drawing, 253
Tankers, types of, 25
  calculation of freeboard for, 84
  stresses on, 110, 125, 126
Tanks, peak, 182, 191
  double bottom, 182, 192
  deep, 182, 192
  settling, 182, 193
  potable water, 182
  anti-rolling, 306
Taylor's Standard Series, 333
Templates, use of, 143
Tests, structural by ABS, 97
  cold-bend, 98
  hardness, 98
  toughness, 98
  steering gear, 368
  anchor gear, 369
  miscellaneous equipment, 369
  welding, by ABS, 172, 174, 176
  structural on ships, 123
Thermit welding, 162
Three-island vessel, 10
Thrust deduction, 347
Timber deck cargoes, load lines for, 81
Tipping, center, 278
  in launching, 224
Tonnage, gross & net register, 6, 35
  displacement, 5, 261
  equipment, 7
  power, 6
  deadweight, 5
  calculations, 45
  well (hatch), 41
Tons per inch immersion, 277
Towing tanks, 318
Towrope resistance, 318
Trailership, 32
Transfer, 200
Transverse, dimensions, 3
  metacenter, 279
  metacentric radius, 281
Trapezoidal Rule, 256
Trepanning, 176
Trial, course, 361
  equipment for, 362
Trials, dock & builders, 359
  standardization, 359
  endurance & fuel economy, 363
  maneuvering, 363
  steering gear, 368
  anchor gear, 369
  miscellaneous, 369
Trim, change in displacement due to, 282
  calculation of displacement when
    trimmed, 282, 269
  moment to change one inch, 284
  effect of on resistance, 328
  change of during turn, 202
  problems of when docking, 242
  effect of on steering, 202
  effect of speed on, 331

Trochoidal wave, 294
  relationship to strength calculations, 110, 116
Tumble home, 3
Turning circle, 200
Types of ships, "C", 18
  private designs, 24
  tankers, 25
  passenger vessels, 26
  special merchant types, 28
  with regard to structure, 75
  with regard to freeboard, 75

Ultimate strength, definition of, 97
  of mild steel, 97
Unionmelt welder, 158
Upper deck, definitions of, 39

Ventilation, of tanks, 194
Vertical, dimensions, 3
  center of buoyancy, 282
  center of gravity, 276
Victory ship, 18
Virtual upright position, 302
Virtual displacement, 303
Volume of displacement, 263

Wake current, types of, 344
  effect on steering, 207
Washing water system, 197
Waterplanes, location of, 1, 135
  coefficient of, 275
  calculation of area of, 256, 277
  calculation of CG of, 278
Waves, motions of ship in, 293, 299
  motion of, 293
  trochoidal, in strength calculations, 110, 116

trochoidal, description of, 294
  effect of on speed of ship, 295
  effect of on yawing, 296
  characteristics of, 296
  propagation of, 297
  shallow water, 298
  set up by ships, 314
Wave resistance, 322
Ways, launching, 215
Weight curve, 112, 115
Welding, principles of, 156
  methods employing fusion, 157
    electric arc, 157
  gas, 161
  thermit, 162
  methods employing pressure, 163
  stud, 164
  definitions, 164
  joints, 166
  Positions, 166
  advantages over riveting, 167
  disadvantages, 170
  intermittent (skip), 172
  sequence of, 173
  inspection of, 175
Welds, fillet, 166
  butt, 164
  plug, 166
  tack & production, 172
Wetted surface, calculation of, 264
  effect of on resistance, 320

X-ray inspection of welds, 175

Yawing, due to waves, 296

Zinc plates, 253
Z-maneuver, 366